LEXICAL
MATTERS

CSLI
Lecture Notes
No. 24

LEXICAL
MATTERS

edited by
Ivan A. Sag and Anna Szabolcsi

CSLI CENTER FOR THE STUDY
OF LANGUAGE
AND INFORMATION

Contents

Introduction   vii

Contributors   xix

1 The Aspectual Interface Hypothesis   1
   CAROL TENNY

2 Thematic Relations as Links between Nominal Reference
   and Temporal Constitution   29
   MANFRED KRIFKA

3 Complex Predicates and Morpholexical Relatedness:
   Locative Alternation in Hungarian   55
   FARRELL ACKERMAN

4 On Obviation   85
   DONKA F. FARKAS

5 Blocking of Phrasal Constructions by Lexical
   Items   111
   WILLIAM J. POSER

6 The Stress and Structure of Modified Noun Phrases in
   English   131
   MARK LIBERMAN AND RICHARD SPROAT

7 Hungarian Derivational Morphology, Semantic
   Complexity, and Semantic Markedness   183
   FERENC KIEFER

8 Focus-Based Inferences in Sentence
   Comprehension   209
   GYÖRGY GERGELY

9 Combinatory Grammar and Projection from the
   Lexicon   241
   ANNA SZABOLCSI

10 The Lexical Entailment Theory of Control and the
Tough-Construction   269
PAULINE JACOBSON

11 A Lexical Analysis of Icelandic Case   301
IVAN SAG, LAURI KARTTUNEN, AND JEFFREY GOLDBERG

Author Index   319
Subject Index   323

Introduction

What is a lexical entry? What information does it include? How are lexicons organized? In the early days of generative grammar, such questions were given relatively simple answers. A lexicon was a list of entries, each of which specified a phonological shape, some representation of its meaning, a grammatical category, and a specification of exceptionality. The excitement concerning the lexicon was minimal, precisely because the grammatical action, so to speak, was elsewhere: lexical entries provided just enough information to satisfy the needs of elaborate syntactic rules.

In the thirty years that have passed since this era, grammatical theories have changed in profound ways, the most striking of which may well be the enhanced role of the lexicon. There is now considerable agreement within the field that lexical representations are highly structured and play an essential role in grammatical description, as many burdens once borne by transformations and other devices are now carried by lexical representations or lexical rules of one sort or another.

In spite of this fundamental agreement, no real consensus has yet been achieved concerning the content of lexical entries, the precise nature of lexical representations, the scope of the lexicon and lexical analyses in general, or the matter of how the lexicon should be structured. It is evident that lexical matters such as these will be of central concern well into the next century, not just within the field of linguistics, but also in the neighboring disciplines where the study of language has assumed an increasingly important role.

The contributions to the present volume, which (with the exception of Gergely's) fall squarely within linguistics proper, illustrate very well the extreme diversity of empirical problems in this domain, as well as the variety of techniques currently employed to investigate lexical matters. Despite their diversity, the papers cluster naturally around four central themes, which we have selected as the organizing foci of the volume:

Lexical Matters. Ivan A. Sag and Anna Szabolcsi, eds.
Copyright © 1992, Stanford University.

1. Argument Structure and the Nature of Thematic Roles
2. Blocking and the Boundaries of the Lexicon
3. The Nature of Lexical Meaning
4. Lexical Alternatives to Syntactic Analyses

1   Argument Structure and the Nature of Thematic Roles

Thematic roles have long been the standard devices for organizing lexical *argument structures*. Substantial theories of thematic roles have been based on the assumption that each individual argument type can be given a grammatical characterization that determines its syntactic behavior. But evidence against this view has been mounting for some time now. It has been observed, for example, that it is difficult to extend the rigorous treatment of thematic roles beyond the core set of Agent, Patient, Experiencer, Stimulus, etc. It is perhaps surprising that certain combinations of these roles, for example, Agent and Patient, are typical, whereas others, like Agent and Stimulus, are not attested at all. Thematic roles, moreover, may be impossible to define in semantic terms (a point already recognized by the grammarians of ancient India and carefully documented by Dowty (1991)) and many important generalizations are statable only with reference to semantically coherent classes of predicates.

It is presumably due to this growing dissatisfaction with the standard notion of thematic roles that Dowty's proposal to take a fresh look at the issue was received with such enthusiasm. Among other things, Dowty suggested to shift the focus to verb meanings and to recognize at most a very limited set of proto-roles. The content of these roles is, to a great extent, characterizable in cognitive, rather than purely grammatical terms. For instance, the Patient proto-role is characterized by (a) undergoing a change of state, (b) being an incremental theme, (c) being causally affected by the event, (d) being stationary, and (e) having a referent whose existence may depend on the action denoted by the verb.

CAROL TENNY's contribution ("The Aspectual Interface Hypothesis") and that of MANFRED KRIFKA ("Thematic Relations as Links Between Nominal Reference and Temporal Constitution") have a close relation. They provide, in fact, an interesting example of how scholars belonging to two quite different research traditions may achieve converging results and insights.

It is well-known that the distinction between cumulative and quantized reference in the domain of nominal interpretation (e.g., *apples* vs. *five apples* parallels the contrast between telic and atelic interpretation in the verbal domain (cf. *run* vs. *run a mile* and, furthermore, that the two interact in grammar. Exactly when and how the properties of the nominal argument affect those of the complex predicate is the subject of both Tenny's and Krifka's contributions.

Using the background assumptions of the MIT Lexicon Project, Tenny proposes the *Aspectual Interface Hypothesis*, according to which (1) the mapping between thematic structure and syntactic structure is governed by aspectual properties and (2) only the aspectual part of thematic structure is visible to syntax. The crucial constraint she proposes is that the internal argument of a simple verb is constrained so that it either undergoes no change or motion, or it undergoes change or motion which measures out the event over time.

The precise interpretation of "measuring out an event over time" may be explicated, at least in a significant subset of the cases, in the terms offered by Krifka, whose work proceeds from the same fundamental insight. Krifka develops a semantic system based on the particular lattice-theoretic properties he assigns to three sorts of entities: objects, events, and times. In his system he is able to give a precise interpretation to notions like cumulative, singular, quantized, and atomic reference. Defining telic predicates as event predicates all of whose subevents have the same terminal point, Krifka goes on to show that all quantized event predicates, and only these, have the property of telicity. The crucial technique that Krifka then introduces to explicate the notion of "measuring out an event over time" is that of a homomorphic mapping from objects to events which preserves lattice structure. Such a mapping exists in the case of drinking wine, for example, but not in the case of drinking a glass of wine, and thus provides a precise model-theoretic construction of the intuitive notion whose empirical utility is argued for by Tenny.

On the grammatical side, Krifka's insights also parallel Tenny's, in that he conceives of cumulativity, uniqueness of events, and graduality as properties of thematic relations. He uses these properties to classify the Patient relations of different verbs and to distinguish them, for example, from Stimulus. The empirical scope of Tenny's informal proposal is significantly broader than Krifka's, however. It extends to objects undergoing change that does not affect the existence of their parts but rather, their color or location (cf. *redden* and *push (the cart) to New York*). Krifka, on the other hand, explores applications of his theory to such problems as Finnish progressivity (marked by the partitive case of the argument) and the interaction of perfectivity and the quantizedness of arguments in Slavic.

Krifka's and Tenny's contributions, both agreeing with Dowty's work in their Davidsonian spirit and their attitude towards thematic roles, address the general question of why and how certain internal arguments determine the aspectual properties of the containing verb phrase. FARRELL ACKERMAN, directly influenced by Dowty's work on roles, explores a set of particularly challenging empirical problems in his paper "Complex Predicates and Morpholexical Relatedness: Locative Alternation in Hungarian".

Ackerman's study is couched in the framework of Lexical Mapping Theory, developed by Bresnan and Kanerva (1989) and Bresnan and Zaenen (1990), inter alia, which seeks to explicate the relation between semantic (or thematic) roles and grammatical relations in terms of a mapping from the former to the latter that obeys certain principles. These principles make reference to a featural decomposition of grammatical relations (subject is decomposed as [-objective] and [-restricted]; objects are all [+objective] and may be (semantically) restricted or not; and oblique dependents are [-objective] and [+restricted]). Among the principles that constrain the role-relation mapping in Lexical Mapping Theory are certain intrinsic feature classifications, for example, the classification of agents as [-objective] (this prevents agents from ever being realized as direct objects, for example).

Ackerman's examination of the systematic correlations between the meanings and grammatical relations associated with various perfective and resultative preverbs in Hungarian leads him to a number of conclusions. First, the intrinsic classifications (following Zaenen (1990)), should be based on Dowty's notion of Proto-Role properties. Second, a clear distinction should be drawn between two kinds of operations: morpholexical (those which affect the lexical semantics of predicates) and morphosyntactic (those which don't). The basic analysis of Hungarian preverbs, Ackerman argues, should all be in terms of morpholexical relatedness (expressed within the word formation component of the grammar), for they involve not only the Proto-Role properties, but also the very kinds of aspectual properties, for example, telicity, explicated in the work of Tenny and Krifka. His paper thus illustrates a new domain (in a third research paradigm) where these basic semantic properties are able to contribute to the explanation of why lexical argument structures are the way they are.

2   Blocking and the Boundaries of the Lexicon

Though syntactic and semantic rules are in general assumed to be independent in their application, there are a variety of cases that indicate that certain grammatical rules must "know about each other." The most striking of these is the phenomenon of *blocking*, whereby the availability of a better-suited form renders a less specific one ungrammatical. In general, these are all cases which can be conceptualized as instances of the Elsewhere Principle (an insight also due originally to the grammarians of ancient India), which states in essence that the existence of particular rules or exceptions blocks the application of more general rules. Although standard examples of this principle seem purely morpholexical in nature (e.g., the existence of *went* blocks the application of the regular past tense suffixation rule (**goed*)), various researchers (Householder, McCawley, Horn, Dowty, Levinson) have studied similar effects in other domains, relating blocking phenomena, for example, to independently motivated aspects of Gricean pragmatic theory. This raises the important theoretical issue of clarifying the nature of the domains in which the Elsewhere Condition applies.

DONKA FARKAS, in her contribution "On Obviation," examines classic examples of obviation, including the impossibility of coreference between matrix subject and pronoun in French examples like *Pierre veut qu'il parte* 'Pierre wants that he leave'. Accounts of this effect have been offered in terms of Chomsky's "avoid pronoun" principle or else Binding Theory. In the latter case, the domain in which the embedded subject is not to be bound is extended to include the matrix clause. Farkas argues, however, on the basis of data from Western Romance—as well as new data from Romanian, Hungarian, and Serbo-Croatian, that these approaches to obviation are unsatisfactory. The alternative she proposes is based on the notion of blocking, thereby tying this phenomenon to her earlier results concerning subjunctives and control.

According to Farkas' proposal, the coreferential reading in the relevant cases is blocked by the availability of a rival infinitival form in the language. This immediately explains why Romanian has no obviation: it minimally differs from Western Romance in lacking rival infinitives completely. A wealth of further, often subtle contrasts are shown to follow from this blocking analysis. For example, coreference of the sort just illustrated is blocked precisely when the infinitive and the subjunctive complement clause both conform to the canonical case of control, that is, cases in which both the matrix and the complement subject bear a *responsibility* relation to the situation denoted by the complement. Farkas argues that such fine distinctions in verb meanings are in general reflected in degrees of obviation, a point she attempts to justify on cross-linguistic grounds.

The mechanism underlying Farkas' analysis, despite its larger effect on coreference relations, is lexical blocking of the familiar sort. Such an analysis is possible precisely because the "competition" in question is between two lexical forms, each subcategorizing for a distinct type of complement. Yet whether or not blocking must be a purely lexical matter is precisely the point taken up in WILLIAM POSER's paper "Blocking of Phrasal Constructions by Lexical Items."

Poser points out three unusual cases where lexical forms block phrasal constructions. The first is that of Japanese "incorporated" periphrastic verbs formed with *suru* 'do'. There is phonological and syntactic evidence that, contrary to the usual assumption, these are phrasal. The fact that these periphrastics cannot be formed directly from deverbal nouns is argued to be a blocking effect, due to the existence of the corresponding lexical verb. The second case is English comparatives and superlatives. The phrasal status of the *more* and *most* forms is clear, yet they are blocked by the availability of the lexical forms with -*er* and -*est*. Third, synthetic expression of tense in Basque blocks periphrastic expression with the defective verb *ari*. The dilemma that these data indicate is this: either blocking is not just lexical, or the lexicon needs to be "extended" to encompass the sorts of phrasal construction discussed.

The first possibility is the pragmatic approach used, for example, by Householder (1971), to explain why the existence of the simpler *pink* blocks more complex *pale red*. This explanation does not extend to morphology, for a number of reasons: (1) *oxen*, for example, is not simpler than *oxes*; (2) the blocking effect in morphology is much stronger than the unacceptability of *pale red*; (3) blocking requires that the two forms be morphologically related; pure semantic relatedness is not enough.

The second possibility is to "extend the lexicon." Poser proposes that a morphological category is one that is potentially instantiated by a word formation rule. Phrasal constructs involving X^0 categories are allowed to instantiate morphological categories. A periphrastic construction is, then, as in grammatical tradition, one in which morphological categories that are typically instantiated lexically are instead instantiated at a phrasal level. This, in turn, allows one to say that if instantiation by a lexical verb is available, phrasal instantiation is blocked.

Poser's notion of phrasal constructs involving X^0 categories may seem unfamiliar to readers steeped in the tradition of modern syntactic theory, yet MARK LIBERMAN and RICHARD SPROAT appeal to just such a notion in their contribution to the present volume, "The Stress and Structure of Modified Noun Phrases in English."

In standard treatments of English modified phrases, the combination of adjective and noun is presumed to be the result of a syntactic rule (building N^1 structures), whereas the combination of noun and noun is taken to be lexical (N^0) in nature. And correlating with this difference in mode of combination, is assumed to be a difference in prosody: in adjective-noun collocations, the noun is stressed, in accordance with the Nuclear Stress Rule; in noun-noun combinations the first noun is stressed, in accordance with the Compound Stress Rule. Standard examples of this contrast include *detéctive novel* versus *defective nóvel*, *bánk check* versus *blank chéck*, and so forth.

On the basis of a detailed examination of a large variety of modified phrases, Liberman and Sproat challenge this standard wisdom. For example, *sóft spot* and *wíld man* are adjective-noun combinations with compound stress, and *steel pláte* and *rice púdding* are noun-noun combinations with nuclear stress. These facts, as the authors show at length, cannot be explained by appeal to discourse factors (differences in inherent contrast) or a distinction between "fixed" expressions and others (e.g., *hard líquor* and *blue moón* are lexicalized adjective-noun combinations bearing nuclear stress). Accent, on Liberman and Sproat's view, is only partly predictable on grounds of category or meaning.

These observations lead in turn to the view that all combinations of modifier-noun in English are in principle ambiguous between N^0 and N^1 structures—a surprising conclusion that raises new questions, only some of which Liberman and Sproat address in detail, about the exact relation among such notions as *being lexicalized*, *being an N^0 expression*, and *being a fixed expression* (i.e., *having a special meaning*).

3 The Nature of Lexical Meaning

The analysis of fixed expressions and the treatment of argument structure are of course only two of the many issues that arise in the area of lexical semantics. Two other notions that have been assumed to play an important role in the organization of the lexicon, in predicting acquisition order, and also with respect to predicting blocking effects of the sort we have already discussed, are *semantic complexity* and *semantic markedness*. Complexity may be thought of simply as the amount of semantic material contained in a lexical item, for example, *sell* is more complex than *give*. Markedness, on the other hand, has to do with how restricted a term is in its utility—basic level terms like *pine* are held to be less restricted, thus more natural and less marked, than either more specific or less specific terms in the same semantic domain.

Since complexity is usually considered with respect to verbs, and basic-level predictions (markedness) with respect to category names, the relation between these two notions is seldom examined. In his paper "Hungarian Derivational Morphology, Semantic Complexity, and Semantic Markedness," FERENC KIEFER investigates precisely this problem. Kiefer seeks to develop an appropriate notion of markedness for verbs and, with that in hand, to examine the interesting circumstance that arises when complexity and markedness make conflicting predictions.

The semantic field he investigates is defined by the rules of Hungarian derivational morphology, involving the formation of causative, passive, frequentative and perfective verb forms (with or without idiosyncratic meanings). Morphological, syntactic and semantic complexity are carefully distinguished from the corresponding kinds of markedness, and the relationship of semantic complexity to syntactic and morphological complexity is examined. What Kiefer finds is that, with an increase of semantic complexity, neither morphological nor syntactic complexity decreases. Furthermore, the semantic complexity relations among derivationally related lexical items which are semantically opaque are the same as those between transparent lexical items.

Kiefer then shows that semantic markedness may conflict with complexity considerations. For instance, verbs with a perfective prefix are less marked than the corresponding iterative/generic verbs, despite the fact that they are semantically more complex. And, similarly, verbs with a directional prefix are less marked than corresponding generic/directionless verbs. In this way, Kiefer argues, the facts of acquisition can be explained: acquisition order is determined by markedness, rather than by complexity (though, if no special markedness relations obtain, semantic markedness may be equated with semantic complexity).

Kiefer's study thus brings rather subtle and indirect evidence to bear on questions having to do with the psychological reality of lexical information. The methodology of GYÖRGY GERGELY, by contrast, is more direct. In his contribution, "Focus-based Inferences in Sentence Comprehension," Gergely is concerned with verifying experimentally the claim that massive incremental integration of diverse types of information takes place rapidly in real-time language processing.

Recent work in sentence comprehension has established that listeners use a variety of cues interactively in the construction of discourse interpretational structures, even before the full syntactic and semantic processing of the sentence is complete. Working within this research paradigm, Gergely investigates the precise on-line effects of some specific cues that have previously only been examined indirectly, using off-line measures. These are: (1) topic-focus (TF) structure, (2) inter-clausal semantic relations, and (3) script-based knowledge.

The initial *though* in sentences like *Though Daddy praised his daughter, she was still not happy* invites script-based inferences concerning cause-effect relations, one of which will be denied in the second clause. Experiments with English speakers have indicated that the pertinent cause-effect relation can only be identified in retrospect, during the processing of the second clause. Gergely's paper is based on experiments with Hungarian speakers, due in large part to the fact that in Hungarian, the TF structure is marked unambiguously by word order and intonation. Gergely hypothesized that listeners can rely on the TF structure of the initial *though* clause to restrict the set of expectable consequences to those that arise from the focused part of the clause. For example, the example just cited is felicitous when the verb *praised*, rather than, for instance, the object *his daughter*, is focused. The reason for this is that praising might be expected to cause happiness.

Gergely's results support this hypothesis. First, naming times for a word probe, whose meaning is in adversative relation to the focus-based consequence of the initial *though* clause, were significantly decreased, even when the probe appeared before the end of the clause. This indicates that before the main clause is processed, subjects have generated predictive inferences about its adversative content. The selective nature of facilitation demonstrates that subjects inferred only those consequences that were based on the focused part of the clause. Such facilitation was not present when the initial clause contained no connective with comparable semantics, suggesting that when focus-based inferences cannot serve a predictive function, they are discarded from working memory at the end of the clause.

Gergely's experiments thus provide key insight into the semantic nature of certain kinds of connectives, as well as the highly integrative nature of language processing in general. In addition, his experiments showed that focus-based inferences directly access pragmatic knowledge structures such as scripts, thus raising the question of whether the probe facilitation here is a further case of lexical priming. In contrast to the automatic and short-lived nature of lexical priming, however, the selective nature of the observed priming effects and their survival even over a clause boundary indicate, as Gergely shows, that they are more like the robust higher-order facilitation of script-associated words.

4   Lexical Alternatives to Syntactic Analyses

As we noted at the outset, a striking trend in contemporary syntactic theory is the lexical analysis of phenomena previously treated in terms of transformational rules or other syntactic devices. With this trend comes, quite naturally, an uncertainty as to which linguistic phenomena should in fact receive lexical treatment. Several of the papers in this volume propose lexically based solutions to problems that have often been assumed to be within the scope of *syntactic* movement theory, binding theory, control theory or case theory. The reason, they argue, is that the standard accounts are descriptively inadequate and/or have theoretically undesirable properties. We have already seen an argument of this type in Farkas's lexical analysis of obviation.

ANNA SZABOLCSI, in her contribution "Combinatory Grammar and Projection from the Lexicon," explores the possibility of articulating assumptions about the lexicon in such a way that they derive a set of generalizations that are traditionally conceived of as purely syntactic. For example, Szabolcsi proposes to eliminate the need for principles pertaining to empty categories and binding by exploring the consequences of the central assumption of categorial grammar, namely, that lexical items with subcategorization frames are to be looked upon as functions.

Her paper first demonstrates the explanatory value of the concept of lexical items as functions, by providing a detailed comparison of the treatments of unbounded dependencies in Government-Binding Theory (GB), Head-driven Phrase Structure Grammar (HPSG), and Combinatory Categorial Grammar (CCG). Taking this concept fully seriously, CCG goes beyond functional application and introduces a set of functional operations, that is, combinators, into the grammar. In this way it can dispense with bound variables corresponding to gaps, and turn the empirical generalizations that GB and HPSG express in terms of constructs like the Empty Category Principle, the Subcategorization Principle, the Nonlocal Feature Principle, etc., into constructive procedures.

The main part of Szabolcsi's paper is devoted to issues that traditionally belong to Binding Theory. These matters pose a special problem for a grammar based on combinatory logic since this logic does not merely allow one to dispense with bound variables, it has no variable binding machinery at all. Szabolcsi argues that this restriction is in fact a virtue of CCG, in that it forces the correct effects to be derived directly from the lexical meanings of anaphors and bound pronouns (crucially involving the duplicator combinator), without invoking the apparatus of a syntactic Binding Theory.

In the last part of her paper, she extends her proposal to VP-ellipsis. The fact that even quantificational antecedents support the strict reading of VP-ellipsis (cf. *Every man mentioned his merits before Mary did* '... before Mary mentioned his merits') has been taken to argue against Reinhart-like approaches like Szabolcsi's and to motivate the introduction of a new logical device, co-parametrization (see Gawron and Peters 1990). Szabolcsi challenges this conclusion, arguing that composition and duplication, the two combinators whose presence in CCG accounts for extraction and anaphora in the general case, are in fact sufficient to derive the strict readings here as well as in examples involving anaphors and gaps.

In her paper "The Lexical Entailment Theory of Control and the *Tough*-Construction," PAULINE JACOBSON presents another purely lexical analysis that challenges conventional syntactic wisdom. Sentences of the type *That rock is hard for me to move* exhibit a set of seemingly contradictory properties. The matrix subject appears to be selected by the infinitive, as in a raising construction; however, the gap following the transitive infinitive resembles *wh*-traces more than NP-traces. One solution to this puzzle, suggested by Chomsky, is to assume that the subject/gap relation is mediated by a null operator.

Building on a number of earlier results (including her own), Jacobson presents a careful examination of data pertaining to these points and to further properties of the construction, and concludes that there is no syntactic relationship between the subject of the *tough*-adjective and the gap. One crucial fact is that there is no syntactic category matching requirement (cf. *That language is learnable is hard for any theory to capture* versus *This theory captures that language is learnable*). On the other hand, the construction allows for null complement anaphora, which is characteristic of control constructions.

Jacobson argues for the following specific assumptions about the lexical, syntactic and semantic properties of the *tough*-adjective: (1) it subcategorizes for an infinitival complement that lacks an object; and (2) its subject is understood as filling the gap position purely in view of some entailment that is part of the lexical meaning of the adjective. This account is modeled after the lexical entailment theory of control, defended by Dowty, Chierchia and others, which holds that *want*, for instance, denotes a relation between individuals and properties, such that for any individual x which stands in the want-relation to a property P, x has the property P in the "want-world" of x. Showing that the same kind of explanation can handle the puzzling relation between the *tough*-subject and the gap, Jacobson suggests an interesting extension of this influential theory.

The final contribution to the volume, "A Lexical Analysis of Icelandic Case," by IVAN SAG, LAURI KARTTUNEN, and JEFFREY GOLDBERG (SKG), provides an essentially lexical treatment of the long-standing problem of "quirky" case in Icelandic complementation.

Although subjects in Icelandic are in general marked with nominative case, and objects are in general accusative, there are three well-studied classes of verbs which are exceptional in requiring (respectively) dative, accusative or genitive case on their subjects. The interesting problem that arises with respect to these quirky-subject verbs is their behavior in raising constructions. The generalizations can be stated simply as follows: (1) the raised subject of a subject-raising verb (e.g., *virðist* 'seems') is nominative if its infinitival complement is headed by a non-quirky verb; (2) the object of an object-raising verb (e.g., *telur* 'believes') is accusative if its infinitival complement is headed by a non-quirky verb; and (3) a raised argument must bear the appropriate quirky case if the head of the complement is a quirky-subject verb.

These facts, well-known in the literature on Icelandic syntax, strongly suggest a two-stage analysis—one where quirky case is lexically assigned in underlying syntactic structures, but structural case (nominative for subjects; accusative for objects) is assigned to very superficial syntactic representations, but *only to those nominals that did not receive (quirky) lexical case at an underlying level of syntactic representation*. The notions of *before transformations have applied* (for quirky case) and *after transformations have applied* (for structural case) appear to be indispensable for an account of these facts.

SKG, motivated by their desire to formulate all of linguistic knowledge as declarative constraints on possible structures, set forth a treatment of these facts that makes no reference to "before" or "after" stages of a transformational derivation. Their analysis posits two attributes—CASE (realized case) and DCASE (default case), and allows the possibility that a particular nominal may bear distinct values for these features. On SKG's analysis, a quirky-subject verb specifies only the CASE value of its subject, but a non-quirky verb specifies only that its subject's CASE value matches its DCASE value. These minimal specifications, together with the independently motivated treatment of realized subjects as [DCASE *nom*] and realized objects as [DCASE *acc*], lead to an account of the data just described that is nonprocedural, monotonic, and constraint-based, as intended, and yet expresses all the relevant generalizations. The SKG analysis is thus another example (like those proposed by Farkas, Szabolcsi, and Jacobson) of how complex data that have been taken to motivate transformational analyses, can be dealt with in alternative terms, without sacrificing either explanation or the design properties that are motivated by processing concerns.

The strong Hungarian presence in the volume at hand is no accident. Several of the papers in this volume were originally presented at the Symposium on Lexical Semantics, held during the 1987 LSA Linguistic Institute at Stanford University, which was attended by a delegation of Hungarian linguists (including one of the editors) and a number of American linguists of Hungarian descent (including the other editor). The editors both regret the various unforeseen delays, in consequence of which the contributions of Tenny, Krifka, Farkas, Kiefer, Gergely, and Szabolcsi, which were complete in 1989, are only now seeing the light of day.

Neither the 1987 symposium nor the present volume would have been possible without the generous support of both the Soros Foundation and the International Research Exchanges Board (IREX) (formerly sponsored by the American Council of Learned Societies and the Social Science Research Council), whose assistance we gratefully acknowledge. In addition, we wish to thank Ferenc Kiefer and András Kornai for their help in organizing the symposium, as well as Dikran Karagueuzian, Jonathan Ginzburg, and Jongbok Kim for their assistance in the preparation of this volume.

Ivan A. Sag and Anna Szabolcsi

References

Bresnan, Joan, and Jonni M. Kanerva. 1989. Locative Inversion in Chichewa: A Case Study of Factorization in Grammar. *Linguistic Inquiry* 20:1–50.

Bresnan, Joan, and Annie Zaenen. 1990. Deep Unaccusativity in LFG. In *Grammatical Relations: A Cross-Theoretical Perspective*, ed. Katarzyna Dziwirek, Patrick Farrell, and Errapel Mejías-Bikandi, 45–57. Stanford: CSLI Publications.

Dowty, David. 1991. Thematic Proto-Roles and Argument Selection. *Language* 67(3):547–619.

Gawron, Jean Mark, and Stanley Peters. 1990. *Anaphora and Quantification in Situation Semantics*. CSLI Lecture Notes No. 19. Stanford: CSLI Publications.

Zaenen, Annie. 1990. Unaccusativity in Dutch: an Integrated Approach. In *Semantics and the Lexicon*, ed. James Pustejovsky. Dordrecht: Kluwer.

Contributors

FARRELL ACKERMAN, Assistant Professor of Linguistics at the University
of California at San Diego, is interested in the interaction between lexical
semantics, morphology and syntax with special attention to the Finno-
Ugric languages.

DONKA F. FARKAS is Associate Professor of Linguistics at the University
of California at Santa Cruz. Her research interests include the interface
between syntax and semantics (in particular, the semantics of complementation), and morphology.

GYÖRGY GERGELY received his Ph.D. in 1986 in experimental psychology
at Columbia University, and has taught in the department of psychology
at the University of Rochester. His current research interests are language
processing, causal and intentional attribution in infancy, and experimental
and psychodynamic approaches to the development of the self.

JEFFREY GOLDBERG, now a resident of Hungary, is a graduate student in
the linguistics department at Stanford University. His research interests
include syntactic theory and computational linguistics.

PAULINE JACOBSON is Professor of Cognitive and Linguistic Sciences at
Brown University. Her research centers largely on the syntax/semantics
interface. She is especially interested in investigating the feasibility of direct
model-theoretic interpretation of (surface) syntactic structures.

LAURI KARTTUNEN is Principal Scientist at the Xerox Palo Alto Research
Center and Consulting Professor of Linguistics at Stanford University. His
linguistic publications include works on pragmatics and semantics. In computational linguistics, he is best known for his contributions to unification-
based grammars and finite-state morphology.

FERENC KIEFER is Senior Research Fellow at the Research Institute for
Linguistics of the Hungarian Academy of Sciences. His main research interests are morphology, semantics and pragmatics.

Lexical Matters. Ivan A. Sag and Anna Szabolcsi, eds.
Copyright © 1992, Stanford University.

MANFRED KRIFKA is currently Assistant Professor in the Department of Linguistics at the University of Texas at Austin. His research interests include the semantics of mass terms, count terms and aspectual classes, polarity phenomena, and focus. He has also worked on the syntax of Swahili.

MARK LIBERMAN obtained a doctorate in linguistics from the Massachusetts Institute of Technology in 1975. From 1975 to 1990, he worked at AT&T Bell Laboratories, for the last three years as head of the linguistics research department. He is now Trustee Professor of Phonetics at the University of Pennsylvania. His current research interests include prosody, phonetics, and computational linguistics, especially the problem of linguistic inference.

WILLIAM POSER is Associate Professor of Linguistics at Stanford University. His interests include the phonetics/phonology interface, the formal properties of phonological rules, phrasal phonology, and Japanese.

IVAN A. SAG is Professor of Linguistics and Symbolic Systems at Stanford University and Vice Chair of the Department of Linguistics. He has worked mostly in the areas of syntax, semantics and language processing.

RICHARD SPROAT holds a doctorate in linguistics from the Massachusetts Institute of Technology. His research interests include morphology, computational morphology, text-to-speech synthesis, Chinese computational linguistics, phonetics, and Celtic syntax. He is a member of the technical staff in the Linguistics Research Department at AT&T Bell Laboratories.

ANNA SZABOLCSI has worked on performatives and focus in Montague grammar, on the structure of the noun phrase in government and binding theory, and on binding and extraction in combinatory categorial grammar. She is currently Associate Professor of Linguistics at the University of California at Los Angeles.

CAROL TENNY is Assistant Professor of Linguistics at the University of Pittsburgh. Her research interests include theoretical syntax, the intersection of syntax and semantics, and the representation of time in natural language.

1

The Aspectual Interface Hypothesis

CAROL TENNY

1.1 Introduction: The Linking Problem

The problem of the linking of thematic roles to syntactic argument positions is of fundamental importance because it is part of the larger problem of the connection between syntax and semantics. Theories of generative grammar have adopted, to a greater or lesser extent, the view of an autonomous syntax operating independently from the semantics of a language. Up to a certain point, this view does seem to characterize the behavior of natural language. However, the problem remains that, in spite of the evidence for the autonomy of syntax and semantics, there are strong generalizations to be made about correspondences between meaning and syntactic structure. There are familiar facts that cannot be ignored; such as the fact that in general, agents are subjects, and themes or patients are objects. Lexical semantics and syntax clearly interact—the problem is how to constrain that interaction. Various mechanisms that have been proposed to deal with this, such as lists of linking rules that connect particular thematic roles with particular syntactic or configurational argument positions, are somewhat stipulative and not entirely satisfactory. More principled approaches to the problem have been presented in the recent literature, in the form of hypotheses that there are uniform and universal constraints on the mapping between syntax and lexical semantics. Perlmutter and Postal (1984) proposed the Universal Alignment Hypothesis (UAH) in the framework of Relational Grammar:

This paper is a 1989 revision of material, some of which was presented at LSA 1987 and NELS 1987 and appears in *Proceedings of NELS 18*, published by University of Massachusetts at Amherst. I am grateful to audiences at these meetings for their comments. I have also benefited from comments by Jane Grimshaw, Beth Levin, James Pustejovsky, Malka Rappaport, Anna Szabolcsi, and Robert Van Valin. This work has been supported by grants from the System Development Foundation and from the Kapor Family Foundation. I am grateful for their support.

Lexical Matters. Ivan A. Sag and Anna Szabolcsi, eds.

Universal Alignment Hypothesis (UAH): There exist principles of universal grammar which predict the initial relation borne by each nominal in a given clause from the meaning of the clause.

And Baker (1985) proposed the Universal Theta Assignment Hypothesis (UTAH), in the framework of Government and Binding Theory:

Universal Theta Assignment Hypothesis (UTAH): Identical thematic relationships between items are represented by identical structural relationships between those items at the level of D-structure.

Both of these hypotheses propose a fundamental connection between "meaning" and some level of syntactic representation. The UAH maintains that general principles constraining the mapping from lexical semantics to syntax do exist, although it gives no indication of what they might be. The UTAH claims that the mapping between thematic and structural relationships is consistent, although it does not explain why the mapping is the way it is. The UAH and the UTAH are elegant ideas that explain a variety of phenomena in a simple way. However, these hypotheses lack an account of the central mechanism by which thematic structures and syntactic structures are connected. The thesis of this paper is that certain aspectual properties mediate between syntax and lexical semantics, and provide a principled basis for hypotheses such as the UAH and the UTAH. The Aspectual Interface Hypothesis (AIH) is proposed to supplant the UAH and the UTAH:

Aspectual Interface Hypothesis: The mapping between thematic structure and syntactic argument structure is governed by aspectual properties. A universal aspectual structure associated with internal (direct), external and oblique arguments in syntactic structure constrains the kinds of event participants that can occupy these positions. Only the aspectual part of thematic structure is visible to the syntax.

This proposal takes a strong stand on the current controversy over whether grammar needs to refer to thematic roles. Under this view, the syntax proper does not need to "see" thematic roles. It only "sees" certain syntactic/aspectual structures the thematic roles are associated with.

This is also in the spirit of much recent work arguing that the thematic content of thematic roles need not be referred to by syntactic operations. (See Belletti and Rizzi 1988; Rappaport and Levin 1988; Levin and Rappaport 1986; Grimshaw 1987a; Rappaport, Laughren, and Levin 1987.)

This paper focuses on the central part of the aspectual structure proposed by the AIH: the correspondence between the argument in a semantic representation which has the special aspectual role of "measuring out the event," and the syntactic argument which may be characterized as the verb's internal argument. The crucial constraint on this correspondence may be stated as:

(1)   The internal argument of a simple verb is constrained so that it either
       undergoes no change or motion, or it undergoes change or motion
       which "measures out the event" over time.

The statement above may be regarded as one clause in a fully articulated
set of principles of aspectual structure. The discussion in this paper is
concerned with simple nonstative verbs (although (1) is true of stative
verbs as well). Verbs with more complicated argument structures, such
as propositional-argument-taking verbs, are unexplored in this paper and
must await further research.

      Section 1.2 outlines some assumptions about lexical and argument
structure on which the discussion in the paper depends. Then in Section 2, various lexical semantic phenomena are discussed which illustrate
the special aspectual role of the internal argument. These include affectedness, unaccusativity, the locative alternation, and psych verbs. Section 3
addresses the question of what the AIH says about thematic roles. Section
4 considers the implications of the AIH for language acquisition, and points
out some constraints it places on the lexicon.

1.2   Some Assumptions

The AIH as stated above adopts a certain view of argument structure and
lexical structure. It employs some ideas developed in the work of the MIT
Lexicon Project. The MIT Lexicon Project has been investigating what
information must be included in the lexical entry for a natural language
predicate; or (to look at it another way) what a native speaker must know
about predicates in his or her language, in order to be able to use them
correctly. (Hale and Keyser 1987; Rappaport and Levin 1986; Rappaport,
Laughren and Levin 1987.) A structured lexical entry has been developed
which has two parts: a structural part and a conceptual part. For example,
Hale and Keyser (1988) show the lexical entry for *cut* as in Figure 1.

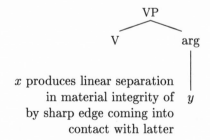

Figure 1 Lexical Entry for English *cut*

      The prose part of the entry expresses the conceptual part of the verb's
meaning, including the number of open arguments and the roles they play

in the event described by the verb. (Notice that thematic roles *per se* are not mentioned.) The structural part indicates how these roles are to be mapped onto syntactic structures. The tree-like structure simply indicates that the "*y*" argument must be the syntactic object of the verb. What is crucial here is that the verbal entry has two parts: a semantic/conceptual part and a syntactic/structural part; and it indicates the nature of the correspondence between them. The AIH drives that correspondence, and it has as a consequence the requirement that the argument linked to the verb's direct object position must be aspectually constrained.

The view of argument structure assumed here includes a distinction between external and internal arguments, and a distinction between direct internal and indirect internal arguments. (See Williams 1980 on external arguments.) External or internal argumenthood is essentially a syntactic property. Argument structures are assumed to map onto syntactic structures in a straightforward way, so that internal and external argumenthood may be equated with syntactic positions. The expression "syntactic argument structure" is used here to refer to these arguments mapped onto their syntactic positions. In this paper the syntactic consequences of the AIH are cast in the framework of Government and Binding Theory, but this is not essential. I believe they may also be expressed in other syntactic frameworks.

Employing the tools of Government and Binding Theory, external arguments are generated outside the verb phrase and are not governed by the verb at D-structure. Internal arguments are generated within the verb phrase. Direct internal arguments are generated as structural objects of the verb, and are assigned structural case by the verb, while internal indirect arguments (oblique arguments) do not receive structural case from the verb. Instead they are assigned inherent case or are assigned case by a preposition. These three argument-types—external, direct, and oblique— are assumed to be associated with these distinctive syntactic positions. I believe these definitions of external, direct and oblique arguments may be translated into other frameworks. What is necessary is simply that there be some representation of argument structure which includes aspectual information, and which has some clear mapping to syntax.

2.1 Aspect and the Internal Argument

In the theory presented here, the crucial aspectual property is associated with the direct internal argument of a verb. The direct internal argument of a verb of change "measures out" over time the event described by the verb. The verb's direct internal argument may be thought of as being converted into a function of time at some level of semantic representation. This is an aspectual property, because aspect refers to the internal temporal organization of an event. The term "measures out" is used here in an informal sense, as a convenient metaphor for uniform and consistent change, such as change

along a scale. The idea of an object measuring out an event can be eluci-
dated using the aspectual property of delimitedness. A delimited event is
one that the language encodes as having an endpoint in time. The aspectual
distinction between delimited and nondelimited events has a long history of
discussion in the philosophical and linguistic literature, dating back to Aris-
totle. (Particularly notable in the recent literature are Vendler 1967, Dowty
1979, Hinrichs 1985, and Verkuyl 1972, 1976, 1978, 1987ab.) The difference
between delimited and nondelimited events is illustrated in (2) and (3).

(2)   Delimited:
       a. destroy the city (in an hour/*for an hour)
       b. climb a tree (in an hour/?for an hour)

(3)   Nondelimited:
       a. like jazz (*in a day/for a day)
       b. push the car (*in an hour/for an hour)

The events described by the verb phrases in (2a) and (2b) are delimited
events; those in (3a) and (3b) are nondelimited events. Temporal adverbial
expressions such as *in an hour* and *for an hour* are useful in distinguishing
between a delimited and a nondelimited reading.[1]

Now consider the verb phrases below. In their salient readings, these
describe delimited events:[2]

(4)   a. perform a play
       b. translate a poem

Not only do these events have temporal bounds, but these bounds are
provided by the referent of the internal argument. In other words, it is the
object that delimits the event. When you perform a play, you perform act
one, then act two, and so on, until you come to the end of the play. The
end of the play is the end of the event. Likewise, in translating a poem,
one may translate the first stanza, then the second stanza, then the third,
until the end of the poem is reached and the translation event is over.

A very coarse test for this idea is provided by certain adverbials such
as *halfway*, which make reference to a kind of measurement:

(5)   a. perform a play halfway
       b. perform half a play
       c. translate a poem halfway
       d. translate half a poem
       e. destroy the city halfway
       f. destroy half the city

---

[1]These adverbial expressions, however, are sensitive to lexical subtleties that make
them imperfect diagnostics of delimitedness. The definition of delimitedness must be
based on the existence of an understood temporal bound to the event, rather than solely
on tests using adverbials.

[2]Some speakers find these to be vague between a delimited and a nondelimited reading.

Although the two verb phrases in each couplet do not mean exactly the same thing, in each pair the second verb phrase represents one possible way to understand the first. That is, *halfway through the event* may be equated with *half of the object*.

In the examples above, the direct internal argument measures out the event through its spatial extent or volume. This makes these examples particularly clear. However, the argument need not measure out the event through its spatial extent or volume; some other property of the object may measure out the event, as in (6) below:

(6)   a. redden the photograph
       b. ripen the fruit

In (6a) it is the redness of the object, and in (6b) it is the ripeness of the object that measures out the event. In both cases the verb names that property of its argument which is to do the measuring.

The direct internal arguments in the verb phrases in (3) through (5) above measure out and delimit the event described by the verb. However, under the theory proposed here, all direct internal arguments undergoing change are constrained to measure out the event, whether or not it is a delimited event.

Consider (7) below:

(7)   a. push the cart (*in an hour/for an hour)
       b. push the cart to New York (in an hour/?for an hour)

In (7a), the verb and its direct internal argument describe a nondelimited event, rather than a delimited one. In (7b) however, with the addition of a goal phrase (an indirect internal argument) the event becomes delimited. Nevertheless, the cart still measures out the event in both of these expressions. The delimitedness of (7b) is achieved through reference to the very property of the direct internal argument that is measuring out the event: namely, its location. The indirect internal argument—or the goal phrase—delimits the event by referring to that property of the direct argument that is undergoing the central change in the event. Example (7) above illustrates how the arguments of verbs that describe nondelimited events may be unified with arguments of verbs describing delimited events such as those in (3), (4) and (5). Verbs such as *push* may be subsumed under the condition that the direct internal argument of the verb is constrained to measure out the event through a change in a single property. The change in the direct internal argument during the course of the event must be describable as a change in a single property. The event may be delimited linguistically through reference to that change or that property.

To summarize the discussion thus far, the following hypotheses have been made. All direct internal arguments undergoing change in the event described by the verb measure out the event. Direct arguments are distinguished arguments in this respect. With some verbs (*perform, translate, destroy*, *redden*, *ripen*) the direct internal argument measures out and delimits the event. With other verbs (*push*) the direct internal argument measures out the event and an indirect internal argument may delimit it. Only internal arguments can delimit the event, and they can do this only by reference to the measuring performed by the direct internal argument.

Various elements of the idea proposed in this paper—that an internal argument measures out an event—may be found in Gruber 1976; Jackendoff 1987; Dowty 1979, 1988; Krifka 1987; Verkuyl 1972, 1976, 1978, 1987ab; Hinrichs 1985; and Pustejovsky 1988.[3] However, none of these authors has extended the idea to include internal arguments in general, or employed the idea as a truly general principle of correspondence between syntactic structure and semantics.

The idea that only the direct internal argument measures out the event explains an asymmetry between internal and external arguments regarding the interaction of the aspectual properties of NP's and VP's. There is an interesting asymmetry between internal and external arguments in the interaction of mass noun arguments with delimitedness. There is a class of verbs which translate count-ness of the internal argument into delimitedness of the event.[4] When the internal argument is a count noun the event is delimited (8a), and when it is a mass noun it is nondelimited (8b). The internal arguments are underlined in (8) below:

(8)   a. Charles drank *a mug of beer* (??for an hour/in an hour). (delimited)
      b. Charles drank *beer* (for an hour/*in an hour). (nondelimited)

To the best of my knowledge there is no corresponding class of verbs that translate count-ness of the external argument into delimited-ness of the event. Whether the external arguments underlined in (9) and (10) are mass or count nouns has no effect on the delimited-ness of the event:

(9)   a. *The heater* melted the candle. (delimited)
      b. *Heat* melted the candle. (delimited)

(10) a. *Snow* surrounds the house. (nondelimited)
      b. *Seven trees* surround the house. (nondelimited)

---

[3]Krifka (1987) and Hinrichs (1985) have written on certain delimiting predicates which, roughly speaking, express homomorphisms from their arguments to the events they describe. Dowty (1991) has employed this idea as one contributing property for the Proto-Patient Role, mapping "incremental themes" (such as *house* in *build a house*) onto the Proto-Patient role. (See Section 2.7.)

[4]It is well known that bare plurals in either subject or object position affect the aspectual properties of a sentence. A bare plural subject or object makes it possible for the sentence to describe some event of indefinite duration. Bare plurals, which behave like mass nouns in many respects, do not exhibit the subject/object asymmetry described above. They must be considered a separate phenomenon for the purpose of this discussion.

Mass/count properties of internal arguments but not of external arguments interact with the aspectual properties of verb phrases and sentences. This asymmetry between internal and external arguments makes sense in light of the requirement that only internal arguments measure out events.[5]

2.2 Affectedness

The property of affectedness has been much discussed in the literature lately. Affectedness is interesting for two reasons: (i) because it is a semantic property that has been implicated in certain syntactic phenomena, and (ii) because it is always associated with direct internal arguments. An affected argument has been generally described as an argument which undergoes some change. Undergoing change is a temporal process. An affected argument can be more adequately described in aspectual terms, as an argument which measures out and delimits the event described by the verb. An affected argument measures out the event by virtue of its being a direct internal argument. What is special about it is that it also delimits the event. The characterization of these arguments as delimiting the event unifies a larger class of verbs having the same syntactic behaviors than does the idea of being affected by some action. Although this fact does not explain why these syntactic behaviors correlate with aspectual properties, it does explain why the crucial aspectual property is associated with the direct internal argument.

The correlation of affectedness with delimited-ness can be illustrated by considering some of the syntactic phenomena in which affectedness has been implicated. Among the syntactic phenomena that affectedness is relevant to are middle formation and NP passivization. (See Anderson 1979, Roberts 1985, and Hale and Keyser 1987 on these topics. The aspectual nature of the affectedness constraint on NP-passivization has also been noted by Fellbaum (1987).) Consider the NP-passives in (11) and (12).

(11) a. The Mongols' destruction of the city.
      b. The city's destruction by the Mongols.
      c. The missionaries' conversion of the natives.
      d. The natives' conversion by the missionaries.

(12) a. John's avoidance of Bill.
      b.*Bill's avoidance by John.
      c. Sally's pursuit of the cat.
      d.*The cat's pursuit by Sally.
         (M. Anderson 1979 (=(51),(53)))

In (11) the arguments are affected and NP passivization is possible. In (12), where the arguments are not affected, NP passivization does not yield good

---

[5]A full account of this phenomenon must be cast in a sound theory of mass- and count-ness, and is beyond the scope of this paper.

expressions. The possibility of NP-passivization correlates closely with the delimited or nondelimited-ness of the event. This is shown in (13) by the applicability of temporal adverbials:

(13) a. destroy the city in a day/*for a day
          (the city's destruction in a day/*for a day)
      b. convert the natives in a month/??for a month
          (the native's conversion by the missionaries in a month/*for a month)
      c. avoid Bill *in an hour/for an hour.
      d. pursue the cat *in an hour/for an hour.

Not only do (13a) and (13b) describe delimited events, but they describe events delimited by the change in the argument. The argument measures out and delimits the events in these examples.

The property that governs NP-passivization is actually an aspectual property. This explains why some verbs like *perform* take NP-passives when they do not actually seem to affect their arguments, as in (14).

(14) a. The company's performance of the play.
      b. The play's performance by the company.
          (M. Anderson 1979 (=(48)))
      c. John's translation of the poem.
      d. The poem's translation by John.

An aspectual definition of an affected argument as a delimiting argument unifies a wider range of relevant data than a definition based on the notion of being affected by some action.

Now consider the middles in (15) and (16).

(15) a. This door opens easily (by pulling on the handle).
      b. This cinch tightens easily (if you give it a good yank).
          (after Hale and Keyser 1987)
      c. This door opens easily in a minute/?for a minute.
      d. This cinch tightens easily in a minute/?for a minute.

(16) a.*The traffic jam avoids easily.
      b.*Fleeing burglars pursue easily.
      c. avoid the traffic jam *in a minute/for a minute
      d. pursue the burglar *in an hour/for an hour

In (15) the arguments are affected arguments, and middles are possible. In (16) they are unaffected and middles are not possible. Again, in (15) the possibility of middle formation correlates with the delimited-ness of the event, and in (16) the impossibility of middle formation correlates with the nondelimited-ness of the event, as shown by the adverbials. The arguments in (15) are delimiting and those in (16) are nondelimiting.

The distinction between delimiting and nondelimiting arguments explains the difference in judgments speakers assign to the sentences in (17).

(17) a. The desert crosses easily for settlers with large wagons.
      b.*The desert wanders easily for settlers with large wagons.
      c. The globe circumnavigates in a day/easily with Pan Am
      d.*The globe travels in a day/easily with Pan Am.
      e. The enemy battalion infiltrated surprisingly easily for the guerrilla
         soldiers.
      f.*The enemy battalion pursued surprisingly easily for the guerrilla
         soldiers.

Although judgments about middles are notoriously murky, most speakers
agree with the relative grammaticality judgments illustrated here.[6]

The examples above show that affected arguments are delimiting arguments, and the notion of delimiting argument is more appropriate than that
of affected argument as a criterion for syntactic behavior. It is well-known
that affected arguments are always direct internal arguments of the verb.
This is predicted by a theory in which direct internal arguments measure
out events. Affected arguments are a subset of the class of direct internal
arguments; they are those arguments that not only measure out but also
delimit the event.

To summarize, the aspectual constraints on internal arguments give us a
handle on the semantic property of affectedness, predict that affected argu-

---

[6]The delimiting argument constraint on middles and NP-passivization predicts that
the same class of verbs will enter into both of these constructions. This prediction is by
and large borne out. Verbs that form middles also form NP-passives:

  (i)   the desert's crossing by settlers with large wagons
  (ii)*the desert's wandering by settlers with large wagons
  (iii) the globe's circumnavigation by Pan Am
  (iv)*the globe's traveling by Pan Am
  (v)   the enemy battalion's infiltration by the guerrilla soldiers
  (vi)*the enemy battalion's pursuit by the guerrilla soldiers

Verbs that form NP-passives (i-iv below) form relatively good middles compared to
verbs which do not form NP-passives (v and vi below), but middle formation is not as
productive as NP-passivization:

  (i) ?Shakespeare's Othello performs more easily with a good company than with a
       bad one.
  (ii) Haiku poetry does not translate at all.
  (iii) ??European explorers found that natives convert with the sword more easily than
        with the word.
  (iv) (??)(*)The munitions research industry predicts that major cities will destroy
        quickly and effortlessly with the weapons of the future.
  (v)*Policemen avoid easily in a crowd.
  (vi)*Burglars pursue easily on foot.

Examples (i), (ii), and (iv) above are poor to unacceptable for most speakers but they
improve with exposure. Middle formation appears to be slightly more constrained than
NP-passivization. Since speakers' judgments about middles show so much variability,
it is likely that there are additional subtle factors at work with middles. It is also
possible that middle formation is more of a lexical phenomenon than NP passivization.
Nevertheless, the delimiting constraint picks out by and large the correct class of verbs
for both middle formation and NP-passivization.

ments should be internal arguments, and substitute the notion of delimiting argument for affected argument as a criterion for certain kinds of syntactic behavior. And although the reason for the interaction of delimited-ness with middle-formation and NP-passivization is still obscure, recognition of the fact that delimited-ness has syntactic properties is a step towards a deeper understanding of the syntax of these constructions.

2.3 Unaccusative and Unergative Verbs

Following the Unaccusative Hypothesis, unaccusative verbs are verbs whose sole argument is an internal direct argument, while unergative verbs have an external argument as their sole argument. (The Unaccusative Hypothesis and the representation of unaccusativity in syntactic theory is discussed by Perlmutter and Postal 1984 and Burzio 1986. For contrasting views and problems, see Van Valin 1987 and Zaenen 1987. For a useful overview of issues see Grimshaw 1987b.) These two classes of verbs constitute a minimal pair with which to investigate the properties of internal and external arguments. The internal or external status of the arguments of unaccusative and unergative verbs is a syntactic fact. However, it is well known that there are strong general semantic tendencies associated with this syntactic distinction. Unergative verbs are usually verbs in which the argument engages in some kind of volitional activity, while unaccusative verbs describe situations in which the argument undergoes some kind of change. Unaccusatives usually assign a patient or theme thematic role to their argument, while unergatives more often than not assign agent thematic roles. These familiar facts are illustrated by the following examples:

(18) a. unergatives: (external arguments; agent)
      run, dance, whisper, bicycle, study
    b. unaccusatives/ergatives: (internal arguments; patient, theme)
      melt, freeze, evaporate, fall, open, collapse

In a model of grammar in which syntax and semantics are strictly autonomous, such a correlation of semantic properties with syntactic structures is difficult to express. In a model in which a wide range of semantic properties is visible to the syntax, the connection between syntax and semantics is difficult to constrain. The semantic generalizations about these verbs are too strong to ignore. The proposal that the internal argument is constrained to measure out the event provides a simple explanation. There are differing aspectual constraints on internal and external arguments, and these aspectual constraints affect what types of thematic roles may occupy those positions. Applying the adverbial *halfway* brings out a difference between unaccusatives and unergatives:

(19) a.*Martha danced halfway.
     *Thomas ate halfway.
     *Jack whispered halfway.

    b. The lake froze halfway.

      The candle melted halfway.

      The barn collapsed halfway.

Halfway applies naturally to the unaccusatives in (19b) but not to the unergatives in (19a).[7]

Adverbial phrases such as *a little bit at a time*, or *a lot at once* provide additional tests. These are illustrated in (20) and (21).

(20)   a. The dancer danced slowly/*a little bit at a time.

       The announcer talked slowly/*a little bit at a time.

       The actress whispered slowly/*a little bit at a time.

     b. The candle melted slowly/a little bit at a time.

       The lake froze slowly/a little bit at a time.

       The barn collapsed slowly/a little bit at a time.

(21)   a.??Martha danced quickly, a lot of her dancing at once.

      ??The announcer talked quickly, a lot of him talking at once.

      ??The actress whispered quickly, a lot of her whispering at once.

     b. The candle melted quickly, a lot of it melting at once.

       The lake froze quickly, a lot of it freezing at once.

       The barn collapsed quickly, a lot of it collapsing at once.

These expressions are awkward when used in conjunction with an unergative verb, but quite natural when used with unaccusative verbs.[8]

The proposal that the internal argument is constrained to measure out the event through some property it possesses, while the external argument is not so constrained, explains the semantic distribution of verb meanings across unergative and unaccusative verb classes. Those verb meanings which become unaccusative verbs describe exactly those event types in which the event participant may be construed as measuring out the event. Verb meanings in which the event participant may not be construed as measuring out the event must become unergative verbs. And finally there will be a class of verb meanings that may be construed in either way, and these will be unaccusative in some languages and unergative in other languages. This is the nature of the correlation that is attested cross-linguistically. (Merlan 1985 examines this question in detail.) The view advanced here of the connection between lexical semantics and syntactic argument structure predicts this. It maintains that there is no absolute mapping from verb meanings to syntactic argument structure. Rather, there is a kind of

---

[7]There is a special sense of *Martha danced halfway* which is acceptable—namely that in which Martha dances halfway to some destination. But in this case the property which is measuring out the event (location), although it is changing in the external argument (Martha), can only be expressed in its pure form through an internal argument, as in *Martha danced half the distance (home)*.

[8]There are some verbs to which these adverbials do not easily apply. Additional tests need to be devised. The reader is reminded that the adverbials serve only to elucidate the aspectual properties of internal arguments. They are not diagnostics.

event template associated with argument structure that acts as a filter on verb meanings. This event template consists of a set of universal aspectual principles of argument structure, including the principle that the internal argument measures out the event.[9]

Van Valin (1987) showed that the aspectual properties of verbs can be used to determine their class membership in the unaccusative or unergative verb classes, and that Dowty's aspectual calculus for lexical decomposition is an effective language for doing so. The theory proposed here has much in common with Van Valin's proposal, but it differs in two crucial ways. In both theories there is a mapping from aspectual properties to syntax, directly or indirectly. But according to Van Valin, the mapping from aspectual properties of verbs to syntax is constrained only in that aspectual properties must be statable in a Dowty-style calculus. These constraints may be language-particular. Under the view advanced here there is one overriding and universal aspectual constraint; that the internal argument, associated with the D-structural object position, measures out the event. The internal argument must be convertible into a (nontrivial) function of time. This overriding aspectual constraint unifies unaccusativity with other verbal phenomena. The two views are not incompatible, however, since within the limits of this general aspectual constraint, there is room for a variety of mappings from Dowty-style aspectual properties into syntax. Secondly, under the theory proposed here (which adopts the Unaccusative Hypothesis) aspectual properties are directly correlated with syntactic structures. This view says that certain aspectual properties are in fact syntactic properties, and predicts that further repercussions of these properties may be found in syntax.

The aspectual properties of internal and external arguments also provide a reason for the familiar fact that agents are never direct internal arguments.[10] Agents are a type of event participant which are inherently

---

[9]One might say, taking this view, that there is a mapping from verb meanings to aspectual structure. However, without a pre-aspectual theory of verb meanings it would be impossible to describe this as an absolute mapping. Even with such a theory it may not be possible, since factors as imprecise as religious or cultural views may influence what type of aspectual properties certain kinds of events are perceived by language speakers to have. It must be emphasized that this theory does not provide the tools for a perfect and absolute mapping from pre-aspectual verb meanings to syntactic structures. In a certain sense it preserves the essential autonomy of syntax and semantics.

[10]Two well-known potential counterexamples to this generalization are syntactically ergative languages, and certain lexical causatives. There is some doubt among researchers on Australian and Eskimo languages that syntactically ergative languages do exist. (Jane Simpson (personal communication) and Alana Johns (personal communication), respectively. Also see Heath 1979 on Dyirbal.) However, if there are true syntactically ergative languages, they pose an interesting problem for the AIH. In most general terms, the AIH requires that there be a distinction between arguments that measure out the event and those that do not, and that this distinction correlates with syntactic structure. Furthermore, the argument that measures out the event

unsuited to measuring out an event on a scale. An agent by its very nature is free to act in unspecified ways to effect something. The actions required of an agent are underspecified and also not necessarily consistent throughout an event, and so are not naturally construable as a scale on which something could be measured.

2.4 The Locative Alternation

Next consider the locative alternation, investigated by Schwartz-Norman (1976), S. Anderson (1977), and Rappaport and Levin (1986). The verbs that participate in this alternation are verbs which take a goal and a theme argument, either of which can be the direct argument of the verb. For example:

(22) a. spray paint on the wall
      b. spray the wall with paint

Either the goal, *wall*, or the theme, *paint*, can be the direct argument of the verb *spray*. Only a very particular class of verbs show this alternation. Not all verbs that have a goal and a theme argument can undergo this alternation. The verb *push* also takes a goal and a theme, but the alternation is not possible in (23):

(23) a. push a cart to San Francisco
      b.*push San Francisco with a cart

The possibility of the locative alternation seems to depend on a very narrow semantic property; the goal must be a flat surface or container, and the theme must be a material which is removed or applied to that surface or container. The verbs in (24) illustrate these properties:

(24) a. load hay on the wagon
      b. load the wagon with hay
      c. clear dishes from the table
      d. clear the table of dishes
      e. cram pencils into the jar
      f. cram the jar with pencils

Furthermore, this generalization holds across a wide variety of unrelated languages. Examples (25) and (26) illustrate the alternation in Dutch and Japanese:

---

must be closer syntactically to the verb than arguments that do not. If there are languages in which the agent is closer to the verb than the theme (under deep syntactic analysis) then this requirement is violated. If such languages exist, the details of this mapping from aspectual structure into syntactic structure would have to be revised. The second case is that of lexical causatives such as *gallop* in *John galloped the horse*, where the internal argument, the horse, has agentive powers. Nevertheless, in this sentence the horse's change of location is measuring out the event. (Consider *John galloped the horse to the edge of the field.*) This example underscores the fact that traditional thematic role labels may be too coarse to express the relevant aspectual properties.

(25)　Dutch:
　　　　a. Jan plant bomen in de tuin.
　　　　　 John plants trees in the garden.
　　　　b. Jan be-plant de tuin met bomen.
　　　　　 John be-plants the garden with trees.
　　　　　 (De Groot 1984, his source Dik 1980)

(26)　Japanese:
　　　　a. kabe ni penki o nuru
　　　　　 wall on paint-ACC paint(VERB)
　　　　　 smear paint on the wall
　　　　b. kabe o penki de nuru
　　　　　 wall ACC paint-with paint(VERB)
　　　　　 smear the wall with paint
　　　　　 (Fukui, Miyagawa, Tenny 1985)

The locative alternation is an alternation in syntactic argument structure that depends on certain characteristics of the theme and the goal. Since we know syntax and semantics to be autonomous to such a large extent, we must ask why such seemingly trivial semantic properties should have syntactic repercussions such as these? The proposal that the direct internal argument is constrained to measure out the event described by the verb provides a simple explanation. These verbs describe exactly those events in which the goal may be construed as measuring out the event. If you apply some material to a flat surface, or fill a container with something, then the material spreads out across the surface or rises up to the top of the container in a consistent and uniform way, and in so doing may be seen to measure out the event.

The aspectual constraints on internal arguments predict certain other familiar facts about the locative alternation. Consider (27) below:

(27)　a. spray the paint in the hole
　　　　b. spray the hole with paint

Phrase (27a) means that the paint is directed into the hole but not necessarily spread around on the surface or wall of the hole. (27b), however, is not an accurate paraphrase of (27a) because it means that the paint is spread around on the surface or wall of the hole. This is because when the goal, the hole, is the direct argument of the verb it is constrained to measure out the event.

The locative alternation is impossible when an instrument thematic role is substituted for the material thematic role. Both material and instrument are possible as indirect objects:

(28)　a. spray the wall with water
　　　　b. spray the wall with a hose

But only the material can be a direct argument:

(29) a. spray water on the wall
      b.*spray a hose on the wall

This is because a material is consumed a little at a time until it is gone, thus measuring out the event, but an instrument does not undergo change in such a way that it can be construed as measuring out the event. In this case it is precisely the aspectual properties of the material and instrument thematic roles which determine how they are mapped into the syntax.

Finally, this approach to the locative alternation can be extended to verbs that take "path" arguments. For example:

(30) a. walk the bridge
      b. walk across the bridge
      c. walk to the bridge

In (30a) *the bridge* is a path argument which measures out the event by virtue of being the verb's direct argument. Although both (30b) and (30c) are acceptable expressions, only (30b) may be a paraphrase of (30a). In (30a) and (30b) the walking event is understood to traverse the bridge, so that a certain amount of bridge correlates with a certain amount of walking. The bridge measures out the walking.

Under this view, it is the aspectual properties of thematic roles that are relevant for syntactic argument structure. The aspectual differences between materials and instruments, and the aspectual properties of certain types of goals, together with the principle that the internal argument measures out the event, are what make the locative alternation possible or impossible.[11]

2.5 Psych Verbs

Next consider psych verbs. These are verbs that have an argument bearing an experiencer thematic role. (The syntax of psych verbs has been discussed by Grimshaw (1987a), Pesetsky (1987), and Belletti and Rizzi (1988), among others.) In the sentences below, John is an experiencer. The experiencer is an external argument in (31a) and an internal argument in (31b):

(31) a. John fears ghosts.
      b. Ghosts frighten John.

---

[11]The aspectual properties of thematic roles determine the possibility of the locative alternation as allowed by a universal semantics. Language-particular lexicalization may allow only a subset of these universal possibilities. We see this for example with *fill*:

  (i) fill the cup
  (ii)*fill the coffee

However, the prediction is that these "universal possibilities" allow *fill* to be re-analyzed as taking the locative alternation:

  (iii)?fill the coffee up to the rim of the cup

Compare this with (23b)repeated below:

  (iv)*push San Francisco with a cart

Psych verbs present interesting minimal pairs in which similar (or identical) verbs assign the same thematic role—experiencer—to the internal or external argument position. At first glance there seems to be no difference in meaning between the members of a pair like *fear* and *frighten*. However, there is an important difference in meaning between verbs with internal argument experiencers and external argument exeriencers, and this is the difference predicted by an aspectual theory of argument structure. When the experiencer is an internal argument it measures out the event, and when it is an external argument it does not.[12] This can be illustrated by adding delimiting expressions to the sentence:

(32) a.* *John$_i$* feared the truth *into drinking$_i$*.
      b. The truth frightened *John$_i$ into drinking$_i$*.

(33) a.??John feared *the truth$_i$ into innocuousness$_i$*.
      b.* *The truth$_i$* frightened John *into innocuousness$_i$*.

Sentence (33a) is problematic because *fear* is a stative verb, and the role of the internal argument as the measure of change is only apparent with verbs of change. (33a) is only acceptable if *fear* is interpreted (or perhaps re-analyzed) as a verb of change. If this is possible (and it may be for a very few speakers) then (33a) means "John made the truth innocuous by fearing it" or "John feared the truth so much it became innocuous for him." This re-analysis is easier with other experiencer-external psych verbs:

(34) a. John resented his neighbor so much, he resented him right into the hospital (by attacking him with a bat).
      b. Mary admires her brother to pieces.

These expressions, facetious and idiomatic as they are, serve to illustrate that if these verbs can be understood as verbs of change, the universal aspectual structure of verbs of change—in which the internal argument measures out the event—is available. This aspectual structure is brought out by delimiting expressions that refer only to the internal argument. The delimiting expressions in (32), (33) and (34) (*into drinking, into innocuousness, into the hospital, to pieces*), are actually resultative secondary predicates. They refer to the central property of the internal argument which is changing and measuring out the event. They delimit the event by picking out some point in that ongoing change at which the event terminates. (The expression *to pieces* does so metaphorically if not literally.) When the experiencer is the external argument, the event may not be de-

---

[12]Belletti and Rizzi (1988) propose a structure for psych verbs with external argument experiencers in which both arguments are generated under the verb phrase, with the experiencer as the highest NP governed by the VP. This is not inconsistent with the theory proposed here since what is important is the correlation of aspectual and syntactic properties. If Belletti and Rizzi are correct, then it is the highest NP generated under the VP which measures out the event.

limited by referring to a property of that experiencer. When it is an internal argument, it is quite natural to do so.

The aspectual constraints on internal arguments provide an explanation for the familiar fact that secondary resultative predicates may refer to the object but not the subject of the sentence. Resultatives are syntactic constructions that depend on the aspectual structure built up by the composition of the verb and its direct argument. Since the external argument is excluded from this aspectual structure, resultatives may not be predicated of external arguments. Consistent with this is the fact that a resultative secondary predicate is constrained not just to refer to the object but to refer to the property of the object that is measuring out the event. The resultative and the internal argument must agree on what property that is. If the delimiting expression in (32b) is changed to a locational goal phrase, the sentence is bad unless it can be interpreted as expressing motion (i.e., change in location):

(35)   The truth frightened John to Ohio.

Sentence (35) is incoherent if it is John's becoming afraid that measures out the event. But it is a good sentence if it is John's changing in location that measures out the event. In the latter case the sentence would be understood to mean that the truth made John go to Ohio by frightening him. Note that this view also unifies resultatives and goal phrases under one aspectual structure. It has been noted (by Simpson (1983), among others) that resultatives and goal phrases pattern together in many ways, and that they do not co-occur. This is not surprising given that they fulfill the same role in the aspectual structure of the sentence.

The case of these psych-verb pairs is particularly telling for a number of reasons. First of all, the thematic role of the arguments in internal and external position is exactly the same. (See Pesetsky 1987 for another view.) The aspectual difference between 'fear' and 'frighten' cannot be traced to differences in thematic structure. They derive only from the difference in syntactic structure.

Secondly, the object-orientation of resultatives is a syntactic fact of great generality. The connection of this fact with the aspectual properties of internal arguments underscores the idea that these properties are syntactically rather than thematically based. The tight connection between aspect and syntax suggests that we may expect to find further repercussions in syntax, of the aspectual properties of syntactic argument structure. And conversely, aspect may be used as a tool in syntactic investigations.

Finally, psych verbs have posed a problem for theories that tightly constrain the mapping of lexical semantics into syntax, because there seems to be no difference in meaning between comparable verbs with experiencers in internal and external argument position. However, there is a difference in meaning that follows from the different aspectual roles of the experiencer in internal and external argument position. The thematic role of experiencer happens to be adaptable to either of the aspectual representations of internal or external argumenthood. In other words, the mapping of lexical semantics into syntax may be tightly constrained only if it is based on aspectual properties, rather than on thematic roles.

2.6 Other Verbs

Unaccusative verbs, locative alternation verbs, and psych verbs provide various kinds of evidence for the AIH. The aspectual properties of argument structure (and particularly of direct internal arguments) are easily apparent with these verbs. There are a few other classes of verbs in which this aspectual structure is less apparent. These include achievement verbs, verbs with goal agents, and verbs with source agents. These verbs may not argue for the AIH in a strong way, but they are not inconsistent with it.

Achievement verbs (e.g., *explode*, *die*) describe events that happen instantaneously (or nearly so). They have internal arguments which measure out the event, even though the measuring has no extended duration:

(36)   The terrorist exploded the bomb.

It is not the duration of the measuring that is important; it is the fact that the internal argument registers the temporal end of the event. This is true in (36) since it is the bomb that undergoes the change that delimits the event, not the terrorist.

Verbs with goal agents (e.g., *acquire*, *buy*, *receive*) are another interesting class. Although the external argument, the agent, seems to be a kind of locational endpoint for the event, it is the internal argument that is actually measuring out the event over time. These verbs behave with rate adverbials in the same way as do unergatives:

(37)   a. John acquired the property slowly, acquiring a little of it at a time.
        b. John acquired the property slowly, *a little of him acquiring it at a time.

Verbs with source agents (e.g., *send*, *give*, *mail*) also describe events in which the external argument seems to mark a significant point of time in the event:

(38)   Christopher sent the package to Bill.

Christopher's act of sending and the package's arrival at Bill's location both seem to mark a potential endpoint of the event. Nevertheless, it is the change undergone by the package and not by Christopher, which is referred to by the delimiting expression (the goal phrase, *to Bill*). In this respect, *send* is similar to *push*, discussed in Section 2.1.[13]

The discussion up to this point has focused on verbs that describe events

---

[13]Double object constructions based on these verbs pose interesting questions for the AIH which I will not address here. See Tenny 1987.

in which the internal argument undergoes some change or motion. It has been argued that with all of these verbs, the change or motion in the internal argument is such that it "measures out the event," or is a function of time. There are many verbs which are not statives, but which describe events in which the internal argument undergoes no change:

(39) a. George pounded the wall.
      b. Mary embraced her sister.
      c. Carla studied the elk population.

The internal arguments of the verbs above do not "measure out the event" in the sense described above. We can state the generalization about internal arguments of verbs of change as follows:

(40) The internal argument of a simple verb is constrained so that it either undergoes no change or motion in the event described by the verb, or it undergoes change or motion which "measures out the event."

Even with verbs where the internal argument undergoes no change or motion, the aspectual structure in which the internal argument measures out the event is sometimes latent. A resultative can be predicated only of the direct internal argument of a verb of contact. A direct internal argument (41a), but not an external argument (41b) or indirect internal argument (41c), can be forced to be understood as undergoing a change that delimits the event:

(41) a. George pounded the wall$_i$ to pieces$_i$.
      b.*George$_i$ pounded the wall to exhaustion$_i$.
      c.*George pounded on the wall$_i$ to pieces$_i$.

Thus the principle that internal arguments can measure out events has wider generality than what might at first appear to be the case. This suggest a bolder hypothesis as a corollary to (40):

(42) All verbs of change (simple nonstative verbs) have latent in them the aspectual structure in which an internal argument can measure out the event.

Principle (42) is proposed here as a direction for research. Whether this universal potential aspectual structure is instantiated or not likely depends on various language-particular conditions. Assuming modular principles of grammar, aspectual structure imposes its own constraints, which then interact with an assortment of other constraints, both in the core and the periphery of the grammar.

2.7 Summary

This section of the paper has argued that there is a strong correlation between aspectual properties and syntactic structures, which constrains the mapping of thematic roles into syntax. The aspect/syntax correlation centers on the verb's internal arguments. With verbs in which the internal argument undergoes any change or motion, all and only direct internal arguments, or D-structural objects of the verb, measure out events. The event is delimited linguistically within the verb phrase, through reference to that "measuring out." These principles constitute the universal aspectual structure of verbs of change, or simple nonstative verbs. This aspectual structure is not always fully realized with all verbs of change, but it is latent in them and potentially realizable.

The correlation between aspectual properties and syntactic argument structure exerts some constraint on the mapping of lexical semantics into syntax, because only certain types of thematic roles are compatible with the requirement that they measure out an event. This theory amounts to a proposal for a certain kind of rigorous connection between lexical semantics, or verb meaning, and syntactic argument structure. However, under this view the essential autonomy of syntax and semantics is preserved, because they interact only through a restricted aspectual vocabulary.

The aspectual theory of argument structure introduces a fundamental semantic asymmetry paralleling the familiar syntactic asymmetry between subjects and objects, or between external and internal arguments. In a sense, this is a rather conservative proposal.

Finally, it must be noted that this aspectual theory of argument structure introduces an unusual view of aspect. Aspectual properties have usually been associated with predicates and predicative expressions, such as verbs, verb phrases, or clauses. But with this approach, we can also talk about the aspectual properties that arguments and noun phrases receive from their governing predicates.

3   The AIH and Thematic Roles

This paper argues for the existence of an aspectual interface between thematic structure and syntactic structure. Under this view, thematic roles are not directly visible to syntactic structure. This does not mean that thematic roles do not exist, or do not need to be characterized in some fashion. What implications does the AIH have for the nature of thematic roles?

The idea that it is the compatibility of various thematic roles with certain aspectual constraints that governs their mapping into syntactic argument positions imparts a view of thematic roles like that propounded in Dowty 1991. Dowty argues that linguistic theory needs to recognize two proto-roles, a Proto-Agent and a Proto-Patient, instead of a set of discrete thematic roles; and these proto-roles are "higher order generalizations about meanings" (Dowty 1991). Associated with these proto-roles are collections of agent-like and patient-like characteristics which are the criteria by which argument selection takes place (from Dowty 1991):

Argument Selection Principle: The argument of a predicate having the greatest number of Proto-Agent properties entailed by the meaning of the predicate will, all else being equal, be lexicalized as the subject of the predicate; the argument having the greatest number of Proto-Patient properties will, all else being equal, be lexicalized as the direct object of the predicate.

Corollary 1: If two arguments of a relation have (approximately) equal numbers of entailed Proto-agent and Proto-patient properties, then either may be lexicalized as the subject (and similarly for objects).

Under this approach thematic roles are essentially generalizations about elements of meaning which map to internal or external argument positions. This view of thematic roles is highly compatible with the AIH.

Dowty lists the properties which contribute to Proto-Agent and Proto-Patient roles as:

Contributing Properties for the Agent Proto-Role:
    a. volition
    b. sentience
    c. cause event
    d. movement
    (e. referent exists independent of action of verb)

Contributing Properties for the Patient Proto-Role:
    a. change of state (including coming-to-being, going-out-of-being)
    b. incremental theme (i.e., determinant of aspect)
    c. causally affected by event
    d. stationary (relative to movement of Proto-Agent)
    (e. referent may not exist independent of action of verb, or may not exist
       at all)

These properties are aligned according to whether or not they can "measure out the event." The Proto-Patient properties are conducive to doing this; the Proto-Agent properties are not. The AIH unifies changes of state, affected theme and incremental theme verbs under one system. In fact, the AIH derives the distinction between Proto-Agent and Proto-Patient roles, which otherwise is unmotivated. Dowty's theory of thematic roles is not only compatible with the AIH, it is motivated by it.

4   Implications for Language Acquisition

The claim that predicates of natural language characterize events in a very particular and constrained fashion has implications for cognitive science in general, and for language acquisition in particular. I will close with some brief speculations about issues relating to language acquisition.

The Aspectual Interface Hypothesis has three specific consequences for language acquisition; it underscores the necessity of syntactic information in the acquisition of verbs, it predicts certain interactions between cognitive and linguistic development, and it makes predictions about what are impossible verbs.

The importance of syntactic information to verb meanings is reflected in the practice of many linguists, of including within the lexical entry of a verb some indication of how the verb's arguments are to be realized syntactically. Because the syntactic information cannot be derived from the core (pre-aspectual) meaning of a verb by any perfect mapping, it must be independent information that has to be acquired and listed in the lexicon. Among researchers on language acquisition, the claim has been made that syntactic information is necessary for verb acquisition. The claim has been made in its general form by Landau and Gleitman (1985) and as a more particular thesis by Gropen, Pinker, and Goldberg (1987). Gropen et al. report on experiments which indicate that children rely on a principle which associates affectedness (an aspectual property) with direct object-hood (a syntactic property), in learning the meanings of the locative alternation verbs.

The importance of the acquisition of syntactic information does not preclude the need for acquiring conceptual information or machinery as well. The AIH predicts that cognitive development will enter into language acquisition in very particular ways. The AIH constrains to some extent the interaction of children's cognitive growth with their linguistic capabilities. Children's understanding of the nature of events and change, and particularly their ability to recognize properties that "measure out events" should affect the difficulty with which they learn various predicates.

A theory proposing a correlation between aspectual and syntactic structure makes strong predictions about possible and impossible verbs. If the view advanced in this paper is correct, verbs that violate the aspectual constraints on argument structure should be impossible verbs. They should not be found in any language, and they should be impossible for children to learn through normal processes of language acquisition. In the next few paragraphs a few "impossible verbs" are described which violate aspectual principles of argument structure.

Verbs with two or more direct internal arguments: Verbs of change describe events measurable on a single scale, which can only be associated with a direct internal argument. A verb with two or more direct internal arguments, both measuring out the event, would violate this principle. Such a verb would describe an event measured out on two independent scales. An example would be a verb meaning "*A* melts and *B* freezes," such that the melting of *A* and the freezing of *B* *independently* define or measure out the event. This event comes to an end when *A* has melted and *B* has frozen. Such a meaning is expressible through conjunction, although it cannot be lexicalized in a single verb. Note that a verb meaning "*A* melts and freezes" would be a possible verb. The scale on which this event is measured out would be a little peculiar to characterize, but it would be a single scale.

Verbs with two or more delimiting oblique arguments: An event described by a verb may be delimited only once. A verb with more than one delimiting argument would violate this principle. This would be a verb taking two or more arguments indicating endpoints to the event—for example, two or more goal arguments. Such a verb would be used as follows: *Push the cart to San Francisco to Mexico*, meaning push the cart to San Francisco and to Mexico. Again, the constraint on this structure is not pragmatic because the meaning can be expressed through conjunction.

Verbs with no internal arguments (including implicit or default arguments): If all verbs of change describe events measurable on some scale, then all verbs of change have potential internal arguments. A verb violating this principle would be a verb which indicates no scale on which the event is measured out. There are many verbs which occur with an external argument and without an overt internal argument, but these verbs can generally take some kind of internal argument such as a cognate object or a reflexive. However, the impossible verb being invented here would have no way of taking any internal argument or direct object. There is a strong claim here; that there may be verbs that can never take external arguments but there are no verbs that can never take internal arguments (including cognate objects and reflexives). This claim may be too strong, but the prediction would be that where default internal arguments are impossible, it is because of stylistic, pragmatic or other extragrammatical or language-particular considerations.

Verbs with two or more external arguments: Although the AIH provides no explanation of why a verb can only have one external argument, it does characterize external arguments aspectually. A verb taking two or more external arguments has not been attested, as far as I know. If there were such a verb it would be a verb which takes two arguments, neither of which measures out the event, or participates in the internal aspectual structure of the event. An example would be a verb that means "some indefinite or incompletely specified change is happening with argument *A and* some indefinite or incompletely specified change is happening with argument *B*." This verb would have as part of its meaning a notion similar to "while." An example would be a verb with arguments *A* and *B*, meaning:

A scratches and *B* dances

A sings while *B* jumps

This does not rule out a verb that means something like "*A* makes *B* dance by scratching," in which case *B*'s traversal of the dance event *is* measuring out the event; and the scratching belongs in a manner clause, without aspectual constraints. (*Dance Bill up the stairs (by scratching)*.) (This is putting aside the special properties of syntactic causative constructions, which are not lexicalized events.)

A verb describing an event in which one argument measures out the event and the other does not is always possible, even if the change or activity of the external argument is seemingly unrelated to the measuring-out change. A verb meaning something like "*A* scratches and *B* gets wetter" is in principle a possible verb, if one of the arguments has the properties of an external argument, and the other of an internal argument. It is only necessary for such a concept to be useful to the speakers of the language for such a verb to be created. Such a verb might mean something like "*A* scratchingly wets *B*."

Several kinds of aspectually "impossible verbs" have been imagined and described above. This kind of prediction about possible or impossible verbs may be testable in language acquisition experiments. I know of no experimental work that sheds light on them, and the appropriate tests may be difficult to design. Nevertheless, the aspectual properties of argument structure introduced by the AIH do make strong, and in principle falsifiable, predictions for natural language acquisition.

References

Anderson, Mona. 1979. *Noun Phrase Structure*. Doctoral dissertation, University of Connecticut.

Anderson, Stephen R. 1977. Comments on the paper by Wasow. In *Formal Syntax*, ed. Peter Culicover, Thomas Wasow, and Adrian Akmajian, 361–378. New York: Academic Press.

Baker, Mark. 1988. *Incorporation: A Theory of Grammatical Function Changing.* Chicago: University of Chicago Press.

Belletti, Adriana, and Luigi Rizzi. 1988. Psych-Verbs and θ-Theory. *Natural Language and Linguistic Theory* 6(3):291–352.

Burzio, Luigi. 1986. *Italian Syntax.* Dordrecht: Reidel.

de Groot, Casper. 1984. Totally Affected Aspect and Three-Place Predicates in Hungarian. In *Aspect Bound: A Voyage Into the Realm of Germanic Slavonic and Finno-Ugrian Aspectology*, ed. Casper de Groot and Hannu Tommola, 133–151. Dordrecht: Foris.

Dik, Simon. 1980. *Studies in Functional Grammar.* London and New York: Academic Press.

Dowty, David. 1979. *Word Meaning and Montague Grammar.* Dordrecht: Reidel.

Dowty, David. 1991. Thematic Proto-Roles and Argument Selection. *Language* 67(3):547–619.

Fellbaum, Christiane. 1987. On Nominals with Preposed Themes. In *Proceedings of NELS 17.* Amherst: University of Massachusetts, GLSA.

Fukui, Naoki, Shigeru Miyagawa, and Carol Tenny. 1985. Verb Classes in English and Japanese: A Case Study in the Interaction of Syntax, Morphology and Semantics. Lexicon Project Working Papers 3. Cambridge, Mass.: MIT Center for Cognitive Science.

Grimshaw, Jane. 1987a. Psych Verbs and the Structure of Argument Structure. Manuscript, Brandeis University.

Grimshaw, Jane. 1987b. Unaccusatives—An Overview. In *Proceedings of NELS 17*. Amherst: University of Massachusetts, GLSA.

Gropen, Jess, Steven Pinker, and R. Goldberg. 1987. Constrained Productivity in the Acquisition of Locative Forms. Talk delivered at Boston University Conference on Language Acquisition, 1987.

Gruber, Jeffrey S. 1976. *Lexical Structures in Syntax and Semantics*. Amsterdam: North Holland. Includes 1965 MIT PhD thesis, *Studies in Lexical Relations*; reissued by Indiana University Linguistics Club (Bloomington, 1970).

Guerssel, Mohamed. 1986. On Berber Verbs of Change: A Study of Transitivity Alternations. Lexicon Project Working Papers 9. Cambridge, Mass.: MIT Center for Cognitive Science.

Hale, Kenneth, and S. Jay Keyser. 1986. Some Transitivity Alternations in English. Lexicon Project Working Papers 7. Cambridge, Mass.: MIT Center for Cognitive Science.

Hale, Kenneth, and S. Jay Keyser. 1987. A View from the Middle. Lexicon Project Working Papers 10. Cambridge, Mass.: MIT Center for Cognitive Science.

Hale, Kenneth, and S. Jay Keyser. 1988. Explaining and Constraining the English Middle. In *Studies in Generative Approaches to Aspect*, ed. Carol Tenny. Lexicon Project Working Papers 24. Cambridge, Mass.: MIT Center for Cognitive Science.

Heath, Jeffrey. 1979. Is Dyirbal Ergative? *Linguistics* 17:401–463.

Hinrichs, Erhard. 1985. *A Compositional Semantics for Aktionsarten and NP Reference in English*. Doctoral dissertation, Ohio State University.

Jackendoff, Ray. 1972. *Semantic Interpretation in Generative Grammar*. Cambridge, Mass.: MIT Press.

Jackendoff, Ray. 1983. *Semantics and Cognition*. Cambridge, Mass.: MIT Press.

Jackendoff, Ray. 1986. Parts and Boundaries. Talk delivered at MIT Lexicon Seminar.

Jackendoff, Ray. 1987. The Status of Thematic Relations in Linguistic Theory. *Linguistic Inquiry* 18(3):369–411.

Krifka, Manfred. 1987. Nominal Reference and Temporal Constitution: Towards a Semantics of Quantity. Manuscript, Universität Tübingen.

Landau, Barbara, and Lila Gleitman. 1985. *Language and Experience: Evidence from the Blind Child*. Cambridge, Mass.: Harvard University Press.

Levin, Beth, and Malka Rappaport. 1986. The Formation of Adjectival Passives. *Linguistic Inquiry* 17:623–661.

Merlan, Francesca. 1985. Split Intransitivity: Functional Oppositions in Intransitive Inflection. In *Grammar Inside and Outside the Clause: Some Approaches to Theory from the Field*, ed. Johana Nichols and Anthony Woodbury, 324–362. New York: Cambridge University Press.

Nwachukwu, P. Akujuoobi. 1987. The Argument Structure of Igbo Verbs. Lexicon Project Working Papers 18. Cambridge, Mass.: MIT Center for Cognitive Science.

Perlmutter, David, and Paul Postal. 1984. The 1-Advancement Exclusiveness Law. In *Studies in Relational Grammar*, ed. David Perlmutter and Carol Rosen, 81–125. Chicago: University of Chicago Press.

Pesetsky, David. 1987. Binding Problems with Experiencer Verbs. *Linguistic Inquiry* 18:126–140.

Pesetsky, David. 1988. Psych Predicates, Universal Alignment, and Lexical Decomposition. Manuscript, University of Massachusetts at Amherst.

Pustejovsky, James. 1988. The Geometry of Events. In *Studies in Generative Approached to Aspect*, ed. Carol Tenny. Lexicon Project Working Papers 24. Cambridge, Mass.: MIT Center for Cognitive Science.

Rappaport, Malka, Mary Laughren, and Beth Levin. 1988. Levels of Lexical Representation. Lexicon Project Working Papers 20. Cambridge, Mass.: MIT Center for Cognitive Science.

Rappaport, Malka, and Beth Levin. 1988. What to Do with Thematic Roles. In *Syntax and Semantics: Thematic Relations*, ed. Wendy Wilkins. New York: Academic Press.

Roberts, Ian. 1985. *The Representation of Implicit and Dethematized Subjects*. Doctoral dissertation, University of Southern California.

Schwartz-Norman, Linda. 1976. The Grammar of 'Content' and 'Container'. *Journal of Linguistics* 12:279–287.

Simpson, Jane. 1983. *Aspects of Warlpiri Morphology and Syntax*. Doctoral dissertation, Massachusetts Institute of Technology.

Tenny, Carol. 1987. *Grammaticalizing Aspect and Affectedness*. Doctoral dissertation, Massachusetts Institute of Technology.

van Valin, Robert. 1987. The Unaccusative Hypothesis vs. Lexical Semantics: Syntactic vs. Semantic Approaches to Verb Classification. In *Proceedings of NELS 17*. Amherst: University of Massachusetts, GLSA.

Vendler, Zeno. 1957. Verbs and Times. *Philosophical Review* 66:143–160. (Also in Vendler 1967, pp. 97–121.).

Vendler, Zeno. 1967. *Linguistics in Philosophy*. Ithaca: Cornell University Press.

Verkuyl, Henk J. 1972. *On the Compositional Nature of the Aspects*. Dordrecht: Reidel.

Verkuyl, Henk J. 1976. Interpretive Rules and the Description of the Aspects. *Foundations of Language* 14:471–503.

Verkuyl, Henk J. 1978. Thematic Relations and the Semantic Representation of Verbs Expressing Change. *Studies in Language* 2:199–233.

Verkuyl, Henk J. 1987a. Aspectual Asymmetry and Quantification. In *Temporalität*, ed. Veronika Ehrich and Heinz Vater. Heidelberg Workshop on Tense and Aspect (Feb. 1986).

Verkuyl, Henk J. 1987b. Nondurative Closure of Events. In *Studies in Discourse Representation Theory and the Theory of Generalized Quantifiers*, ed. Jeroen Groenendijk, Martin Stokhof, and Frank Veltman. Dordrecht: Foris.

Williams, Edwin. 1980. Predication. *Linguistic Inquiry* 11(1):203–238.

Zaenen, Annie. 1987. Are There Unaccusative Verbs in Dutch? In *Proceedings of NELS 17*. Amherst: Univeristy of Massachusetts, GLSA.

2

Thematic Relations as Links between Nominal Reference and Temporal Constitution

MANFRED KRIFKA

This paper treats the correspondence between the reference type of NPs (i.e., mass nouns, count nouns, measure constructions, plurals) and the temporal constitution of verbal predicates (i.e., activities, accomplishments). A theory will be developed that handles the well known influence of the reference type of NPs in argument positions on the temporal constitution of the verbal expressions, assuming an event semantics with lattice structures and thematic roles as primitive relations between events and objects. Some consequences for the theory of thematic roles will be discussed, and the effect of partitive case marking on the verbal aspect, as in Finnish, and of aspectual marking on the definiteness of NPs, like in Slavic, will be explained.

1 Introduction

It has been observed for some time that semantic distinctions in the nominal domain and in the verbal domain show certain resemblances to each other, namely the distinction between mass and count terms on the one hand and the distinction between "aspectual classes" or "aktionsarten" on the other.

Concerning the nominal domain, I think that one should not contrast mass nouns like *wine* to count nouns like *apple* directly, because they dif-

The theory developed in this paper represents parts of my doctoral thesis at the University of Munich (Krifka 1986). I learned a lot from my supervisors, Theo Vennemann and Godehard Link. And there are many more people who helped to clarify my ideas and their presentation: Rainer Bäuerle, David Dowty, Hana Filip, Franz Guenthner, Sebastian Löbner, Jan Tore Lønning, Uwe Mönnich, Barbara Partee, Craige Roberts, Arnim von Stechow, Henk Zeevat, Barbara Zimmermann, Ede Zimmermann, and surely more. Thanks to them all.

fer in their syntactic distribution and in their semantic type; the first can serve as an NP, whereas the second cannot. One should contrast instead expressions like *wine* and *an apple*, or *apples* and *five apples*, or *wine* and *a glass of wine*. The first element in each of those pairs has the property of referring cumulatively (cf. Quine 1960): whenever there are two entities to which *wine* applies, this predicate applies to their collection as well. The second member in each pair does not have this property: whenever there are two (different) entities to which *an apple* applies, this predicate does not apply to their collection. Let us subsume these properties under the heading of *nominal reference*. Predicates like *wine* will be called *cumulative*, and predicates like *five apples* will be called *quantized*. As for "aspectual classes" or "aktionsarten," I would like to use another name for this concept, because these terms were originally coined for related, but quite different phenomena in the morphology of the Slavic and Germanic languages. I will call the notion we are after *temporal constitution*, which was invented as the German term "Zeitkonstitution" by François (1985) and covers a concept which was treated perhaps most prominently by Vendler (1957). I will concentrate here on what Vendler calls *activities* and *accomplishments*, which I call *atelic* and *telic* expressions, following Garey (1957). To give a preliminary definition: A verbal expression is atelic if its denotation has no set terminal point (e.g., *run*), and it is telic if it includes a terminal point (e.g., *run a mile*). This well-known semantic distinction is supported by a battery of tests (cf. Dowty 1979). For example, in ordinary, e.g., non-iterative interpretations, atelic expressions allow for durative adverbials like *for an hour*, but do not allow for time-span adverbials like *in an hour*, whereas with telic expressions the situation is reversed.

(1) a. John ran (for an hour)/(*in an hour).
     b. John ran a mile (*for an hour)/(in an hour).

That nominal reference and temporal constitution are related became clear in two ways. First, the two concepts are felt to be semantically similar. For example, a quantized NP like *an apple* denotes an object with precise limits, just as *run a mile* denotes an event with precise limits. On the other hand, a cumulative NP like *wine* denotes something without clear limitation, just like what *run* denotes also has no clear limitation. Second, it was observed that the reference types of verbal arguments often determine the temporal constitution of complex verbal expressions, insofar as a quantized argument yields a telic verbal predicate, and a cumulative argument yields an atelic verbal predicate:

(2) a. John drank wine (for an hour)/(*in an hour).
     b. John drank a glass of wine (*for an hour)/(in an hour).

However, we cannot observe this effect with any verbal predicate, as the following examples show:

(3)   a. John saw a zebra (for an hour)/(*in an hour).
       b. John saw zebras (for an hour)/(*in an hour).

This suggests that the lexical semantics of the verb plays a crucial role in the way the nominal reference type of the arguments affects the temporal constitution of the complex expression. More specifically, it seems that the *thematic role* of the argument is responsible for this effect; for example, we find it with arguments which can be described as "consumed object" as in (2), but not with arguments which can be described as "observed objects" as in (3). Therefore, a theory which explains this effect will have consequences for the theory of thematic roles.

Some historical remarks: The similarity between nominal and verbal distinctions was observed already by Leisi (1953). The effect of verbal arguments was investigated first by Verkuyl (1972) in his work on aspectual composition, who dealt with features like [+SPECIFIED QUANTITY] that are projected from the argument to the verb phrase. Another approach relying on feature projection is Platzack 1979. Dowty (1979) criticized these feature-based approaches, as they merely describe the facts and do not really explain them. Dowty himself, as well as Hoepelman (1976) and Hoepelman and Rohrer (1980), developed theories in the paradigm of model-theoretic semantics to capture the facts in a more explanatory way. See Krifka 1986 for a detailed criticism of their approaches. It seems to me that the general insight of the feature-based approach, that the arguments and the complex expression have something in common, is lost in these model-theoretic approaches. The theory presented here and in Krifka 1986, 1989 is more in the spirit of ter Meulen 1984 and Bach 1986, who tried to characterize the similarities of noun denotations and verb denotations by model-theoretic means, but they remain at a rather informal level. There is one explicit model-theoretic approach which looks similar to the one developed here, namely Hinrichs 1985. But Hinrichs' theory crucially depends on the notion of a stage of an individual, which complicates his formalizations and has some unintuitive side effects. The theory presented here comes most closely to Dowty 1987, 1989, and Link 1987.

2   The Semantic Representation Language and Its Interpretation

In this section, I will introduce the semantic representation language and the basic facts about the model structure of its interpretations. I assume a type-theoretic language with function symbols and identity. For reasons of simplicity, it is assumed to be extensional.

To handle the semantics of cumulative and quantized reference, we must provide for the semantic operation of joining two individuals to a new individual. This means that our model structure must be of the form of a *lattice* (cf. Link 1983). Here, I can simplify Link's approach to aspects relevant to my argument; for example, I will not distinguish between individual entities and quantities of matter. But I will extend Link's approach to cover event predicates as well.

Assume that we have two non-overlapping sorts of entities, *objects* (characterized by a predicate $\mathcal{O}$), *events* (characterized by a predicate $\mathcal{E}$), and *times* (characterized by a predicate $\mathcal{T}$). The extensions of $\mathcal{O}$, $\mathcal{E}$ and $\mathcal{T}$ have the structure of a complete join semi-lattice without a bottom element. Let $\sqcup$ be a two-place operation (join), and $\sqsubseteq$, $\sqsubset$, $\circ$ two-place relations (part, proper part, overlap). Then the following postulates must hold for admissible interpretations of the semantic representation language:

(P1) $\forall x, y, z[(x \sqcup y = z) \rightarrow [\mathcal{O}(x) \wedge \mathcal{O}(y) \wedge \mathcal{O}(z)] \vee [\mathcal{E}(x) \wedge \mathcal{E}(y) \wedge \mathcal{E}(z)] \vee [\mathcal{T}(x) \wedge \mathcal{T}(y) \wedge \mathcal{T}(z)]]$ \hfill (restriction to $\mathcal{O}$, $\mathcal{E}$, $\mathcal{T}$)

(P2) $\forall x, y \exists z[x \sqcup y = z]$ \hfill (completeness)

(P3) $\forall x, y[x \sqcup y = y \sqcup x]$ \hfill (commutativity)

(P4) $\forall x[x \sqcup x = x]$ \hfill (idempotency)

(P5) $\forall x, y, z[x \sqcup [y \sqcup z] = [x \sqcup y] \sqcup z]$ \hfill (associativity)

(P6) $\forall x, y[x \sqsubseteq y \leftrightarrow x \sqcup y = y]$ \hfill (part)

(P7) $\neg \exists x \forall y[x \sqsubseteq y]$ \hfill (no $\bot$ element)

(P8) $\forall x, y[x \sqsubset y \leftrightarrow x \sqsubseteq y \wedge \neg x = y]$ \hfill (proper part)

(P9) $\forall x, y[x \circ y \leftrightarrow \exists z[z \sqsubseteq x \wedge z \sqsubseteq y]]$ \hfill (overlap)

We can generalize the join operation to the fusion operation, which maps a set P to its lowest upper bound:

(P10) $\forall x, P[[(P \subseteq \mathcal{O} \vee P \subseteq \mathcal{E} \vee P \subseteq \mathcal{T}) \rightarrow FU(P) = x]$
$\leftrightarrow \forall y[P(y) \rightarrow y \sqsubseteq x] \wedge \forall z[\forall y[P(y) \rightarrow y \sqsubseteq z] \rightarrow x \sqsubseteq z]]$ \hfill (fusion)

We now define some higher-order predicates and relations to characterize different reference types.

(P11) $\forall P[CUM(P) \leftrightarrow \forall x, y[P(x) \wedge P(y) \rightarrow P(x \sqcup y)]]$
\hfill (cumulative reference)

(P12) $\forall P[SNG(P) \leftrightarrow \exists x[P(x) \wedge \forall y[P(y) \rightarrow x = y]]]$ \hfill (singular reference)

(P13) $\forall P[SCUM(P) \leftrightarrow CUM(P) \wedge \neg SNG(P)]$
\hfill (strictly cumulative reference)

(P14) $\forall P[QUA(P) \leftrightarrow \forall x, y[P(x) \wedge P(y) \rightarrow \neg y \sqsubset x]]$ \hfill (quantized reference)

(P15) $\forall P[SQUA(P) \leftrightarrow QUA(P) \wedge \forall x[P(x) \rightarrow \exists y[y \sqsubset x]]]$
\hfill (strictly quantized reference)

(P16) $\forall x, P[ATOM(x, P) \leftrightarrow P(x) \wedge \neg \exists y[y \sqsubset x \wedge P(y)]]$ \hfill (x is a P-atom)

(P17) $\forall P[ATM(P) \rightarrow \forall x[P(x) \rightarrow \exists y[y \sqsubseteq x \wedge ATOM(y, P)]]]$
\hfill (P has atomic reference)

Postulate (P17) says that if P is atomic, then every x which is P contains a P-atom. The following theorems hold, as can be easily checked:

(T1) $\forall P[SNG(P) \rightarrow QUA(P)]$

(T2) $\forall P[SNG(P) \rightarrow CUM(P)]$

(T3) $\forall P[QUA(P) \rightarrow \neg SCUM(P)]$

(T4) $\forall P[QUA(P) \rightarrow ATM(P)]$

We have to postulate some structure for events and times. First, we assume that the time lattice is atomic, that is, $ATM(\mathcal{T})$, with $\mathcal{T}_a$ as the set of atoms (*time points*). (I leave the question open as to whether objects and events are atomic as well). Second, we assume a *temporal order* relation $\leq$, which is a linear order for time points. With these notions, we can define convex times, or *time intervals*. (In the following, I will use t, t', etc., as variables for times, and e, e', etc., as variables for events.)

(P18) $ATM(\mathcal{T}) \wedge \forall t[\mathcal{T}_a(t) \leftrightarrow ATOM(t, \mathcal{T})]$

$\qquad\qquad\qquad\qquad\qquad\qquad$ ($\mathcal{T}_a$ is the predicate of time points)

(P19) $\forall t, t', t''[\mathcal{T}_a(t) \wedge \mathcal{T}_a(t') \wedge \mathcal{T}_a(t'') \rightarrow [t \leq t \wedge [t \leq t' \wedge t' \leq t'' \rightarrow$
$\qquad t \leq t''] \wedge [t \leq t' \vee t' \leq t] \wedge [t \leq t' \wedge t' \leq t \rightarrow t = t']]]$

$\qquad\qquad\qquad\qquad\qquad\qquad$ ($\leq$ is a linear order for time points)

(P20) $\forall t, t'[t \leq t' \leftrightarrow \forall t'', t'''[t'' \sqsubseteq t \wedge t''' \sqsubseteq t' \rightarrow t'' \leq t''']]$

$\qquad\qquad\qquad\qquad\qquad\qquad$ (extension of $\leq$ to times in general)

(P21) $\forall t[CONV(t) \leftrightarrow \forall t', t'', t'''[t' \sqsubseteq t \wedge t'' \sqsubseteq t \wedge t' \leq t''' \leq t'' \rightarrow t''' \sqsubseteq t]]$

$\qquad\qquad\qquad\qquad\qquad\qquad$ (convex times, or intervals)

Third, we assume a function τ from the extension of $\mathcal{E}$ to the extension of $\mathcal{T}$, the *temporal trace* function; this function maps an event to its "run time," or temporal trace. It is a homomorphism relative to the join operation:

(P22) $\forall e, e'[\tau(e) \sqcup \tau(e') = \tau(e \sqcup e')]$

That is, the join of the temporal traces of two events equals the temporal trace of the join of these events.

3 Cumulativity and Quantization for Object and Event Predicates

In this section, we will apply the notions we have developed so far to the semantic description of certain predicate types. First, we will look at predicates on objects, and then at predicates on events.

Characterizing object predicates like *wine* versus *a glass of wine*, or *apples* versus *five apples*, is straightforward. If we represent these expressions by predicates in the semantic representation languages, we have:

(4)   a. $wine \subseteq \mathcal{O} \wedge CUM(wine)$

       b. $a.glass.of.wine \subseteq \mathcal{O} \wedge QUA(a.glass.of.wine)$

       c. $apples \subseteq \mathcal{O} \wedge CUM(apples)$

       d. $five.apples \subseteq \mathcal{O} \wedge QUA(five.apples)$

(4a) says that *wine* is a predicate on objects (note that we make no distinction between stuff and objects for reasons of simplicity), and that it is cumulative. (4b) says that *a.glass.of.wine* is also a predicate on objects, but that this predicate is quantized. Similarly, *apples* is a cumulative object predicate, and *five.apples* is a quantized object predicate. I will not go into the semantic composition of predicates which are syntactically or morphologically complex, like *a.glass.of.wine*, *apples*, or *five.apples*; see Krifka 1986, 1989 for a treatment.

Now look at expressions like *run* and *run a mile*. In the standard treatment (5i), one-place verbal predicates are reconstructed as applying to objects, just as object predicates. For example, *run* is analyzed as applying to every object that runs. However, there are good reasons to assume that these predicates have also an argument place for events (cf. Davidson 1967), as in (5ii), or even that they are predicates on events, and that the participants are related to these events by thematic relations like Agent, Theme, etc. (cf. Parsons 1980, Carlson 1984, Bäuerle 1988), as in (5iii):

(5) *Mary runs.*   i. $run(Mary)$
                     ii. $run(Mary, e)$
                     iii. $run(e) \land AG(e, Mary)$

Obviously, if we want to model the temporal constitution of verbal expressions, we should choose either (5ii) or (5iii) as a representation format, because the temporal constitution can most easily be formulated with the help of the event argument e. Furthermore, it will turn out that the rules can be more easily formulated in the format (5iii), which factorizes a verbal predicate into an event property and the thematic information. So I will base what follows on this representation format.

How can we characterize an atelic event predicate like *run* and a telic event predicate like *run.a.mile* within our theoretical framework? We may say that the first is cumulative and the second is quantized: If we have two events of running, then they form together an event of running; and if we have an event of running a mile, then no proper part of it is an event of running a mile. So we can reconstruct atelic and telic expressions by cumulative and quantized event predicates, respectively:

(6.)   a. $run \subseteq \mathcal{E} \land CUM(run)$
       b. $run.a.mile \subseteq \mathcal{E} \land QUA(run.a.mile)$

We might ask how this characterization of telic and atelic predicates relates to the traditional one, that telic predicates have a set terminal point and atelic predicates lack such a set terminal point. There is, in fact, a close relationship:

The notion of a "set terminal point" cannot be defined for bare events or "event tokens", but only for events with respect to a certain description, event predicates, or "event types." For consider a concrete event of running and a concrete event of running a mile; then surely both events have a terminal point (both events might be even identical). The difference is that an event of running might be a part of another event of running which has a later terminal point, whereas this is not possible for an event of running a mile.

We can define the notion of a telic event predicate like follows. First, let us define a function TP which maps events to the last time point in their run time. Then we can define the notion of event predicates which have a set terminal point, STP.

(P23) $\forall e, t[TP(e) = t \leftrightarrow T_a(t) \wedge t \sqsubseteq \tau(e) \wedge \forall t'[t' \sqsubseteq \tau(e) \rightarrow t' \leq t]]$

(the terminal point of an event)

(P24) $\forall P[STP(P) \leftrightarrow \forall e[P(e) \rightarrow \forall e'[P(e') \wedge e' \sqsubseteq e \rightarrow TP(e) = TP(e')]]]$

(event predicates with set terminal point)

An STP event predicate, then, applies to events such that all subevents which fall under the predicate have the same terminal point. In a natural interpretation of *run* and *run.a.mile*, we can assume the following properties:

(7) a. *run* $\subseteq \mathcal{E} \wedge \neg STP(run)$
     b. *run.a.mile* $\subseteq \mathcal{E} \wedge STP(run.a.mile)$

That is, *run.a.mile* is a predicate with a set terminal point, as every subevent of an event of running a mile has the same terminal point. This is different for *run*. In general, we may characterize telic predicates P as $STP(P)$, and atelic predicates P as $\neg STP(P)$.

If we defined a mapping from objects to spatial regions and define the notion of a border of regions, and hence, of objects, then we could characterize nominal predicates like *a.glass.of.wine* and *wine* similarly, as implying a set border or as not implying a set border. In this way, we could capture the similarity between expressions like 'run' and 'run a mile' with 'wine' and 'a glass of wine', respectively.

It turns out, however, that a good deal of the similarity can already be covered by the notions of cumulative and quantized predicates. The reason is that there is a relation between predicates with a set terminal point and an interesting class of cumulative event predicates. This class can be defined as follows: With the exception of singular event predicates (that refer to one event only), event predicates in natural language typically have the property that they apply to events which have different terminal points. For example, a predicate like *run*, or *run a mile*, refers to events that end at different times. Let us define the notion of *natural event predicates*, *NEP*, as an event predicates with that property:

(P25) $\forall P[NEP(P) \leftrightarrow P \subseteq \mathcal{E} \wedge \exists e, e'[P(e) \wedge P(e') \wedge \neg TP(e) = TP(e')]]$

Now we can prove that cumulative natural event predicates cannot have a set terminal point:

(T5) $\forall P[CUM(P) \wedge NEP(P) \rightarrow \neg STP(P)]$

Proof: Assume an event predicate P with $CUM(P)$ and $NEP(P)$. As P is natural, there are two events e_1, e_2 such that $P(e_1)$, $P(e_2)$, and $\neg TP(e_1) = TP(e_2)$. Assume that $TP(e_1) \leq TP(e_2)$. As P is cumulative, it holds that $P(e_1 \sqcup e_2)$. As $\tau(e_1 \sqcup e_2) = \tau(e_1) \sqcup \tau(e_2)$, we have $\neg TP(e_1) = TP(e_1 \sqcup e_2)$. But it holds that $e_1 \sqsubseteq e_1 \sqcup e_2$. Consequently, we have $\neg STP(P)$.

This means that, under the assumption that P is cumulative, $CUM(P)$, and not singular, $\neg SNG(P)$, we can normally assume that P has no set terminal point, $\neg STP(P)$. That is, strictly cumulative event predicates can safely be taken as atelic under the traditional definition (lacking a set terminal point).

On the other hand, whenever we have a quantized event predicate P, $QUA(P)$, this will have a set terminal point, $STP(P)$. This is because when $QUA(P)$ and $P(e)$, then e has no proper part; so all parts e' of e will have the same end point, as e' and e are in fact identical. Therefore all quantized event predicates will be telic, under the traditional definition. But note that there are predicates with set terminal points that fail to be quantized. One example is 'walk to the station': If this predicate applies to an event e, then it will also apply to the latter half of e; so it is not quantized.

In the following, I will view telic predicates simply as quantized event predicates, and atelic predicates as strictly cumulative event predicates.

4 A Framework for Object and Event Reference

Before we turn to a formal description of the influence of nominal arguments to verbal predicates, I will sketch the syntactic and semantic framework I am assuming by way of an example (see Krifka 1986 for a more explicit treatment).

I assume a categorial-like syntactic representation; this is, however, not essential. Verb argument places come with features such as category (like NP), case (like *subj*, *obj*), and theta-roles (like *ag*, *pat*). The expressions that fill these arguments must have the same values for these features. The value of the theta feature is interpreted semantically by corresponding thematic relations. In the derivation tree in (8), I specify the expression, its syntactic category, and its semantic interpretation. The general syntactic operation is concatenation, and the semantic operation is functional application.

A verb is interpreted as a one-place predicate of events; the syntactic argument slots have no counterpart in its semantic representation, but only in its syntactic categorization. The theta-role information, which is specified with the argument slots in syntax, is passed to the subcategorized NPs, where it is realized as a part of the semantic representation of the determiners (e.g., *pat* is realized as $PAT(e,x)$). With free adjuncts like *in a pen*, the thematic relations are specified within the adjunct. Here I assume that the theta role is specified in the preposition; the NP governed by the preposition only has a dummy theta feature "empty" that is not realized in the interpretation of the determiner.

(8) $drank$; S/NP[$subj, ag$], NP[obj, pat] ; $\lambda e[drink(e)]$

| $water$; N ; $water$

| | $\emptyset$; NP[obj, pat]/N ; $\lambda P' \lambda P \lambda e \exists x[P(e) \wedge PAT(e, x) \wedge P'(x)]$

| $water$; NP[obj, pat] ; $\lambda P \lambda e \exists x[P(e) \wedge PAT(e, x) \wedge water(x)]$

$drank\ water$; S/NP[$subj, ag$] ;
| $\lambda P \lambda e \exists x[P(e) \wedge PAT(e, x) \wedge water(x)](\lambda e[drink(e)]) =$
| $\lambda e \exists x[drink(e) \wedge PAT(e, x) \wedge water(x)]$

| in ; [S/S]/NP[$obj, empty$] ; IN

| | pen ; N ; pen

| | | a ; NP[$obj, empty$]/N ; $\lambda P' \lambda R \lambda P \lambda e \exists x[P(e) \wedge R(e, x) \wedge P'(x)]$

| | $a\ pen$; NP[$obj, empty$] ; $\lambda R \lambda P \lambda e \exists x[P(e) \wedge R(e, x) \wedge pen(x)]$

| $in\ a\ pen$; S/S ; $\lambda P \lambda e \exists x[P(e) \wedge IN(e, x) \wedge pen(x)]$

$drank\ water\ in\ a\ pen$; S/NP[$subj, ag$] ;
| $\lambda P \lambda e \exists x[P(e) \wedge IN(e, x) \wedge pen(x)](\lambda e \exists x[drink(e) \wedge PAT(e, x)$
| $\wedge\ water(x)]) =$
| $\lambda e \exists x, y[drink(e) \wedge PAT(e, x) \wedge water(x) \wedge IN(e, y) \wedge pen(y)]$

| pig ; N ; pig

| | a ; NP[$subj, ag$]/N ; $\lambda P' \lambda P \exists x[P(e) \wedge AG(e, x) \wedge P'(x)]$

| $a\ pig$; NP[$subj, ag$] ; $\lambda P \exists x[P(e) \wedge AG(e, x) \wedge pig(x)]$

$a\ pig\ drank\ water\ in\ a\ pen$; S ;
| $\lambda P \lambda e \exists x[P(e) \wedge AG(e, x) \wedge pig(x)](\lambda e \exists x, y[drink(e) \wedge PAT(e, x)$
| $\wedge\ water(x) \wedge IN(e, y) \wedge pen(y)]) =$
| $\lambda e \exists x, y, z[drink(e) \wedge AG(e, x) \wedge pig(x) \wedge PAT(e, y) \wedge water(y)$
| $\wedge\ IN(e, z) \wedge pen(z)]$

After all free variables are bound, we obtain a predicate on events without free variables, the *sentence radical* (S). This can be transformed to a sentence (S') by the application of a *sentence mood operator*, e.g., the declarative operator, which simply binds the event variable with an existential quantifier.

(9)   ...

    ⌐ . ; S'/S ; $\lambda P \exists e P(e)$

A pig drank water in a pen. ; S' ;
$\exists e \exists x, y, z[drink(e) \land AG(e, x) \land pig(x) \land PAT(e, y) \land water(y)$
$\land IN(e, z) \land pen(z)]$

This representation of declarative sentences thus conforms to the truth scheme of Austin (1961), who assumed that a declarative sentence consists of two basic semantic constituents, namely a specification of an event type and a reference to a specific event, which is claimed to be of the specified type. Types of events I capture by event predicates, and the reference to a specific event by the existential quantifier. Surely, both reconstructions will turn out to be too simple, but they suffice for the present purpose, and the analysis to be developed hopefully can be recast in more complex representations.

5   The Impact of Arguments

In this section, which repeats part of Krifka 1989, I will show how the impact of the nominal reference of arguments on the temporal constitution of verbal predicates can be captured formally.

The basic idea is that, with certain thematic relations, the reference properties of the syntactic arguments carry over to the reference properties of the complex construction. There is a way to visualize this transfer of reference types, namely space-time diagrams. In these diagrams, space is represented by one axis, and time by the other. Objects, with their spatial extension, can be represented as lines, and events can be mapped to the time axis. Now consider e, the event of drinking a quantity of wine w (which is gradually disappearing during the drinking):

(10)

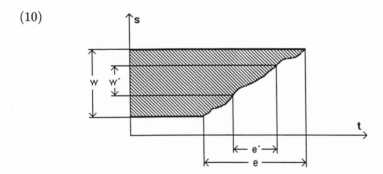

By this picture the intuitive notion that the object is subjected to the event in a gradual manner should become clear. Consider two possible descriptions of w and, consequently, e. First, let w be described as *wine*, and hence e as *drink wine*. As *wine* is cumulative, it is normally the case that it can also be applied to proper parts of w, like w'. But then it should be possible to apply the predicate *drink wine* to the corresponding proper part of e, namely e', as well. Secondly, let w be described as *a glass of wine*, and e consequently as *drink a glass of wine*. As *a glass of wine* is quantized, no proper part of w can be described as *a glass of wine*. But then no proper part of e can be described as *drink a glass of wine* either.

Technically speaking, we have to assume a *homomorphism* from objects to events which preserves the lattice structure. This should follow from the properties of the thematic relation that mediates between event and object. To characterize these properties, I assume the following notions:

(P26) $\forall R[SUM(R) \leftrightarrow \forall e, e', x, x'[R(e,x) \wedge R(e',x') \rightarrow R(e \sqcup e', x \sqcup x')]]$
(summativity)

(P27) $\forall R[UNI\text{-}O(R) \leftrightarrow \forall e, x, x'[R(e,x) \wedge R(e,x') \rightarrow x = x']]$
(uniqueness of objects)

(P28) $\forall R[UNI\text{-}E(R) \leftrightarrow \forall e, e', x[R(e,x) \wedge R(e',x) \rightarrow e = e']]$
(uniqueness of events)

(P29) $\forall R[MAP\text{-}O(R) \leftrightarrow \forall e, e', x[R(e,x) \wedge e' \sqsubseteq e \rightarrow \exists x'[x' \sqsubseteq x \wedge R(e',x')]]]$
(mapping to objects)

(P30) $\forall R[MAP\text{-}E(R) \leftrightarrow \forall e, x, x'[R(e,x) \wedge x' \sqsubseteq x \rightarrow \exists e'[e' \sqsubseteq e \wedge R(e',x')]]]$
(mapping to events)

Summativity (that is, cumulativity for two-place relations) provides the basic connection between thematic relations and the join operation $\sqcup$. For example, two (distinct) events of drinking a glass of wine yield an event of drinking two glasses of wine. *Uniqueness of objects* captures the fact that an event is related to a specific object, for example, a drinking of a glass of wine is related via the patient role to this glass of wine, and to nothing else. *Uniqueness of events* says that there is only one event related to the object by the thematic relation; for example, for a specific glass of wine there can be only one drinking event. *Mapping to objects* can be exemplified by our example as follows: every part of a drinking of a glass of wine corresponds to a part of the glass of wine. And *mapping to events* says in the example at hand that every part of the glass of wine being drunk corresponds to a part of the drinking event. These are just informal characterizations of the properties of thematic relations; they will be discussed in more detail below.

The following postulate covers the notion of *iterativity*. It is a relation between an event e, an object x and a thematic relation R saying that at least one part of x is subjected to at least two different parts of e. This notion applies to, e.g., the reading of a book if at least one part of the book is read twice. It is more permissive than the usual notion of iterativity, which would claim in the example at hand that the whole book must have been read at least twice.

(P31) $\forall e, x, R[ITER(e, x, R) \leftrightarrow R(e, x) \land \exists e', e'', x'[e' \sqsubseteq e \land e'' \sqsubseteq e$
$\land \neg e' = e'' \land x' \sqsubseteq x \land R(e', x') \land R(e'', x')]]$ (iterativity)

Which properties must we assume for thematic relations to derive their homomorphism properties? Let us translate an expression like *read a letter* by predicates ϕ,

(11) $\phi = \lambda e \exists x[\alpha(e) \land \delta(x) \land \theta(e, x)]$

where α represents the verbal predicate (*read*), δ represents the nominal predicate (*a letter*), and θ represents a thematic relation (here, a specific patient relation). In the following, I will examine the effects of some properties of δ and θ on ϕ. The verbal predicate α will be considered to be cumulative throughout.

We start with the question: What are the conditions for ϕ to be cumulative? One set of conditions is: ϕ is cumulative if δ is cumulative and θ is summative (an example is *read letters*). Proof: Assume e_1, e_2 (not necessarily distinct) with $\phi(e_1)$, $\phi(e_2)$. According to the definition of ϕ, there are two objects x_1, x_2 with $\alpha(e_1)$, $\delta(x_1)$, $\theta(e_1, x_1)$ and $\alpha(e_2)$, $\delta(x_2)$, $\theta(e_2, x_2)$. Because α and δ are cumulative, it holds that $\alpha(e_1 \sqcup e_2)$ and $\delta(x_1 \sqcup x_2)$, and because θ is summative, it holds that $\theta(e_1 \sqcup e_2, x_1 \sqcup x_2)$. Hence $\phi(e_1 \sqcup e_2)$, that is, ϕ is cumulative:

(T6) $\forall P, Q, R[CUM(P) \land CUM(Q) \land SUM(R) \to CUM(\lambda e \exists x[P(e) \land Q(x) \land R(e, x)])]$

As singular predicates (e.g., *the letter*) are cumulative as well, albeit in a somewhat pathological way, this result holds for them, too. Consider the following example, with *the.letter* as a predicate with singular reference applying to the letter.

(12) *read the letter*
    $\lambda e \exists x[read(e) \land PAT(e, x) \land the.letter(x)]$

But if we want to understand *read the letter* as atelic, as in *he read the letter for an hour*, then we clearly have to assume either a partitive reading or an iterative reading. Partitive readings will be treated in Section 7. As for the iterative reading, it can be shown that if ϕ is strictly cumulative, θ is summative, and δ has singular reference, then we get an iterative interpretation.

Proof: If ϕ is strictly cumulative, then we have two distinct e_1, e_2 with $\phi(e_1)$, $\phi(e_2)$. According to the definition of ϕ, there are two objects x_1, x_2 with $\delta(x_1)$, $\theta(e_1, x_1)$ and $\delta(x_2)$, $\theta(e_2, x_2)$. Because θ is summative, it holds that $\theta(e_1 \sqcup e_2, x_1 \sqcup x_2)$, and because δ has singular reference, it holds that $x_1 = x_2$. With $\theta(e_1 \sqcup e_2, x_1)$, $\theta(e_1, x_1)$, $\theta(e_2, x_1)$ and $\neg e_1 = e_2$, the conditions for iterativity (P31) are met, as x_1 is subjected to two different parts of the event $e_1 \sqcup e_2$, namely e_1 and e_2. So the following theorem holds:

(T7) $\forall P, R, e, x[SNG(P) \land SUM(R) \land SCUM(\lambda e \exists x[P(x) \land R(e,x)]) \rightarrow$
$ITER(e, x, R)]$

If we exclude the iterative interpretation and retain singular reference of δ and summativity of θ, then it follows that ϕ cannot be strictly cumulative:

(T8) $\forall P, R, e, x[SNG(P) \land SUM(R) \land \neg ITER(e, x, R) \rightarrow$
$\neg SCUM(\lambda e \exists x[P(x) \land R(e,x)])]$

Hence a verbal predicate like *read the letter*, under a non-iterative and non-partitive interpretation, cannot be strictly cumulative, and hence cannot be atelic.

Sometimes the iterative interpretation is excluded in the first place, namely with *effected* or *consumed* objects, as in *write the letter* or *drink the wine*. The reason is that an object can be subjected to an event of drinking or writing a maximum of one time in its career. Therefore, uniqueness of events should be postulated for the respective thematic relations. And this excludes an iterative interpretation. Proof: Assume to the contrary that θ is unique for events, $\theta(e_0, x_0)$ and $ITER(e_0, x_0, \theta)$. Because of iterativity, it follows that there are e_1, e_2, x_1 with $e_1 \sqsubseteq e_0, e_2 \sqsubseteq e_0$, $\neg e_1 = e_2$ and $x_1 \sqsubseteq x_0$ for which it holds that $\theta(e_1, x_1)$ and $\theta(e_2, x_1)$. But this contradicts uniqueness of events.

(T9) $\forall R, e, x[R(e, x) \land UNI\text{-}E(R) \rightarrow \neg ITER(e, x, R)]$

Let us now investigate the influence of quantized nominal predicates like *a letter*. Under which conditions can we assume that they cause the complex verbal predicate to be quantized as well? One set of conditions is that the thematic role θ must satisfy uniqueness of objects and mapping to objects, and that iterative interpretations are excluded. Proof: We assume to the contrary that δ is quantized, $\phi(e_1)$, $\phi(e_2)$ and $e_2 \sqsubset e_1$. Then there are x_1, x_2 with $\delta(x_1)$, $\theta(e_1, x_1)$ and $\delta(x_2)$, $\theta(e_2, x_2)$, according to the definition of ϕ. Because $e_2 \sqsubset e_1$ and θ satisfies mapping to objects, there is an x_3 such that $x_3 \sqsubseteq x_1$ and $\theta(e_2, x_3)$. Because uniqueness of objects, it holds that $x_3 = x_2$, and therefore $x_2 \sqsubseteq x_1$. As we have $\theta(e_2, x_2)$, $e_2 \sqsubset e_1$ and $\neg ITER(e_1, x_1, \theta)$, we can infer that $\neg x_1 = x_2$. With $x_2 \sqsubseteq x_1$, this yields $x_2 \sqsubset x_1$, but this contradicts the assumption that δ is quantized. Hence there are no e_1, e_2 as assumed above, and that means that ϕ is quantized.

(T10) $\forall P, R, e, x[QUA(P) \land UNI\text{-}O(R) \land MAP\text{-}O(R) \land \neg ITER(e, x, R)$
$\rightarrow QUA(\lambda e \exists x[P(x) \land R(e,x)])]$

As a special case of (T10), we have the following theorem for thematic relations which satisfy uniqueness of events (e.g., effected and consumed objects), as this property excludes an iterative interpretation in the first place:

(T11) $\forall P, R[QUA(P) \land UNI\text{-}O(R) \land MAP\text{-}O(R) \land UNI\text{-}E(\theta) \rightarrow$
$QUA(\lambda e \exists x[P(x) \land R(e,x)])]$

Even in the iterative case it holds that examples like 'read a letter' are atomic. The conditions for thematic relations which are relevant for this result are that they satisfy uniqueness of objects and mapping to events. We have to assume δ not only to be quantized, but to be strictly quantized, which is not a substantial limitation. Proof: Assume an e_1 with $\phi(e_1)$, hence an x_1 with $\delta(x_1)$ and $\theta(e_1, x_1)$. Because δ is strictly quantized, x_1 contains a proper part x_2, that is, $x_2 \sqsubset x_1$, with $\neg\delta(x_2)$. Because of mapping to events, there is an e_2 with $e_2 \sqsubseteq e_1$ and $\theta(e_2, x_2)$. Because of uniqueness of objects, x_2 is the only object with this property. Hence there is no x with $\delta(x)$ and $\theta(e_2, x)$. But then $\neg\phi(e_2)$ holds, and this means that e_1 contains a ϕ-atom, e_2. As we made no special assumption for e_1, it follows that ϕ is atomic.

(T12) $\forall P, R[SQUA(P) \wedge MAP\text{-}E(R) \wedge UNI\text{-}O(R) \rightarrow$
$\quad ATM(\lambda e \exists x[P(x) \wedge R(e, x)])]$

In Krifka 1986, 1989, I have shown how we can explain with the help of these results why durative adverbials like *for an hour* select for atelic verbal predicates, whereas time-span adverbials like *in an hour* select for telic predicates. The underlying reason is that durative adverbials presuppose that the verbal predicate they are applied to is strictly cumulative, and time-span adverbials presuppose that the verbal predicate they are applied to is atomic. Now, quantized verbal predicates ($\approx$ telic predicates) are atomic and not strictly cumulative; hence their distribution with respect to those adverbials is explained. Strictly cumulative verbal predicates ($\approx$ atelic predicates) can be combined with durative adverbials, and they can also be combined with time-span adverbials under the presupposition that they are atomic. Normally, this presupposition is not warranted, and hence the combination with time-span adverbials sounds odd.

To conclude this section, let us use the properties of thematic relations to classify the patient relations of different verbs. It is useful to introduce a new notion that says that the object is subjected to the event in a gradual manner, as visualized by the space-time diagram (10). I call this *graduality*; it comprises uniqueness of objects, mapping to objects, and mapping to events.

(P32) $\forall P[GRAD(P) \leftrightarrow UNI\text{-}O(P) \wedge MAP\text{-}O(P) \wedge MAP\text{-}E(P)]$ (graduality)

The criteria for the classification of thematic roles can be applied to transitive verbs. This yields at least three interesting classes; two classes can be further subdivided for independent reasons.

(13)	example	summa-tivity	gradu-ality	uniqu.events	label
	write a letter	×	×	×	gradual effected patient
	eat an apple	×	×	×	gradual consumed patient
	read a letter	×	×	−	gradual patient
	touch a cat	×	−	−	affected patient
	see a horse	×	−	−	stimulus

I think the conditions of summativity, graduality and uniqueness of events are intuitively plausible for the respective patient relations. In the next section, I will discuss the transfer properties for thematic relations in greater detail.

6 Some Consequences for the Theory of Thematic Relations

In this section, we will discuss some consequences which follow from the assumption of properties of thematic relations, as discussed in the last section.

The most general property is *summativity*, which obtains for all patient relations, and probably for all thematic relations whatsoever. This means that thematic relations are not sensitive to the "size" of the entities they relate to each other.

One thing which summativity can buy us is a simpler and intuitively more appealing treatment of *cumulative readings* than the one offered in Scha 1981. For example, if there are two events, one to be described with (14a), the other with (14b),

(14) a. John saw three zebras.
      b. Mary saw four zebras.

and if the zebras John and Mary saw do not overlap, then the sentence *John and Mary saw seven zebras* can be derived if one assumes summativity for the experiencer relation and the stimulus relation, and that the count noun relation contains extensive measure functions compatible with the object lattice, a notion introduced in Krifka 1986, 1989. *EXP* and *STI* should represent the experiencer and stimulus relation, and *zebra(x,n)* says that x and n are zebras.

(15) $see(e_1) \wedge EXP(e_1, John) \wedge STI(e_1, x_1) \wedge zebra(x_1, 3)$
      $see(e_2) \wedge EXP(e_2, Mary) \wedge STI(e_2, x_2) \wedge zebra(x_2, 4)$

$$\frac{\neg \; x_1 \circ x_2}{see(e_1 \sqcup e_2) \wedge EXP(e_1 \sqcup e_2, John \sqcup Mary) \wedge STI(e_1 \sqcup e_2, x_1 \sqcup x_2)}$$
      $\wedge zebra(x_1 \sqcup x_2, 7)$

Note that the derived sentence has rather weak truth conditions, as it remains unspecified how the zebras relate to John and Mary individually. This is as it should be, as the different possibilities are not different "readings" of the sentence. In contrast to other theories of cumulative predication, for example the one by Gillon (1987), this is a natural outcome of a very simple rule and need not be stated by a complicated rule involving quantification over partitions of sets and the like.

An objection against this treatment might be that a sentence like *John and Mary saw seven zebras* are understood as saying that they saw exactly seven zebras, a reading which is not captured by $\exists e, x[see(e) \wedge EXP(e, John \sqcup Mary) \wedge STI(e, x) \wedge zebra(x, 7)]$, as this representation allows for John and

Mary to have seen more than seven zebras. But this problem can be handled if we assume a pragmatic rule that enforces maximally informative readings, as the sentence x *saw n zebras* is more informative than x *saw n′ zebras*, if $n > n'$ (cf. Krifka 1986, 1989).

To cover collective readings, as e.g., *John and Mary (jointly) own three houses*, we need of course a different representation, which will not be developed here. And it should be clear that distributive readings can be treated in this framework as well (cf. Link 1983 for distributivity in lattice model structures).

Uniqueness of objects has been discussed by several authors. For example, it corresponds to "thematic uniqueness" in Carlson 1984 and "uniqueness of role-bearers" in Dowty 1987, and it is a requirement for the treatment of thematic relations as functions, as e.g., in Link 1987. Furthermore, Carlson suggests that thematic roles may serve to discriminate events from one another on the basis of this property and the discrimination of objects involved in the events: If θ is unique for objects, then we can infer from $\theta(e_1, x_1) \wedge \theta(e_2, x_2) \wedge \neg x_1 = x_2$ that $\neg e_1 = e_2$. But note that I do not assume uniqueness of objects for every thematic relation, as these authors seem to do. Obviously, it does not hold for the stimulus relation, as e.g., I can see a zebra and, with the same event of seeing, see the mane of the zebra as well. And it does not obtain with affected objects, as e.g., I can touch a shoulder and a person with the same event of touching.

Next, consider *mapping to events* and *mapping to objects*, the two relations which constitute the core of the construction of the homomorphism from objects to events. They seem to be sound assumptions for gradual patient relations. Take as an example the reading of a book; every part of the book corresponds to a part of the reading and vice versa. With other thematic relations, these properties normally do not obtain; for example, there is no correspondence between parts of the person that is reading and the reading event. But note that as we can have sum individuals, it is possible that mapping to events and mapping to objects (as well as uniqueness of objects) apply to other thematic relations in certain circumstances as well. As an example, consider *see seven zebras*. Even if a single experiencer is involved, this predicate can be applied to events with different temporal structures, for example to events where seven zebras are seen simultaneously, or to the sum of seven consecutive events, in each of which a single zebra was seen. Now, in the second case, it does make sense to speak of mapping to events and mapping to objects, as for every part of the complex seeing event (down to the observings of single zebras) there is a part of the sum individual of the zebras which is seen in this event. Note that in cases like this one, predicates as 'see seven zebras' can be understood as telic; for example, (16) can be understood to say that the seven zebras were not seen simultaneously.

(16)   John saw seven zebras in an hour.

Time-span adverbials like *in an hour* select for atomic verbal predicates (cf. Krifka 1986, 1989). The simplest way to get an atomic reading of *see seven zebras* is that in the relevant event, the zebras were seen in some temporal succession.

The fact that the object roles of verbs like *see* sometimes have the same mapping properties as the object roles of verbs like *eat* indicates that the properties we have discussed so far are not "hard-wired" in the thematic relations, but follow from other knowledge sources. Consequently, we should assume that even the object role of verbs like *eat* does not exhibit graduality as some grammatical feature, but simply because the normal way of eating enforces the graduality properties.

However, there are some problems with the mapping properties. With mapping to events, it is often the case that only a certain class of parts of the object are relevant. As an example, consider *eat the apple* and *peel the apple*; in the first case, all the parts of the apple are involved, whereas in the second case, only the surface parts are. Another example is *read the book* and *burn the book*; surely, there are parts of the book which are relevant in the second case (e.g., the cover of the book) which do not count as parts of the book in the first case. To handle these phenomena, we may assume that the verb selects specific *aspects* of an object (e.g., only its surface).

Perhaps more problematic is mapping to objects. As an example, consider *build the house*. There are surely parts of the event of building a house which cannot be mapped to parts of the house. An example is the erection of the scaffold, which is clearly part of building the house, but the scaffold is not a part of the house, and even vanishes when the house is finished. Therefore, mapping to objects does not hold in a strict sense for complex events.

This problem can be solved if we assume that predicates like *build the house* refer to events consisting of events which themselves fall under different quantized predicates. A list of such predicates may be called a *scenario*, after Link 1987. For example, the building of a house consists in raising a loan, buying a place, and so on. This can be captured by a predicate $\phi = \lambda e \exists e_1 \ldots e_n[\phi_1(e_1) \wedge \ldots \wedge \phi_n(e_n) \wedge e = e_1 \sqcup \ldots \sqcup e_n]$, where all the ϕ_i are quantized and disjoint from each other. It can be shown that ϕ is then quantized as well. Proof: Assume to the contrary that $\phi(e_1)$, $\phi(e_2)$ and $e_1 \sqsubseteq e_2$; then there is at least one ϕ_i, $1 \leq i \leq n$, and e_3, e_4 such that $\phi_i(e_3)$, $\phi_i(e_4)$ and $e_3 \sqsubseteq e_4$, which contradicts the assumption that ϕ_i is quantized.

However, an objection to this solution may be raised, as many events lack a standard scenario (cf. Link 1987). For example, with the building of a house, there need not be an erection of a scaffold. Therefore, we have to assume that a complex event of a certain type has to be related to *some* scenario of quantized subpredicates which need not be exactly specified, but which at least must qualify as being quantized, and this is all we need.

Uniqueness of events, finally, characterizes those patient relations which describe the coming into being and disappearing of objects, because there can be only one such event for every object. This is another property that should not be considered as a grammatical feature, but as an external fact about the world.

Note that with many *verba efficiendi*, we find a certain ambiguity: They can be either token-oriented and type-oriented, so to speak. For example, it is possible to write the same letter more than once, if one refers to the letter type, not to the letter token. Such type-oriented verbs were called "performance verbs" by Verkuyl (1972). The approach outlined here can be extended to type reference. Types may be considered as abstract entities with a part relation that corresponds to the part relation for concrete entities we considered so far. For example, if y, y' are types and $y' \sqsubseteq y$, and if a concrete object or event x realizes the type y, then there should be an object or event x', $x' \sqsubseteq x$, that realizes type y'. The specific patient relation of performance verbs then describes the realization of a type. Verbs like *play* and *compose* (as in *play/compose a sonata*) have patient relations relating an event to types, whereas *write* can be analyzed as either token-oriented or type-oriented. We cannot assume uniqueness of events for the type-oriented patient relation of *write* and *play*, and therefore we can understand a predicate as *write a letter* as atelic in its performance reading and under an iterative interpretation, as e.g., in (17a). On the other hand, with the patient relation of *compose*, we should assume uniqueness of events, which explains why (17b) is bad.

(17) a. The secretary wrote this letter for three years.
      b.*Scarlatti composed this sonata for three years.

In this paper, I cannot go into the semantics of types, or kinds, and their relation to tokens; see Krifka 1986 for a more elaborate treatment.

7 Progressive and Partitive

The framework developed so far can be extended in many different directions and applied to interesting problems. Here, I will treat two topics, namely the marking of progressives in Finnish and German and an interaction between aspect and definiteness in Slavic languages.

I start with *progressives*. There are two ways to mark progressives in natural language. Most often, it is marked by verbal morphology, or by a periphrastic verbal construction, as in Czech or English. Sometimes, it is marked by some special prepositional or partitive case marking of an NP, as in German or Finnish (cf. Moravcsik 1978 for the meaning of different object markings in general and Heinämäki 1984 for the partitive objects in Finnish):

(18) a. John *snědl* rybu.

 b. John *jedl* rybu když Mary vztoupila.

(19) a. John *ate* a fish.

 b. John *was eating* a fish (when Mary came in).

(20) a. John aß *einen Fisch.*

 b. John aß *an einem Fisch* (als Mary hereinkam).

(21) a. John söi *kalan.*

 b. John söi *kalaa* (kun Mary tuli sisään).

Progressivity normally is considered to be a verb-oriented category. How is it possible, then, that it is marked on an argument of the verb? The theory developed here provides an answer, because it predicts that a change of the reference type of the nominal predicate will affect the temporal constitution of the complete construction. This I want to show more precisely.

Although progressivity seems to elude a satisfying model-theoretic semantic description, it is clear since Bennett and Partee 1972 that some notion of partiality is involved in it. As a first approximation, which suffices for our purposes, we can consider a predicate like *be drinking a glass of wine* as applying to events which are parts of events to which *drink a glass of wine* applies. That is, progressivity is associated with the following operator:

(22) $PROG = \lambda P \lambda e' \exists e[P(e) \wedge e' \sqsubseteq e]$

On the other hand, one can assume that partitivity can be associated with a similar operator (cf. Bach 1986). For example, the partitive of 'fish' can be analyzed as referring to parts of a fish.

(23) $PART = \lambda P \lambda x' \exists x[P(x) \wedge x' \sqsubseteq x]$

Although the partitive may be analyzed like this in languages as Finnish which have a clear partitive case marking, the German case probably has to be handled differently because partitive objects like *an einem Fisch* have a rather limited distribution. They should instead be analyzed as prepositional objects governed by the verb. We have to assume a lexical restructuring rule which takes verbs like (24a) with an accusative object and a patient theta role and transforms them into verbs like (24b) with a prepositional object and a "partitive" patient relation. The partitive patient relation is related to the normal patient relation as in (24c):

(24) a. *essen* S/NP[*nom, ag*], NP[*acc, pat*]

 b. *essen* S/NP[*nom, ag*], NP[*an-obj, part-pat*]

 c. $\forall e, x[PART\text{-}PAT(e, x) \leftrightarrow \exists x'[PAT(e, x') \wedge x' \sqsubseteq x]]$

Now, consider the following two expressions, (25a) representing a verbal progressive (English style, e.g., *be eating a fish*), and (25b) representing a nominal progressive (Finnish or German style, e.g., *an einem Fisch essen*), with α as verbal predicate (*eat*), δ as nominal predicate (*a fish*), and θ as the specific thematic relation.

(25) a. $\phi_v = \lambda e' \exists e, x [\alpha(e) \wedge \delta(x) \wedge \theta(e, x) \wedge e' \sqsubseteq e]$

  b. $\phi_n = \lambda e \exists x, x' [\alpha(e) \wedge \delta(x) \wedge \theta(e, x') \wedge x' \sqsubseteq x]$

We assume that θ is gradual and unique for events. At least in German, the progressive marking by prepositional phrase is possible only with verbs like *drink* or *write*, marginally possible with *read*, but impossible with *see* or *pat*:

(26) a. Hans schrieb/?las an einem Brief.

  b.*Hans sah/streichelte an einer Katze.

Furthermore, the verbal predicate α should be divisive, that is, if it applies to an event, it applies to every part of it as well. Even if this is not exactly true, we can assume it in the general case.

A final point is worth mentioning. In (25), I used the general part relation instead of the proper part relation. I think that this captures the semantics of progressivity, but pragmatically one can infer from the use of the progressive form, which is more complex than the corresponding simple form, that the proper part relation holds. Therefore, we have to show that ϕ_v is similar to ϕ_n using the proper part relation.

Proof: First I show that for all e, $\phi_v(e) \rightarrow \phi_n(e)$. Let $\phi_v(e_2)$, then there is an e_1 with $\alpha(e_1)$ and $e_2 \sqsubseteq e_1$, and an x_1 with $\delta(x_1)$ and $\theta(e_1, x_1)$. Because α is divisive, it holds that $\alpha(e_2)$. With mapping to objects, uniqueness for objects and uniqueness for events, there is an x_2 with $x_2 \sqsubseteq x_1$ and $\theta(e_2, x_2)$. But then $\phi_n(e_2)$ holds, too. Secondly I show that for all e, $\phi_n(e) \rightarrow \phi_v(e)$. To do this, we have to make an additional assumption, namely that with all nominal progressives, the whole object is eventually subjected to the event (this means ignoring the problems of the imperfective paradox). Let $\phi_n(e_2)$, then $\alpha(e_2)$ holds, and there are x_2, x_1 with $\delta(x_1)$, $\theta(e_2, x_2)$ and $x_2 \sqsubseteq x_1$. Now the additional assumption is that there is an e_1 with $\alpha(e_1)$ and $\theta(e_1, x_1)$. Because of mapping to events, there is an e_3 with $\theta(e_3, x_2)$ and $e_3 \sqsubseteq e_1$. Because of uniqueness of objects, x_2 is the only x for which $\theta(e_3, x)$ holds, and because of uniqueness of objects, e_3 is the only e for which $\theta(e, x_2)$ holds, hence $e_3 = e_2$ and $\neg e_2 = e_1$ (because $\neg x_1 = x_2$), and therefore $e_2 \sqsubseteq e_1$. But then it holds that $\phi_v(e_2)$.

By this method, it can be explained how it is that a marking on the noun can serve to mark an essentially verbal category. Note that in Finnish the partitive is used in many more cases; it serves to express the progressive even with nouns like *read* and *buy*, and it may be employed to mark irresultative verbs, as e.g., *to shoot and wound* versus *to shoot dead*. This can be explained by an analogical extension of this type of marking to conceptually similar cases. The *tertium comparationis* of this extension is that the expression with a partitive object denotes an event which is not as complete as an event denoted by the corresponding expression with an accusative object.

8 Perfective and Definiteness

Let us now look at *definiteness in Slavic*. We have seen how a nominal predicate operator can have an effect that is similar to a verbal predicate operator. As the transfer of reference properties works in both directions, we should not be surprised to find the converse case as well, that is, a verbal predicate operator affecting the meaning of a nominal predicate. We observe this most clearly in Slavic languages. The observation and data in this section are based on Wierzbicka 1968 for Polish and Filip 1985 for Czech.

As it is well known, Slavic languages mark perfective aspect (or aktionsart; the difference does not matter here), whereas they do not mark definiteness of the NP. For example, the Czech NP *víno* can mean either 'wine' or 'the wine', *hruška* can mean either 'a pear' or 'the pear', and *hrušky* can mean either 'pears' or 'the pears'.

(27) a. *vno*   i. $\lambda x[wine(x)]$
          ii. $\lambda x[x = FU(wine) \land wine(x)]$
      b. *hruška* i. $\lambda x[pear(x, 1)]$
          ii. $\lambda x[x = FU(\lambda x pear(x, 1)) \land pear(x, 1)]$
      c. *hrušky* i. $\lambda x[pears(x)]$
          ii. $\lambda x[x = FU(pears) \land pears(x)]$

I represent definite NPs on the basis of a predicate P as predicates applying to the fusion of all P-elements, given that the predicate P applies to the fusion. For example, *the wine* will apply to the fusion of all wine quantities (which is a wine quantity as well, as *wine* is cumulative). Similarly, *the pears* will apply to the fusion of all pears. And *the pear* will apply to one pear if there is only one; otherwise, the fusion of the objects which fall under the predicate *(a) pear* would not fall under that predicate.

According to this interpretation, *hruška* is a quantized predicate in both readings, whereas the two readings of *víno* and *hrušky* differ in their reference type: in the definite reading, they are quantized (as they have singular reference), whereas in the indefinite reading, they are cumulative.

Now consider the following examples:

(28) a. Ota pil víno.
          'Ota drank wine/?the wine' (imperfective)
      b. Ota vypil víno.
          'Ota drank the wine/*wine' (perfective)

(29) a. Jedl hrušku.
          'He ate a pear/?the pear' (imperfective)
      b. Snědl hrušku.
          'He ate a pear/the pear' (perfective)

(30) a. Jedl hrušky.
        'He ate pears/?the pears' (imperfective)
     b. Snědl hrušky.
        'He ate the pears/*pears' (perfective)

These data can be interpreted as follows: (28) and (30) show that aspect marking can distinguish between the indefinite and the definite reading of mass nouns and bare plurals, as the perfective aspect is compatible only with the definite interpretation of the object. (29) shows that a verb in the perfective aspect may have an indefinite object if this object is quantized. Hence it is not definiteness, but quantization which is required by the perfective aspect marking.

The data can be explained as follows: Let us assume that the perfective operator has scope over the complex verbal predicate. One of its meaning components is that the predicate it applies to is quantized. That is, at least part of the meaning of the perfective can be captured by the modifier $\lambda P \lambda e[P(e) \wedge QUA(P)]$. This follows from the usual assumptions for perfectivity which says that it conveys the meaning that an event is "completed." This makes sense only for events which are quantized (or have a set terminal point), as events under a cumulative description have no set terminal point and hence cannot be said to be completed.

If we assume the normal transfer properties for the object role of verbs like *eat* and *drink*, then we see that only with a quantized object the complex verbal predicate will be quantized as well. If the perfective aspect forces a quantized interpretation of the complex verbal predicate, the complex verbal predicate will again force a quantized interpretation of the object NP. This means in the case of (28b) and (30b) the definite interpretation of the object, as this is the only quantized interpretation (note that all singular predicates are quantized). In the case of (29b), we can assume both the definite and the indefinite interpretation, as the latter one will also yield a quantized object.

In a similar way, the imperfective aspect may force a non-quantized interpretation of the verbal predicate, which consequently enforces a non-quantized interpretation of the object NP. However, this requirement seems to be much weaker.

Note that the treatment of the Slavic definiteness marking proposed here is essentially compositional, although the phenomenon itself seems not to be compositional at first sight, as the interpretation of *víno* depends on other constituents. It is simply that the unwelcome reading is excluded by general principles, just as in *rob the bank* the unwelcome readings of *bank* are excluded by the lexical meaning of *rob*.

It should be stressed here that perfectivity is not just an expression of quantization. If it were just this, we could not explain why languages typically use a variety of perfectivity markers, even for the same verb, with slight meaning differences. But quantization is at least a component of the meaning of perfectivity. There seem to be interesting variations between languages in what has been called "perfectivity." Singh (1991), for example, argues that perfectives in Hindi are not related to quantization, but to atomicity of the basic predicate.

9 Some Final Remarks

To summarize, I hope to have made it clear that a semantic representation is feasible in which the intuitive similarities between the reference type of noun phrases and the temporal constitution of verbal expressions is captured in a simple way. I have shown how the reference type of a noun phrase can affect the temporal constitution of a verbal expression and vice versa. I have discussed the properties of thematic relations that allow this transfer of reference properties. Finally, I have applied these insights to explain the marking of progressives by the case of NPs, and the effects of aspect to the definiteness of NPs.

In Krifka 1989, I have shown how the theory can be extended to cover quantification and negation. Furthermore, I have explained why durative adverbials like *for an hour* and time-span adverbials like *in an hour* select for cumulative and quantized event predicates, respectively. In Krifka 1986, I also treated the influence of locative and directional adverbials on the temporal constitution of a complex verbal expression with examples such as *walk to the school in/*for an hour* versus *walk towards the school *in/for an hour*. In Krifka (1990), I have shown how measure expressions in nominal constituents can express a measure on events. For example, the sentence '4000 ships passed through the lock last year' has a reading in which it does not imply that there are 4000 ships that passed through the lock, but that there were 4000 events of passing of a single ship. Another area of application is the semantics of the frequentative aktionsart; in many languages, it remains unspecified whether a sentence with a frequentative predicate claims that there is more than one event or more than one participant in an event, an ambiguity which can be rendered easily in our semantic representation.

References

Austin, John. 1961. Truth. In *Philosophical Papers*, 117–133. Oxford: Oxford University Press.

Bach, Emmon. 1986. The Algebra of Events. *Linguistics and Philosophy* 9:5–16.

Bäuerle, Rainer. 1979. *Temporale Deixis, Temporale Frage*. Tübingen: Gunter Narr.

Bennett, Michael, and Barbara Partee. 1972. *Toward the Logic of Tense and Aspect in English*. Bloomington: Indiana University Linguistics Club.

Carlson, Gregory N. 1984. Thematic Roles and their Role in Semantic Interpretation. *Linguistics* 22:259–279.

Davidson, David. 1967. The Logical Form of Action Sentences. In *The Logic of Decision and Action*, ed. Nicholas Rescher, 81–95. Pittsburgh: Pittsburgh University Press.

Dowty, David. 1979. *Word Meaning and Montague Grammar*. Dordrecht: Reidel.

Dowty, David. 1987. Events, Aspects, and NP Semantics. Paper presented at the Conference on Logic and Linguistics, July 1987, Stanford University.

Dowty, David. 1989. On the Semantic Content of the Notion "Thematic Role". In *Properties, Types and Meaning, Vol. 2: Semantic Issues*, ed. Gennara Chierchia, Barbara Partee, and Raymond Turner. Dordrecht: Kluwer.

Fauconnier, Gilles. 1978. Implication Reversal in a Natural Language. In *Formal Semantics and Pragmatics for Natural Language*, ed. Franz Guenthner and S. J. Schmidt, 289–301. Dordrecht: Reidel.

Filip, Hana. 1985. Der Verbalaspekt und die Aktionsarten dargelegt am Beispiel des Tschechischen. Master's thesis, Universität München.

Fillmore, Charles. 1968. The Case for Case. In *Universals in Linguistic Theory*, ed. Emmon Bach and Robert T. Harms, 1–90. New York: Holt, Rinehart and Winston.

François, Jean. 1985. Aktionsart, Aspekt und Zeitkonstitution. In *Handbuch der Lexikologie*, ed. Christopher Schwarze and Dieter Wunderlich, 229–249. Kronberg: Athenaeum.

Garey, Howard B. 1957. Verbal Aspects in French. *Language* 33:91–110.

Gillon, Brendan S. 1987. The Readings of Plural Noun Phrases in English. *Linguistics and Philosophy* 10:199–220.

Gruber, Jeffrey S. 1976. *Lexical Structures in Syntax and Semantics*. Amsterdam: North Holland. Includes 1965 MIT PhD thesis, *Studies in Lexical Relations*; reissued by Indiana University Linguistics Club (Bloomington, 1970).

Heinämäki, Orvokki. 1984. Aspect in Finnish. In *Aspect Bound: A Voyage into the Realm of Germanic, Slavonic and Finno-Ugrian Aspectology*, ed. Casper de Groot and Hannu Tommola, 153–178. Dordrecht: Foris.

Hinrichs, Erhard. 1985. *A Compositional Semantics for Aktionsarten and NP Reference in English*. Doctoral dissertation, Ohio State University.

Hoepelman, Jakob. 1976. Mass Nouns and Aspects, or: Why We Can't Eat Gingercake in an Hour. In *Amsterdam Papers in Formal Grammar 1*, ed. Jeroen Groenendijk and Martin Stokhof, 132–154. Universiteit van Amsterdam. Centrale Interfaculteit.

Hoepelman, Jakob, and Christian Rohrer. 1980. On the Mass-Count Distinction and the French Imparfait and Passé Simple. In *Time, Tense, and Quantifiers*, ed. Christian Rohrer. Tübingen: Niemeyer.

Krifka, Manfred. 1986. *Nominalreferenz und Zeitkonstitution. Zur Semantik von Massentermen, Pluraltermen und Aspektklassen*. Doctoral dissertation, Universität München. Published 1989, München: Fink.

Krifka, Manfred. 1989. Nominal Reference, Temporal Constitution and Quantification in Event Semantics. In *Semantics and Contextual Expressions*, ed. Renate Bartsch, Johan van Benthem, and Peter van Emde Boas, 75–115. Foris: Dordrecht.

Krifka, Manfred. 1990. Four Thousand Ships Passed Through the Lock: Object-Induced Measure Functions on Events. *Linguistics and Philosophy* 13:487–520.

Leisi, Ernst. 1953. *Der Wortinhalt. Seine Struktur im Deutschen und Englischen.* Heidelberg: Quelle und Mayer.

Link, Godehard. 1983. The Logical Analysis of Plurals and Mass Terms: A Lattice-Theoretical Approach. In *Meaning, Use, and Interpretation of Language,* ed. Rainer Bäuerle, Christopher Schwarze, and Arnim von Stechow, 302–323. Berlin: Mouton.

Link, Godehard. 1987. Algebraic Semantics for Event Structures. In *Proceedings of the 6th Amsterdam Colloquium,* ed. Jeroen Groenendijk, Martin Stokhof, and Frank Veltman, 243–262. University of Amsterdam. Institute for Language, Logic, and Information.

Lønning, Jan Tore. 1987. Mass Terms and Quantification. *Linguistics and Philosophy* 10:1–52.

Moravcsik, Edith. 1978. On the Case Marking of Objects. In *Universals of Human Languages, Vol. 4,* ed. Joseph H. Greenberg, 249–289. Stanford University Press.

Parsons, Terence. 1980. Modifiers and Quantifiers in Natural Language. *Canadian Journal of Philosophy* (Suppl) 4:29–60.

Platzack, Christer. 1979. *The Semantic Interpretation of Aspect and Aktionsarten: A Study of Internal Time Reference in Swedish.* Dordrecht: Foris.

Quine, Willard V. 1960. *Word and Object.* Cambridge, Mass.: MIT Press.

Scha, Remko. 1981. Distributive, Collective, and Cumulative Quantification. In *Formal Methods in the Study of Language, Vol. 2,* ed. Jeroen Groenendijk, Theo Janssen, and Martin Stokhof, 483–512. Amsterdam: Mathematisch Centrum.

Singh, Mona. 1991. The Perfective Paradox, or: How to Eat a Cake and Have It, Too. In *Proceedings of the 17th Annual Meeting of the Berkeley Linguistic Society.* University of California at Berkeley.

ter Meulen, Alice. 1984. Events, Quantities, and Individuals. In *Varieties of Formal Semantics,* ed. Frederick Landman and Frank Veltman, 259–280. Dordrecht: Foris.

Vendler, Zeno. 1957. Verbs and Times. *Philosophical Review* 66:143–160. (Also in Vendler 1967, pp. 97–121.).

Vendler, Zeno. 1967. *Linguistics in Philosophy.* Ithaca: Cornell University Press.

Verkuyl, Henk J. 1972. *On the Compositional Nature of the Aspects.* Dordrecht: Reidel.

Wierzbicka, Anna. 1967. On the Semantics of the Verbal Aspect in Polish. In *To Honor Roman Jakobson: Essays on the Occasion of his Seventieth Birthday,* Vol. 2, 2231–2249. Den Haag: Mouton.

3

Complex Predicates and Morpholexical Relatedness: Locative Alternation in Hungarian

FARRELL ACKERMAN

1 Introduction

This paper examines Hungarian locative alternation predicates as well as restrictions on prenominal deverbal adjective formation in this language. Sentences exhibiting *Locative Alternation* are familiar in the linguistic literature:

(1) a. The peasant loaded (the) hay onto the wagon.
                             OBJ_{theme} OBL_{goal}
  b. The peasant loaded the wagon with (the) hay.
                             OBJ_{goal} OBL_{theme}

Accounts of these constructions commonly address two issues. First, there is an observable alternation of grammatical functions (GFs) for the ostensible *theme* and *goal* arguments of participating predicates: the *theme* alternates between OBJ and OBL while the *goal* alternates between OBL and OBJ. Second, there are semantic (or, aspectual) differences associated with each variant of this construction: there is argued to be a *holistic* effect associated with the variant in which the *goal* appears as OBJ or as SUBJ depending on the transitivity of the predicate.[1] Both the recurrence

---

The present analysis of locative alternation follows the general outlines of a joint presentation of this material by Ackerman and Komlósy at the Stanford LSA Lexical Semantics Workshop 1987. The present analysis supersedes the analysis found in Ackerman 1990. The discussion of deverbal adjectives is based on Laczkó and Ackerman 1984—Cf. Laczkó and Szabolcsi 1988 for further discussion.

[1]Cf. Fillmore 1968, Anderson 1971, Salkoff 1983, Pinker 1989, Levin and Rappaport 1986, Rappaport and Levin 1988, among others.

Lexical Matters. Ivan A. Sag and Anna Szabolcsi, eds.

of this phenomenon and its arresting cross-linguistic similarities make it a perennial issue within the lexical semantic literature.

Rappaport and Levin (1988) argue quite cogently that an adequate account of these phenomena in English should be formulated in terms of *Predicate Argument Structures* (PAS). This level of representation is interpreted as a projection of the syntactically relevant aspects of the compositional semantic representations typified by the *lexical conceptual structures* of Jackendoff (1983) and the MIT lexicon project. They argue explicitly against the viability of a feature based analysis.

Contrary to their claims, I propose that a feature based analysis does extend explanatorily to the phenomena at hand.[2] In particular, I demonstrate that a particular interpretation of the feature based mapping theory of Lexical Functional Grammar yields an instructive insight into the organization of the lexicon. Moreover, this model of the lexicon provides lexical entries for both simple and complex predicates with precisely the right sorts of information to account for relatedness between predicates, differences between related predicates, correct grammatical function assignment to arguments and constraints on prenominal deverbal adjective formation. This model does not appeal to underlying levels of syntactic representation. The basic proposal constitutes a synthesis of the views of mapping from semantic proto-role features to grammatical function features found in Zaenen 1990 and the monostratal proposal to capture unaccusativity effects found in Bresnan and Zaenen 1990.

I suggest that the architecture of mapping theory yields a natural partitioning of lexical operations within the lexicon. The first type of operation, referred to as *Morpholexical, affects the lexical semantics of predicates by altering the semantic properties (SP) associated with predicates*: locative alternation and causativization are two phenomena effected by morpholexical operations. This type of operation has consequences for the assignment of the *intrinsic features* or ICs within lexical mapping theory.[3] It will be shown that, in determining intrinsic (IC) feature classification, lexical semantic properties *indirectly* constrain the Grammatical Function (GF) realization of arguments. Locative alternation predicates will be related by *morpholexical* rule: in effect, a *morpholexical* rule is a function which takes one verbal form and associated information as an argument and yields another verbal form and associated information as a value. The second type of operation, referred to as *Morphosyntactic*, assigns features supplemental

---

[2] I leave to another forum the question as to how the present proposal explains the English data: as will be seen, the distributions of data in English and Hungarian are sufficiently similar to entertain an extension of the present analysis to English.

[3] *Morpholexical* operations correspond to what Simpson (1983) refers to as *semantic redundancy rules*, while *Morphosyntactic* operations correspond to her *relation-changing rules*. Both types of rules are lexical rules, i.e they apply within the lexicon, on her account as well as on the account developed here.

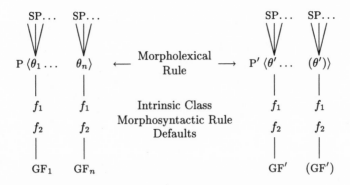

Figure 1 Model of (Modified) Mapping Theory

to those supplied by IC assignment: these operations can effect the final GF assignments to arguments but cannot affect the lexical semantics or consequent IC feature assignment of predicates: passive and locative inversion are two phenomena affected by morphosyntactic operations. These operations will play no role in the present paper. In general, the bifurcation of lexical operations stipulated in a theory such as that proposed by Zubizarreta (1987) follows naturally on the present account. The model of mapping advanced here has the shape shown in Figure 1.

The immediately relevant information in this diagram concerns the functions performed by morpholexical and morphosyntactic rules. Morpholexical rules manipulate semantic properties (SP) of arguments, i.e., these are roughly the proto-role features of Dowty 1991. Arguments are interpreted as hierarchically organized valence slots represented here as θ. Assemblages of semantic properties associated with arguments determine the intrinsic (or, IC) feature assignments of arguments, i.e., the values for f_1. Morphosyntactic rules and defaults further determine the feature matrices of individual arguments, i.e., the values for f_2, within the limits defined by monotonicity: this principle basically insures that the operations responsible for complementing the IC features of arguments will neither alter IC features nor align IC features with incompatible and contradictory features. The entire feature composition of arguments determines their GF status: grammatical functions are not atomic, they are feature matrices.

The treatment of locative alternation phenomena as well as the well-known unaccusative effects exhibited by constraints on prenominal deverbal adjectives, e.g., *the yellowed leaf* vs. **the limped man*, will be derived from the operation of *morpholexical rules*. On the present account, locative alternation alters semantic information associated with lexical entries with consequences for grammatical function realization, while deverbal adjective formation appeals to the reflexes of this information contained in lexical entries: syntactic effects are attributed to manipulation of featural information in lexical entries.[4] The information accessed concerns the lexical aspect ([±TELIC]) and the IC feature composition (specifically, the [−o] vs. [−r] status) of lexical entries.[5]

The paper is organized as follows. Section 1 introduces the Hungarian locative alternation constructions. Section 2 proposes a version of LFG mapping theory appropriate for treating locative alternation phenomena in terms of complex predicate formation. As will be seen, Hungarian locative alternation constructions contain complex predicates consisting of a *PreVerb* (PV) and a verb stem: the relevance of PVs for establishing lexical aspect and for IC feature determination will be discussed. Section 3 examines constraints on prenominal deverbal adjective formation in Hungarian and explains the observed unaccusative effects associated with these constraints in terms of the interaction between lexical aspect and the IC feature composition of arguments motivated in Section 2.

2 Locative Alternation and Complex Predicates

Hungarian exhibits a productive means of predicate formation via prefixation: a *prefixal preverb*[6] is juxtaposed to a verbal stem and—modulo the (semantic class of the) preverb and the (semantic class of the) verb—the combination results in an alteration of lexical meaning, changes in valence and/or case government and/or changes in the GF status of arguments, as contrasted with these properties of the simple verb stem. The constitutive pieces of such morpholexical compositions, i.e., the prefixal preverb and verbal stem, are separable under specifiable syntactic conditions.[7]

I turn now to a restricted domain of complex predicate formation, namely, the domain of locative alternation. The Hungarian variants exhibit all the characteristics of locative alternation constructions mentioned previously: grammatical functions change, while the semantics of the variants remains basically similar but differs along the so-called *holistic* dimension. Consider the Hungarian constructions presented below.[8]

---

[4]The treatment of deep unaccusativity in Bresnan and Zaenen 1990 informs the present speculations in this domain: they propose a way in which a monostratal theory with rich lexical assumptions can accommodate the types of effects generally attributed to underlying syntactic relations.

[5]The present proposal parallels the position propounded in Zaenen 1990 and was proposed in previous versions of the present paper. For the most, I will rely on Zaenen's formulations here.

[6]In Ackerman 1987 I distinguish between two basic types of PVs, specifically, those which bear no synchronic syntactic relation to the verbal stem, i.e., prefixal preverbs, and those that do bear some synchronic syntactic relation to the stem, i.e., argumental preverbs interpretable as incorporated elements. For the most part this paper will concentrate on prefixal preverbs.

[7]This syntactic behavior of verbal prefixes explains the earlier reference to *juxtaposition* rather than affixation.

[8]Intransitive variants will be ignored in the present work although the basic analysis proposed here extends without complication to them as well. The following abbreviations

(2) a. a paraszt   (rá=)rakta   a szénát
           the peasant (onto)loaded-3sg/DEF the hay-ACC

a szekérre
the wagon-SUBL

The peasant loaded the hay onto the wagon.

b.*a paraszt   (rá=)rakta   a szekeret
    the peasant (onto)loaded-3sg/DEF the wagon-ACC

szénával
hay-INSTR

'The peasant loaded the wagon with hay.'

(3) a. a paraszt   meg=rakta   a szekeret
           the peasant PERF-loaded-3sg/DEF the wagon-ACC

(szénával)
(hay-INSTR)

'The peasant loaded the wagon (with hay).'

b.*a paraszt   meg=rakta   a szénát
    the peasant PERF-loaded-3sg/DEF the hay-ACC

a szekérre
the wagon-SUBL

'The peasant loaded the hay onto the wagon.'

(4) a. a paraszt   tele=rakta   a szekeret   szénával
           the peasant full-loaded-3sg/DEF the wagon-ACC hay-INSTR
           'The peasant loaded the wagon full with hay'.

b.*a paraszt   tele=rakta   a szénát
    the peasant full-loaded-3sg/DEF the hay-ACC

a szekérre
the wagon-SUBL

'The peasant loaded the hay full onto the wagon'.

In contrast to their English analogues, the Hungarian locative alternation predicates are complex, i.e., they consist of a *PreVerb* (PV) and a verb stem. The preceding sentences illustrate the types of complements permitted to co-occur with three representative verb forms: (2) contains verb forms with an optionally present directional preverb, (3) contains verb forms with the *Perfective* preverb *meg*, and (4) contains verb forms with the *Resultative* preverb *tele*.

The presence or absence of prefixes correlates with differences in case government and function assignment for nominal complements as well as

---

and conventions are employed in the Hungarian examples: ACC = accusative, SUBL = sublative, INSTR = instrumental, DEL = delative, ABL = ablative, IN = inessive, PERF = perfective, DEF = definite conjugation, and '=' is employed as a juncture marker between PV (preverbs) and verbal stems.

with aspectual differences in the meaning associated with alternative patterns. In particular, whereas *hay* must be marked in the ACC and function as the OBJ complement of the simple verb or complex verb with directional prefix (*rá* 'onto'), it must bear INSTR marking and function as an OBL when it co-occurs with complex predicates containing either the PERF (*meg*) or resultative prefix (*tele* 'full'). Conversely, *wagon* must appear with a locational case marker and function as an OBL with simple verbs or complex predicates containing directional prefixes, while it must bear ACC marking and function as an OBJ when it co-occurs with complex predicates containing either a PERF or resultative prefix.

There is evident systematicity in the correlation of prefix, case-marking and grammatical function: nominals functioning as *loc* arguments are always marked with LOC case and bear the OBL relation in conjunction with directional preverbs, while these nominals are marked ACC and function as an OBJ when they co-occur with PERF or resultative preverbs. In a similar fashion, nominals functioning as *th* arguments are marked with the ACC case and bear the OBJ relation when they co-occur with directional preverbs, while these nominals are marked with the INSTR case and function as OBLs when they co-occur with PERF or resultative preverbs.

It remains to be observed that the juxtaposition of preverbs and verb stems in Hungarian is traditionally assumed to alter the aspectual status of the affected predicate. In particular, the presence of a preverb generally confers *perfective* or *completive* aspect on the predicate. There are certain preverbs such as *meg* which appear devoid of lexical semantic meaning and seem to function almost exclusively as aspectual markers, while there are other preverbs such as *tele* which simultaneously contribute lexical semantic and aspectual values to the predicate. For present purposes I will assume that the presence of a preverb correlates with alteration of the lexical aspect of a predicate and that this is registered in the lexical entry for a predicate. Following Zaenen 1990 I will assume that the preverb makes the affected predicate [+TELIC].

Distribution of time adverbials

There is standard evidence which can be adduced for the claim that the presence of a preverb correlates with the aspect of a predicate. Following Vendler 1967 and Dowty 1979 (among others) there is a rich tradition devoted to the interaction between predicates and temporal adjuncts. Consider the tabular representation of predicate and adverb interactions presented below:[9]

---

[9]It should be observed that Hungarian possesses a construction in which a directional PV follows a verbal stem and conveys *progressivity*. Example (5a) below reflects this reading, e.g. *raxta rá a szérát* 'was loading the hay onto'.

(5)

		egy órán át 'for an hour'	egy óra alatt 'in an hour'
a.	rakta (rá) a szénát 'loaded the hay'	+	−
b.	rá=rakta a szénát 'onto=loaded the hay'	−	+
c.	tele=rakta a szekeret 'full-loaded wagon'	−	+
d.	meg=rakta a szekeret 'PERF-loaded wagon'	−	+

From the present perspective it is important to observe that the simple verb stem (or verb stem with postposed directional prefix, cf. preceding footnote) and prefixed verb stems display different co-occurrence options. The particular correlation of adverbial and verb is significant for the present thesis: prefixed verbal stems co-occur with an adverbial generally acknowledged to correlate with perfective aspect, while the simple stem (or, stem and postposed directional prefix) co-occur with adverbials generally acknowledged to correlate with progressive aspect.[10]

In summary, the assumption that prefixes are associated with aspectuality is borne out in the co-occurrence constraints of time adverbials and certain predicates. As previously mentioned, I will assume with Zaenen (1990) that the relevant aspectual value is [+TELIC]: Dutch verbs containing separable preverbs of direction are like Hungarian verbs in this respect. Having seen the importance of preverbs for determining lexical aspect, semantic interpretation of the variants and the grammatical function status of arguments, it is necessary to investigate how complex predicate formation should figure in our theory of grammar.

3   A Version of Mapping Theory

In the version of mapping theory advanced here the slots representing the valence of a predicate, i.e., expediently expressed here in terms of *thematic role labels*, are associated with *Semantic Properties* and these semantic properties are partially determinative of the *Grammatical Function* status of these arguments. All of this information is contained in lexical entries as will be amply illustrated below.

The lexical mapping theory developed in Bresnan and Kanerva 1989 decomposes grammatical functions (GFs) into (sometimes underspecified) feature bundles. Two binary-valued features are postulated, namely, [±o] for *Objective* and [±r] for *(Semantically) Restricted* and these feature bun-

---

[10]Differences between perfective vs. progressive aspect will also be relevant in the discussion of constraints on deverbal adjective formation in Section 4.

dles define natural classes of functions. Both the feature composition of GFs and the natural classes defined by these features are listed below.[11]

Feature Composition of Grammatical Functions

$$\text{SUBJ} = \begin{bmatrix} -o \\ -r \end{bmatrix} \quad \text{OBJ} = \begin{bmatrix} -r \\ +o \end{bmatrix} \quad \text{OBJ}_\theta = \begin{bmatrix} +o \\ +r \end{bmatrix} \quad \text{OBL}_\theta = \begin{bmatrix} -o \\ +r \end{bmatrix}$$

Natural Classes Defined by Features

$$[-r] = \text{SUBJ, OBJ} \quad [+r] = \text{OBL}_\theta, \text{OBJ}_\theta$$
$$[-o] = \text{SUBJ, OBL}_\theta \quad [+o] = \text{OBJ, OBJ}_\theta$$

The basic question with respect to these features concerns the principles which are responsible for associating them with the valence positions of a predicate. One claim advanced in Bresnan and Kanerva is that a certain class of features are determined by lexical semantic properties of the predicate. This is formulated by them in terms of *Intrinsic Classification* or IC feature classification: certain features are assigned to arguments by virtue of the thematic role of those arguments. This assignment is presented below:

I(ntrinsic) C(lassification)

agent $= [-o]$, patient/theme $= [-r]$ or $[+o]$[12], other $= [-o]$

3.1 Partial Lexical Entries

In the present paper IC feature classification will also be keyed to lexical semantic properties of elements in the predicate's valence structure. However, I will be assuming (along with Zaenen 1990) that thematic roles are not atomic, but are rather abbreviations for constellations of semantic properties as on the analysis of Dowty 1991. Dowty proposes that verb meanings entail the existence of arguments defined schematically as constellations of a small set of recurring semantic properties.[13] The semantic properties employed here follow those suggested by Dowty:[14]

---

[11]For the intuitive motivations underlying the postulation of these features see Bresnan and Kanerva 1989.

[12]The optional assignment of $[+o]$ to *th* is proposed for Chicheŵa double object constructions in Alsina and Mchombo 1989. Since Hungarian does not contain double object constructions this option will not play a role here.

[13]Cf. Ladusaw and Dowty 1988 and Culicover 1989 for further discussion.

[14]The particular properties germane to the present discussion will be *causally affected*, *change of state* and *incremental theme* so I will, for the most part, take no stand on the precise repertoire of properties listed above. The delimitation of a reliable and explanatory set of semantic properties, as Dowty acknowledges, is as fraught with vagueness as the defense of particular collections of (atomic) thematic or semantic roles: in the present paper I have nothing illuminating to say about these issues. For present purposes it is sufficient to suggest that there is a natural partition of operations and that morpholexical operations as defined here are driven by lexico-semantic properties of predicates irrespective of whether these be atomic thematic roles or features constitutive of such arguments.

Proto-Role Properties

Proto-Agent	*Proto-Patient*
volition	change of state
sentience	incremental theme
causes event	causally affected
movement	stationary
referential	possibly referential

On such a view, traditional thematic role labels are (misleading) abbreviations for particular constellations of properties. That is, thematic roles are interpretable as feature bundles.[15] On Dowty's account, the algorithm for the grammatical function realization of feature ensembles is as follows:

Argument Selection Principle

The argument of a predicate having the greatest number of Proto-Agent properties entailed by the meaning of the predicate will, all else being equal, be lexicalized as the subject of the predicate: the argument having the greatest number of Proto-Patient properties will, all else being equal, be lexicalized as the direct object of the predicate.

A corollary relevant to locative alternation, among other constructions containing OBL(ique) complements, is formulated as follows:

Corollary

With a three place predicate, the non-subject argument having a greater number of entailed Proto-Patient properties will be lexicalized as the direct object, the non-subject argument having fewer entailed Proto-Patient properties will be lexicalized as an oblique or prepositional object ...

In sum, the system of mapping proposed by Dowty directly associates an unweighted inventory of semantic properties with specific syntactic roles via Argument Selection Principles[16] and various corollaries.

On the present account, as in Zaenen 1990, I will be assuming that (possibly weighted) constellations of properties determine the value for the *Intrinsic Classification* feature of arguments: as will become clear below, this means that semantic properties *indirectly* constrain the GF realization of arguments.

The previous assumptions will yield partial lexical entries for predicates as shown in Figure 2.

A constellation of semantic properties is associated with a valence position, i.e., θ, and determines the values for the IC features, i.e., f_1.

---

[15]That the entities reified into role labels are organized into hierarchies will be assumed in Section 3.5 below.

[16]Cf. Fillmore 1977a, 1977b and Gawron 1983 for discussion of SUBJ and OBJ selection principles which are keyed to hierarchically arranged lexico-semantic features.

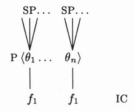

Figure 2 Schematic Partial Lexical Entry

3.2 Basic lexical entries: unmarked IC assignment

The principles for determining specific IC feature assignments for basic or underived predicates, i.e., for simple verb stems without PVs, roughly follow those proposed by Zaenen (1990).

Principles of IC Feature Assignment

(1) The argument with the most or most heavily weighted proto-patient properties is intrinsically classified as $[-r]$.

(2) The argument with the most or most heavily weighted proto-agent properties is intrinsically classified as $[-o]$.

(3) All other arguments are intrinsically classified as $[-o]$.

These feature specification principles yield the following partial lexical entry for the basic or underived predicate *rak* 'load': the first argument has a preponderance of proto-agent properties and is therefore assigned $[-o]$, the second argument has a preponderance of proto-patient properties and is therefore assigned $[-r]$, while the third argument has fewer of the preceding properties or different properties and is therefore assigned $[-o]$.[17]

(6)   rak   ⟨ ag,   th,   loc⟩
              $[-o]$ $[-r]$ $[-o]$ Intrinsic Classification (IC)

I will assume that the arguments expediently labelled as *th* and *loc* in the preceding examples share the proto-patient property *causally affected*. The proposed IC feature assignment principles obtain, by hypothesis, for *basic predicates*. The crucial characteristic of Hungarian locative alternation predicates, however, is that they contain *derived complex predicates*. As mentioned previously, the presence of a preverb correlates with the alteration of inherent lexical aspect and depending on the preverb and the (class of the) verb stem, with an alteration of the lexical semantics, case government and grammatical function assignment to arguments as well.

---

[17]I will employ thematic role labels for convenience, but they should be understood as abbreviations of semantic properties in the same way that grammatical function names should be considered as abbreviations for feature matrices.

3.3 Complex lexical entries: marked IC assignment

I will assume that complex predicate formation with preverbs is a morpholexical operation. This means that the combination of a preverb and verb stem can alter the lexical semantics of a basic predicate: this alteration is registered in the lexical entry of the complex predicate. Since IC feature assignment is keyed to lexical semantic properties of predicates, the application of such an operation can alter IC feature assignment. These morpholexical operations are a way of relating predicates, i.e., of accounting for observed similarities, while also accounting for whatever differences they may display: the differences are attributable to divergent inventories of semantic properties and whatever reflexes of these may be exhibited as a function of different IC feature assignments. We have already seen that the presence of a preverb alters lexical aspect: the correlate of this will be that the relevant complex predicate will be associated with the feature [+TELIC]. In addition, each preverb will confer certain other semantic properties on arguments of the complex predicate. In general, morpholexical operations responsible for complex predicate formation will lead to a *marked* IC feature assignment viz. the principles proposed for feature assignment with basic predicates.

There are two marked feature assignments associated with preverbs which are relevant for locative alternation. The preverbs will be divided into two types. There are (uses of) preverbs which contribute a specification of directionality to the action denoted by the verb stem: these PVs will be subscripted with the diacritic [+dir]. This type is exemplified by the PVs *rá* 'onto', *be* 'into', *ki* 'out of', etc. There are also (uses of) preverbs which do not contribute any directional sense to the action denoted by the verb stem. This type is exemplified by the PVs *meg* 'PERF' and *tele* 'full'. Whereas both types of preverb determine that the lexical aspect of the complex predicate is [+TELIC], each type yields a different distribution of lexico-semantic properties to the arguments of the complex predicate.

3.3.1 PV$_{[+dir]}$

PV$_{[+dir]}$s establish motional and topological constraints on the *loc* argument of the complex predicate. The motional notions and topological constraints are reflected in the repertoire of surface case and postpositions which can be employed to encode the *loc* complement. These considerations become evident with respect to locative alternation in the contrast between the lexical entries for complex predicates based on the verbal stem *rak* 'load' when composed with either the directional preverb *ki* 'out of' or *be* 'into'. Each of these PVs require their *loc* complement to be expressed by cases or adpositions which encode certain features. For example, the PV *ki* requires its *loc* complement to be expressed by a morpheme which has the features [−goal, +containment].[18] Two representative markers compati-

---

[18]The case features utilized here are intended to be heuristic: their theoretical status

ble with this requirement are the case marker *-ból* 'from out of' and the postposition *alól* 'from under'. Similarly, the PV *be* constrains its *loc* complement to be expressed by any member of a set of morphemes which bear the features [+goal, +containment]. Representative markers from this set are the case marker *ba* 'into' and the postposition *alá* 'to under'. The presence of these PVs also determines the telicity value of the complex predicate. The relevant lexical entries might be represented roughly as follows, where the annotation for the function OBL is intended to convey the requirement that this function must be encoded by markers that bear the stated features:

$$\text{ki=rak} \quad \text{V} \quad \text{'unload'} \quad \langle \text{ag, th, loc} \rangle$$
$$\text{OBL}_{\text{case}} = \alpha \in [-\text{goal}]$$
$$[+\text{containment}]$$
$$\text{TELIC} = +$$

$$\text{be=rak} \quad \text{V} \quad \text{'into load'} \quad \langle \text{ag, th, loc} \rangle$$
$$\text{OBL}_{\text{case}} = \alpha \in [+\text{goal}]$$
$$[-\text{containment}]$$
$$\text{TELIC} = +$$

In summary, $\text{PV}_{[+\text{dir}]}$'s alter the lexical aspect of a predicate and specify the motional and topological features of *loc* arguments. This results in a complex predicate with a lexical entry that contains the aspectual feature [+TELIC]. The lexical entry for the complex predicate will differ minimally from that for the basic or simple predicate: whereas the former will contain a negative telicity feature value, the latter will have a positive value for this feature. The partial representation of *rá-rak* 'onto-load' is presented below:

$$\text{rá-rak} \quad \text{V} \quad \text{'onto-load'} \quad \langle \ \text{ag,} \quad \text{th,} \quad \text{loc} \rangle$$
$$[-\text{o}] \quad [-\text{r}] \quad [+\text{r}]$$
$$\text{TELIC} = +$$

3.4 $\text{PV}_{[-\text{dir}]}$

I will assume here that $\text{PV}_{[-\text{dir}]}$s correlate both with the association of [+TELIC] and with a distribution of semantic properties among arguments. The resultative or purely aspectual [−dir] preverbs associate the property *change of state* with an argument containing the feature *causally affected* which is associated with [−o] in basic predicates. The argument now exhibiting a preponderance of proto-patient properties will be assigned the [−r] IC feature value, while the argument with fewer (or less heavily weighted) proto-patient values will receive [−o].

The motivation for assigning [−o] to the *th* is based on three interrelated

---

is both arguable and irrelevant to the point at issue. [+goal] is intended to designate centripetal or afferent motion, [−goal] designates centrifugal or efferent motion, [+containment] designates that the location is construable as denoting a bounded space with an interior.

considerations: (1) [−o] is the feature assignment which follows from the principles of IC feature assignment presented previously, (2) Hungarian is a language whose predicates can only have a single [−r] intrinsically classified argument (following the parametric difference between languages proposed in Alsina and Mchombo 1989, and (3) the assignment of [−o] avoids a violation of the constraint against multiple [−r] IC arguments, while yielding the correct function assignments for both transitive and intransitive[19] variants of the locative alternation predicates.

In the predicates at issue, these assignments mean that the argument which is roughly correlative with the *loc* role will receive [−r], while the argument roughly correlative with the *th* will receive [−o]. The PV_{dir} also determines the telicity value for the complex predicate as +. The resulting partial lexical entry is presented below.

$$\text{meg-rak} \quad \text{V} \quad \text{`onto-load'} \quad \langle \text{ ag,} \quad \text{th,} \quad \text{loc} \rangle$$
$$\qquad\qquad\qquad\qquad\qquad\qquad [-\text{o}] \quad [-\text{o}] \quad [-\text{r}]$$

$$\text{TELIC} = +$$

3.5 Full Lexical Entries

Since grammatical functions, on the present interpretation, are tiered feature bundles, there must be additional ways to complement the IC feature composition of arguments. Within mapping theory there are essentially two ways to do this: there are morphosyntactic operations such as passive which determine the argument inventory which will be syntactically expressed and there are default assignments of features which are dependent on the IC features of arguments. These alternative ways of assigning features are presented below:

Morphosyntactic Operations

$$\text{e.g., Passive} \; — \quad \langle \hat{\theta} \rangle$$
$$\qquad\qquad\qquad\qquad |$$
$$\qquad\qquad\qquad\qquad \emptyset \quad \text{i.e., suppress the highest argument}$$

The effect of passive is to "suppress" the highest argument (cf. below). This means that this argument will not be expressed syntactically. The suppression of this argument would lead to the ostensible *th* playing the role of SUBJ, given the well-formedness conditions stated below.

The basic default assignments are presented below:

Defaults (a) Subject default $\hat{\theta}$ (b) Elsewhere default θ
$$\qquad\qquad\qquad\qquad\qquad | \qquad\qquad\qquad\qquad\qquad\qquad\qquad |$$
$$\qquad\qquad\qquad\qquad [-\text{r}] \qquad\qquad\qquad\qquad\qquad\qquad [+\text{r}]$$

---

[19]Though I ignore here the treatment of intransitive variants of this construction, there is one aspect of their analysis with respect to the alignment of *th* with [−o] which will be addressed after the presentation of default assignments below.

These defaults function as instructions to associate arguments with particular features. The arguments are organized in terms of a hierarchy. In particular, the argument with the most proto-agent properties is higher than the argument with the most proto-patient properties. Other arguments are arrayed within a hierarchy such as that presented below. The hierarchy can be stated in terms of thematic role labels:

Argument hierarchy (partial)

$$\text{ag} < \text{exp} < \text{ben/goal} < \text{th/pat} < \text{loc}$$

The highest argument will be referred to as $\hat{\theta}$. The SUBJ default associates the highest argument with the feature $[-r]$, while the (b) default associates other arguments with $[+r]$, as long as this doesn't conflict with the argument's IC feature assignment (cf. below for monotonicity). This procedure leaves the argument with $[-r]$ IC underspecified and therefore able to assume either the SUBJ or OBJ function (cf. below for well-formedness conditions).

The assignment of features to complement IC features is constrained by *Monotonicity*:

Monotonicity Constraint on Feature Assignment

Feature assignment is additive, i.e., neither rules nor defaults can alter feature assignments nor result in contradictory assignments of features for arguments.

Once the assemblages of features have been determined, there are two well formedness conditions on final lexical entries for predicates:

Well-formedness Conditions on Lexical Forms

(1) Functional Uniqueness: Every grammatical function and every functional feature must have a unique value.

(2) SUBJ condition: Every lexical form must contain a SUBJ function.[20]

The manner in which features are associated with arguments and result in assignments of GFs can be illustrated in the case of the basic Hungarian verb *rak* 'load'.

(7)   rak

	⟨ag,	th,	loc⟩	
	$[-o]$	$[-r]$	$[-o]$	Intrinsic Classification (IC)
	$[-r]$		$[+r]$	Default
	SUBJ	SUBJ/OBJ	OBL	Bi-Uniqueness Constraint
	SUBJ	OBJ	OBL	
	TELIC = −			

The verb *rak* 'load' is associated with a thematic argument inventory consisting of an *ag*, *th* and *loc*. The arguments are associated with features

---

[20]A lexical form is the lexical representation that results from the mapping of arguments into grammatical functions. The SUBJ condition is possibly parametric: there may be some languages for which it does not obtain.

following the algorithm for semantic determination of IC feature assignment. Specifically, the *ag* argument is associated with a [−o] IC since it exhibits the most proto-agent properties, the *th* argument is associated with a [−r] IC since it contains the most proto-patient properties, while the *loc* argument is associated with the IC [−o] since it is the remaining argument in the argument structure. Since there are no (morphosyntactic) operations such as passive which apply here, the defaults then apply: the SUBJ default requires that the highest argument is associated with the feature [−r], while the elsewhere default, states that all other arguments are associated with the feature [+r] as long as this assignment does not violate the monotonicity constraint. In the case of 'load', the highest argument is *ag* which is associated with [−r], while the *loc* is associated with the feature [+r]. The *th* cannot be associated with [+r] without violating monotonicity, so it remains underspecified. The object created by the assignment of features to arguments, namely, a *Lexical Form* is constrained to conform to the two well-formedness conditions (1) functional uniqueness and (2) the SUBJ condition. The result of assigning features to 'load' is a representation in which the *ag* is fully specified and must appear as SUBJ, the *th* is underspecified and can, consequently, appear as either a SUBJ or an OBJ, while the *loc* is fully specified and must appear as an OBL. The SUBJ condition, which obtains in Hungarian, applies and determines that the *th* is OBJ. The final GF assignments are indicated in the text: *ag* is mapped into SUBJ, *th* mapped into OBJ and *loc* into OBL.

The assignment of features to the basic verb 'load' is straightforward: *ag* receives [−o] IC, *th* the [−r] IC, and loc the [−o] IC, then defaults apply fully specifying the *ag* with [−r] by the SUBJ default, and fully specifying the *loc* with [+r] by the elsewhere default, and leaving the *th* underspecified. These assignments result in the *ag* as SUBJ, *th* as OBJ and *loc* as OBL.

In the present instance, as in all others, the interaction between intrinsic classification, rules and default assignments lead to an increasing specification of the features associated with semantic roles and this results in GF realizations for arguments.

The lexical entries for complex predicates containing PVs are derived in the following way. Since both *tele* and *meg* are [−dir] the *loc* argument is associated with [−r] IC, while the *th* argument is associated with [−o] IC. The *ag* argument receives the [−o] IC. The SUBJ default applies to the *ag* assigning it [−r], while the elsewhere default applies to the *th* argument assigning it [+r]: the *loc* argument remains underspecified. Since the *ag* is fully specified as [−o] and [−r] it surfaces as the SUBJ. Likewise the *th* is fully specified as [−o] and [+r] and therefore surfaces as an OBL$_\theta$. The *loc* is underspecified and in principle could assume either the SUBJ or OBJ function. However, a violation of functional uniqueness would ensue if the *th* appeared as a SUBJ, so it assumes the OBJ function. The entire predicate is, of course, associated with the feature TELIC = +.

Composition of Complex Predicates

$$rà{=}rak \quad \text{'onto-load'} \quad \langle \text{ ag,} \quad \text{th,} \quad \text{loc } \rangle$$

	ag	th	loc	
	[−o]	[−r]	[+r]	IC
	[−r]		[−o]	Default
	SUBJ	OBJ	OBL	
TELIC = +				

$$tele{=}rak \quad \text{'full=load'} \quad \langle \text{ ag,} \quad \text{th,} \quad \text{loc } \rangle$$

	ag	th	loc	
	[−o]	[−o]	[−r]	IC
	[−r]	[+r]		Default
	SUBJ	OBL$_\theta$	OBJ	
TELIC = +				

$$meg{=}rak \quad \text{'PERF-load'} \quad \langle \text{ ag,} \quad \text{(th),} \quad \text{loc } \rangle$$

	ag	(th)	loc	
	[−o]	([−o])	[−r]	IC
	[−r]	([+r])		Default
	SUBJ	(OBL$_\theta$)	OBJ	
TELIC = +				

The derivation is somewhat different for complex predicates containing [+dir] PVs. The *th* argument in predicates containing a [+dir] PV is associated with [−r], while the *loc* argument receives the [−o] IC feature. After the defaults have applied the *ag* is fully specified as [−o] and [−r], the *th* is underspecified as [−r], and the *loc* is fully specified as [−o] and [+r]. These feature specifications, in conjunction with the well-formedness conditions, result in GFs assignments whereby the *ag* is SUBJ, the *th* is OBJ and the *loc* is an OBL$_\theta$.[21]

---

[21]The astute reader may have calculated that the conventions for default feature assignment might lead to incorrect function assignments for intransitive locative alternation predicates. The apparent problem can be illustrated with reference to the intransitive locative alternation predicate *tele=folyik* 'full flow' which is associated with the following argument structure and presumable IC feature assignments:

$$tele{=}folyik \quad \text{'full flow} \quad \langle \text{th,} \quad \text{loc} \rangle \text{'}$$
$$\qquad\qquad\qquad\qquad\qquad [−o] \quad [−r]$$

The straightforward application of the SUBJECT and elsewhere defaults would associate [-r] with the highest argument, e.g., *th*, while the *loc* argument would remain underspecified. This would yield function assignments where the *th* would be the SUBJECT and the *loc* would be the OBJECT: locative alternation, in this instance, would appear to be a transitivizing operation. These are, unfortunately, the wrong assignments: the intransitive locative alternation predicates remain intransitive with the *th* functioning as an OBL and the *loc* functioning as the SUBJECT. This situation might be explained, as suggested by an anonymous reader, if we follow the spirit of Bresnan and Zaenen's attempt to yield an external versus internal argument distinction within lexical mapping theory. If we assume that an external argument $\hat{\theta}$ must bear a preponderance of proto-agent properties, while arguments with a preponderance of proto-patient properties are always internal irrespective of the IC features they bear, then the SUBJECT default can be interpreted as an instruction to associate an external argument with [−r]. For the case at hand, the predicate *tele=folyik* 'full=flow' does not have an external argument,

In this section we have seen that the conventions for composing [±dir] PVs with predicates act in conjunction with various assumptions of mapping theory to yield the correct assignment of GFs to arguments of transitive predicates. I turn now to an investigation of how this analysis interacts with observed constraints on deverbal adjective formation.

4 Deverbal Adjective Formation

The morpholexical relatedness analysis of locative alternation constructions refers criterially to the effects of composing complex predicates in the lexicon: this composition process determines the aspectuality of predicates in terms of the feature [+TELIC] as well as the distribution of semantic properties determinative of IC feature assignment. In this final section I will demonstrate that reference to these features (or more accurately, to the properties they denote) is central for explaining otherwise puzzling constraints on deverbal adjective formation in Hungarian. In the course of this presentation I will argue that proposals based on thematic roles, grammatical function (surface or deep), or morphology, i.e., the presence or absence of PVs, are inadequate.

Consider the following examples of deverbal adjectives formed from locative alternation verbs:[22]

(8)   a.   a *rára*kott   széna$_{th}$/*szekér$_{loc}$
              the onto-loaded   hay/wagon
       b.   a *tele*rakott   szekér$_{loc}$/*széna$_{th}$
              the full-loaded   wagon/hay

The examination of restrictions on perfect adjective formation in English have led to the hypothesis that there is a *thematic constancy* constraint underlying a similar distribution of judgments in that language:[23] roughly, a verb can be adjectivalized only if it contains a *th*(eme) in its argument array. The *th* argument functions as the head (or *externalized* argument) of the NP in which the derived attributive adjective appears. This proposal has been challenged in Levin and Rappaport 1986 where it is argued that data such as:

(9)   the stuffed pillow$_{loc}$ vs. *the stuffed feathers$_{th}$

i.e., it's *th* argument is still internal despite its [−o] IC feature. The elsewhere default applies to the *th* providing a [+r] feature and insuring that it assumes an OBL function, while the *loc* argument must assume the SUBJECT function in order to satisfy the SUBJECT condition. It can do this since it is the underspecified argument associated with a [−r] IC. The proposal to distinguish between external and internal arguments on the basis of semantic properties and independent, in some sense, of the IC features borne by the relevant arguments leads to various empirical consequences for phenomena other than locative alternation. I will not explore these consequences here.

[22]The prefixal preverb in these examples is italicized and the diacritic for juxtaposition, i.e., '=', has been omitted since in these adjectival forms the prefix is not separable from the nominal stem.

[23]Cf. Wasow 1977, Bresnan 1982.

run afoul of the such a hypothesis: among other problems, certain *loc* arguments can inexplicably head nominals containing deverbal adjectives, while certain *th* arguments inexplicably cannot. Levin and Rappaport propose that this distribution can be explained by the Sole Complement Generalization:

Sole Complement Generalization

> An argument that may stand as a sole NP complement to a verb can be externalized by APF (= Adjectival Passive Formation)

This generalization attempts to relate the observation that acceptable adjectival passive constructions correlate with acceptable clauses containing a single internal argument. In other words, we find clauses of the following sort correlative with the previously cited judgments for adjectival passive forms:

(10) Henry stuffed the pillow$_{loc}$ vs. *Henry stuffed the feathers$_{th}$

Two questions arise with respect to this sort of explanation for the observed judgments: (1) if such a generalization actually obtains then it represents a mystery easily as arresting as the constraint on deverbal adjectivalization which it is supposed to explain, and (2) it is not clear how or whether this sort of "explanation" can be extended to account for similar constraints in languages with null complements, i.e., languages in which the notion "sole complement" is difficult to define.

In the following discussion I will argue that featural distinctions previously referred to in order to account for locative alternation predicates are likewise crucial for the explanation of constraints on deverbal adjectivalization in Hungarian. In effect, we will see that neither thematic constancy nor the sole complement constraint provide explanations for these data: in particular, the thematic constancy proposal, arguably, founders on data such as those presented by Levin and Rappaport (1986) while the basic effects of the sole complement generalization as well as constraints on adjective formation follow from a featural treatment of the relevant data.

The Hungarian constructions (8a) and (8b) conflict with the thematic constancy condition in much the same fashion as the English examples cited above: the *loc* argument is head of the NP, while the *th* cannot be the head of this NP. In Hungarian, unlike in English, complements of the verb may be omitted in surface syntax:

(11) a paraszt rá=rakta
      the peasant onto=loaded-3sg/DEF
      'The peasant loaded (something determinate) (somewhere determinate)'.

(12) a paraszt   tele=rakta
      the peasant full=loaded-3sg/DEF
      'The peasant full-loaded (something determinate) (with something
      determinate).'

Whereas the notion of sole complement is difficult to define in such a language, the notion of argument associated with a [−r] IC feature is quite
transparent. Specifically, the complex verbs presented above have [−r] associated with the *th* argument of verbs containing a directional prefixal
preverb and with the *loc* argument for complex verbs containing *tele* or
meg. In other words, appeal to the feature [−r] explains the present distribution of grammaticality judgments. This treatment can be formulated as
follows:

[−r] Condition on Adjectivalization (Preliminary)

A verb α a is related to an adjective β if the argument structure of
α a contains an argument annotated with [−r].

This condition claims that the presence of [−r] constitutes a necessary
condition on deverbal adjectivalization in Hungarian.[24]

Given the fact that the arguments associated with [−r] in the preceding
examples are realized as ACC marked complements, it might be claimed
that surface OBJ(ecthood)) (correlative with accusative marking in the
present instances) is the determinant of adjectivalization rather than the
presence of [−r]. The inadequacy of this line of speculation becomes apparent by examining two types of evidence. First of all, there are verbs which
govern the ACC case for their OBJ complements but which cannot undergo
the relevant adjectivalization process. Examples of this sort suggest that
neither case marking nor the surface relation OBJ provide sufficient conditions for the formulation of a constraint on adjective formation. Second,
there are some intransitive verbs whose nominative marked SUBJ argument
appears as the modified head in an NP containing its deverbal adjectival
form.[25] These examples suggest that surface OBJecthood is not a necessary condition on the formulation of a constraint on adjective formation. I
examine each of these cases in turn below.

There are numerous simple (i.e., unprefixed) transitive verbs which govern the ACC case for their OBJ *th* arguments. Consider the two representative lexical entries below:

---

[24]We will see below that restrictions on perfect adjective formation for one of the intransitive variants of the locative alternation predicates precludes a stronger formulation,
i.e., one in terms of both necessary and sufficient conditions.

[25]This latter phenomenon, obviously, raises the question about *unaccusativity* or underlying objecthood in Hungarian. We will see below that the presumable unaccusative
verbs in Hungarian are those that bear an aspectual feature [+TELIC] and contain a
[−r] argument.

(13) készít 'to prepare' ⟨ag, th⟩
                            [−o] [−r]

(14) sárgít 'to yellow' ⟨ag, th⟩
                           [−o] [−r]

The account of deverbal adjective formation presented thus far predicts that verbal forms such as these should undergo perfect adjectivalization: they contain arguments which have a [−r]. The judgments associated with the following constructions are therefore surprising.

(15) *a készített   ruha
       the prepared   clothes

(16) *a sárgított   levél
       the yellowed   leaf

The presence of [−r] in the lexical entries for these predicates make it mysterious why such forms are prohibited. However, it turns out that predicates related to those presented above can participate in adjective formation of the relevant sort. Consider the following partial lexical entries and nominal constructions in this regard:

(17) el=készít 'to prepare' ⟨ag, th⟩
                               [−o] [−r]

(18) meg=sárgít 'to yellow' ⟨ag, th⟩
                               [−o] [−r]

(19) az elkészített   ruha
       the PERF-prepared   clothes
       'the prepared clothes'

(20) a megsárgított   levél
       the PERF-yellowed   leaf
       'the yellowed leaf'

In these constructions the [−dir] PV confers [+TELIC] lexical aspect on the complex predicate. In addition, the complex predicate contains an argument with a [−r] IC feature. A revised version of the constraint on adjective formation might be formulated as follows:

Condition on Adjectivalization (Revised)

A predicate α is related to an adjective β iff (i) the argument structure of α contains an argument annotated with a [−r] IC feature and (ii) the predicate bears the feature [+TELIC].

The preceding discussion clearly demonstrates that a constraint on adjective formation keyed to ACC case marking and/or the surface OBJ function status of an argument alone is inadequate. The inadequacy of such a formulation becomes even more evident upon examining the behavior of certain intransitive verbs with respect to perfect adjective formation.

Consider the following partial lexical entries for the intransitive variants of the transitive verbs presented in (17) and (18).

(21) a. készül 'to get prepared' ⟨th⟩
                                     [−r]

      b. el=készül   ⟨th⟩
                                     [−r]
                                     TELIC = +

(22) a. sárgul 'to yellow' ⟨th⟩
                               [−r]

      b. meg=sárgul   ⟨th⟩
                                [−r]
                                TELIC = +

The revised analysis predicts that only adjectives based on the (b) variants will be well-formed since only these forms contain both the aspectual feature [+TELIC] and an argument annotated with the [−r] IC feature. The correctness of this prediction is exemplified by the following constructions.[26]

(23) a.*a készült   ruha
         the prepared   clothes
      b. az elkészült   ruha
         the PERF-prepared   clothes
         'the prepared clothes'

(24) a.*a sárgult   levél
         the yellowed   leaf
      b. a megsárgult   levél
         the PERF-yellowed leaf
         'the yellowed leaf'

The preceding distributions not only conform to the predictions of the revised condition on adjective formation, but they illustrate clearly that surface OBJecthood is not a determinant of candidacy for adjectivalization. Some notion of "deep" or underlying OBJecthood would seem to be at issue: such phenomena are ordinarily interpreted as indicative of *unaccusativity*.

---

[26]It should be observed that there are other ways to save the ill-formed constructions found in the text other than by providing simple verb stems with prefixes. In particular, as observed in Laczkó and Ackerman 1984 it is often possible to provide the simple verbal stem with an adverbial; *a bálra készült ruha*, 'the clothes prepared for a ball' (lit. the for a ball prepared clothes) or, *az elsőként futott fiú*, 'the boy who ran and came in first' (lit. 'the first run boy'). In addition, there are certain constructions which are acceptable without either prefixes or adverbials of the sort alluded to above. For example, *füstölt hús* 'smoked meat' and *vagdalt hús* 'ground meat' exemplify such constructions. These forms raise questions which cannot be addressed here.

This is the nature of the analysis proposed by Rappaport and Levin (1988) for somewhat similar distributions of data in English. The present analysis yields the observed unaccusative effects by appealing to the presence of the IC feature [−r] in the condition on adjective formation. Bresnan and Zaenen (1990) argue for independent reasons that "deep" unaccusativity effects can be captured by appealing to the IC feature [−r]. The present analysis adduces the present distributions as further support for their proposal. As on their analysis, there is no need in the present case to appeal to a distinction between underlying vs. surface grammatical relations.

Given the determinative role attributed to aspectual considerations in the analysis, one might ask whether aspectual considerations are relevant for the other deverbal formations as well. The relevance of aspect becomes clear when we see that forms such as *készül* and *sárgul* can function as *progressive active* adjectives, while their prefixed partner cannot:[27]

(25) a. a készülő   ruha
         the preparing clothes
         'the clothes being prepared'
     b.*az elkészülő   ruha
         the PERF-preparing clothes

(26) a. a sárguló   levél
         the yellowing leaf
         'the yellowing leaf'
     b.*a megsárguló   levél
         the PERF-yellowing leaf

It is likely that constraints on the formation of deverbal adjectives such as those listed above are keyed to aspectual properties of the base predicate. For example, the base predicate arguably is associated with the feature [−TELIC]. For present purposes it is sufficient to suggest that aspectual properties of predicates are, at least partially, determinative of constraints on word-formation.

In this section we have seen that constraints on perfect adjective formation rely on the joint presence of [+TELIC] and a [−r] IC feature: only if these features are co-present is it possible to form perfect adjectives.

4.1   Preverbs and Transitivity

The preceding section argued for the inadequacy of IC featural information alone to explain the observed constraints on adjective formation. Aspectual considerations appear to play a pivotal role. Since we have seen the importance of aspectual information in constraining adjective formation it

---

[27]The present examples illustrate the adjectives in their attributive use. These same adjectives can be employed predicatively with attendant progressive aspectual distinctions, e.g., *a ruha készülöben van* 'the clothes are being prepared' (lit. the clothes in-preparing are) vs. *a ruha **meg**=készülöben van.*

might well be asked whether aspectual information alone could explain the relevant distributions. In the present section I investigate another class of cases that contain complex predicates but which exhibit a restriction on perfect adjective formation: perfect adjective formation is permitted with complex predicates containing [−dir] PVs but prohibited with those containing [+dir] PVs: in both instances we are dealing with [+TELIC] predicates but we find differences in grammaticality along the line predicted by the hypothesis that both aspectual and IC feature information play a central constraining role.

There are clusters of verbs in Hungarian where the PV$_{[-dir]}$ correlates with a change in transitivity for an associated verbal stem: the simple stem or complex predicate with PV$_{[+dir]}$ are intransitive, while the complex predicate containing a PV$_{[-dir]}$ is transitive. These predicates generally denote contrasts between activities vs. accomplishments/achievements following the Vendler/Dowty typology of aspectual types. These pairs are exemplified by the constructions below:

(27) a. a paraszt   (rá=)célzott   a madárra
          the peasant   (at-)aimed-3sg   the bird-SUBL
          'The peasant aimed at the bird.'

     b.*a paraszt   (rá=)célozta   a madarat
          the peasant   (at-)aim-3sg/DEF   the bird-ACC

     c. a paraszt   meg=célozta   a madarat
          the peasant   PERF-aim-3sg/DEF   the bird-ACC
          'The peasant aimed at the bird.'

     d.*a paraszt   meg=célzott   a madárra
          the peasant   PERF=aim-3sg   the bird-SUBL

(28) a. a paraszt   (rá=)nevetett   a fiúra
          the peasant   (at-)laughed-3sg   the boy-SUBL
          'The peasant laughed at the boy.'

     b.*a paraszt   (rá=)nevette   a fiút
          the peasant   (at-)laughed-3sg/DEF   the boy-ACC

     c. a paraszt   ki=nevette   a fiút
          the peasant   PERF=laughed-3sg/DEF   the boy-ACC
          'The peasant made fun of the boy.'

     d.*a paraszt   ki=nevetett   a fiúra
          the peasant   PERF=laughed-3sg   the boy-SUBL

The verbs in the preceding constructions yield the following distribution with respect to perfect adjective formation:

(29) a.*a rácélzott   madár
          the at-aimed   bird

  b. a megcélzott madár
     the aimed   bird
     'the aimed at bird'

(30) a.*a ránevetett   fiú
         the at-laughed boy
      b. a kinevetett   fiú
         the PERF-laughed boy
         'the made fun of boy'

This is precisely the expected scatter of grammaticality judgments, given a condition which contains reference both to telicity and the IC feature [−r]. It is not the distribution to be expected if reference to aspectual properties alone was a sufficient condition on adjectivalization. Consider the lexical entries for the relevant verbs:

(31) (rá$_{[+dir]}$=)céloz 'aim at' ⟨ag, loc⟩
                                        [−o] [−o]

(32) meg$_{[−dir]}$=céloz 'aim' ⟨ag, loc⟩
                                    [−o] [−r]

(33) (rá$_{[+dir]}$=)nevet 'laugh at' ⟨ag, loc⟩
                                          [−o] [−o]

(34) ki$_{[−dir]}$=nevet 'make fun of' ⟨ag, loc⟩
                                           [−o] [−r]

The argument inventories of the preceding verbs resemble the inventories of locative alternation predicates with one crucial difference: they do not contain a *th*. Recall the conventions for associating features with arguments of locative alternation predicates: [−dir] PVs specify the association of [−r] with *loc*, while for [+dir] PVs [−r] is associated with the *th*, i.e., the argument with most proto-patient properties. In the present instances, these conventions will assure that the *loc* arguments of (32) and (34) are associated with [−r], while [−r] will not be associated with any argument in (31) and (33) since these latter arguments are *goals*.[28] This contrasts with *meg=céloz* 'shoot down' and *ki=nevet* 'make fun of': the prefixes *meg* and *ki* determine the [−r] IC features for the original *loc* argument. Since the argument structure of these verbs contain the requisite aspectual and IC feature specifications they can serve as a base for perfect adjective formation.

    In summary, the analysis of the present data set suggests that a condition relying on the mere presence of aspectual specifications in complex predicates is not sufficient to yield the observed constraints on perfect adjective formation. Instead, the analysis proposed for locative alternation constructions extends explanatorily into this domain. The empir-

---

[28] Given our feature assignment conventions *loc* argument of the basic verb will assigned a [−o] IC feature, while the variant with a PV [+dir] will be assigned a [-o] IC feature.

ical predictions of an analysis based on the mere presence of preverbs vs. an analysis based on the presence of both aspect and a [−r] IC feature are further distinguished in the two classes of predicates examined below.

4.2 Relatedness Between Manner of Motion and Change of Location Predicates

Hungarian contains many intransitive verb clusters related by morpholexical rule. In these complex predicates a [+dir] PV is composed with a verb denoting motion. The preverb specifies the directionality of the motion and sets constraints on the topological nature of a *loc* complement in the same fashion as it does for locative alternation predicates. This phenomenon is illustrated in the following constructions utilizing the *manner of motion* predicate *fut* 'run'.

(35) a. a paraszt   futott   a szobában
      the peasant   ran   the room-IN
      'The peasant ran (around) in the room.'

    b. a paraszt   be=futott   a szobába/*szobából
      the peasant   into-ran   the room-ILL/*room-EL
      'The peasant ran into the room.'

    c. a paraszt   ki=futott   a szobából/*szobába
      the peasant   out-ran   the room-EL/*room-ILL
      'The peasant ran out of the room.'

The presumable lexical entries for these verbs are as follows:

(36)   fut   'run' $\langle$ag, (loc)$\rangle$
                [−o]   [−o]

(37)   be$_{[+dir]}$=fut   'run-into' $\langle$ag, loc$_{goal}\rangle$
                          [−o]   [−o]

(38)   ki$_{[+dir]}$=fut   'run-out' $\langle$ag, loc$_{source}\rangle$
                          [−o]   [−o]

As in all previous instances, the directional preverb adds the aspectual feature [+TELIC] to the lexical entry of the complex predicate. Both *be* 'into' and *ki* 'out of' are [+dir] (in their use with the present class of motion predicates) so that they correlate with the assignment of [-o] IC to their *loc* arguments. The absence of [−r] in the lexical entries of these predicates predicts that they cannot serve as a base for perfect adjective formation. Consider the following constructions containing the perfect adjective forms based on the predicate *fut* 'run'.

(39) a.*a futott   szoba
      the run   room
      'the run-in room'

    b.*a be-futott   paraszt/szoba
       the into-run   room
       'the peasant who ran in/the run-into room'
    c.*a ki-futott   paraszt/szoba
       the out-run   room
       'the peasant who ran out/the run-out-of room'

As predicted, these prefixed *manner of motion* predicates cannot serve
as bases for perfect adjective formation. Once again, it is clear that the
presence of a preverb does not constitute a sufficient condition for the
application of deverbal perfect adjective formation.

The behavior of a final class of intransitive dyadic predicates likewise
suggests that the mere presence of a preverb is insufficient to license perfect
adjective formation. There are numerous unprefixed dyadic intransitive
verbs in Hungarian which govern an oblique case for their OBL complement.
Their government pattern and GF selection requirements remain unaltered
when they compose with a [−dir] PV. This class is exemplified in the
following constructions containing the verb *(meg=)árt* 'harm, hurt' which
governs the DAT case for its *th* argument.

(40) a. a nedvesség   (meg=)ártott   a papírnak
         the dampness   (PERF=)damaged-3sg the paper-DAT
         'The dampness damaged the paper.'
      b.*(meg)ártott papír
         'the damaged paper'

As can be seen, the mere presence of the [−dir] PV is insufficient to license
perfect adjective formation.[29]

5   Conclusions

In this paper I have argued for a mapping theory which yields a natural
partitioning between operations which affect the lexical semantics of predicates, that is, *Morpholexical* vs. those which don't, that is, *Morphosyntactic*. I have argued that Hungarian locative alternation constitutes a
case of *Morpholexical Relatedness*. The clusters of predicates which participate in this alternation are created in the word formation component
of the grammar. The semantic properties which characterize the arguments associated with these predicates are determinative of the *Intrinsic
Classification* features assigned to these arguments. The particular semantic properties conferred on arguments as well the value for the aspectual
feature [TELIC], are correlative with the presence of ± directional uses of
PreVerbs.

---

[29]I will not speculate here about the relation between lexical semantics, IC feature
assignment and invariant case government with these predicates. It is not to clear
at this time whether the interaction between these phenomena is principled or simply
idiosyncratic.

Finally, the basic ingredients for the thesis of morpholexical relatedness between locative alternation predicates is extended explanatorily to the treatment of constraints on perfect adjective formation in Hungarian. In particular, the independently required necessity to refer to telicity values of predicates as well as the specific way in which PV types help determine IC feature values for arguments appears to be required for explaining observed constraints on deverbal adjective formation. This reliance is encoded in the proposed condition on adjectivalization. In sum, this analysis relies on the interaction between semantic properties of arguments, aspectual values of predicates and the feature decomposition of grammatical functions.

References

Abraham, Werner, and Sjaak de Meij. 1986. *Topic, Focus, and Configurationality.* Amsterdam: John Benjamins.

Ackerman, Farrell. 1987. *Miscreant Morphemes: Phrasal Predicates in Ugric.* Doctoral dissertation, University of California at Berkeley.

Ackerman, Farrell. 1990. Locative Alternation vs. Locative Inversion. In *Proceedings of the 9th Annual West Coast Conference on Formal Linguistics*, ed. Aaron L. Halpern. Stanford: CSLI Publications.

Ackerman, Farrell, and András Kómlosy. 1987. Relatedness in Hungarian Spray/Load Verb Clusters. Presented at LSA Lexical Semantics Workshop, Stanford University.

Alsina, Alex, and Sam Mchombo. 1989. Object Asymmetries in Chichewa. Manuscript, Stanford University and University of California at Berkeley.

Anderson, Stephen R. 1971. On the Roles of Deep Structure in Semantic Interpretations. *Foundations of Language* 6:197–219.

Anderson, Stephen R. 1977. Comments on the paper by Wasow. In *Formal Syntax*, ed. Peter Culicover, Thomas Wasow, and Adrian Akmajian, 361–378. New York: Academic Press.

Brassai, Samuel. 1860, 1863-65. The Hungarian Sentence. *Magyar Akadémiai Értesítö.* 1:279–399, 3:3–128, 173–409 (in Hungarian).

Bresnan, Joan. 1982. Control and Complementation. In *The Mental Representation of Grammatical Relations*, ed. Joan Bresnan. Cambridge, Mass.: MIT Press.

Bresnan, Joan, and Jonni M. Kanerva. 1989. Locative Inversion in Chichewa: A Case Study of Factorization in Grammar. *Linguistic Inquiry* 20:1–50.

Bresnan, Joan, and Lioba Moshi. 1989. Applicative Constructions in Ki-Chaga. Manuscript, Stanford University and University of Georgia.

Bresnan, Joan, and Annie Zaenen. 1990. Deep Unaccusativity in LFG. In *Grammatical Relations: A Cross-Theoretical Perspective*, ed. Katarzyna Dziwirek, Patrick Farrell, and Errapel Mejías-Bikandi, 45–57. Stanford: CSLI Publications.

Channon, Robert. 1980. On Place Advancements in English and Russian. In *Morphosyntax in Slavic*, ed. Catherine V. Chvany and Richard D. Brecht. Columbus: Slavica Publishers.

Culicover, Peter. 1989. On Thematic Relations. MIT Working Papers in Linguistics 10. Massachusetts Institute of Technology: Department of Linguistics.

Dowty, David. 1979. *Word Meaning and Montague Grammar*. Dordrecht: Reidel.

Dowty, David. 1989. On the Semantic Content of the Notion "Thematic Role". In *Properties, Types and Meaning, Vol. 2: Semantic Issues*, ed. Gennara Chierchia, Barbara Partee, and Raymond Turner. Dordrecht: Kluwer.

Dowty, David. 1991. Thematic Proto-Roles and Argument Selection. *Language* 67(3):547–619.

Fillmore, Charles. 1968. The Case for Case. In *Universals in Linguistic Theory*, ed. Emmon Bach and Robert T. Harms, 1–90. New York: Holt, Rinehart and Winston.

Fillmore, Charles. 1977a. Topics in Lexical Semantics. In *Current Issues in Linguistic Theory*, ed. Roger W. Cole. Bloomington: Indiana University Press.

Fillmore, Charles J. 1977b. The Case for Case Re-opened. In *Syntax and Semantics, Volume 8*, ed. Peter Cole. New York: Academic Press.

Foley, William, and Robert Van Valin. 1984. *Functional Syntax and Universal Grammar*. New York: Cambridge University Press.

Fukui, Naoki, Shigeru Miyagawa, and Carol Tenny. 1985. Verb Classes in English and Japanese: A Case Study in the Interaction of Syntax, Morphology and Semantics. Lexicon Project Working Papers 3. Cambridge, Mass.: MIT Center for Cognitive Science.

Gawron, J. Mark. 1983. *Lexical Semantics and the Semantics of Complementation*. Doctoral dissertation, University of California at Berkeley. Also appearing in Garland Outstanding Dissertations in Linguistics, 1989.

Gawron, J. Mark. 1986. Valence Structure Preservation and Demotion. In *Papers from the 22nd Regional Meeting of the Chicago Linguistic Society*. University of Chicago.

Jackendoff, Ray. 1983. *Semantics and Cognition*. Cambridge, Mass.: MIT Press.

Jackendoff, Ray. 1985. Multiple Subcategorization and the θ-criterion. *Natural Language and Linguistic Theory* 3(3):271–295.

Jászay, László, and László Tóth. 1987. *Az orosz igeaspekusról magyar szemmel*. Budapest: Tankönykiadó.

Kiefer, Ferenc. 1982. The Aspectual System of Hungarian. In *Hungarian Linguistics*, ed. Ferenc Kiefer. Amsterdam: John Benjamins.

Kiss, Katalin É. 1987. *Configurationality in Hungarian*. Budapest: Academic Press and D. Reidel Publishing Company.

Laczkó, Tibor, and Farrell Ackerman. 1984. Nominal Passives and Thematic Roles. Manuscript, Hungarian Academy of Sciences, Budapest.

Laczkó, Tibor, and Anna Szabolcsi. 1988. A főnóvi csoport szerkezete (The Structure of Noun Phrases). In *Magyar mondattan*, ed. Ferenc Kiefer. Akadémiai Kiadó.

Ladusaw, William, and David Dowty. 1988. Toward a Nongrammatical Account of Thematic Roles. In *Syntax and Semantics: Thematic Relations*, ed. Wendy Wilkins, 61–73. New York: Academic Press.

Levin, Beth, and Malka Rappaport. 1986. The Formation of Adjectival Passives. *Linguistic Inquiry* 17:623–661.

Levin, Lori. 1986. *Operations on Lexical Forms*. Doctoral dissertation, Massachusetts Institute of Technology.

Pinker, Steven. 1989. *Learnability and Cognition: the Acquisition of Argument Structure*. Cambridge, Mass.: MIT Press.

Pollard, Carl, and Ivan A. Sag. 1987. *Information-Based Syntax and Semantics, Vol. I: Fundamentals*. CSLI Lecture Notes No. 13. Stanford: CSLI Publications.

Rappaport, Malka, and Beth Levin. 1988. What to Do with Thematic Roles. In *Syntax and Semantics: Thematic Relations*, ed. Wendy Wilkins. New York: Academic Press.

Salkoff, Morris. 1983. Bees are Swarming in the Garden. *Language* 59:288–346.

Simpson, Jane. 1983. *Aspects of Warlpiri Morphology and Syntax*. Doctoral dissertation, Massachusetts Institute of Technology.

Vendler, Zeno. 1967. *Linguistics in Philosophy*. Ithaca: Cornell University Press.

Wasow, Thomas. 1977. Transformations and the Lexicon. In *Formal Syntax*, ed. Peter Culicover, Thomas Wasow, and Adrian Akmajian. New York: Academic Press.

Wasow, Thomas. 1981. Major and Minor Rules in Lexical Grammar. In *Lexical Grammar*, ed. Teun Hoekstra et al. Dordrecht: Foris.

Zaenen, Annie. 1990. Unaccusativity in Dutch: an Integrated Approach. In *Semantics and the Lexicon*, ed. James Pustejovsky. Dordrecht: Kluwer.

Zubizaretta, Maria-Luisa. 1987. *Levels of Representation in the Lexicon and Syntax*. Dordrecht: Foris.

4

On Obviation

DONKA F. FARKAS

1 Introduction

This paper addresses the question of why, in many languages, the subject of certain subordinate clauses must be disjoint in reference from certain NPs in the immediately higher clause, as illustrated by the following French example.

(1)   Pierre$_i$ veut qu'il$_{*i/j}$ parte.
        P. wants that he leave.SUBJ(unctive)

In what follows, the complements whose subjects obey this restriction will be called *obviative*.

This problem has been discussed in recent Government and Binding literature especially in connection with Romance languages (see Picallo 1984, 1985; Meireles and Raposo 1983; Kempchinsky 1985; Bouchard 1982, 1983; among others). Common to all these works is the attempt to account for obviative complements within Binding Theory (BT). In Section 2 I will review previous solutions and then argue that the BT approach is empirically inadequate. In Section 3 I will propose a new treatment, one in which the restriction on the interpretation of the subject pronoun in (1) appears as a consequence rather than as a cause. The solution I will argue for rests on Kiparsky's notion of blocking applied in the realm of subcategorization, as well as on lexico-semantic considerations involving the semantic relations that obtain between the arguments of a verb in virtue of its meaning. Under the analysis presented in Section 3 the phenomenon of obviation is crucially connected to control.

I wish to thank Larry Horn, Nirit Kadmon, John Goldsmith, Nicolas Ruwet, and Draga Zec for useful comments and criticisms of earlier drafts. Earlier versions of this paper were presented at Stanford University, University of Illinois at Urbana-Champaign, Yale University, and at the 1988 winter LSA meeting.

2 Previous solutions

2.1 The Pragmatic Approach

The simplest possible way of disposing of the problem illustrated in (1) would be to invoke the Chomskian "avoid pronoun" commandment (or the more general Gricean "be as concise as possible" maxim), given that the infinitive is used instead of the subjunctive in examples like (1) in French, as well as in Spanish, Catalan and Portuguese. (Throughout this paper I will use French for illustrative purposes.)

(2)   Pierre veut partir.
        P. wants to leave

As noted by Picallo (1985), the immediate problem with a simple-minded "avoid pronoun" approach is that the infinitive does not always block the use of a finite form in these languages. The verb *promettre* 'to promise', for instance, may take both infinitive and indicative complements:

(3)
$$\text{Pierre}_i \text{ a promis} \begin{cases} \text{qu'il}_{i/j} \text{ partira.} \\ \text{that he}_{i/j} \text{ will leave.} \\ \text{de partir.} \\ \text{Prep. leave.INF} \end{cases}$$
$$\text{P}_i \text{ promised}$$

Since in Romance languages all obviative complements are in the subjunctive, one could dispute the relevance of (3) by claiming that the effect of the "avoid pronoun" commandment is somehow restricted to subjunctive complements. As shown in (4), however, there are subjunctive complements which are nonobviative although an infinitive alternant is possible as well:

(4)   a.
$$\text{J'ai proposé à Jean}_i \begin{cases} \text{qu'il}_i \text{ s'en aille.} \\ \text{that he}_i \text{ leave.SUB} \\ \text{de s'en aller.} \\ \text{Prep. leave.INF} \end{cases}$$
$$\text{I have suggested to J.}_i$$

      b.
$$\text{Je regrette} \begin{cases} \text{que je n'aie pas pu te voir.} \\ \text{that I not have.SUBJ been able to see you} \\ \text{de ne pas avoir pu te voir.} \\ \text{Prep. not have.INF been able to see you} \end{cases}$$
$$\text{I regret}$$

I will nonetheless argue below that the ungrammaticality of (1) is indeed connected to the grammaticality of (2); the correct solution has to account both for this connection and for the data in (3) and (4). (A more complex "avoid pronoun" solution will be discussed below.)

Finally, note that, although (5b) is slightly worse than (5a),

(5)   a.*Je veux que je parte.
        I want that I leave.SUB
      b.*Il$_i$ veut qu'il$_i$ parte.
        He$_i$ wants that he$_i$ leave.SUB

one cannot explain the problem away by invoking the Gricean "avoid ambiguity" maxim either, since there is no danger of ambiguity in (5a).

2.2 The BT Approach

Researchers working in the GB framework have been exploring the attractive possibility of assimilating the phenomenon illustrated in (1) to the well-known case in (6), covered by principle B of Binding Theory, which forbids a pronominal from selecting an antecedent within its binding domain.

(6)   *John$_i$ saw him$_i$.

In order to implement this idea, one has to analyze obviative subjunctive clauses as not constituting a binding domain as far as their subjects are concerned. Since obviative clauses in Romance languages are a subset of subjunctive complements, one has to find some special characteristic of this subset which distinguishes its members from nonobviative subjunctive complements as well as from indicative ones, and the boundaries of binding domains have to be made sensitive to this characteristic. If the analysis is correct, the characteristic in question should be connected to obviation in other languages as well.

Picallo (1984, 1985), Meireles and Raposo (1983), and Salamanca (1981) suggest that the distinctive feature of obviative clauses is located in the Tense component of their I(nflection) node. (AGR, the other component of I cannot be responsible for obviation because its properties are the same for all subjunctive clauses, and therefore it cannot be used to isolate any subset thereof.) The main idea behind all of these proposals is that the Tense of obviative clauses is somehow dependent on the Tense feature of the immediately higher clause, and it is this dependency that the definition of binding domains is sensitive to.

In order for any solution based on this idea to work, the set of obviative clauses must turn out to be coextensive with the set of clauses whose Tense is dependent. Suñer and Padilla-Rivera (1984) and Zaring (1985, chap. II), convincingly argue that there is no notion of "dependent" Tense which isolates the right class of clauses for Spanish, French, and Brazilian Portuguese. Sequence of tense restrictions, for instance, hold not only in obviative clauses but also in some nonobviative subjunctive clauses and in certain indicatives. Strengthening the requirement to *subsequent* time reference does not work for the same reason. Both complement clauses in (7) have subsequent time reference and yet they are nonobviative.

(7)   a. Marie$_i$ promet à Paul qu'elle$_i$ partira tôt.
          M.$_i$ promises P. that she$_i$ will leave soon
       b. J'ai proposé au professeur que je fasse l'expérience moi-même.
          I proposed to the professor that I perform.SUB the experiment
          myself.

The independently detectable properties of Tense in obviative clauses in Romance languages do not distinguish them from nonobviative ones and therefore obviation cannot be a consequence of any of these properties.

Before abandoning this approach I will discuss two further empirical challenges to it. The first comes from Romanian, where subjunctive clauses have semantic and morphological properties similar to those in other Romance languages (except for the fact that the subjunctive is used in a wider range of complements, a point we will return to below). Crucially, however, subjunctive clauses are not obviative:

(8) Ion_i vrea $[e_{i/j}$ să plece].
       Ion_i wants $[pro_{i/j}$ SUBJ leave]

(The 'e' above marks the dropped pronominal subject.)[1]

Now the Romanian facts come as a complete surprise under any BT approach relying on Tense because there is no independently justified reason for treating Tense in (8) as essentially different from the Tense in (1).

The next problem is brought up in Ruwet 1984, where it is noted that the strength of obviation in French depends on the semantics of both the matrix and the obviative clauses. The relevant generalization is that obviation is weakened if the degree of "agentivity" of the subordinate or main clause subject decreases:

(9)   a. Je veux que je puisse partir.
          I want that I can.SUB leave

       b. Je veux que je sois autorisé à partir tôt.
          I want that I be.SUB authorized Prep. leave early

       c. Je veux que je guérisse aussi vite que possible.
          I want that I recover.SUB as soon as possible

       d. Je voudrais bien que je parte tôt.
          I would like it well that I leave.SUB early

of agentivity is the same as the notion of *responsibility*, (RESP), which, as argued in Farkas 1988, is involved in controller choice with verbs like *promise* and *persuade*. Following Farkas 1988, I will assume that the RESP relation obtains between an individual and a situation if the individual brings the situation about. The sentences in (9a)–(9c) differ from (1) in that the embedded subject is understood as not being responsible over the situation denoted by the complement. The switch to the conditional and the addition of the adverb in (9d) affect the responsibility of the matrix

---

[1]The fact that an overt pronoun is not possible in (8) under the coreferential reading is not specific to subjunctive clauses:

(i) Ion_i ştie că $e_{i/j}/el_{j/*i}$ e deştept.
       Ion knows that he is clever.

The problem of obviation as defined above is connected to the alternation between null and overt pronouns but the two issues are distinct and I will not deal with the latter here. For discussion, see Montalbetti 1984 and Levinson 1987.

subject over the complement situation. Thus, one would say (9d) rather than (1) just in case it is not up to the speaker whether he leaves or not. Ruwet notes that, while judgments differ with respect to the acceptability of examples like those in (9), they are all significantly better than (1). He further notes that by removing responsibility from both subjects, one arrives at practically perfect sentences, like the example in (10).

(10)   Je voudrais bien que je puisse partir dès aujourd'hui.
        I would like well that I can.SUB leave already today

Ruwet's data are incompatible with any solution based on Tense since there is no plausible way of making the contents of the Tense of the embedded clause depend on the factors discussed above. As Ruwet correctly argues, these data cannot be handled by any purely configurational account.

An altogether different BT solution is proposed in Kempchinsky 1985. She assumes that subjunctive clauses contain a subjunctive operator which moves to their COMP at LF just in case the matrix verb subcategorizes for the subjunctive clause. In Spanish or French this means that the whole I node moves to COMP. As a result, the embedded clause is no longer a binding domain for its subject (because it no longer contains a governor of the subject). Kempchinsky notes that the Romanian data are explained under the assumption that the subjunctive operator in this language is not under I and therefore its movement to COMP does not affect the binding domain of the subject, which is governed by I.

The crucial ingredient of this analysis is the movement of the subjunctive operator to COMP at LF. This movement is supposed to be triggered by the fact that subcategorization requirements must be met at LF and therefore, if a verb subcategorizes for a subjunctive complement, the head of the complement must fulfill the subcategorization requirement. Assuming that COMP is the head of S', this means that the COMP of subcategorized subjunctive complements must contain a subjunctive element at LF.

The main shortcoming of this solution is that it incorrectly predicts that the class of obviative complements is coextensive with the class of subcategorized subjunctive complements in languages like Spanish or French. There are, however, plenty of subcategorized subjunctive complements in these languages which are nonobviative, such as the complements of negative epistemic verbs (*nier* 'deny', *douter* 'doubt') or of factive-emotives (*être heureux*, 'be happy', *regretter* 'regret'). Note also that Ruwet's data constitute just as much of a problem for this analysis as for the one discussed previously. I therefore conclude that the BT solutions proposed so far are inadequate because they fail to predict the class of obviative complements in Romance languages and because they fail to account for the role the semantic factors discussed by Ruwet play in obviation. These shortcomings are shared by the pragmatic approach as well.

Yet another approach is proposed in Bouchard 1982, 1983. Bouchard takes obviation to be the manifestation of his own version of "avoid pronoun," suggestively called the Elsewhere Principle. According to it, a pronoun cannot be used in a position where an anaphor is possible, i.e., in a position where the pronoun will be interpreted as coreferential with an NP that governs it.[2] Hermon (1985), in discussing obviation in Imbabura Quechua, proposes a version of Bouchard's Elsewhere Principle where the presence or absence of [AGR] is the crucial factor in determining whether PRO is an anaphor or a pronominal. In order to explain why only subjunctive clauses are obviative, Bouchard makes reference to the fact that both subjunctives and infinitives have "unrealized tense" (see Bresnan 1972). It is not made clear, however, how and why this property comes to play a role in obviation, and therefore there is no account of why *promettre* 'promise', for instance, takes nonobviative complements, although their tense is also unrealized.

Picallo (1985) correctly notes that Bouchard's solution fails to account for the fact that in French, as well as in Catalan, obviation is Su(bject) oriented, i.e., its effect is weakened if the matrix argument involved is not the Su, as in (4a) or (11):

(11) ?Marie a convaincu Paul$_i$ qu'il$_i$ s'en aille./de s'en aller.
      M. has convinced P.$_i$ that he$_i$ leave.SUBJ/Prep. leave.INF

Finally, note that this solution does not fare any better than the previous ones with respect to the data discussed in Ruwet 1984. Hermon's version, if extended to Romance languages, would have the additional problem of positing an abstract and unmotivated [AGR] difference between obviative and nonobviative subjunctive clauses.

3   Towards a Solution

3.1   Data To Be Accounted For

Below I will summarize the main facts discussed so far and bring in some new data from two non-Romance languages, Hungarian and Serbo-Croatian.

Within Romance

(i) We have seen above that in those Romance languages that have them, obviative clauses are a subset of subjunctive complements. We therefore have to account for the fact that indicative clauses are nonobviative (recall the *promettre* 'promise'/*vouloir* 'want' contrast). We also have to distinguish obviative clauses from nonobviative subjunctives (recall the *nier* 'deny', *regretter* 'regret'/*vouloir* 'want' contrast as well as the data discussed by Ruwet).

---

[2]For Bouchard PRO is an anaphor when referentially dependent on a governing NP and a pronominal otherwise.

(ii) We also have to give an account of the difference between Romanian and the other Romance languages.. Such an account should link the non-existence of obviation to some other feature of Romanian, which distinguishes it from its better known Romance sisters.

(iii) Next, we have to account for the fact that obviation tends to be Su oriented, i.e., the argument that the complement subject must be disjoint in reference from tends to be the matrix subject. Recall the contrast between (1) and (4a) or (11).[3]

(iv) Finally, one has to predict the locality of the phenomenon, i.e., one has to predict that the two NPs that must be disjoint in reference are in adjacent clauses:

(12) Marie$_i$ souhaite que Jeanne$_j$ veuille qu'elle$_{i/*j}$ parte.
       Marie wishes that Jeanne want.SUBJ that she leave.SUBJ

Beyond Romance

The correct account of obviation for Romance languages should extend to other languages as well. Below, we will consider the relevant data in Serbo-Croatian, which is a Balkan language, and Hungarian, which is neither Balkan nor Romance.

In what follows, the complements of verbs like *convince*, *try*, or *begin*, whose Su arguments are necessarily referentially dependent on a matrix NP, will be called *dependent Su clauses*. The term *accidental Su dependency* will be used for cases where the subject of a complement happens to be referentially dependent on a matrix argument.

Hungarian

Hungarian has both infinitive and subjunctive complements. The infinitive is the only possible complement form in dependent Su clauses when the controller is the matrix subject:

(13)
    János
    J.
    $\begin{cases} \text{elkezdett beszél-ni.} \\ \text{started talk-INF} \\ \\ \text{igyekszik kedves len-ni.} \\ \text{tries nice be-INF} \end{cases}$

When the controller is a non-Su, verbs subcategorize for either infinitive or subjunctive complements:

(14) a.
    János$_i$ meggyőzte Marit$_j$,
    J. convinced M.
    $\begin{cases} \text{hogy e}_{j/*i,*k} \text{ men-jen vele.} \\ \text{that (she) go-SUB with him.}^4 \\ \\ ^*\text{men-ni vele.} \\ \text{go-INF with him} \end{cases}$

---

[3]Subject orientation is only a tendency, rather than a clear cut phenomenon because judgments concerning finite clauses whose subjects are coreferential with a non-Su matrix argument and which have an infinitive counterpart show considerable variation from speaker to speaker and from verb to verb.

b.

$$\text{János elküldte Marit}_i \begin{cases} \text{vásárol-ni.} \\ \text{shop-INF} \\ {}^*\text{hogy e}_i \text{ vásárol-jon.}^5 \\ \text{that (she) shop-SUBJ} \end{cases}$$

J. sent M.

In case of accidental *Su* dependency, the complement is either in the infinitive or in the subjunctive and is obviative, i.e., the subject of the subjunctive complement is disjoint in reference from the matrix subject:

(15) János moziba akar men-ni.
      J.   movie-into wants go-INF

      János$_i$ azt akarja, hogy e$_{*i/j}$ moziba men-jen.
      J.   it-ACC wants that (he/she) movies-into go-SUB

Not all subjunctive complements are obviative, however. The verb *követel* 'demand', for instance, is like *akar* 'want' except that it takes only subjunctive complements. As shown in (16), its complement is nonobviative:

(16)

$$\text{János}_i \begin{cases} \text{követeli, hogy e}_{i/j} \text{ kap-jon több ételt.} \\ \text{demands that (he/she) get-SUB more food} \\ {}^*\text{követel kap-ni több ételt.} \\ \text{demands get-INF more food} \end{cases}$$

J.

Obviation in Hungarian is influenced by the following factors. First, in certain contexts in which the whole complement is focused an otherwise obviative clause becomes nonobviative:

(17) Ha az-t   akarod, hogy velünk gyere,
      if that-ACC want   that us-with come.SUBJ,

      viselked-j   szépen.
      behave-SUBJ well

If you want to come with us, behave well.[6]

In this case the demonstrative pronoun *az-t* 'that-ACC', whose antecedent is the clause, has to be used. The exact syntactic analysis of the construction exemplified above is immaterial for present purposes. What matters is that this construction is not possible with infinitival complements:

---

[4]Hungarian is a *Su* pro drop language too.

[5]Examples like (14b) were brought to my attention by A. Szabolcsi. It is not clear, however, that the relation between the infinitive and the direct object of the matrix in (14b) is the same as in obligatory control cases but I will not pursue this issue any further here. The subjunctive in (14b) is grammatical under an interpretation in which the complement is understood as a purpose clause.

[6]Thanks again to A. Szabolcsi for bringing this type of examples to my attention. Exactly which contexts allow a focused nonobviative subjunctive clause is not clear to me at present. The mere presence of the pronoun *az* 'that' appears to be insufficient, since (i) is bad, or at least significantly worse than (17).

(i)   *János$_i$ az-t akarja, hogy e$_i$ jöjjön velünk.
       J. that-ACC wants that (he$_i$) come.SUBJ with us.

(18) *János azt akarja velünk jön-ni.
    J.   that wants with us come-INF

Obviative complements become nonobviative also if the complement subject is focused. In this case the subject must occur immediately before the subjunctive verb and it receives special stress, indicated by capitals.

(19) János$_i$ (azt) akarja, hogy Ő$_i$ menjen Marival (és nem László).
    J$_i$ (it)   wants that he$_i$ go.SUB M. with (and not L.)

Serbo-Croatian[7]

The relevant facts in Serbo-Croatian (Belgrade dialect) can be summarized as follows. In case the complement subject is obligatorily controlled by the matrix subject or direct object, the complement form is a so-called "da_2 complement" whose subject must be null. (Serbo-Croatian is a Su pro drop language as well.)

(20) a. Petar$_i$ je pokušao da   e$_{i/*j}$ dodje.
        P.   Aux tried   Comp (he) come

     *Petar$_i$ je pokušao da on$_i$ dodje.
      P.   Aux tried   Comp he come[8]

b.

Ana je naterala Mariju$_i$
A. Aux forced M.$_i$
$$\begin{cases} \text{da } e_{i/*k} \text{ dodje} \\ \text{Comp (she) come} \\ \text{*da ona}_i \text{ dodje.} \\ \text{Comp she}_i \text{ come} \end{cases}$$

"Da_2 complements" in Serbo-Croatian are not formally distinguished from so-called "da_1 complements" with respect to either the complementizer or verbal inflection. However, da_2 complements are special in that they obey tense restrictions and have modal connotations characteristic of subjunctive complements (see Zec 1987 and references quoted therein).

Now in case the subject of a da_2 complement is accidentally dependent on some NP in the matrix, it must necessarily be null:

(21)

Petar$_i$ je želeo
P.$_i$ Aux wants
$$\begin{cases} \text{da } e_{i/j} \text{ dodje.} \\ \text{Comp (he}_{i/j}) \text{ come} \\ \text{da on}_{j/*i} \text{ dodje.} \\ \text{Comp he}_{j/*i} \text{ come} \end{cases}$$

Obviation in Serbo-Croatian reduces then to the null/overt pronoun choice in da_2 complements. In case the complement subject is accidentally dependent in reference the null pronoun must be chosen, i.e., the overt pronoun is obviative.

---

[7]The data below come from Zec 1987.

[8]In case the matrix verb is an auxiliary, the infinitive is used. The use of a finite verb form in obligatorily controlled complements is a Balkan trait that the Belgrade dialect of Serbo-Croatian shares with Romanian.

In Serbo-Croatian, just like in Hungarian, the obviation effect disappears in case the complement subject is emphatically stressed: the examples in (20b) and (21) lose their stars if there is emphatic stress on the complement subject.

Since the facts from Hungarian and Serbo-Croatian are strongly reminiscent of the Romance obviation data, we should seek a unitary account. The main new facts concern the effect of emphasis on obviation and the fact that in Serbo-Croatian obviation reduces to the contrast between a null and an overt pronoun.

3.2 The "Blocking" Approach

I suggest that we should view obviation as the manifestation of a constraint on the use of certain complement forms rather than as a problem pertaining to pronoun use or interpretation.[9] According to this claim, in Romance languages and in Hungarian obviation is due to the old rivalry between the subjunctive and the infinitive. Under this proposal, (1) is ungrammatical not because a pronoun selects its antecedent in the wrong domain but rather because a subjunctive complement is used instead of an infinitive one. This claim is different from Bouchard's in that it does not refer to the choice between a pronominal and an anaphor directly. Recall now that in Serbo-Croatian the two rival complement forms differ only with respect to whether the subject is obligatorily null or not. What is common to the infinitive in Romance and Hungarian, and da_2 complements with null subjects in Serbo-Croatian is that they are the complement forms used in dependent Su clauses. We can then start from the preliminary generalization in (I):

(I)   The complement form used to mark dependent Su clauses blocks the use of the subjunctive under certain circumstances.[10]

The term 'blocking' is used here in the sense used in lexical semantics and morphology. Thus, Horn (1984), in discussing semantic relationships between items in the lexicon, notes that "the meaning, use, or very existence of a given word or expression is affected by the existence and range of a related and more basic or specific entry in the lexicon" (p. 111). (For relevant work in lexical semantics, see McCawley 1977 and Horn 1978, and in morphology, Aronoff 1976 and Kiparsky 1983.) The existence of a more specific lexical item or construction is said to block the use of the more general one in cases where a choice is theoretically possible. My claim is that the same phenomenon is responsible for the obviation effect discussed here, where the two competing expressions are complement forms. In case the more specific complement form, the one that marks Su depen-

---

[9]This suggestion is in the spirit of the pragmatic approach outlined in Section 2.1. The differences will become clear below. Under the present proposal the term 'obviation' is a misnomer for the phenomenon exemplified by (1) but I will continue to use it nonetheless.

[10]The term 'subjunctive' is used loosely here. It will be eliminated below.

dence, can be used the use of the less specific form, the subjunctive, is not allowed.

Below I will first point out the immediate advantages of this approach; I will then briefly comment on the subjunctive/infinitive rivalry, and finally, I will turn to the mysterious "certain circumstances" in (I).

Viewing obviation as one complement form (the infinitive) blocking another (the subjunctive) allows us to correctly predict that subjunctive clauses will be obviative only in contexts in which an infinitive is also possible, i.e., that obviative clauses are a subset of those subjunctive clauses which can in principle alternate with infinitives. The following facts are thus accounted for:

(i) Romanian subjunctive clauses are nonobviative because in this language the complement form used to mark Su dependency *is* the subjunctive.

(22) Ion_i a încercat $e_{i/*j}$ să plece.
         I. tried SUBJ leave[11]

         Ion_i a forțat-o pe $Maria_j$ $e_{j/*i,*k}$ să plece.
         I. forced M. SUBJ leave

The difference between Romanian and the other Romance languages concerning obviation is thus connected to the difference in the role played by the infinitive. The relevant difference between Romanian and Serbo-Croatian is that in Romanian the null pronoun is more widely used than in the Belgrade dialect of Serbo-Croatian and therefore there is no special complement form indicating Su dependency and no significant difference between indicative and subjunctive complements with respect to the null/overt subject pronoun contrast.[12]

(ii) The complement of *követel* 'demand' in Hungarian is nonobviative because this verb, unlike *akar* 'want', takes only subjunctive complements. Subjunctive complements controlled by non-subjects in Hungarian are nonobviative for the same reason.

(iii) The disappearance of obviation under emphasis in Hungarian and Serbo-Croatian is also explained. In Hungarian, in certain contrastive contexts illustrated in (17) in which the complement may not be infinitive, the subjunctive is nonobviative. Note also that in both Hungarian and Serbo-Croatian emphatic subjects are nonobviative because they may not be null.

So far, the blocking approach shares advantages with the "avoid pronoun" solution, except that the former can account for obviation in Serbo-Croatian while the latter cannot. The problem raised by Serbo-Croatian

---

[11]For details see Joseph 1983 and Farkas 1985b.

[12]Comorovski (1985) finds that the "avoid pronoun" principle seems stronger in subjunctive complements than in indicative ones. She connects this difference to the fact that the use of an overt subject in subjunctive complements triggers the use of the complementizer *ca* as well.

for the "avoid pronoun" approach is to explain why the force of the commandment is so much stronger in obviative clauses than in nonobviative ones. Of course, we have not accounted for the Serbo-Croatian data either until the term 'subjunctive' is eliminated in (I) and until the "certain circumstances" are specified.

The fact that indicative clauses are nonobviative is stipulated in (I). Below I will offer some justification for treating infinitive and subjunctive complements in a class that contrasts with indicative complements.

3.3 On the Infinitive/Subjunctive Rivalry

It was proposed above that obviation in Romance and Hungarian should be accounted for by claiming that the possibility of using an infinitive complement blocks the use of a subjunctive one under certain circumstances. We have also seen that the infinitive does not block the indicative in these languages. I will now attempt to justify this contrast by arguing that certain subjunctive complements share with infinitive complements semantic characteristics that set them apart from indicative complements. Under the assumption that we have the same type of blocking here as lexical blocking, which requires the two forms involved to be semantically close, we have some explanation for why the infinitive blocks the subjunctive but not the indicative.

In what follows, I will assume that sentences, as well as infinitival complements, can be used to denote *situations*, i.e., individuals having properties and standing in various relations at various spatio-temporal locations.[13] I will also assume that verbs are lexically associated with predicate-argument structures, where the arguments identify participants in the situations denoted by clauses involving the predicate in question. The arguments of the predicate end up being associated with syntactic constituents. The details of this association are irrelevant for present purposes.

Now in the case of complex sentences, one of the arguments of the matrix predicate, namely the one linked to the complement, denotes a situation. The situation denoted by the complement (s_c) is a constituent of the situation denoted by the matrix (s_m). The matrix predicate may impose various restrictions on s_c as part of its lexical meaning since s_c is one of its arguments. These restrictions may involve the immediate constituent parts of s_c, i.e., the participants in s_c, as well as its spatiotemporal location. The more such restrictions are imposed on s_c, the more dependent it is on s_m. The parameters of semantic dependency that are most consequential for linguistic phenomena are (i) Su dependency and (ii) world dependency. The most important consequence of semantic dependency is its correlation with the use of moods.[14] Below, I will briefly discuss each dependency

---

[13]The term 'situation' is borrowed from Barwise and Perry 1983.
[14]Noonan (1985) and Ransom (1986) discuss the same question from different perspec-

parameter and in the process, I will argue that a third parameter, time reference dependency is less basic.

A. *Su* Dependency

There are predicates which require that the "external" argument of s_c, i.e., the argument that would be linked to the subject of the complement, be necessarily referentially dependent on some argument of the matrix predicate. This means that these arguments are referentially dependent on some participant in s_m.[15] Complements realizing such arguments have been called here *dependent Su* complements. Examples of verbs requiring dependent *Su* complements are "aspectuals," such as *begin, start, try*, and 'directives', such as *persuade* or *convince*.

Note now that it is frequent for languages to use a special complement form to indicate *Su* dependency, a form in which the *Su* is not expressed. In languages that have infinitival complements, they are crucially connected to *Su* dependency. These languages use infinitival complements in at least some dependent *Su* complements. Concerning the languages discussed here, in Western Romance the verb form in dependent *Su* complements is the infinitive and there are no infinitival complements whose *Su* argument is free in reference. The situation is similar in Hungarian, the major difference being that in Hungarian the infinitive is exclusively used only in *Su* dependent clauses controlled by a subject;[16] recall that if the controller is a non-subject the subjunctive may be the only possibility (cf. (14a)).[17] Note also that the time reference of dependent *Su* complements is also dependent on that of the matrix but there are complements whose *Su* reference is free and whose time reference is dependent, such as the complements of *promise*, or *foresee*. The claim that the infinitive is associated with *Su* dependency rather than time reference dependency is justified by the fact that these verbs may always take indicative complements. There

---

tives. They both treat time-reference dependency as basic and do not discuss world-reference dependency at all.

[15]The two arguments are nevertheless different qua arguments, each being constrained by its own predicate.

[16]The difference is actually less sharp: in dependent *Su* complements where the controller is a non-subject the subjunctive is not ruled out in Western Romance either, as illustrated in (i):

(i)

?J'ai convaincu Marie
I convinced M.

$\begin{cases} \text{qu'elle vienne.} \\ \text{that she come.SUBJ} \\ \text{de venir.} \\ \text{Prep. come.INF} \end{cases}$

[17]Nothing in what follows depends crucially on the syntactic status of complements and therefore the remarks below are compatible with a syntactic treatment in which at least some of these complements are VPs, as well as with one in which they are all sentential. An important question which I will not address here is how to ensure that only subjects (i.e., external arguments) can be controlled.

are no languages that use the infinitive just in case s_c is dependent in time reference and free in Su reference.

B. World Dependency

In order to introduce the notion of world dependency two more general assumptions have to be stated. First, unlike in "situation semantics," I assume that collections of situations, called "worlds" play a central role in the interpretation of sentences. A sentence is true in a world w iff the situation it denotes is part of w. Second, the possible worlds framework assumed here differs from most in that *partial* worlds are admitted. (For a discussion of partiality, see Landman 1986.) Thus, a sentence may be true, false or undecided in a particular world.

In the case of verbs taking situation-denoting complements, it often is the case that the world in which the complement is evaluated is different from the world in which the matrix is evaluated. Thus, it may well be the case that (23a) is true in the real world (w_R), while (23b) is not.

(23) a. John thinks that Mary is home.
      b. Mary is home.

What is required, however, is for (23b) to be true as far as John is concerned, i.e., to be true in what John takes Reality to be. If *know* is substituted for *think*, (23b) has to be true in both worlds.

What world the complement is interpreted in depends on the lexical meaning of the matrix predicate, which is said to "introduce" (or "create") this world. In what follows the introduced world will be called "the new world," while the world in which the matrix sentence is evaluated will be called "the base world." In the cases we will consider here the base world will always be w_R. The type of semantic dependency under discussion has to do with the properties of the new world.

I will briefly argue now that there are two distinct ways of introducing a world. One is to introduce a world whose situations are independent of the base-world or any other world in the sense that the new world is not assumed to inherit any parts from any world. I will call such worlds *independent*. Another way of introducing a world is to, in a sense, modify another world, i.e., introduce a world w' that is just like some other world w, except that a particular situation, s_c holds in w'. I will say that in this case w' inherits from w all those situations that do not conflict with s_c and I will say that w' is *dependent* on w. One gets from w to w' by adding s_c to w and performing all the accommodating changes required to maintain consistency. I will call s_c in such cases a highlighted situation for which w' is a background world.

Independent Worlds

As an example of independent worlds, consider the worlds introduced by "cognitive" verbs such as *think*, *believe*, and *know*, exemplified in (23a).

(The former two are taken here in their "strong" sense, in which the referent of their Su takes the complement to be true.) The base world in this case is w_R and the new world is one that represents Reality as John sees it, a world that I will denote by $w_R(J)$. In what follows, I will call the referent of the (active) subjects of predicates introducing worlds *anchors* of those worlds. If instead of *think* we had *know*, the world introduced would be part of $w_R(J)$. The point that is of interest here is that the world introduced by these verbs is independent of the base-world or any other world, in the sense that all we know about the new world on the basis of sentences like (23) is that s_c holds in them. There are no situations in the base world, or any other world, that the new world inherits. Other verbs that introduce independent worlds are *dream, imagine, fantasize*. The world introduced by them is not Reality anchored to the referent of their subject but is a world that plays that role under limited circumstances. The point again is that these worlds are independent. No situations from w_R or $w_R(a)$, where a is the anchor, are inherited by these worlds.[18]

Dependent Worlds

Things are quite different in the case of desideratives like *want, wish*, and *desire*, exemplified in (24).

(24)   John wants Mary to leave.

As noted in McCawley 1977, one cannot speak of a single buletic alternative introduced by *want* since one may hold contradictory wishes simultaneously without thereby being guilty of logical inconsistency. (This, of course, is not so with cognitives.) I will therefore assume that desideratives introduce a *set* of buletic alternatives anchored to the referent of their subject, and that their complement holds in some world of this set. The point that is of relevance here is that in this world s_c is a highlighted situation whose background is $w_R(a)$, i.e., the world in which s_c holds is one where s_c is added to $w_R(a)$. Viewing things this way helps us account for several semantic properties of desideratives, which distinguish them from cognitives.

First, note that (25a) does not entail (25b) even if John is fully aware that being away from one's wife entails having a wife.

(25)   a. John wants to be away from his wife.
       b. John wants to have a wife.

The highlighted situations are different in the two cases and therefore the two worlds are different. In (25a) the situation added to $w_R(J)$ is one in which John is away from his wife, while the situation added to $w_R(J)$ in the case of (25b) is one in which John has a wife.

---

[18]The question of inheritance is independent from the pragmatic assumption, mentioned in McCawley 1977 and discussed at length in Fauconnier 1985, according to which worlds are not supposed to differ in relevant respects, unless explicitly stated.

Second, having a background world and a highlighted situation helps us account for the role s_c plays in specifying the buletic alternative introduced by the verb. Thus, note that the buletic alternative introduced by a desiderative cannot be just any world in which s_c holds, i.e., the realization of s_c cannot count as a sufficient condition for a world to be a buletic alternative of the anchor's. Presumably, a world in which John cannot bear to be separated from his wife and in which he is away from her is not a buletic alternative of John's even if (25a) is true. The buletic alternative introduced in (25a) is one where John's marriage is the way John thinks it is in Reality. As mentioned before, realizing s_c cannot count as a necessary condition for a world to be a buletic alternative of the anchor's because one may hold two contradictory wishes simultaneously without wanting them to be realized simultaneously.

Thus, if (26) is true of John, there is a buletic alternative of John's in which he is a lawyer and not a marine, and another, in which he is a marine and not a lawyer.

(26)   John wants to become a lawyer but if he can't get into a good school, he wants to join the marines.

The two alternatives have different background worlds. The background world of the first is $w_R(J)$, while that of the latter is one in which the situation denoted by the *if* clause has been added to $w_R(J)$.

I will end the discussion of desideratives by drawing attention to a difference between *want* and *wish* concerning the nature of s_c. Consider the contrast in (27):

(27)   a. I want it to be Friday.
       b. I wish it were Friday.

said by an ordinary person in our ordinary world. I suggest that (28a) is strange because *want* imposes a further restriction on s_c, namely that it should be possible, for all that the anchor knows, for s_c to be realized and therefore s_c cannot be counterfactual as far as the anchor is concerned. The fact that it cannot be factual either follows from pragmatic considerations, since if it were, the conditions would be met for the use of an emotive factive. The verb *wish* does not impose this requirement on s_c. Note that this difference correlates with time reference restrictions, since one can know how things turned out in the past but usually one can only conjecture about the future. The complement of *want* is acceptable with past time reference in English, at least for some people, if the anchor does not know whether the situation it denotes is factual or not.

There is cross-linguistic variation with respect to the details of the constraints particular desideratives impose on s_c. For French, Ruwet (1984) claims that the use of *vouloir* 'want' in the indicative implies that the anchor is ready to do what it takes in order to bring s_c about, while *souhaiter* 'wish' implies that the anchor's attitude towards the fulfillment of his wish is passive.

"Directives," such as *ask, order, demand, request* can be analyzed as similar to *want* except that the person responsible for bringing about s_c is the individual denoted by the internal argument of the verb (the direct object or the object of the preposition *of* or *from*).

With respect to time dependency, we have seen that it is associated with Su dependency and that it may accompany world dependency as well, as a result of a constraint on the realizability of s_c. We have already seen that not all world-dependent complements have dependent time reference (cf. *wish*). Conversely, there are complements whose time reference is dependent but which are neither world nor Su dependent. Consider, for instance, the complements of *promise* and *foresee*. Their time reference is dependent: it must necessarily be non-anterior to the time reference of the matrix. As noted above, they are not, however, dependent Su complements and they do not introduce a new world, and therefore certainly not a dependent one. Their complements are supposed to hold in the base world at some non-anterior time. *Promise* differs from the other two in that it imposes the realizability condition on the referent of its (active) subject and s_c, and therefore these two arguments must be in the RESP relation.

Going back to the main point of all this, namely the subjunctive/infinitive rivalry, note that world dependency, just like Su dependency, and unlike time reference dependency, is associated with the use of a special "non-indicative" mood. Thus, languages that have mood distinctions use a non-indicative mood in world-dependent complements. In languages that have a subjunctive, this is the mood used to mark world dependency, except, of course, under special circumstances, when the infinitive blocks it.[19]

Common to the infinitive and the subjunctive then, is that they mark semantic dependency. The "rivalry" between them manifests itself in the tendency of one "dependent" mood to take over the rightful domain of the other. The existence of the rivalry is not surprising in view of the fact that the domains of the two moods often overlap, as for instance in the case of a verb like *try* or in the case of directives that take dependent Su complements, like *persuade*. Thus, we have already noted that in Balkan languages the subjunctive has supplanted the infinitive to a large extent, and therefore the subjunctive has come to be used to mark not only world dependency but subject dependency as well. In English the reverse has happened: the subjunctive has almost disappeared, its place having

---

[19]Marking world dependency is only one of the uses the subjunctive may be put to. Thus, in French it is used to mark subordination, in preposed complements, as well as non-assertiveness, in emotive-factives (cf. Palmer 1986).

been taken by the infinitive. Consequently, we have infinitive complements whose subject reference is free, as in (28):

(28)   John wants (for) Mary to leave.

Recall also that in Hungarian and Western Romance the situation is mixed, the infinitive marking Su dependency and the subjunctive marking world dependency. In cases of overlap, the infinitive tends to win in case of Su control, while the subjunctive has at least a chance in case of non-Su control. (In Hungarian in these cases verbs select either the subjunctive or the infinitive, while in Western Romance both complement types are possible.) The case of Serbo-Croatian is different since there only Su dependency is formally marked (by an obligatorily null subject pronoun); recall that world-dependent complements (da_2 complements) are only semantically distinguished from independent ones (da_1 complements).

We are ready now to return to obviation. Languages which have obviative complements are languages which distinguish dependent Su complements from world-dependent ones. The battleground between the two forms is limited to those cases where the complement meets the semantic requirements for both Su and world dependency, i.e., s_c is world dependent and the participant connected to its subject is referentially dependent on some participant in s_m. The generalization in (I) can then be reformulated as in (II), which now covers Serbo-Croatian as well.

(II)   In certain world-dependent complements, the form used to mark subject dependency blocks the form used in world-dependent complements.

For French, for instance, (II) requires the choice of the infinitive over the subjunctive in certain world-dependent complements, while in Serbo-Croatian the choice will be between an obligatorily null pronoun over a potentially overt one. This gives the disjoint reference effect in both languages. Blocking, of course, presupposes the existence of two complement forms, and therefore no obviation effect exists in Romanian.

Note that calling this preference for the dependent Su construction "blocking" is appropriate because this construction is semantically more specific than the world-dependent one. Recall that obviation manifests itself in case of accidental Su dependency. Now the fact that the complement is world dependent is predictable from the meaning of the matrix verb but the fact that its Su is referentially dependent is not. The use of the dependent Su form in this case is therefore more informative than the use of the world-dependent one. The less informative complement form may be chosen only in case the conditions are not met for the use of the more informative one, which results in the disjoint reference effect under discussion here. Let us turn now to a less mysterious characterization of the "certain" complements involved.

3.4 The Semantic Role of the Controller and of the Controlled Argument

So far we have narrowed the range of obviation to world-dependent complements whose subjects are accidentally dependent on a matrix argument. Obviation was treated here as the result of one complement form blocking another in these cases. Note, however, that nothing we have said so far accounts for Ruwet's weakening factors. Recall that based on examples such as (10), repeated here as (29),

(29)   Je voudrais bien que je puisse partir dès aujourd'huis.
       I would like well that I can.SUBJ leave already today

Ruwet concludes that the semantic role of the two arguments involved affects obviation. The remarks that follow are elaborations of ideas in Suñer and Padilla-Rivera 1984, Zaring 1985 and Ruwet 1984.

We have seen above (cf. examples (9a)–(9c)) that obviation is weakened in case the complement is passivized, or if it contains a modal or a "non-agentive" main verb. Common to all these cases is the fact that the controlled argument (the complement subject) is not seen as bringing s_c about, i.e., it is not in the RESP relation with the situation of which it is a participant. The tendency of obviation to disappear when the complement is passivized, or when it contains a modal or a "non-agentive" main verb leads me to conclude that the controlled argument must bear the RESP relation to the situation denoted by the complement. This means that the controlled argument is the *initiator* of the situation in which it is a participant.

It was also noted above that obviation is weakened if the controller is not seen as being in the RESP relation with s_c (cf. example (9d)). Relevant here is Ruwet's observation that obviation is weaker in the complement of *souhaiter* 'wish' than in that of *vouloir* 'want'. As mentioned in Section 3.3 above, Ruwet also notes that the Su argument of the latter is more likely to be interpreted as being in the RESP relation with s_c than the Su argument of the former. Ruwet also notes that the complement of *exiger* 'demand' is not obviative. The relevant characteristic of this verb is that its Su argument may *not* be in the RESP relation with s_c. I conclude therefore that the obviation effect is most robust if both controller and controlled argument are in the RESP relation with s_c, the former as a result of the characteristics of s_m, the latter as a result of the characteristics of s_c. (We have here, of course, two distinct arguments of two distinct predicates even though they happen to be referentially dependent.)

This situation is reminiscent of facts pertaining to controller choice, discussed in Farkas 1988. It was argued there that the unmarked controller choice for infinitival complements falls on the matrix argument that bears the RESP relation to s_c, when the controlled argument bears this relation to s_c as well. This suggests that there is a correlation between the use of dependent Su constructions and the RESP relation, which is the link between obviation and control. I suggest that there is a "canonical control case," canonical for the use of a dependent Su complement. The semantic characteristic of the canonical control case is that both the complement Su and the matrix argument it is referentially dependent on bear the RESP relation to s_c. We expect then that if a language has a complement form marking Su dependency, it will use it in complements conforming to this characteristic and that if the characteristic is not met we will find cases in which the dependent Su construction is not used. A case in point is the Hungarian equivalent of *exiger*, *követelni*, which, as seen in (16) above, may not take infinitival complements but only subjunctive ones. This property, I claim, is not accidental but rather, it is the result of the fact that the controller may not be in the RESP relation with s_c.

It is therefore not surprising that obviation is strongest in case the semantic characteristics of the "canonical control case" are met, in view of the fact that obviation is the result of preferring the dependent Su complement form over some other complement form. The generalization in (II) can now be rendered more precise:

(III) In world-dependent complements that conform to the canonical control case, the form used to mark Su dependency blocks the form used for world dependency.

The generalization as formulated now accounts for Ruwet's weakening factors. The proposal made here elaborates the suggestions in Ruwet 1984. It differs from both Suñer and Padilla-Rivera 1984, and Zaring 1985. According to Suñer and Padilla-Rivera 1984 obviation is connected to the semantic feature [+WILL] of the matrix predicate. In discussing this proposal, Zaring 1985 correctly notes that the role of the complement subject is also relevant and proposes that a complement is obviative when the matrix subject is an "instigator" and the complement subject, an "instigatee." Zaring does not, however, elaborate on the meaning of these terms. In particular, it is not clear how to postulate a semantic relationship between the matrix subject and the complement subject since they are not arguments of the same predicate. In the analysis suggested above, the two subjects are related by both bearing the RESP relation to the same situation, the situation denoted by the complement.

The question to be addressed next is that of why the RESP relation should play such a prominent role in control and obviation. The answer is suggested by Ruwet (1984), who notes that when a matrix argument is in what we call here the RESP relation to s_c there is a crucial difference between the case when it is coreferential with the complement argument bearing the RESP relation to the same situation and the case when it is not. Let us call the matrix argument i_m (the matrix initiator) and the complement argument i_c (the complement initiator). If the two initiators are referentially independent, i_m is indirectly responsible for s_c in that it has to act on i_c, who brings s_c about. If the two initiators are referentially dependent, on the other hand, the realization of s_c depends on a single individual and the i_c has direct responsibility over s_c. It is therefore not surprising that languages will tend to mark this difference. What we have called obviation here is one way of marking it. The generalization in (III) then can be seen as a rule that limits the freedom allowed by subcategorization restrictions whose effect, besides limiting the number of ways one can say the same thing, is to mark a relevant semantic difference.

3.5   Locality and *Su* Orientation

There are two more characteristics of obviation that have to be accounted for, locality and *Su* orientation.

Locality

Recall that the disjoint reference effect characteristic of obviation always involves an argument of a matrix verb and the subject of its immediate complement. This follows in our analysis from the fact that obviation is dependent on semantic characteristics of a matrix argument and s_c, characteristics that are imposed by the lexical meaning of the matrix verb. It follows therefore that s_c must be an argument of that V since only the immediate arguments of a verb may be affected by the verb's meaning. Now imposing semantic constraints on a situation may involve imposing semantic constraints on its participants. Further details of the situation in question are unavailable.

Su Orientation

As noted before, *Su* orientation refers to the strong cross-linguistic tendency of obviation to disappear in case the controller is not the subject of the matrix clause. Recall that in French, *vouloir* 'want' contrasts with *persuader* 'persuade' or *convaincre* 'convince' in that the complements of the latter are nonobviative, (or less obviative) as shown in (11), repeated here as (30).

(30)

?Marie a convaincu Paul$_i$
M. has convinced P.$_i$

$\begin{cases} \text{qu'il}_i \text{ s'en aille.} \\ \text{that he}_i \text{ leave.SUBJ} \\ \text{de s'en aller.} \\ \text{Prep. leave.INF} \end{cases}$

The same appears to hold in Serbo-Croatian, as seen in (31).

(31)

Petar$_i$ je molio Mariju$_j$
P.$_i$ Aux asked M.$_j$

$\begin{cases} \text{da e}_{i/j} \text{ ostane na večeri.} \\ \text{Comp (he/she) stay at dinner} \\ {}^*\text{da on}_i \text{ ostane na večeri.} \\ \text{Comp he}_i \text{ stay at dinner} \\ ?{}^*\text{da ona}_j \text{ ostane na večeri.} \\ \text{Comp she}_j \text{ stay at dinner} \end{cases}$

I suggest that this property of obviation is connected to the general tendency of languages to formally mark coreference with a subject more explicitly than coreference with a non-subject. Thus, note that cross-linguistically, reflexive pronouns may always be bound by a subject but not always by a non-subject. Second, in "switch reference" languages it is again coreference with the subject that matters. Last, note that there is a cross-linguistic tendency for the infinitive to act as a "same subject" construction. Recall that in French and Hungarian, for instance, dependent Su complements may be in the subjunctive only if controlled by a non-subject.

We can account for these facts as well as for the Su orientation of obviation by restricting the notion of canonical control case to cases of Su control. The definition of canonical control case will then have a semantic side, pertaining to the semantic role of the controller and the controlled argument, and a syntactic side, pertaining to the grammatical role of the controller. The blocking effect we have discussed here is strongest when both requirements are met.

4 Conclusion

It has been argued here that obviation is the effect of a blocking mechanism that limits the choice between two complement types subcategorized for by a verb. The range of the phenomenon is limited to semantically dependent complements and is most robust in canonical control situations. The disjoint reference effect discussed here thus reduces to the requirement of using a control construction, if possible, in canonical control situations. The blocking mechanism we have invoked is the same as lexical blocking, discussed in McCawley 1977, and Horn 1978, 1984, where it is argued that the existence and interpretation of a lexical item may be affected by the existence and interpretation of another. In these works it is shown that the choice of a formally more complex and semantically less specific form is restricted to cases where the use of a formally less marked and semantically more specific form is not possible. What we have seen here is that, not surprisingly, the same is true with respect to the choice of complement forms. The generalization in (III) can thus be seen as a principle operating in the lexicon, which limits the choice between two subcategorized complement forms, a principle driven by the same mechanism as lexical, morphological or phonological blocking, expressed by some adequately generalized version of the Elsewhere Principle.

Note that our proposal differs from that in Bouchard 1983 in that no mention is made of anaphors and pronominals here. As a result, we lost the direct connection between obviation and the effects of principle B of Binding Theory, a connection that is present in all the analyses of obviation formulated within Government and Binding theory. Note, however, that if one adopts an analysis of the coreference properties of anaphors and pronominals along the lines proposed by Bouchard or Reinhart 1983, the connection is regained. The fundamental reason for the ungrammaticality of (1) and (6), repeated here as (32a) and (32b),

(32) a. Pierre$_i$ veut qu'il$_{*i/j}$ parte.
    P. wants that he leave.SUBJ
    b.*John$_i$ saw him$_i$.

would then be the same: a less specific form has been chosen when a more specific one was available, and as a result, one has failed to formally mark coreference with a subject. The difference in range between obviation and the anaphor/pronominal choice results from the fact that the former concerns the choice between subcategorized forms, a choice sensitive to the semantic characteristics of the two situations involved. The principle governing the pronominal/anaphor choice and our generalization (III) are then members of a family of constraints on choice, whose common denominator is the Elsewhere Principle.

References

Aronoff, Mark. 1976. *Word Formation in Generative Grammar*. Cambridge, Mass.: MIT Press.

Barwise, Jon, and John Perry. 1983. *Situations and Attitudes*. Cambridge, Mass.: MIT Press.

Bouchard, Denis. 1982. *On the Content of Empty Categories*. Doctoral dissertation, Massachusetts Institute of Technology.

Bouchard, Denis. 1983. The Avoid Pronoun Principle and the Elsewhere Principle. In *Proceedings of NELS 13*, 29–36. Amherst: University of Massachusetts, GLSA.

Bresnan, Joan. 1972. *Theory of Complementation in English Syntax*. Doctoral dissertation, Massachusetts Institute of Technology.

Comorovski, Ileana. 1985. Control and Obviation in Romanian. In *Proceedings of the 2nd Annual Eastern States Conference on Linguistics*.

Farkas, Donka. 1985a. *Intensional Descriptions and the Romance Subjective Mood*. New York: Garland Publishers.

Farkas, Donka. 1985b. Obligatory Controlled Subjects in Romanian. In *Papers from the 21st Annual Meeting of the Chicago Linguistic Society*, 90–100. University of Chicago.

Farkas, Donka. 1988. On Obligatory Control. *Linguistics and Philosophy* 11:27–58.

Fauconnier, Gilles. 1985. *Mental Spaces: Aspects of Meaning Construction in Natural Language*. Cambridge, Mass.: MIT Press.

Hermon, Gabriela. 1985. *Syntactic Modularity*. Dordrecht: Foris.

Horn, Laurence R. 1978. Lexical Incorporation, Implicature, and the Least Effort Hypothesis. In *Proceedings of the Parasession on the Lexicon*, ed.

Donka Farkas, Wesley M. Jacobsen, and Karol W. Todrys, 196–209. Chicago: Chicago Linguistic Society.

Horn, Laurence R. 1984. Ambiguity, Negation, and the London School of Parsimony. In *Proceedings from NELS 14*, ed. Charles Jones and Peter Sells, 108–31. Amherst: University of Massachusetts, GLSA.

Joseph, Brian. 1983. *The Synchrony and Diachrony of the Balkan Infinitive*. New York: Cambridge University Press.

Kempchinsky, Paula. 1985. The Subjunctive Disjoint Reference Effect. In *Proceedings of the 15th Symposium on Romance Languages*.

Kiparsky, Paul. 1982. Word Formation and the Lexicon. In *Proceedings of the 1982 Mid-America Linguistics Conference*, ed. Frances Ingemann, 3–29, 47–78. Lawrence: University of Kansas.

Landman, Frederick. 1986. Towards a Theory of Information. In *GRASS 6*. Dordrecht: Foris.

Levinson, Stephen. 1987. Pragmatics and the Grammar of Anaphora: a Partial Pragmatic Reduction of Binding and Control Phenomena. *Journal of Linguistics* 23:379–434.

McCawley, James. 1977. Conversational Implicature and the Lexicon. In *Syntax and Semantics 9: Pragmatics*, ed. Peter Cole, 245–259. New York: Academic Press.

Meireles, J., and Eduardo Raposo. 1983. Subjunctives and Disjoint Reference in Portuguese: Some Implications for Binding Theory. Paper presented at the Colloqui International de Linguistica Teorica i Llengues Romanicas, Barcelona.

Montalbetti, Mario. 1984. *After Binding: On the Interpretation of Pronouns*. Doctoral dissertation, Massachusetts Institute of Technology.

Noonan, Michael. 1985. Complementation. In *Language Typology and Syntactic Description Vol. II*, ed. Timothy Shopen, 42–140. New York: Cambridge University Press.

Palmer, Frank. 1986. *Mood and Modality*. New York: Cambridge University Press.

Picallo, Carme. 1984. The Infl-node and the Null Subject Parameter. *Linguistic Inquiry* 15:75–102.

Picallo, Carme. 1985. *Opaque Domains*. Doctoral dissertation, City University of New York.

Ransom, Evelyn. 1986. Complementizers: How Do They Mean. In *Proceedings of the 2nd Annual Meeting of the Pacific Linguistics Conference*, ed. Scott DeLancey and Russell S. Tomlin. University of Oregon.

Reinhart, Tanya. 1983. Coreference and Bound Anaphora: A Restatement of the Anaphora Questions. *Linguistics and Philosophy* 6:47–88.

Ruwet, Nicolas. 1984. Je veux partir/*Je veux que je parte. In *Cahiers de grammaire*, chapter 7. Toulouse: Le Mirail.

Salamanca, D. 1981. Subjunctive Syntax. Manuscript, Massachusetts Institute of Technology.

Suñer, Margarita, and J. Padilla-Rivera. 1984. On the Subjunctive and the Role of the Features of INFL: Evidence from a Null Subject Language. Manuscript, Cornell University.

Zaring, L. 1985. *The Syntactic Role of Verbal Inflection in French and Brazilian Portuguese.* Doctoral dissertation, Cornell University.

Zec, Draga. 1987. On Obligatory Control in Clausal Complements. In *Working Papers in Grammatical Theory and Discourse Structure*, ed. Masayo Iida, Stephen Wechsler, and Draga Zec, 136–168. Chicago: University of Chicago Press.

5

Blocking of Phrasal Constructions by Lexical Items

WILLIAM J. POSER

Introduction

Blocking is the widely observed phenomenon where the existence of one form prevents the creation and use of another form that would otherwise be expected to occur.[1] Perhaps the most prominent cases are those in which the existence of an irregular form prevents the corresponding regular form from being used. In English for example, the existence of the irregular plural *men* for *man* is said to block the regular form **mans*.

Since the inception of the idea (Paul 1896), and in virtually all work on morphology over the past sesquidecennium, blocking has been taken to be restricted to the word-formation component (Esau 1973, Aronoff 1976, Allen 1978, Clark and Clark 1979, Tomán 1980, Zwanenburg 1981). Cases of non-lexical blocking are not cited as examples of the phenomenon.[2] Moreover, the theoretical proposals that have been put forward account only for blocking of one lexical form by another. For example, Miyagawa (1980) proposes that the morphological categories of a language define a set of slots in the lexicon, each of which, in the normal case, may be instantiated only once, so that if a more specific rule (of which the extreme case is the existence of an irregular form) applies to instantiate a category, a more general rule may not apply. Similarly, Kiparsky (1982a) proposes that morphological rules are subject to the Elsewhere Condition (Anderson

This is a revised version of a paper presented on 27 April 1986 at the Southern California Conference on General Linguistics, University of California, San Diego, California. Thanks to Steve Anderson, Joe Emonds, Paul Kay, Paul Kiparsky, Alec Marantz, Mariko Saiki, and Michael Wescoat for discussion of these issues and comments on the draft.

[1]The term *blocking* is due to Aronoff (1976, 41) who defines it as "... the nonoccurrence of one form due to the simple existence of another."

[2]Exceptions are Di Sciullo and Williams 1987 and Hualde 1988, to which we will refer later.

Lexical Matters. Ivan A. Sag and Anna Szabolcsi, eds.
Copyright © 1992, Stanford University.

1969, Kiparsky 1973) so that a more specific rule instantiating a complex morphological category will apply disjunctively with a more general rule instantiating the same category, thus producing the blocking effect. On both accounts, blocking is expected only internal to the lexicon, under Miyagawa's proposal because the set of morphological categories is simply the structured part of the lexicon, and under Kiparsky's proposal because morphological rules are by definition lexical. I argue here on the basis of three examples that the blocking phenomenon is not restricted to the lexicon, that is, that it is possible for lexical forms to block phrasal constructions.

1 The Existence of Phrasal Blocking

In this section I present three examples in which lexical items block phrasal constructs, in each case offering evidence for the lexicality of the blocker, the phrasal status of the blocked item, and the claim that the relationship between the two is that of blocking.

Example I: Japanese Periphrastic Verbs

The Periphrastic Construction

Japanese has a very large number of periphrastic verbs consisting of a nominal part followed by the verb *suru* 'do'. The majority of such verbs are based on loans from Chinese, as are the examples in (1).

(1)   denwa suru   to telephone
       sanpo suru   to take a walk
       kenkyuu suru   to do research

This periphrastic construction is the usual way of borrowing verbs from foreign languages; rather than adapting a foreign verb directly to Japanese verbal morphology Japanese normally borrows a nominal form and then creates a periphrastic verb. Some examples of periphrastics based on loans from English are given in (2).

(2)   doraibu suru   to drive
       nokku suru   to knock

Periphrastics based on native nouns, such as those in (3), also exist but are relatively uncommon; one reason for this will be discussed below.

(3)   tatigare suru   to be blighted
       tatiuti suru   to cross swords

The nouns that appear in periphrastic verbs are never restricted to the periphrastic context; they invariably may appear in Noun Phrases in other contexts.[3] For example, the noun *kenkyuu* that forms the base of the periphrastic verb *kenkyuu suru* 'to study, to do research' may also appear

---

[3]There are a number of superficial exceptions to this statement, but these are all examples of the historically related but synchronically quite distinct lexical pseudo-periphrastics, described in detail in Poser 1991.

as the head of the subject NP of a sentence, as in (4), or as the head of a relative clause serving as a predicate nominal, as in (5).

(4) Sono kenkyuu-ga taisetu-da.
     that   research-N   important-be
     That research is important.

(5) Sore-wa Tanaka-san-ga site-iru   kenkyuu-da.
     that-T   Tanaka-Mr.-N   doing-be   research-be
     That is the research that Mr. Tanaka is doing.

Periphrastic verbs come in two forms, referred to as the "incorporated" and "unincorporated" forms. In the incorporated form, the nominal component is not case-marked, as in (1), (2) and (3), while in the unincorporated form it bears accusative case, as in (6).

(6) denwa-o suru   to telephone
     sanpo-o suru   to take a walk
     tatigare-o suru to cross swords

More generally, in the unincorporated form the nominal behaves like an ordinary direct object NP, so that if the unincorporated periphrastic has a logical object, the logical object appears as a genitive modifier of the nominal component of the periphrastic, as in (7). In contrast, the logical object of an incorporated periphrastic, like other direct objects in Japanese bears accusative or dative case, as in (8), and cannot be modified.

(7) Eigo-no   benkyoo-o site-iru.
     English-G study-A   doing-be
     (He) is studying English.

(8) Eigo-o   benkyoo site-iru.
     English-A study   doing-be
     (He) is studying English.

The unincorporated periphrastics are unequivocally phrasal but the incorporated periphrastics have been treated in most of the literature as single words, whether lexically derived (Inoue 1976, Poser 1980, Miyagawa 1987, 1990, Grimshaw and Mester 1988), or derived by incorporation in the syntax (Kageyama 1977). However, there is considerable evidence that they too are phrasal in character (Hasegawa 1979, Poser 1989). The evidence for phrasal status may be briefly summarized as follows:

(a) Periphrastic verbs are accented like phrases rather than like any other sort of verb (Poser 1989).

(b) Reduplication affects only the *suru* component of the periphrastic (Kageyama 1977).

(c) Periphrastic verbs do not undergo even highly productive lexical nominalizations (Poser 1989).

(d) Sentence-internally periphrastics are analyzable into the nominal and verbal portions, in that the nominal may be omitted in *whether*-constructions, which require repetition of the verb (Poser 1989).

(e) It is possible to Right Node Raise the *suru* portion alone (Poser 1989).

(f) It is possible to delete the verbal noun in the second conjunct of a pair of conjoined sentences (Kageyama 1977).

(g) Periphrastics are analyzable across sentence-boundary in that the nominal part may be omitted in *too*-clauses, in which the verb of the first sentence is repeated in the second sentence (Poser 1989).

(h) Periphrastic verbs are analyzable at the discourse level across speakers into the nominal and *suru*, in that the nominal part may be omitted in responses to yes-no questions (Poser 1989).

True phrasal periphrastic verbs contrast in these properties as well as a number of others with historically related forms that have now been lexicalized (Poser 1991).[4]

Given that periphrastic verbs are phrasal constructions, we do not expect it to be possible to block them, but in fact there is reason to believe that such blocking takes place.

Deverbal Noun Formation

Japanese has a fairly productive process of simple deverbal noun formation.[5] The deverbal noun is segmentally identical to the verb stem if the verb is a vowel-stem verb, and consists of the verb stem followed by the vowel /i/ if the verb is a consonant-stem verb.[6] Some examples are given below in (9).

(9)   Simple Deverbal Nouns

Verb Stem	Derived Noun	Gloss
ir	iri	parching
kari	kari	borrowing
mamor	mamori	protection
oyog	oyogi	swimming
sabak	sabaki	judgment

---

[4]The astute reader may find it peculiar that I attribute the hypothesis that incorporated periphrastics have a phrasal structure to Hasegawa (1979) but in addition to my own work cite only Kageyama (1977), who treats periphrastics as single words, for arguments to this effect. The reason for this apparent paradox is that Hasegawa, whose paper constitutes a reply to Kageyama's arguments for incorporation in the syntax, contributed no new arguments for phrasal status but rather argued, contra Kageyama, that incorporation never takes place at all.

[5]I use the term *simple* to refer to the least specialized kind of deverbal noun formation in Japanese. There are others, for example the manner nominals derived by suffixation of -*kata*.

[6]Although treated in much past work as a suffix, Yoshiba (1981) proposes that this /i/ be inserted by a morphological epenthesis rule, and Poser (1984) proposes that it be inserted by a phonological epenthesis rule.

This kind of nominalization appears to be a lexical process. The precise meaning taken on by the noun varies considerably, from the abstract 'act of V-ing' through the agent noun, as illustrated by the examples in (10).

(10)   Thematic Types of *renyoomeisi*

Verb	Gloss	Noun	Gloss	Thematic Type
iru	parch	iri	parching	action
kariru	borrow	kari	borrowing	action
kumoru	become cloudy	kumori	cloudiness	result
moru	serve, dish up	mori	a serving	theme
oou	cover	ooi	a cover	instrument
tetudau	help	tetudai	helper, help	agent
tumu	load	tumi	shipment, load	theme

Moreover, in a number of cases deverbal nouns are accented irregularly, further indicating they are lexical. In general, deverbal nouns are accented on the ultima if the verb stem is accented and non-compound. Otherwise, they are unaccented (Kawakami 1973). But as the examples in (11) show, there are a number of exceptional cases in which the accent falls on the first syllable rather than on the ultima. Moreover, as the examples in (12) show, there are also cases in which a deverbal noun that ought, if regular, to be accented, is in fact unaccented.

(11)   Initial Accented Deverbal Nouns

domóru	stammer	dómori	stammering, a stammerer
hanaréru	separate	hánare	isolation
nagásu	sing from door to door	nágasi	strolling musician
orósu	sell at wholesale	órosi	wholesale trade
sabáku	judge	sábaki	judgment
sawágu	make noise	sáwagi	noise, hubbub
séku	dam up	séki	dam
súru	pick pockets	súri	pickpocket
tanómu	request,ask	tánomi	a request, favor
tatáru	curse	tátari	curse
tómu	become rich	tómi	riches

(12)   Unaccented Nouns Derived from Accented Verbs

takurámu	scheme, plan	takurami	a design, a trick
takuwaéru	store, lay in	takuwae	store, hoard
todoróku	roar, peal	todoroki	a roar, a peal
tumúgu	spin	tumugi	pongee
tutusímu	be discreet	tutusimi	discretion

Blocking of Periphrastic Verbs

We might expect that we would be able to take a native verb, derive from it a noun, and form a periphrastic with this deverbal noun as its nominal base, yielding forms like those in (13). However, this turns out to be impossible; with rare exceptions, incorporated periphrastics may not be formed directly from deverbal nouns.[7]

(13) Periphrastics Based on Root Deverbal Nouns

*irí suru	parch
*mamorí suru	protect
*oyogí suru	swim
*sábaki suru	judge
*ukétori suru	receive

Note that the claim here is that the incorporated periphrastics are impossible. As I note below, the same is not true of their unincorporated counterparts. This means that one must be careful to distinguish between true incorporated periphrastics and unincorporated periphrastics in which the accusative case particle has been elided by the process referred to as O-Ellipsis.[8] In the transitive case this can readily be determined by the case-marking of the object: accusative in the case of a true incorporated periphrastic but genitive in the case of an unincorporated periphrastic that has undergone O-Ellipsis. Another diagnostic is whether the form with a caseless nominal base is considered appropriate in writing and in formal speech, since O-Ellipsis is permissible only in casual speech.

I propose that this is a blocking effect, that is, that the periphrastic forms are unacceptable because a corresponding lexical verb already exists, as also suggested by Kageyama (1982).

One alternative explanation that we must consider is that we have here only an ordering effect, that is, that periphrastic verbs based on deverbal nouns are impossible simply because periphrastic verb formation occurs at a point at which the deverbal nouns have not yet been created. But there is good reason not to accept this proposal. One argument is theory-internal. This is the fact that deverbal noun formation is lexical and periphrastic

---

[7]There are a small number of exceptions, real and apparent, to the blocking of periphrastic verbs by their lexical counterparts. An apparent exception is *sakadati suru* 'stand on end, stand on one's head', which has the non-periphrastic counterpart *sakadatu*. In this case the two forms have different meanings. The periphrastic form cannot be used to refer to inanimate things, such as hair, standing on end, while the lexical form has precisely this use. Real exceptions include *tatigare suru* 'be blighted' which coexists with its lexical counterpart *tatigareru*, *tabenokosi suru* 'leave food behind' < *tabenokosu*, *fumitaosi suru* 'cheat' < *fumitaosu*, *torisimari suru* 'check on', < *torisimaru*, and *norikae suru* 'change trains' < *norikaeru*. Saiki (1987) observes that the blocking effect seems to be weakening among younger speakers.

[8]In casual speech it is possible for the accusative case-marker *o* to be omitted. This is known as O-Ellipsis.

formation is post-lexical. Since lexical rules precede post-lexical rules, deverbal noun formation must precede periphrastic formation, and hence the deverbal nouns must be available. Secondly, there is direct evidence that the deverbal nouns are available at the point at which periphrastic formation applies. In (14) we have a number of examples of periphrastic verbs whose nominal component is a compound the second member of which is deverbal.

(14) Periphrastic Verbs with Compound Deverbal Nominal Component

Periphrastic	Gloss	Analysis
amamori suru	leak rain	rain + leak
amayadori suru	take shelter from the rain	rain + take shelter
asibumi suru	stamp	foot + tread on
atomodori suru	retreat	after + turn back
atozusari suru	flinch	after + withdraw
hitobarai suru	clear a room of people	person + sweep
hitomisiri suru	be bashful	person+see+know
hitoriaruki suru	be independent	one-person + walk
hitotigai suru	mistake a person for another	person + mistake
iede suru	leave home	house + leave
igui suru	live in idleness	live + eat
kantigai suru	misjudge	perception + differ
kimayoi suru	waver	spirit + be confused
maeoki suru	make introductory remarks	front + put
mizuarai suru	wash with water	water + wash
nebumi suru	appraise	price + evaluate
senobi suru	straighten one's back	back + straighten
tatiuti suru	cross swords	sword + strike
tukimi suru	engage in moon-viewing	moon + see
yukimi suru	engage in snow-viewing	snow + see

In addition to the many more-or-less random examples of this type, certain first members are quite common. For example, periphrastics meaning 'do V in advance' are created rather freely from nominals formed by compounding the noun *mae* 'front, before' with the deverbal noun. Some examples are given in (15).

(15) Periphrastic Verbs with Nominal Component Containing *mae*

Periphrastic	Gloss	Analysis
maebarai suru	prepay	front + pay
maegari suru	draw (money) in advance	front + borrow
maegasi suru	advance (money)	front + lend
maeuri suru	sell in advance	front + sell

Similarly, periphrastics meaning 'do V a little' are formed fairly productively by compounding the deverbal noun with the number 'one', *hito*.[9]

(16) Periphrastic Verbs with Nominal Component Containing *hito*

Periphrastic	Gloss	Analysis
hitohasiri suru	go for a run	one + run
hitomawari suru	go round	one + go around
hitonemuri suru	nap	one + sleep
hitooyogi suru	swim a little bit	one + swim
hitoyasumi suru	take a short rest	one + rest

The existence of such periphrastics suffices to demonstrate that deverbal nouns must be available for periphrastic verb formation. The reason that these are acceptable while other periphrastic verbs based on deverbal nouns are not, is that these have no corresponding lexical verbs. That is, there are no verbs *amamoru, *amayadori, *asibumu, *atomodoru, *atozusaru, *hitobarau, *hitohasiru, *hitomawaru, *hitomisiru, *hitonemuru, *hitooyogu, *hitoriaruku, *hitotigau, *hitoyasumu, *iederu, *iguu, *kantigau, *kimayou, *maebarau, *maegariru, *maegasu, *maeoku, *maeuru, *nebumu, *senobiru, *tatiutu, *tukimiru, or *yukimiru. The great majority of the nominals on which periphrastics of the type illustrated in (14), (15), and (16) are based are Noun-Noun compounds whose first component is a non-deverbal noun.[10] Although there are sporadic examples of the type, Japanese does not productively generate verbs by compounding a noun with a verb, so these nominals cannot be derived by nominalizing a verb with this structure. Moreover, as shown in Poser (1984, 93), the accentuation of these nominals is consistent with a derivation in which the second member is nominalized and then compounded with another noun, but not with a derivation in which a compound verb is created and then nominalized. Thus, periphrastics based on nominals containing non-deverbal nouns suffer no competition from non-periphrastic verbs, and hence, are not blocked.

Periphrastics may also be based on deverbal nouns to which the suffix *bakari* 'only' has been attached, as in (17), or to which the topic-marking suffix *wa* has been attached to focus the verb, as in (18).

(17) Yomi-bakari site imasu.
Reading-only do-ing be
I am only reading.

---

[9] I am grateful to Yo Matsumoto for pointing out the relevance of the compounds of *hito*.

[10] Of the examples cited, the sole exception is *igui suru*, whose nominal base, *igui*, is a compound both of whose members are deverbal. (The first member is derived from the verb *iru*, 'be located in a place, live'.) However, even this example conforms to the larger generalization, as there is no compound verb *iguu*.

(18) Yomi-wa   site   imasu.
     Reading-TOP do-ing   be
     I am **reading**.

These too show that the deverbal noun must be available for periphrastic formation. They are not blocked since their meaning differs from that of the simplex verbs from which they are derived.

In sum, the acceptability of periphrastics based on compound nouns with a deverbal member, and the acceptability of periphrastics based on simplex deverbal nouns to which *bakari* and *wa* have been suffixed demonstrate that the ordering explanation is untenable, while the blocking hypothesis makes exactly the correct prediction.

Still another explanation might be based on the fact that not every noun can enter into the incorporated periphrastic construction—the noun must have a suitable argument structure and other syntactic properties. We might suppose that deverbal noun formation creates nouns which, unlike the non-derived loans from Chinese and English, lack the syntactic properties necessary to enter into the periphrastic construction. But this is belied by the fact already demonstrated that deverbal nouns can form the basis for periphrastic verbs provided that there be no corresponding non-periphrastic verb. Moreover, there is no syntactic property that the non-native nominal bases of periphrastic verbs exhibit that the native ones do not, other than, of course, the ability to enter into the periphrastic construction. Thus, just as non-native nominals can assign case in the absence of the verb *suru* in certain constructions, such as purpose clauses (19), so can native deverbal nouns (20). There is no evidence that the properties of the deverbal nouns themselves are in any way distinct from those of the non-deverbal nouns from which periphrastic verbs may be formed.

(19) Hanako-wa eigo-o   benkyoo-ni amerika-e   itta.
     Hanako-T English-A study-D   America-AD went
     Hanako went to America to study English.

(20) Taroo-wa Hanako-kara hon-o   uketori-ni   dekaketa.
     Taroo-T   Hanako-ABL   book-A   receiving-D went-out
     Taroo went out to get a book from Hanako.

In sum, periphrastic verbs based on deverbal nouns are not possible so long as there is a corresponding lexical verb. Alternative explanations for this behavior being untenable, this appears to be a case in which lexical items block a phrasal construction.[11]

---

[11]The blocking analysis proposed here eliminates the need for the Japanese analogue of Do-Support proposed by Kuroda (1965). Kuroda proposed that sentences like (18) have a deep structure in which the particle *wa* appears to the right of the entire verb.

Example II: English Comparatives and Superlatives

Comparative and superlative adjectives in English may be formed in two ways. There is a lexical construction, involving the suffixation of the morphemes *-er* and *-est*, and a periphrastic construction, in which the adverbs *more* and *most* precede the adjective.

The lexicality of the affixation of *-er* and *-est* seems clear. They exhibit no behavior inconsistent with lexical status: their phonology is that of words, the affixes are bound, and nothing not itself a suffix may intervene between the adjective and these affixes. Moreover, comparative and superlative adjectives are in certain cases formed by suppletion, clear evidence of lexicality. Thus, we have *better* for **good+er* and *best* for **good+est*, *worse* for **bad+er*, *worst* for **bad+est*.[12] *-er* and *-est* also occur inside of compounds, as in *surer-footed, fairer-minded, lightest-skinned*.

Similarly, the phrasal status of the periphrastics in *more* and *most* seems clear. *more* and *most* can be followed by arbitrary conjunctions of adjectives, as in (21), and it is possible to interpolate appositive material between *more* and *most* and the following adjective, as in (22).

(21)   Periphrastic Comparatives and Superlatives of Conjoined Adjectives:

      (a) more [curious and inquisitive]

      (b) most [economical, efficient, and frugal]

The *si*-Insertion transformation (p. 63, ex. 121), which takes the form V-AUX-*wa* → V-*wa-si*-AUX, moves *wa* to the right of the verb stem and inserts the verb *suru*. The subsequent discussion suggests that he intended to generalize this rule to other particles as well, though he does not state the more general form of the rule. Leaving aside the open question of how *si*-Insertion is to be formulated in a more restrictive theory than classical Transformational Grammar, the blocking account seems clearly superior to that based on *si*-Insertion. First, since the periphrastic construction exists independently, the rule of *si*-Insertion is simply unnecessary. Second, the blocking account provides a complete account of when *suru* appears and when it does not, while it is an arbitrary stipulation that certain morphemes trigger *si*-Insertion. Kuroda says that the purpose of *si*-Insertion is to carry the AUX. However there is no explanation of why a verb to which these particles are attached cannot itself bear the AUX. Third, the blocking analysis explains why it is that the accentuation of the V is that of the verbal noun, which is left unexplained on Kuroda's account. Finally, the blocking analysis provide a cleaner account of what *wa* and similar morphemes can attach to. These morphemes basically attach to NP, though some of them can attach to S-bar complements and to participles. They cannot attach to adjectives or adverbs. On the blocking analysis, this distribution is maintained, as the form to which *wa* and its ilk attach in the periphrastric construction is a noun. On the *si*-Insertion analysis, these morphemes must be allowed to attach underlyingly to tensed verbs. Note that the blocking issue would arise even if we were to accept Kuroda's proposal. Given the independent existence of the periphrastic construction, we would still need an account of why some but not all peripherastics based on deverbal nouns are acceptable.

[12]One conceivable, though unattractive alternative would be to claim that the non-suppletive forms were phrasal and that only suppletive forms are lexical. In this case we would have a different argument for phrasal blocking, since the suppletive forms block the regular forms **gooder* and **goodest*.

(22) Interpolation into Periphrastic Comparatives and Superlatives:
  (a) This situation is more, I suppose the term is delicate, than I had thought.
  (b) Watson, this is the most, how shall I say, curious case that I have ever seen.

This is not true of the lexical forms. In (23) we see that each term in a conjunct requires its own comparative or superlative suffix. When the comparative suffix falls on the last term the sentence is grammatical, but the comparison is restricted to the last adjective. When it is on a non-final term the example is simply ungrammatical.[13]

(23) Interpolation into Periphrastic Comparatives and Superlatives:
  (a) He is taller, slimmer, and handsomer than John.
  (b) He is tall, slim, and handsomer than John.
  (c) *He is taller, slim, and handsome than John.
  (d) *He is tall, slimmer, and handsome than John.

The lexical forms are possible only in a fairly small range of cases, determined in a way not fully understood by the length or stress pattern of the stem. Generally speaking, lexical comparatives and superlatives of adjectives with mono- and di-syllabic stems are perfect, while lexical forms derived from adjectives with longer stems are unacceptable. On the other hand, while it is always possible to form periphrastic comparatives and superlatives from adjectives with longer stems, periphrastic forms of adjectives with mono- and di-syllabic stems are generally unacceptable.[14] The crucial observation is, then, that whatever the nature of the principles governing the well-formedness of lexical comparatives and superlatives, the acceptability of the periphrastic forms is inversely related to that of the lexical forms, as illustrated in (24). As far as I can see, the only plausible explanation for this is that the periphrastic forms are blocked by the lexical forms.[15]

---

[13]It is also true that interpolation between the adjective and the comparative or superlative suffix is impossible, in the sense that there are no acceptable examples of it, but the unacceptability of these examples is not of great probative value since I have been able to find no circumstances in which, were the comparative and superlative affixes clitics or even independent words, we would expect the interpolation to be acceptable.

[14]One systematic exception to this generalization occurs in such metalinguistic constructions as *It's more big than good*, where the periphrastic form is not only acceptable but obligatory (cf. *It's bigger than better*). What distinguishes such sentences from ordinary comparatives is that the nature of the comparison is different from that conveyed by lexical comparatives. In the usual case, saying that *A is Adj-er than B* means that on some scale of Adj-ness, A lies farther from the reference point than B. In contrast, when we say *A is more Adj$_1$ than Adj$_2$* we mean something like "It is more accurate or appropriate to say that A is Adj$_1$ than to say that A is Adj$_2$." In other words, the comparison is here between the appropriateness of two utterances rather than between two situations in the world.

[15]Di Sciullo and Williams (1987) have also noted this example.

(24)   English Comparatives

Base	Lexical	Periphrastic
big	bigger	*more big
small	smaller	*more small
good	better	*more good
fun	funnier	*more funny
silly	sillier	*more silly
childish	*childisher	more childish
regal	*regaler	more regal
damaging	*damaginger	more damaging
symmetric	*symmetricer	more symmetric
vivacious	*vivaciouser	more vivacious

Example III: Basque

A third example of blocking of a phrasal construction by lexical items is found in Basque, as described by Hualde (1988, 38–41). In Basque, progressive aspect is normally expressed by means of periphrasis with the defective verb *ari*. Thus, the progressive counterpart of (25) is (26), in which *ari* appears between the verb stem and the auxiliary.

(25) Jon   abiatzen   da.
      John   leave-*imf*   AUX-*intr*
      John leaves.

(26) Jon   abiatzen   ari   da.
      John   leave-*imf*   ari   AUX-*intr*
      John is leaving.

However, a handful of verbs have synthetic (non-periphrastic) present and past tense forms, and these lack periphrastic progressive forms in *ari*. Hualde provides the examples in (27), where the grammatical, synthetic form in the first column contrasts with the ungrammatical but expected periphrastic form in the third column.

(27) daki   he knows   *jakiten ari da
      doa   he goes   *joaten ari da
      dakar   he brings   *ekartzen ari da
      dabil   he walks   *ibiltzen ari da
      dator   he comes   *etortzen ari da
      dauka   he possesses   *edukitzen ari da

The existence of the lexical tense-aspect forms of these verbs apparently blocks the corresponding periphrastic forms.

As evidence that the periphrastic forms are indeed phrasal, that is, that *ari* is not lexically attached to the main verb, Hualde offers the fact that in negative constructions *ari* need not be adjacent to the verb stem at all. In (28) *ari* precedes the verb *kantatzen* and is separated from it by the direct object *madrigalak*. This appears to be compelling evidence for the phrasal status of *ari* periphrastics, and hence for the claim that we have here another case of blocking of a phrasal construction by lexical items.

(28) Jon ez da ari madrigalak kantatzen
 John NEG AUX ari madrigals sing-*imf*
 John is not singing madrigals.

In sum, Japanese, English, and Basque appear to provide real examples of blocking of phrasal constructs by lexical items.[16]

2 Implications

The three examples of blocking of phrasal constructions by lexical items presented here are problematic for the existing theory of blocking since they cannot be accounted for in terms of unique instantiation of complex morphological categories, at least if we take such morphological categories to be those filled by the word-formation component. Either we must find some other account of blocking, one under which we do not expect blocking to be restricted to the lexicon, or we must in some way "extend" the lexicon to encompass the sorts of phrasal construction that we have discussed here.

2.1 The Pragmatic Approach

There is, in fact, one proposal in the literature that does not predict the restriction of blocking to the lexicon. This is the proposal, due to Householder (1971) and McCawley (1977), that effects very much like those that are usually ascribed to blocking are to be attributed to pervasive Gricean principles, to wit the principle that *ceteris paribus* the speaker expends as little effort as possible to say what he wants to say and therefore chooses the simplest available form. For example, Householder (1971) observes that it is awkward to say *pale red*. He proposes that the reason for this is that English has a simpler way of expressing the same notion, namely the word *pink*. Insofar as *pink* and *pale red* express the same meaning, the speaker will minimize his expenditure of effort and choose the former. *pale red* will be chosen only when *pink* is for some reason inappropriate, as when the hearer does not know the meaning of *pink* and *pale red* is given as a definition.

Neither Householder nor McCawley uses the term *blocking* or discusses the usual cases of morphological blocking, nor are their works cited in the

---

[16]Di Sciullo and Williams (1987) cite the relationship between the synthetic and periphrastic forms of the Latin passive as an example of lexical blocking of a phrasal construct, which it may well be, though to be sure it is necessary to offer evidence of the phrasal character of the periphrastic construction and to rule out alternative explanations of the relationship. In general, paradigms containing both synthetic and periphrastic forms are good candidates for instances of lexical blocking of phrasal constructs.

literature on morphological blocking. Thus it does not seem that their proposal was intended to extend to these cases, nor has it been so interpreted. However, Di Sciullo and Williams (1987) suggest such an approach to blocking, without citing Householder or McCawley, or going into any detail.

This proposal has the advantage that it is not restricted to the lexicon. Thus, we must entertain the possibility that the unique instantiation account of blocking is incorrect, and that it is rather a pragmatic effect due to minimization of effort.

Although this proposal is attractive, it does not solve our problem. To begin with, it fails to account for a number of the classical examples of morphological blocking, since it predicts that form A will block form B only if form A involves a lesser expenditure of effort. This means, other things being equal, that we expect blocking only if the blocker contains less phonological material than the blocked form. But this prediction is incorrect. For example, we cannot appeal to the pragmatic proposal to explain the blocking of English *oxes by the irregular oxen, since both forms are of equal phonological and morphological complexity. Similarly, in Japanese, the verb kuru 'come' has the irregular present neutral negative stem kona- in place of the regular *kina. The fact that kona- blocks kina- is inexplicable on the pragmatic hypothesis, since the two stems are of equal complexity. Even worse is the present neutral affirmative form of the Japanese verb 'to do'. The irregular present neutral affirmative form suru is actually longer than the expected but incorrect *su.[17] A parallel example in English is the irregular plural children, which is surely not simpler than the regular *childs. Examples such as these show that the pragmatic hypothesis does not handle the traditional cases of blocking.

A second problem with extending the pragmatic hypothesis to all cases of blocking is the fact that in the typical case of blocking the judgments are much stronger than in Householder's pale red example. While it is true that pink is generally preferable to pale red, it is still possible to use the latter when there is sufficient motivation, as, for example, in defining pink for someone who does not know its meaning. In contrast, we cannot explain the irregular form men to a person learning English by equating it with *mans. This latter form is not simply verbose; it is impossible.

The very property that makes the pragmatic hypothesis attractive, namely that it predicts the existence of blocking outside the lexicon, also provides an argument against it. Under the pragmatic hypothesis, it should be possible for phrasal constructs of any size to be blocked. But in point of fact the examples of blocking of phrasal constructs known to me all involve

---

[17]The stem of 'do' throughout most of its paradigm is simply /s/. The addition of the present neutral affirmative suffix /ru/ to this stem will yield *su.

blocking of small phrases; there appear to be no examples of blocking of large syntactic units. For example, *the red book* does not block *the book which is red*.

A further difficulty for the pragmatic approach arises from the fact that the correspondence between two forms depends only on their meaning—if two potential forms have the same meaning, the simpler form should block the other one whether or not they are morphologically related, as is indeed the case in Householder's example of *pale red*, which has only a semantic relation to *pink*.[18]

In general, there is no blocking effect when two forms are not related.[19] Thus,

(29) John is smarter than Tom.

blocks

(30) *John is more smart than Tom.

but not such synonymous but structurally unrelated sentences as:

(31) John's intelligence exceeds Tom's.

(32) John has more intelligence than Tom.

or

(33) John has greater intelligence than Tom.

The pragmatic approach therefore fails to provide a fully adequate account of blocking, partly because it cannot account for the classical observation that irregular forms block regular forms, and partly because it fails to restrict blocking effects to structurally related forms where the blocked form comprises a small syntactic unit.

2.2 Morphological Constructions

These problems with the pragmatic hypothesis suggest that we ought to try the other available route, namely finding some way to characterize certain phrasal constructs as instantiating morphological categories in spite of their non-lexical status. Roughly speaking, what we want to do is to

---

[18]Another apparent counterexample is that of doublets of a type common in Japanese, where there is both a native simplex verb and a periphrastic verb based on a loan from Chinese, where on the pragmatic account we might expect the simplex verb to block the periphrastic. In many cases the members of these doublets appear to be perfectly synonymous. An example is *manabu* 'study', the native counterpart to the Sino-Japanese periphrastic *benkyoo suru*. In most if not all of these cases, however, the members of the pair belong to different stylistic registers. It is usually the Sino-Japanese periphrastic that belongs to the higher register, but there are exceptions, such as *manabu*, which is the higher register member of the pair. Insofar as the pragmatic constraint is to use the simplest available form, the absence of blocking here is expected if we take availability to be relative to the chosen register.

[19]The difficulty of determining which utterances count as relevant alternatives is discussed in some detail by Horn (1978) in a critique of the proposal of McCawley's of which we here consider an adaptation.

extend the boundary of the lexicon, so that we can treat a class of phrase formation rules as essentially morphological in character, in the sense that they instantiate morphological categories.

The question that arises is how to instantiate this idea. I will tentatively propose that we should distinguish between morphological rules, by which I mean processes that instantiate morphological categories, and word-formation rules, by which I mean the non-phonological rules that operate within the lexicon. Since word-formation rules all instantiate morphological categories, all word-formation rules are morphological rules, but the converse need not be the case. Insofar as there are syntactic rules that instantiate morphological categories, these rules are morphological rules but not word-formation rules.[20] This provides us with a reconstruction of the traditional notion of periphrasis: a periphrastic construction is one in which morphological categories which are typically instantiated lexically are instead instantiated at a phrasal level.

The question then arises as to how to define a morphological category other than by saying that it is something that is instantiated by a word-formation rule. Suppose that we say that a morphological category is a category *potentially* instantiated by a word-formation rule. Then we would say that the category of comparative adjectives is a morphological category because in some languages it is instantiated by word-formation rules. The fact that it may be instantiated by a phrasal construction as well, as in English, does not affect the claim that this category is morphological in nature.

This distinction between morphological rules and word-formation rules permits a straightforward account of the English comparative adjective. The morphological category of comparative adjective may potentially be filled either by a lexical form or by a periphrastic form. If the lexical form exists, the category is instantiated and so the periphrastic form is blocked.

Similarly, in the case of the periphrastic verbs, the morphological category is the verb with the argument structure and other properties of the related noun. If this category is instantiated by a lexical verb, the periphrastic form is blocked, but if it is left empty it may be instantiated by a phrasal construction.

One question that arises is what kinds of phrasal constructs may instantiate morphological categories, and hence be blocked by lexical forms. The three examples that we have seen both involve phrasal categories that are in a certain sense "small." As I pointed out above, one defect of the pragmatic proposal is that it predicts that it should be possible to block any sort of phrasal construction. We should like to avoid the same problem here. I conjecture that it is only what I will call *small categories* that can instantiate morphological categories. By a *small category* I mean a cate-

---

[20]A theory with this property is that of Anderson (1991).

gory that dominates only zero-level projections. The English periphrastic comparatives and superlatives are presumably categories of type A^1 and contain only categories of type ADV^0 and A^0. The Japanese incorporated periphrastics are "small" since, on the analysis of Poser 1989, they are of category V^0 and contain only categories of the same level, namely V^0 and N^0.

This definition helps us to explain a fact about the Japanese periphrastics that would otherwise seem problematic. As I have noted, although incorporated periphrastics are blocked by corresponding lexical verbs, their unincorporated counterparts are not. This contrast follows immediately once we recognize that the unincorporated periphrastics are not "small"; the nominal part of an unincorporated periphrastic is a full NP, as illustrated in example (7) above as well as in (34).

(34) Butyoo-ga suru yoo-ni meirei sita
     Boss-NOM do   so   ordered

     kenkyuu-o   mada sinakatta.
     research-ACC still do-*neg-past*

He still hasn't done the research that his boss ordered him to do.

Since the unincorporated periphrastic contains a full NP it is not a "small" category and so cannot instantiate a morphological category.[21]

Whether it is possible to derive the restriction of phrasal blocking to "small" phrases is unclear. It may well be that this restriction can be derived from principles governing the distribution of morphological features, but I am not at present prepared to defend this position.

The proposal that morphological rules be considered to be a superset of the word-formation rules, with blocking applicable to morphological categories, not to words, provides an account both of the classical blocking cases and of the attested cases of phrasal blocking, without falsely predicting blocking to be a more general phenomenon than it is. In this sense, it seems that the proposal is on the right track. However, as presented here the proposal is also excessively vague, and its viability depends on whether subsequent research provides an adequate theory of morphological categories and how they are instantiated. If this approach is correct, it

---

[21]Let me note briefly two inadequate alternatives that I considered. First, it is not adequate to say that "small" categories are merely non-recursive. The incorporated periphrastics, on the analysis given here, are recursive in that they contain another category of the same type (V^0 contains another V^0). Second, we might define the "small" categories as those that are monotonic in the sense that they contain no projections higher than themselves. The incorporated perphrastics and the periphrastic comparative and superlative adjectives satisfy this definition since they contain only zero-level projections, but this definition fails to distinguish between the incorporated perphrastics and their unincorporated counterparts. Insofar as the latter are of category V^2 they should count as "small' even if they dominate full NPs. This definition might, however, be tenable if the unincorporated periphrastics were of category V^1, a possibility that I am not at present prepared to rule out conclusively.

provides reconstructions of the traditional notions of periphrasis and construction, notions used regularly for descriptive purposes, but which have no home in current morphological and syntactic theory.[22]

3 Summary

Although the current literature on blocking is restricted to the lexicon, there appear to be cases of blocking of phrasal constructions by lexical items. Three examples are presented here, namely the blocking of Japanese periphrastic verbs by their lexical counterparts, the blocking of English periphrastic comparative and superlative adjectives by lexical comparative and superlative forms, and the blocking of Basque periphrastic progressive verb forms by lexical progressives. These examples require a modification of the theory of blocking. One possibility is a purely pragmatic account, along the lines suggested by Householder (1971), McCawley (1977), and Di Sciullo and Williams (1987). This, however, is subject to a number of objections. Instead I propose an extension of existing lexical accounts of blocking to encompass blocking of phrasal constructions that instantiate morphological categories.

References

Allen, Margaret R. 1978. *Morphological Investigations.* Doctoral dissertation, University of Connecticut.

Anderson, Stephen R. 1969. *West Scandinavian Vowel Systems and the Ordering of Phonological Rules.* Doctoral dissertation, Massachusetts Institute of Technology.

Anderson, Stephen R. 1991. *A-morphous Morphology.* New York: Academic Press.

Aronoff, Mark. 1976. *Word Formation in Generative Grammar.* Cambridge, Mass.: MIT Press.

Clark, Eve, and Herbert Clark. 1979. When Nouns Surface as Verbs. *Language* 55:767–811.

Di Sciullo, Anne-Marie, and Edwin Williams. 1987. *On the Definition of Word.* Cambridge, Mass.: MIT Press.

Esau, Helmut. 1973. *Nominalization and Complementation in Modern German.* Amsterdam: North Holland.

Fillmore, Charles J., Paul Kay, and Mary Catherine O'Connor. 1988. Regularity and Idiomaticity in Grammatical Constructions. *Language* 64:501–538.

---

[22]The work of Fillmore, Kay, and O'Connor (1988) on Construction Grammar is an exception. Although one might entertain the idea that what can be blocked are constructions, it appears that from the point of view of Construction Grammar every phrasal collocation is a construction—there is no distinction made between phrasal collocations that instantiate morphological categories and other phrasal structures—so that their notion of construction is too general to be useful for the purpose of delimiting the scope of blocking.

Grimshaw, Jane, and Armin Mester. 1988. Light Verbs and Theta-Marking. *Linguistic Inquiry* 19:205–232.

Hasegawa, Nobuko. 1979. A Comparison of Two Approaches to a Class of Japanese Constructions. Manuscript, University of Washington, Seattle.

Horn, Laurence R. 1978. Lexical Incorporation, Implicature, and the Least Effort Hypothesis. In *Proceedings of the Parasession on the Lexicon*, ed. Donka Farkas, Wesley M. Jacobsen, and Karol W. Todrys, 196–209. Chicago: Chicago Linguistic Society.

Householder, Frederick W. 1971. *Linguistic Speculations*. New York: Cambridge University Press.

Hualde, José Ignacio. 1988. *A Lexical Phonology of Basque*. Doctoral dissertation, University of Southern California.

Inoue, Kazuko. 1976. *Henkei Bunpoo to Nihongo (Transformational Grammar and the Japanese Language)*. Tokyo: Taishukan.

Kageyama, Taroo. 1977. Incorporation and Sino-Japanese Verbs. *Papers in Japanese Linguistics* 5:117–156.

Kageyama, Taroo. 1982. Word Formation in Japanese. *Lingua* 57:215–258.

Kawakami, Shin. 1973. Doosi kara no tensei meisi no akusento (Accentuation of Deverbal Nouns). *Imaizumi Hakase Koki Kinen Kokugogaku Ronsoo* 55–70.

Kiparsky, Paul. 1973. Elsewhere in Phonology. In *A Festschrift for Morris Halle*, ed. Stephen R. Anderson and Paul Kiparsky. New York: Holt, Rinehart, and Winston.

Kiparsky, Paul. 1982a. From Cyclic Phonology to Lexical Phonology. In *The Structure of Phonological Representations (Part I)*, ed. Harry van der Hulst and Norval Smith, 131–175. Dordrecht: Foris.

Kiparsky, Paul. 1982b. Word Formation and the Lexicon. In *Proceedings of the 1982 Mid-America Linguistics Conference*, ed. Frances Ingemann, 3–29, 47–78. Lawrence: University of Kansas.

Kuroda, Sige-yuki. 1965. *Generative Grammatical Studies in the Japanese Language*. Doctoral dissertation, Massachusetts Institute of Technology. Reprinted 1979 by Garland Publishers, New York.

McCawley, James. 1977. Conversational Implicature and the Lexicon. In *Syntax and Semantics 9: Pragmatics*, ed. Peter Cole, 245–259. New York: Academic Press.

Miyagawa, Shigeru. 1980. Complex Verbs and the Lexicon. In *Coyote Papers, I*. Tucson: Department of Linguistics.

Miyagawa, Shigeru. 1987. Lexical Categories in Japanese. *Lingua* 73:29–51.

Miyagawa, Shigeru. 1990. Light Verbs and the Ergative Hypothesis. *Linguistic Inquiry* 20:659–688.

Paul, Hermann. 1896. Über die Aufgaben der Wortbildungslehre. *Sitzbungsberichte der königl. bayer. Akademie der Wissenschaften* (philosophisch-philologische und historische Classe) 692–713.

Poser, William J. 1980. Periphrastic Verbs in Japanese. Manuscript, Massachusetts Institute of Technology.

Poser, William J. 1984. *The Phonetics and Phonology of Tone and Intonation in Japanese*. Doctoral dissertation, Massachusetts Institute of Technology.

Poser, William J. 1989. Japanese Periphrastic Verbs and Noun Incorporation. To appear in *Natural Language and Linguistic Theory*.

Poser, William J. 1991. Lexical and Phrasal Periphrastic Verbs in Japanese. Manuscript, Stanford University.

Saiki, Mariko. 1987. *On the Manifestations of Grammatical Functions in the Syntax of Japanese Nominals*. Doctoral dissertation, Stanford University.

Scalise, Sergio. 1984. *Generative Morphology*. Dordrecht: Foris.

Szymanek, Bogdan. 1985. Disjunctive Rule Ordering in Word Formation. In *Papers and Studies in Contrastive Linguistics, Vol. 20*, ed. Jacek Fisiak, 45–64. Poznan: Adam Mickiewicz University.

Tomán, Jindrich. 1980. *Wortsyntax*. Doctoral dissertation, University of Cologne.

Yoshiba, Hiroshi. 1981. The Mora Constraint in Japanese Phonology. *Linguistic Analysis* 7:241–262.

Zwanenburg, Wiecher. 1981. Le principe du blocage dans la morphologie derivationelle. In *Linguistics in the Netherlands 1981*, ed. Saskia Daalder and Marinel Gerritsen, 65–72. Amsterdam: North Holland.

6

The Stress and Structure of Modified Noun Phrases in English

MARK LIBERMAN AND RICHARD SPROAT

1 Introduction

Our topic is the stress pattern of English noun phrases in which the head noun is preceded by a sequence of modifiers.[1] We assume a context of use that is rhetorically stress-neutral; the phenomena of FOCUS, CONTRAST and ANAPHORA—henceforth FCA—are taken to be perturbations of the patterns that we discuss. We attempt to establish the basic regularities that shape the complex data in this area, against the background of a broad (and thus complex) description. Our purpose is to establish an adequate set of descriptive categories, able to support a formal model of the syntax, semantics and prosody of complex nominals. We would like such a model to be adequate for parsing and assigning stress to modified noun phrases in unconstrained English text. We start with a careful description of the phenomena, followed by a more formal account of the proposed syntactic analysis, and a sketch of the implications for parsing and stress-assignment algorithms.

Many syntacticians (e.g., Jackendoff 1977) have noted the existence of at least four distinct prenominal positions, arranged in a right-branching structure:

(1)

4	3	2	1	0
the	three	exotic	chess	boards
John's	many	large	book	bags
those	few	Chinese	store	owners

Position 4 is stereotypically occupied by articles, demonstratives, and possessive phrases; position 3 by certain quantifiers and numerals; position

[1]The authors would like to thank an anonymous reviewer for useful comments, and Julia Hirschberg and Mats Rooth for some discussion.

2 by adjectives; and position 1 by nouns making up the initial element of a compound word. We will refer to items in positions 1 and 2 as MODIFIERS.

Each of the positions in (1) may be occupied by an item that has internal structure of its own: *John's brother's* (position 1), *distressingly few* (3), *more exotic* (2), *liquor store* (1). Items characteristic of positions 1 and 2 are often repeated, either in parallel or a layered fashion: *powerful, luxurious automobiles*; *powerful economic forces*. Normally, a strict ordering of these positions is required—phrases like *large many John's book bags* are about as wrong as arrangements of English words can be.

The lefthand edge of English noun phrases is more complex than the simple pattern (1) indicates. For instance, certain quantifiers cannot substitute in position 3 of the pattern, co-occurring with articles, demonstratives and possessive phrases only in so-called *partitive* constructions: *John's all/some/any/each large book bags*, *all/some/any/each of John's large book bags*; see Jackendoff 1977, pages 104ff for some discussion. Other complexities arise in the handling of pronouns, *such*, definiteness, and so forth. However, we will not discuss the intricacies of material to the left of position 2 in (1); our concern is with the complexities of the inner structure, and their influence on stress patterns.

1.1 A Sketch of Our Conclusions

We take a traditional view of modifiers in positions 1 and 2 of (1): a position 1 modifier combines with a noun to form a compound noun, whereas a position 2 modifier forms a phrasal category. Expressed in terms of X-bar theory, position 1 is filled by modifiers of N^0 whereas position 2 contains modifiers of N^1. The structure of *large exotic chess boards* is thus:

(2) $[_{N^1}$ large $[_{N^1}$ exotic $[_{N^0}$ chess boards$]]]$

Position 1 modifiers—COMPOUND MODIFIERS—are thus adjunctions to N^0, whereas position 2 modifiers—PHRASAL MODIFIERS—are daughters of N^1, modifying a right sister that is either N^1 or N^0.[2]

We shall agree with the traditional generative view (Chomsky and Halle 1968, Liberman and Prince 1977, Hayes 1980) that constructions involving positions 1 and 2 in (1) are assigned different default stress patterns due to the difference in category of their parent node. English stress is normally assigned recursively to rightmost elements, but the stress rule for nouns, simple or compound, will ignore a single non-complex element at each level. This implies that N^1 constructions are "right dominant"—i.e., have main stress on the head noun—while N^0 constructions are "left dominant"—i.e., have main stress on the modifier—as long as the head is

---

[2]We know of no distinction in types of modification that would motivate maintaining these two alternative categories for the right sister of position 2 modifiers, so one could assume that such modifiers are always adjoined to N^1. Under that assumption, the sister of *exotic* in (2) would be more correctly given as $[_{N^1} [_{N^0}$ chess boards$]]$.

a single word. We thus disagree with the view (Bolinger 1972, Ladd 1984) that the difference between compound and phrasal stress is derivable from FCA effects.

Position 1 modifiers are usually taken to be joined with their heads in a separate lexical or morphological component, whereas position 2 modifiers are taken to be syntactic in origin; a recent expression of this view is given in Di Sciullo and Williams 1987. We agree that constructions dominated by N^0 are words, but we see no good evidence for assuming that they should be considered anything other than syntactic constructions in English. We shall return in a later section to a fuller discussion of the theoretical issues in English noun phrase modification.[3]

We also agree with the traditional view that the two different types of syntactic modification imply different sorts of semantic relationship as well. However, as will become clear from the discussion below, there does not seem to be a single, clean semantic distinction such that all nominals with lefthand stress will fall into one semantic class and all nominals with righthand stress will fall into the other.

The main novelty of our position is this: we argue that both position 1 and position 2 may be occupied by modifiers of a wide variety of categories. We show in particular that positions 1 and 2 may be filled by both adjectives and nouns or phrases made up of these and other categories, sometimes linked with the possessive *'s*. This implies that for any modifier-noun sequence, both N^0 and N^1 structures are always available in principle. Thus the contextually appropriate parsing of such phrases may require a judgment as to the relative plausibility of the semantic relations implied by the structural choices. This is at least somewhat consistent with Bolinger's (1972) dictum that "accent is predictable (if you're a mind reader)". However, we will suggest that there are some strategies that can achieve fairly high accuracy without telepathic assistance.

1.2 The Problem

It is common in running text or speech in English to find PREMODIFIED NOMINALS containing one or more modifiers, such as the examples in (1). Depending on the style of the material and on the definition of 'phrase', something like 30 to 70 percent of all phrases can be expected to end in such units. As a matter of practice, the location of the main stress in these sequences is quite variable. Although the final noun is the commonest location, pre-final main stress is also quite frequent. Depending on the type of material studied, somewhere between 10 and 60 percent of the premodi-

---

[3]For those readers familiar with the work of Abney 1987, we note that we shall use the terms 'noun phrase' and 'NP' in their traditional sense for the bulk of this paper. Also, we shall generally use 'XP' (e.g., NP, AP,...) to refer to the (contextually) maximal projection of the category in question with no commitment to the bar level of this projection.

fied noun constituents show pre-final main stress, with 30-40 percent being typical of newspaper writing.

There are several sorts of reasons why the main stress in a noun group might fall before the head. We distinguish cases where the preterminal stress serves to underline an important word, or to avoid stressing a redundant one, from cases where a preterminal stress pattern is normal or natural for the phrase in neutral contexts of use. In the following example, and henceforth in this paper, boldface is used, where needed, to mark the word that bears the main stress:

(3)　　a. Stress pattern "natural" for the phrase:

　　　　　　i. At 9:00, there is an important **meeting**.
　　　　　　ii. At 9:00, there is a **staff** meeting.
　　　　　　iii. John was wearing a red **jacket**.
　　　　　　iv. John was wearing a **life** jacket.

　　　　b. Stress pattern determined by "FCA" considerations

　　　　　　i. We're only concerned with **solvable** problems.
　　　　　　ii. He replaced his **low-interest** bonds with **high-interest** bonds.

While FCA effects are not uncommon and cannot be ignored, it is nonetheless true that FCA phenomena must in turn interact with other principles—such as the lexical stress pattern of polysyllabic words—to produce observed stress patterns; see Hirschberg 1990 for some recent discussion of issues in modeling some FCA effects and their interaction with lexical stress placement. In particular, a familiar generalization seems to underlie the stress pattern of cases like those in (3a), where [A N] phrases typically show main stress on the head noun (righthand stress), while [N N] units typically show stress on the noun in the lefthand position. These simple generalizations hold true more often than not. We can provide a rough experimental check by having someone read some text, and counting up the stress patterns employed for constituents of the appropriate kinds. In our experience, more than 90% of [A N] units will be read with righthand main stress, while around 75% of [N N] units will show lefthand main stress. .

Although the contrary cases remain fairly frequent, we might suppose that they represent the expected effect of the phenomena of FCA. Because theories of FCA phenomena are not very well developed, it is hard to check this notion with total assurance. However, one typically has some feeling for the application of such analyses in particular cases, and we can look for them in all the textual examples whose stress patterns are contrary to the predictions of part of speech sequence. On this basis, FCA-type explanations do not seem to help very much, especially for the [N N] anomalies.

The exact statistics depend very much on the style of the material surveyed, but two sample cases will give the flavor of the situation. In one text (taken from a book on computer vision), 190 out of 214 [A N] constituents showed righthand stress, while 76 out of 92 [N N] constituents showed lefthand stress.[4] A plausible explanation in terms of FCA could be found for 18 of the 24 left-stressed [A N] units, and for none of the 16 right-stressed [N N] units. Thus we are left with about 3% anomalous left-stressed [A N] expressions and about 17% anomalous right-stressed [N N] expressions. In a second text (several stories from the main section of the *New York Times*), 153 out of 169 [A N] constituents had the expected righthand stress, while 102 out of 138 [N N] constituents had the expected lefthand stress. FCA-type explanations applied to 8 of the 16 left-stressed [A N] units, and to none of the 36 [N N] units, leaving about 5% non-FCA left-stressed [A N] expressions, and about 26% non-FCA right-stressed [N N] expressions. In these two sample texts, only 60% of the "anomalous" [A N] cases (and none of the anomalous [N N] cases) had a plausible FCA explanation.[5] This means that in 6.7% of all [A N] sequences there was a useful FCA explanation for the stress pattern (be it left or right), and in none of the [N N] cases.

So, while the stress pattern of an [X N] expression is strongly correlated with the lexical category of the word preceding the head noun, there are quite a few apparent exceptions, most of which cannot be attributed to discourse effects. Theories which explain patterns of modifier-noun stress mostly or solely on the basis of FCA factors (such as that of Ladd 1984), are unlikely to be correct. We shall return to this issue at subsequent points in the paper. We devote the body of the paper to a survey of the "standard" pattern, as well as the systematic classes of exceptions to it.

2   The Standard Pattern

Before we take up the minority cases of left-dominant [A N] expressions and right-dominant [N N] expressions, it will be helpful to survey the standard forms of these constructions. Nearly all of the material discussed in this section is familiar from the literature, but since the full range of issues is rarely found discussed in one place it seems useful to review the facts here.

---

[4]We require that both the head noun and its modifier be content words, thus disallowing anaphors and excluding a few easily predictable [A N] FCA examples involving head words like *one*.

[5]Maidment (1989) has noted that news reporters often tend to place righthand stress on [N N] sequences that he feels should properly be left-stressed, and speculates (p. 187) that "this feature of broadcast speech is due to a desire ... on the part of the broadcaster to defer the intonational 'payoff' for as long as possible in order to create suspense or to make the news item sound more portentous." Indeed, Bolinger (1972, p. 643) notes that similar effects can even interfere with normal lexical stress for non-compound words. This possibility adds another possible dimension to FCA effects on which we will not comment further.

2.1 Standard Compound Nouns: N^0 $[N\ N]$ Expressions

It is a well-known fact that English permits the free formation of compound nouns, the commonest type being of the form $[N\ N]$. The orthographic conventions for encoding compounding are varied. Short, frequent or fossilized compounds are often written as single words:

(4)   drugstore, icewater, postman, gamecock, basketball, bathroom, ashcan, bartender, poolhall, earwax, lawnmower, flagpole, marshmallow, wallpaper, keyboard, waveform

Sometimes (especially in attributive position) a hyphen is used, and sometimes the two words are written separately: *masthead, mast-head, mast head*. The correlation between typographical practice and the semantic regularity of the resulting compound is at best imperfect. Some compounds that are commonly written as single words have a meaning that seems fairly compositional (5a), while other cases that must be written as two words have a special meaning that surely must be lexically listed (5b):

(5)   a. phonecall (a call on the phone)
         b. overseas cap (a particular style of cap)

The frequency of the compound, and the length of its constituent words, seem to be more important factors than semantic compositionality.

To some extent, the typography is a matter of style. Some writers prefer words written solid, while others like hyphens, or find pleasure in spaces. However, the typographical usage in actual text is quite variable. Even individual writers are not always consistent—within a single chapter of a textbook on the automobile electrical system, we have found *spark plug*, *spark-plug*, and *sparkplug*. However they may be spelled, such compound nouns are generally pronounced with primary stress on the first element. Indeed when the compound is run together or spelled with a hyphen, first-element stress is almost inevitable.

Because noun compounding is an easy way to create terms of art, technical writing, in the broad sense, is especially prone to such coinages. However, ordinary life also provides plenty of examples—a few days of recording those that came up in reading and listening produced over 5,000 examples, a few of which are given below:

(6)   drug abuse, line backer, tool cabinet, feast day, knife edge, crop failure, dart game, body hair, shoe imports, phone jack, tea kettle, heat lamp, utility man, node name, post office, soap pad, printer queue, boat race, cocktail sauce, folk tale, land use, property value, star wars, junk yard, combat zone

2.2 Semantic Relations in N^0 Compound Nouns

The productive types of N^0 $[N\ N]$ compounds fall into a number of different categories. As an initial cut, we will distinguish two broad classes on the basis of the semantic relation that holds between the two nouns. In the first type, a paraphrase of the meaning has the first noun providing an argument for a predicate associated with the second (head) noun; we will call this type ARGUMENT-PREDICATE compounds. A typical example would be *lion tamer*, paraphrased as 'one who tames lions'. Extensive work has been done within theoretical linguistics on these so-called SYNTHETIC COMPOUNDS; see for example, Roeper and Siegel 1978, Selkirk 1982, Lieber 1983, Sproat 1985, Levin and Rappaport 1992, Marantz 1989. All of this work treats the relation between the lefthand member and the head in argument-predicate compounds by analogy to the relation between verbs and their objects.

In the second type of compound, paraphrases of the meaning involve a predicate not implicit in either word, with a meaning like POSSESSION, PURPOSE, etc., for which the two elements of the compound provide arguments. We will call this type ARGUMENT-ARGUMENT compounds. Some examples are *pie chart*, paraphrased as 'a chart that is like a pie', and *keyhole saw*, paraphrased as 'a saw used to make keyholes'. The semantics of these has been much less extensively studied, but Lees 1960 and in particular Levi 1978 are two works which discuss these compounds at length.

2.3 Argument-Predicate Compounds

The head noun in the *argument-predicate* type of compound may be an "agentive" -*er* nominal, a gerund, a derived nominal, or a noun without a verbal counterpart whose meaning nevertheless seems to put it in this category. A generalization which holds over all of these cases is that when the lefthand member is assigned an internal thematic role—typically whatever argument is normally assigned to the direct object of the verb from which the compound's head is derived—the main stress is on the lefthand member of the compound. The compound is therefore an N^0 by our assumptions.

Compounds with "agentive" heads. By these we mean, of course, examples such as the following, where in each case the lefthand member is interpreted as the internal argument of the verb from which the righthand member is morphologically derived via affixation of -*er*:

(7)   shock absorber, torch bearer, syntax checker, car dealer, grain exporter, fire extinguisher, lens grinder, door knocker, deer hunter, rocket launcher, steel maker, can opener, music publisher, paint remover, knife sharpener, opium taker, window washer

It is easy to find (or think of) hundreds of other natural and familiar-seeming examples. There are a number of cases where quite large sets of objects will go nicely with a particular head. In the cases in (8), X could quite plausibly be any one of thousands of things:

(8)   a. X maker: X = anvil, arrow, battery, bobbin, buckle, button, car, carriage, cheese ...

b. X supplier: X = asbestos, cable, copper, leather, lumber, paper, pipe, steel ...

c. X collector: X = art, book, car, clock, coin, mirror, pottery, stamp ...

There are relatively few values of X for which it might not, under some circumstances, be appropriate to speak of an X *maker*, an X *supplier*, or an X *collector*.

All of the above agentive compounds have lefthand main stress since their lefthand members function as internal arguments to the head. Needless to say, any agentive nominal that can occur alone, can also occur in constructions in which a preceding noun does not function as an object for the agentive's underlying predicate, but instead has one of the other sorts of relation possible in noun phrases. These constructions may show main stress on either member, depending on their nature:

(9) a. Left-dominant cases: ghost writer (does not write ghosts), baseball writer (does not write baseballs)

b. Right-dominant cases: Virginia creeper (does not creep Virginia), gas drier (does not dry gas), girl swimmer (does not swim girls)

This is expected given that agentive nouns are (after all) nouns, and should therefore be able to function like non-agentive nouns no matter what other properties they may have. So, parallel to *girl swimmer* there are other right-dominant N^1 constructions with appositive interpretations, such as *boy athlete*. Examples such as those in (9) cause problems for computational analysis, since it is often hard to be sure that an argument-predicate interpretation is wrong.

Agentive-headed argument-predicate compounds are not ordinarily well-formed if the left member is a measure noun or other pseudo-object. Nor is there normally any way to incorporate arguments whose expression normally requires a preposition or particle (though one finds a few examples like *city-dweller*, *church-goer* and *looker-upper*):

(10) *This meeting looks like a day-laster.
      *Smoking-stoppers tend to be irritable.
      *a water-looker-for
      *a for-water-looker
      *a water-looker

The lefthand member of agentive compounds may be modified in various ways, but it usually may not be quantified, usually may not be plural, and certainly may not have its own determiner or other noun phrase specifiers. Absence of determiners and other specifiers for modifiers is generally required in English, and this is a point we will take up again later. On its face, this suggests that the modifier for agentive nominals may be either N^0 or N^1, but no higher projection of N (and no projection of D) is allowed (see Fabb 1984):

(11)   a toxic waste dumper
    *a three dog owner
    *a dogs owner
    *a the Grand Canyon admirer

Compounds with gerunds as heads. English gerunds participate in a variety of constructions; in the one that concerns us here, a gerund is the head of a compound noun, whose lefthand member (usually) functions as the object:

(12)   cattle breeding, ale brewing, carpet cleaning, number crunching, cost cutting, tape dubbing

Note that these cases are sometimes difficult in practical contexts to distinguish from the phrasal *NP V-ing* construction and it is certainly not difficult to construct genuinely ambiguous examples:

(13)   The man eating shark was repulsive.

Sometimes an *-ing* nominal acquires an additional meaning that partly or entirely supersedes the act/process one; this meaning often denotes the result of the act or process—e.g., *dropping, building, writing*—or some materials or methods central to the process or action—*caulking*. Such cases do not usually form compounds of the type exemplified in (12), although (like all nouns) they participate freely in other sorts of compounding and modification. That is, a preceding noun will not serve as object if a gerund head is used in the "result" sense. Thus a *mouse dropping* is normally a dropping that comes from a mouse. If punk pilots adopted the practice of showering public gatherings with thousands of live mice, *mouse dropping* would be a natural way to refer to this unnatural act, but would not serve to denote its pitiful result, which we would have to call *dropped mice*.

As in the case of agentive-headed compounds, the argument-predicate compound constructions are typically ill-formed with pseudo-objects or with arguments expressed by means of prepositions:

(14)   *He is capable of day-waiting.
    *Cigarette-quitting is hard work.
    *Oil-drilling-for is chancy.

Argument-predicate compounds with derived nominals as heads. As is well known (see Chomsky 1970, Thomason 1985, Sproat 1985, Safir 1987, among many others), derived nominals can have meanings that relate to an act or process associated with the related verb, or to the cause, instrument, method, resulting state of such an act or process. The second type of meaning—result, etc.—seems more erratic, while the first type—act, process or event—is more regularly found and its gloss is more easily predicted. We will follow such previous work by distinguishing these two types of meanings as PROCESS NOMINALS and RESULT NOMINALS.

In a compound noun headed by a process-nominal, the left member may correspond to a noun phrase in various syntactic relations with the related verb:

(15) a. Subject: cell division, commando raid, sunrise, police action, snake bite, proton decay, ether drift, moon glow

  b. Object: nest construction, dream analysis, haircut, birth control, dress design, steel production, office management, heart massage, heat regulation, trash collection

The subject types often have (though clearly do not always have) right-dominant stress patterns:

(16) enemy invasion, police intervention, staff attempts, faculty decision, student inventions

Argument-predicate compounds without a deverbal head? There are many examples of [N N] compounds whose head is not deverbal (and indeed may not have any corresponding verb) but seem nevertheless to correspond semantically to a predicate that takes other nominal constituents as arguments. Such words seem to form compounds of the argument-predicate type. Sometimes there is a corresponding expression with a postnominal PP expressing the argument, and sometimes not:

(17) expert in ballistics   ballistics expert
  critic of music   music critic
  format of data   data format
  department of chemistry   chemistry department
  ?broker of commodities   commodities broker
  *buff of opera   opera buff
  *thief of cars   car thief

Of course, as we shall see in Section 2.4, the range of argument-argument compounds is so broad that it is hard to be sure that examples such as those in (17) are not included in it.

Compounds whose left member is _self_. Compounds headed by agentives and derived nominals can freely occur with the word _self_ as lefthand member. In all cases, the normal stress pattern is right dominant, for the same reasons—presumably FCA reasons—that reflexive pronouns are generally deaccented in phrasal contexts. Compounds headed by _V+ing_ nominals do not so easily take _self_ as a left member, although the corresponding compound adjectives are common:

(18) self-starter, self-promotion, self-igniting

2.4 Argument-Argument N^0 Compounds

We now turn to N^0 compounds where a paraphrase links the two words in the compound with a predicate not implicit in either one. We are limiting this category to endocentric compounds, so that their English paraphrase will be something like 'an *N1 N2* is an N2 *relative-clause-containing-N1*, e.g., 'an *ankle bracelet* is a bracelet that is worn on the ankle,' or '*rubbing alcohol* is alcohol that is used for rubbing'. The range of predicates implied by such paraphrases is very large. Since this type of compound-formation can be used for new coinages, any particular compound will in principle be multiply ambiguous (or vague) among a set of possible predicates.

Consider *hair oil* versus *olive oil*. Ordinarily, *hair oil* is oil for use on hair, and *olive oil* is oil derived from olives. But if the world were a different way, *olive oil* might be a petroleum derivative used to shine olives for added consumer appeal, and *hair oil* might be a lubricant produced by recycling barbershop floor sweepings.

A coherent categorization is hard to find. In their everyday meanings, the compounds *olive oil* and *hair oil* resonate with many similar examples:

(19) a.   Like *olive oil*

pattern SOURCE-PLANT SUBSTANCE-THEREFROM-DERIVED				
peanut oil	sesame oil	safflower oil	soybean oil	corn oil
palm oil	cottonseed oil	corn syrup	bean paste	wheat bran
wheat flour	chickpea flour	rice flour	wheat bran	barley malt
corn starch	mango pulp	orange juice	lemon juice	apple juice
carnauba wax	guar gum	beet sugar	cane sugar	pine tar

       b.   Like *hair oil*

pattern BODY-PART SUBSTANCE-THEREON-USED				
hand cream	skin cream	face powder	foot powder	lip gloss
eye drops	nail polish	underarm deodorant	hairspray	toothpaste

Such broad resonances have been the driving force behind classificatory schemes for argument-argument compounds of the type most fully developed in Levi 1978. A practical problem, discussed by Downing (1977), is that the set of patterns that would be required to achieve complete coverage appears to be open ended.

A more fundamental problem is that there does not seem to be any non-arbitrary way to decide on a single, coherent categorization of such patterns. The *olive oil* type of pattern exemplified in (19a),

SOURCE-PLANT SUBSTANCE-THEREFROM-DERIVED

covers substances such as oil, flour, syrup, bran, juice and so on, which are extracted by a variety of methods, use various portions of the source plant, and so on. This much generalization seems unproblematic—almost everyone would agree that these examples are instances of a type. However, the set can be extended in many directions. Each extension seems natural, but the resulting set is less and less coherent. One set of extensions (20a)–(20c) gradually relaxes the limitation of N1 to particular plants, allowing for plants in general, to living things in general and finally to inanimate sources of materials; another (20d) allows N2 to be a count rather than a mass noun:

(20) a. *SOURCE-PLANT* is a more general category:
          fruit juice, vegetable oil, grain alcohol
      b. N1 is an animal:
          whale oil, fish oil, chicken fat, horse hair, goose down
      c. N1 is inanimate:
          rock dust, river water, bread crumbs
      d. N2 is a subpart that can be extracted or removed rather than a derived substance:
          peach pit, chicken wing, rose petal, pine cone, coca leaf, corn cob, fish scale, corn husk, peanut shell

Plausibly, a general pattern to cover all the cases in (20) and the

> *SOURCE-PLANT SUBSTANCE-THEREFROM-DERIVED*

instances in (19) would be

> *SOURCE SUBSTANCE-OR-PIECE-WHICH-COMES-FROM-SOURCE*,

in which *COMES-FROM* includes derivation of a "new" substance by pressing, grinding, and so forth, of the source, and also by separation of a part from the whole.

Now consider the common cases where N1 is the whole of which N2 is a part:

(21) tire rim, mountain peak, arrow head, door knob, bed post, piano keys, shirt sleeve, table leg

These examples certainly are analogous to *peanut shell* or or *fish scale*, since both fit the rough schema **N2 is part of N1**. The examples like *olive oil*, in turn, are analogous to *peanut shell*, since both fit the pattern *N2 comes from N1*. But it seems less plausible that *olive oil* and *mountain peak* are in the same category. Each example, taken as a nucleus of generalization, yields several sets with which it shares some properties, but which may not share any properties with one another. A related example will give us new sets of neighbors, which overlap with the previous sets but are not exactly the same. Because of arguments like this, we doubt that an approach such as that proposed in Levi 1978 can be coherently and systematically pursued.

The 'connected-with' theory. As several writers have noted—e.g.; Dowty (1979)—the facts are consistent with a linguistic rule of argument-argument compounding that contributes only a vague 'connected-with' predicate, the more specific meanings arising from lexicalization and from the usual contextual circumscription of linguistically vague expressions. On this view, there is no well-defined hierarchical categorization of such examples, since a given form may have analogical connections in many directions.

Thus the core meaning of *olive oil* would be something like 'oil connected with olives', and *hair oil* would be 'oil connected with hair'. In the case of these particular expressions, it is likely that their more specific meanings should be lexically listed. Novel cases—e.g., *thistle oil* or *moustache oil*—cannot get more specific meanings from a direct dictionary entry, but they can get a predisposition to go in one direction or another from analogy with the patterns in (19), the meanings of their component words, and common sense.

Words and fixed phrases easily acquire special meanings; utterances are always interpreted in context; and analogy with fixed expressions is a powerful determinant of everyday phraseology. So the mechanisms required by the connected-with theory are in any case available. By the nature of this theory, it cannot be disproved by positive examples, since (by some argument or another) it licenses any compound in any meaning. To show that this theory is wrong, we must show that some meaning relations are systematically excluded, and that some alternative hypothesis will distinguish those that occur from those that don't. This is nearly impossible to do without a precise account of such meaning relations,[6] which no one can at present provide.

A survey of argument-argument compounds. Our task is to distinguish the $[N\ N]$ constructions with lefthand stress (N^0) from those with righthand (N^1) stress. Since the part-of-speech categories give us no help, any successful algorithm must rely in part on the semantic relationship between the words. The argument-predicate compounds previously considered were nearly all left-dominant. In this section, we will survey some common types of argument-argument compounds, limiting consideration to examples that are also left-dominant. After right-dominant expressions of form $[N\ N]$ have been treated in a later section, we will discuss possible sources of the distinction.

Since any $[N\ N]$ form could in principle have many meanings, we have chosen examples that rely on the existence of a meaning that is frozen through common use, that is implied by common sense given the word meanings, or that is strongly preferred due to the existence of a "schema" emerging from the analogical force of many related forms. It is an open question if such schemata achieve the technical status of linguistic "constructions" or formation rules, whether of morphology, syntax, or semantics. In practice, new instances of such compounds may usually be coined freely, whether by analogy or by rule. We divide the cases into categories that are designed mainly for expository convenience, and that are definitely far from complete. Fudge 1984 contains discussion of some of these classes.

---

[6]Though see Downing 1977 for some discussion.

(22) pattern *ELEMENT-IN-CAUSAL-CHAIN RESULT*:
      drug deaths, heat rash, job tension, snow blindness, food poisoning,
      hay fever, tire track

For some reason, the head nouns in the pattern in (22) are usually negative in connotation. Persuasive examples with positive heads are hard to
construct, and are generally right dominant, as in the example *for your
listening pleasure*.

(23) pattern *TYPICAL-RESULT-OR-PRODUCT ELEMENT-IN-CAUSAL-
      CHAIN*:
      disease germ, polio virus, growth hormone, honey bee, silkworm,
      song bird, oil well, sob story

(24) pattern *SUBTYPE TYPE*:
      a. N1 a name, N2 virtually redundant (hence the construction is
         almost exocentric):
         pine tree, cactus plant, collie dog, lilac bush, ivy vine
      b. N1 specifies species or type:
         preacher man, tree shrew, girlfriend, man servant, sports activ-
         ities, tape measure, soldier ant

Note that *polio virus* is like *pine tree*, in that N2 is a generic biological
classifier and N1 is a name for a particular type; however, a polio virus
causes polio but is not a polio, while a pine tree does not cause pine, but
is a pine.

(25) pattern *N1 THING-MADE-OUT-OF-N1*:
      daisy chain, cable network, mountain range, grape arbor, chocolate
      bar, snowball, sugar cube (but cf. (68))

(26) pattern *POWER-SOURCE MECHANISM*:
      steam engine, water wheel, vacuum cleaner, air brake, cable car (but
      cf. (75))

(27) pattern *INSTRUMENT ACTION* or *INSTRUMENT RESULT*
      head butt, sword thrust, tank attack, knife wound, pot roast, pan
      fries, shovel cakes (but cf. (75))

(28) a. pattern *PLACE-WHERE-N2-IS-FOUND N2*:
         field mouse, mountain lion, desert rat, sea cruise, surface tension,
         farm boy, marsh gas, field trial, pond scum, house fly, street cop,
         city folk, alley cat
      b. pattern *TIME-WHEN-N2-OCCURS N2*:
         morning sickness, night blindness, Easter bunny, birthday party,
         Christmas present, morning coat, Sunday school (but cf. (70))

(29) pattern *N1 SOMETHING-WITH-PURPOSE-ASSOCIATED-WITH-N1*:
      horse doctor, nose drops, fly paper, test pattern, cooking utensils,
      arms budget, plant food, face towel
      (This is a large and diverse set that could be further subdivided.)

(30) a. pattern *THING-CONTAINED CONTAINER*:
picture book, photo album, gunboat, bear country
b. pattern *CONTENTS CONTAINER*:
parts bin, gin bottle, butter dish, olive jar, milk can, juice glass, garbage can, water bucket, stock drawer, linen closet, coffee mug, laundry basket, punch bowl, water tumbler, oil tank
c. pattern *N1 SHELTER-OR-TRANSPORTATION-FOR-N1*:
dog kennel, horse barn, cow shed, guest room, hay loft, corn crib, grain elevator, hay wagon

(31) pattern *SUBJECT-MATTER THING-FOR-WHICH-SUBJECT-MATTER-IS-RELEVANT*: tax law, abortion vote, budget debate, adventure story, love song, detective novel, oil crisis

(32) pattern *N1 THING-LIKE-N1*:
catfish, dragonfly, hermit crab, spider monkey, garter snake, kettledrum, frogman, cat burglar

Types and subtypes could be multiplied. For the reasons that we gave earlier, the categories are not disjoint and do not have sharp boundaries.

2.5 Compound Nouns whose Heads are not Nouns

English can also make compound nouns from various combinations of verbs, prepositions and nouns; see, for example, Selkirk 1982. Almost always, the stress pattern of these constructions is left-dominant. Also, most are written with a hyphen or as a single typographical word. These cases mostly fall outside the topic of this paper, but we list them briefly for completeness.

Phrasal verbs (verbs that combine with a "particle" or intransitive preposition) are nominalized freely. Common examples often have an idiosyncratic meaning:

(33) fall-away, run-away, throw-away, tear-away, slow-down, melt-down, come-down, splash-down, walk-out

Prepositions can also combine with verbs in the opposite order, although this type of combination is less productive:

(34) downdraft, downfall, downpour, downturn, downtrend, outburst, outbreak, outcast, outlook, outreach

Erratically, a verb may combine with a noun to form a noun. One [*V N*] pattern produces an exocentric compound whose referent is the (unexpressed) subject. This type is common in Romance languages but not in Germanic ones. It is no longer very productive in English, although it seems to have been popular in earlier times:[7]

---

[7]Marchand (1969, pp. 37–39) makes the interesting observation that such constructions are almost invariably pejorative, which seems to be true of the examples in (35) with the exception of *dreadnought*, which might explain its tendency to be less well-known.

(35) cut-throat, pick-pocket, pinch-penny, do-nothing, kill-joy, know-nothing, dreadnought, sawbones

A second [V N] compound type is endocentric (that is, the referent is identified with the head noun). The semantic relation between the verb and the head noun is quite varied. Furthermore, it is often difficult to be sure that the lefthand member is indeed a verb and not the homophonous noun. New examples of this type of compound are frequently coined, but not all attempts are plausible. Thus a punch intended to stun might be called a *stun punch*, but a remark intended to offend could not be called an *offend remark*:

(36) searchlight, dancehall, springboard, workbench, grindstone, plaything, push pin, stuff bag, dive plane, trim tab, thrust plate, stab wound, snap bean, pitchfork, stun gun, hit man, push rod, lock washer

2.6 Compounds with Complex Parts, and the Compound Stress Rule

We have discussed binary nominals which are syntactically N^0 and which are therefore assigned lefthand stress. We now wish to consider the stress properties of N^0 constructions which have more than two leaf nodes. It is common to find compounds made up of subconstituents with internal structure. When the first member is itself a noun compound, and the second member is lexically simple, we generally find stress on the left:

(37) Air Force Academy, football game, money-market account, post-office box, data acquisition board, flashlight battery, X-ray film, bit vector machine, fund-raising operations

In each of the examples in (37), a compound noun is combined with another noun on its right, in a second level of compounding. In the result, the main stress is typically on the leftmost element. Sometimes, we find another recursion on the same pattern, in which a doubly compound lefthand member is further compounded with a single word after it. These are mercifully rare:

(38) water supply network repairs, windshield wiper blade replacement, error correction code logic

It is also possible to combine a noun on the left with a compound noun on the right, in a right-branching structure. These are perhaps slightly less common than the comparable left-branching structures shown in (37).[8] They often occur with a compound lefthand member as well:

(39) radio direction finder, spark-plug heat range, sink spray head, VAX instruction set

---

[8]For Swedish, Blåberg (1988, p. 68) claims that the right branching structure is significantly less common than the left branching structure in ternary nominals.

In such constructions, the primary stress is typically found on the penulti-
mate member. In general, for a noun compound [*N1 N2*], if N2 is not itself
a compound, then it will give up its claim to main stress in favor of N1.
However, if N2 is a compound, then it will retain main stress within itself.
This rule was called the COMPOUND STRESS RULE (CSR) in Chomsky and
Halle 1968; we shall also use the traditional term NUCLEAR STRESS RULE
(NSR) to refer to "phrasal" or righthand stress.

Liberman and Prince (1977) suggested that this rule was the same one
that assigns main stress in nouns in general. As they observed, the righthand element of a noun is stress-dominant if and only if it branches, where
the nodes of the relevant tree are words in the case of compound nouns,
and syllables or feet in the case of simple nouns. Hayes (1980) suggested
that this regularity should be recast as a simple final-stress rule, with the
rightmost unit ignored (extrametrical) in the case of nouns. Again, one
(simple) word is ignored in the case of compounds, and one syllable in the
case of simple nouns. Under any formulation, the rule may be applied recursively to generate patterns of stress. (The effects of the so-called RHYTHM
RULE, which shifts some non-final stress relations in order to create a more
regularly alternating pattern, must also be taken into account.)

Across many types of noun sequences, the predictions of the CSR are
fairly well verified. In (40) we give a set of typical examples containing
four or more nouns, with the contextually implied grouping indicated by
parentheses. The reader is invited to consider the predictions of the CSR,
and compare them to his or her own intuitions about how the examples
should be read:

(40) a. [[starter [drive gear]] clearance]
      b. [[[gear selector] [control rod]] adjustment]
      c. [[[power generating] station] [[control room] complex]]
      d. [government [[tobacco [price support]] program]]

We note in passing that the CSR's determination of main stress position
underdetermines the phrase structure in such cases—for instance, the pairs
of structures shown below yield the same main stress location (marked in
boldface) in each case:

(41) [A [[**B** C] D]]   [[A [**B** C]] D]
      [A [B [**C** D]]]   [[A B] [**C** D]]

Due to the semantically protean nature of the compound construction,
it is also not always clear what the structure of complex compounds is.
Thus *tobacco price supports* might be *price supports* for *tobacco*, or (almost
equivalently) *supports* for *tobacco prices*. Putting the main accent on *price*
(which seems to be most people's preference) settles the matter in favor of
the first option. The example *government tobacco price support program*,
however, might be either [*government* [[*tobacco* [*price support*] *program*]]]
or [[*government* [*tobacco* [*price support*]] *program*]], without any effect on

the main stress location. Of course, the situation is usually much clearer. In the context of use from which we took it, the parsing of *starter drive gear clearance* is unambiguous.

Having now considered some of the types of N^0 $[N\ N]$ constructions in English, and further elaborating on the stress facts for such constructions which have more than two leaf nodes, we return to the examination of binary modifier-noun constructions.

2.7 Adjective-Noun Expressions

The canonical sequence $[A\ N]$ differs from $[N\ N]$ in that its parent is N^1 rather than N^0. Usually an $[A\ N]$ sequence takes main stress on the right, in contrast to the left-stressed pattern of the $[N\ N]$ sequences in (6):

(42)   clear advantage, miserable bastard, comfortable chair, small difficulty, bitter end, special feature, ample girth, heavy heart, complete idiot, last judgment, fluorescent lamp, slender margin, arrant nonsense, smooth operation, wonderful person, stupid question, hasty retreat, great skill, worthless trash, enriched uranium, macroscopic Volvox, useful widgets, rare yak, melodious zither

2.8 An Explanation for the Basic Pattern

The High Road of Phrasal Stress is: CSR in $[N\ N]$, NSR in $[A\ N]$. Syntactic category is a very good predictor of stress patterns for $[A\ N]$, and a fairly good predictor for $[N\ N]$. Given this observation, the simplest account would appear to be one which derives stress placement from some syntactic property of the construction. The account we have been assuming wherein CSR applies in N^0 constructions and NSR in N^1 constructions, is just such an account. To be sure, there are complications with this story. One complication is that we must assume that exceptions to the general pattern, to which we turn in the next section, are exceptional from a syntactic rather than purely from a prosodic point of view. However, as we shall see, the alternatives to this assumption seem even less attractive.

3 Exceptions to the "Standard Pattern"

We will present a catalog of exceptions to the High Road to Phrasal Stress, with some commentary on its meaning.

3.1 Left-dominant $[A\ N]$ Sequences

Lexicalized $[A\ N]$ sequences. Some of the left-stressed $[A\ N]$ cases are apparently lexically re-analyzed as nouns—i.e., as N^0. Some of these are written as a single word, or separated by a hyphen rather than a space; as with $[N\ N]$ compounds, the typographical conventions are variable. Some of these cases are metonymic epithets[9]—*hardhat, red neck*—but many are not:

---

[9]Often known as *bahuvrihi compounds*, after the traditional Sanskrit terminology.

(43)   square knot, soft spot, sticky bun, wild man, tonic water, pink slip, red line, black belt, blue book, golden boy, cold chisel, blind spot, sweet spot, dry dock, straight edge, whitewash, clean room

Examples like those in (44) below, which take the usual NSR pattern (unless contrast or whatever intervenes), show that the CSR does not automatically apply to fixed expressions of the form $[A \ N]$, even if their meanings are partly or entirely idiosyncratic:

(44)   white lead, red oak, green onions, brown sugar, Irish stew, hard liquor, red herring, brown betty, blue moon, black death, musical chairs, crazy eights, heavy metal, old maid

In order to attribute the stress pattern difference to the parent category, we must accept that the expressions in (43) are complex words of category N^0, while those in (44) are fixed expressions or semantically idiosyncratic phrases of category N^1. The alternative, however, is to add some feature like [±CSR] to the lexical entries of phrases.

For a few phrases of this type—indeed, for nominals of almost any type—some speakers have lefthand stress while others have righthand stress or can say the phrase either way. This demonstrates that any description must make it possible to effectively specify the stress pattern of such phrases without changing their meaning very much. However, there are a number of subregularities suggesting that the stress pattern in these examples should normally be determined from the parent category, so that the left-dominant expressions will be of category N^0, while the right-dominant ones will (mostly) be of category N^1. In particular, constructions for which it is reasonable to assume an N^0 analysis in the general case also tend to be pronounced with the stress predicted by the CSR. For example, $[A \ N]$ sequences that are adopted as epithets (vocative or otherwise) tend to acquire compound-type stress, even if the same phrase can easily also be used as a normal phrase with righthand stress:

(45)

Epithet context	Non Epithet context
Hey, **big** mouth!	You've got a big **mouth**.
Hey, **fat** head!	You've got a fat **head**.
No more Mr. **Nice** Guy!	You're really a nice **guy**

A reasonable analysis of such cases, it seems to us, is that epithet-formation involves turning a phrase into a word—an N^0—and that it is this fact alone which accounts for the typical accentual pattern of such phrases.

Brand names, place names and plant or animal names with $[A \ N]$ structure also have quite a strong tendency to develop lefthand stress. This tendency is especially pronounced for metonymic names, but many others show it as well:

(46)   a. Long Beach, Hungry Horse, Red Wing, Old Town

b. Big Boy, Redbook, Green Stamps, Pure Aire, Smooth Pore, Kleen Flex, Ful Flo, Final Air, Dri-Pak, Hi-Flo, E Z Kleen, Tiny C, Soft Cote, Common Lisp, Rite Aid

c. yellowtail, bluefin, bluebird, blackbird, redwood, yellowjacket, bluebell, bluefish, redfish

Again, it is reasonable to assume that in the general case, such terms have become lexicalized and re-analyzed as N^0, and that this fact accounts for their accentual patterns.

Right-dominance is normal, however, in plant and animal names that are semi-compositional; that is, where the righthand element is a class name such as *oak* and the lefthand element is a descriptive adjective such as *red*. By our analysis, such cases would have to be analyzed as N^1. This pattern generally requires a head of some specificity, such as *leek* or *eagle*—more general heads such as *fish* or *bird* are more likely to be found in the class (46):

(47)   red oak, curly dock, wild leek, bushy aster, common flax, bald eagle, American coot, spotted rail

Some place names seem also to be semi-compositional, in this sense:

(48)   Big Bend, American Falls

Finally, although most [A N] brand names are left-dominant, as exemplified in (46), a few are right-dominant. Many of these have polysyllabic righthand members; a few may be considered semi-compositional:

(49)   Orange Julius, Best Western, Dutch Masters, Big Mac, Leading Edge, Silver Cloud

We suggest that the nominals that we are calling "semi-compositional" retain their N^1 structure, despite becoming a fixed expression with a special meaning.

What is lexicalization? Note that not all lexicalized two-word nominals wind up with left-word main stress. In connection with the issue under discussion, there are in principle three types of lexicalization that a phrase can undergo.

First, a phrase may acquire a special meaning or association that requires it to be listed in a phrasal lexicon of some sort (see Di Sciullo and Williams 1987). Thus the compositional meaning of some topical phrase, say *mutually assured destruction* or *album-oriented rock*, is not enough to pin down the extra associations or technical meanings that it has acquired. Under the present analysis, however, the fact that these phrases are normally given phrasal stress means that they must be (minimally) N^1.

Second, a phrase may be treated as dominated by a lexical category, although presumably retaining its internal structure, or at least its divisions into words.

Finally, a former phrase may loose some or all of its internal structure as well as becoming a lexical category. There is no question that this long ago happened to *Worcester* on its way to being pronounced as if it were written <wuster>. A more current example is *high school*. One of the authors speaks a dialect that raises and fronts the diphthong [ai] when it precedes a voiceless consonant within the same word, so that the vowel in *fife* is quite different from the vowel in *five*. This raising applies obligatorily to the first vowel in *high school*, but not typically to the first vowels of, say, *fly paper* or *pie plate*, suggesting that the common word *high school* has lost its internal word boundary.

There is an interesting twist to this account which we merely mention here. As we have noted, the normal rules of English word stress, for nouns without internal word-level structure, say roughly to put the main word stress on the last non-final heavy syllable. Thus for an (originally) two-word phrase whose second word has at least one post-tonic syllable, the stress pattern predicted for the third stage of lexicalization, in which the internal word boundary is lost, is in effect, main stress on the second word. So if, for example, *red herring* were a noun without internal word boundaries, its main stress location would be the same as if it were a noun phrase. The preponderance of monosyllabic or final-stressed head words in (46), and of trochaic head words in (49), suggests that these lexicalized [A N] sequences may generally lack internal word-level structure, at least for purposes of stress assignment. That is, one can readily explain the distribution of stress patterns most simply by considering such cases to belong to the third stage of lexicalization outlined above.

Adjectives as substantives in [A N] "compounds." In other cases, left-dominant [A N] sequences seem perhaps to involve an adjective used as a substantive; see Levi 1978 for further discussion:

(50)   athletic facilities, circulatory system, regulatory agency, electrical tape, erogenous zone, legal work, medical department, primary school, professional organization, solar system, tidal zone

All these are plausibly instances of productive patterns, in which a variety of other adjectives and nouns can occur in the lefthand position, with similar meaning. In some cases—e.g., *professional*—the adjectival form can also be used as a substantive, but often there is no common independently-usable substantive—e.g. *legal*, or the independent substantive has a different meaning—e.g., *primary*. Thus we cannot claim that the lefthand member of the examples in (50) is a true, independent substantive—a noun that happens to look like an adjective. However, the semantic connection between the two words in these examples seems similar to the relations that apply in analogous [N N] examples with left-dominant stress. So, the phrase *medical building* is essentially parallel to *chemistry building* or *office building*, except that 'medical stuff' has to be understood for *medical*.

Presumably the word *medicine* is avoided because of the confusion with the kind of medicine that comes in bottles.

The inadequacy of "implicit contrast": further arguments against FCA-only theories. We might try to explain left-stressed examples like those in (50) in terms of an "implicit contrast" between the modifier and its alternatives. This idea has no predictive value: there is no greater amount of "implicit contrast" in **legal** *work* than there is in *left* **lane**. To use the phrase *left lane* almost surely implies the alternatives *right* and *center*, and yet the main stress still falls on the second word. Here are some other examples of normally right-dominant [A N] sequences where the adjective is in "implicit contrast" with a small set of known alternatives:

(51)   silver medal, heavy crude, young man, big business, large family, fresh bread

Without a definition of "implicit contrast" that can distinguish between the examples in (50) and those in (51), such explanations must be rejected as vacuous.

In some of the examples in (50) the head noun is a relatively empty one, so that one might appeal to some sort of redundancy-triggered deaccentuation. However, other [A N] expressions, with head nouns that seem equally empty, work more normally (i.e., by the NSR). In (52) we have tried to use heads that are both general and common, yet in all of these examples the primary stress falls on the righthand member:

(52)   an enormous area, a nice person, a special place, a funny thing, a strange man, a loathsome object, the thirteenth time

Again, without a definition of "redundant head" that can distinguish (50) from (52), this account must also be considered to have no predictive value.

Conclusions about the left-dominant [A N] cases. So, we are left with two fairly clear patterns and some unanswered questions about them. There is clearly a pattern of adjectives-masquerading-as-substantives forming [N N]-like compounds with nominal heads, as in (50). There also seems to be a pattern of [A N] sequences becoming single words, and acquiring the stress patterns thus predicted, as shown by the examples in (46) and (45), and presumably the examples in (43).

What determines the set of adjectives that can be used as quasi-substantives? It is surely not a random choice. Why is the substantival usage often (not always) restricted to attributive position? Why do the examples with monosyllabic heads in (44), such as *Big Ben, blue moon, hard times*, fail to "collapse" into the single noun stress pattern along with *Big Foot, blue bird, hard ball*, and all the others? In order to make progress with these questions we probably need a substantial fragment of the relevant "phrasal lexicon," giving us a large enough list of examples to be able to see patterns and test predictions.

We have motivated a distinction between "semantic" lexicalization (that is, a fixed expression with a non-compositional meaning) and "syntactic" lexicalization (that is, a fixed expression that is stressed as if its parent category was N^0 rather than N^1). It appears that the second implies the first, but not vice versa. Finally, we have distinguished the category of "morphophonemic lexicalization," in which a lexicalized compound word loses its internal word structure, and becomes subject to phonological and phonetic processes that would ordinarily only apply word-internally. We assume that this can only happen to expressions that are already syntactically lexicalized. We have also suggested that many of the lexicalized [A N] sequences, discounting the cases discussed above where the adjective is functioning as a noun, may fall into this third category, though it may be difficult in particular cases to distinguish between this possibility, and the possibility that the case in question really belongs to the semantic or syntactic lexicalization class.

3.2 Some Other Left-dominant Phrasal Units

Besides the atypical [A N] units just discussed, there are a few other cases of non-[N N] noun phrase structures that are left-dominant. We survey them below.

Compound-like cases with possessives as left member. Sometimes a phrase of the form [N's N] or [[N N's N] regularly prefers stress on the first member, although such phrases normally are stressed by the NSR:

(53)   cashier's check, bachelor's degree, servant's entrance, pig's feet, ram's horn, chef's knife, lubber's line, user's manual, goat's milk, bosun's chair, machinists' union, sheep's wool, auto workers' union, meat cutters' union, bull's eye, crow's nest

A familiar set of accounts are available here: lexicalization; implicit contrast of the left constituent; low information content for the right constituent. As in the case of left-dominant [A N]] expressions, all of these accounts have predictive problems.

Thus, although many of the expressions in (53) are semantically lexicalized, there are other fixed or idiomatic [N's N] expressions that are nevertheless right dominant:

(54)   pope's nose, cat's pajamas, fool's errand, busman's holiday, blind man's buff, Zipf's Law

So, as outlined for the [A N] examples discussed above, lexicalization in and of itself does not predict N^0 status.

Still, there is some evidence that lexicalization has a part in such examples: again [N's N] epithets are often left-dominant (though one of the authors has righthand stress in *horse's ass*) as are brand names, idiomatic plant names, etc.:

(55)   a. momma's boy, cat's paw, dog's body

  b. Boar's Head, Bird's Eye, Woman's Day

  c. Bachelor's-button, Baby's-breath, Lady's-slipper, Solomon's-seal, Shepherd's-purse, Dutchman's-pipe, Prince's-feather, Tinker's-weed, Lamb's-quarters, Goat's-rue, Lion's-foot, Virgin's-bower

It is interesting that metaphorically descriptive names, such as those in (55c), are inevitably left dominant, while a right-dominant treatment is given to species names in which the discoverer's name possessively particularizes the name of the larger class. These cases are identical in spirit to the "semi-compositional" [A N] names surveyed in (47):

(56) Swainson's thrush, Lincoln's sparrow, Kirtland's warbler, Catesby's Trillium

The parent node of left-dominant possessives. The possessives in left-dominant [N's N] expressions have the distributional properties of position 1 modifiers: certainly, at least, they can be preceded by articles, quantifiers, adjectives, and nominal modifiers. This is in striking contrast to the evidence supporting the view that possessive phrases normally occupy the same peripheral determiner position as articles and demonstratives—what we called position 4 in (1):

(57) a. the fresh mare's milk

  b. 16 Unix user's manuals

  c. a physics master's degree

  d.*the red Sam's car

  e.*16 well-thumbed Knuth's books.

Since *Unix manual* and *physics degree* are ordinarily left-dominant, examples like (57b) and (57c) suggest position 1 as opposed to position 2 status for *Unix* and *physics*, respectively, and from this we conclude that *user's* and *master's* must also occupy position 1.

The possessive phrases in (56) pattern more like position 2 elements than like normal possessives, occurring inside position 3 and other position 4 elements:

(58) a. the three Catesby's Trilliums

  b. yesterday's innumerable Swainson's thrushes

We have not found any convincing examples to suggest that these right-dominant possessives, as opposed to the left-dominant ones, can occur inside position 1 modifiers. Some of the other right-dominant lexicalized [N's N] expression are similarly distributed:

(59) the coveted pope's nose, an obvious fool's errand

These striking distributional differences make it reasonable to treat lexicalized possessive phrases as having a different parent category from normal possessive phrases. The most plausible candidates seem to be N^0 for the left-stressed cases and N^1 for the right-stressed cases.

Implicit contrast in left-dominant possessives? In many of the expressions in (53), the possessive is in some sense implicitly contrastive; thus *lamb's wool* may be distinguished from the wool of sheep, goats, or whatever. However, the same thing may be said of nearly any [*N's N*] construction. In the film title *The President's Analyst*, the expression might be said to distinguish the President's analyst from the analyst associated with anyone else, but the expression is stressed on the final word. The same can be said for any of the right-dominant possessive phrases in (54) or (56). Thus the "implicit contrast" treatment of these expressions has no predictive value, nor any apparent descriptive appropriateness, and should be rejected as a general explanation.

Left-dominant [*N PP*] expressions. There are a fair number of compound-like *N PP* words that take main stress on the lefthand element:

(60) jack-in-the-box, brother-in-law, mother-in-law, free-for-all, hole-in-the-wall, good-for-nothing, stick-in-the-mud, snake-in-the-grass

These cases are probably related to the general tendency of NP-locative sequences to deaccent the locative phrases, regardless of whether or not the phrase is idiomatic, and of whether the locative is a modifier of the preceding *NP* or an adjunct of an earlier verb:

(61) a. Here's **mud** in your eye.
  b. He's got a **bee** in his bonnet.
  c. He's got a **chip** on his shoulder.
  d. I've got a **spot** on my shirt.
  e. There's a multi-legged **creature** on your shoulder.

However, many fixed or idiomatic expressions of the form *N PP* (or perhaps *NP PP*) take righthand stress:

(62) man of the world, bolt from the blue, chip off the old block, drop in the bucket, grant-in-aid, jack of all trades, king of the hill, man in the moon, man o' war, manna from heaven, pie in the sky, piece of cake, tug of war, word of mouth

Again, epithets seem disposed to be left-dominant:

(63) Little Miss Nose-in-the-air, Mr. Full-of-fun, light-of-my-life

Other cases. Occasionally a verb phrase or similar collocation takes on an idiomatic nominal meaning, along with main stress on its leftmost word. These examples are probably related to the cases in (35):

(64) forget-me-not, thank-you-ma'am, know-it-all

However, most verb phrase nominalizations are right-dominant. Game names are a common source:

(65) spin the bottle, pin the tail on the donkey, squeak-piggy-squeak, go fish, beggar my neighbor, follow the leader, catch-me-if-you-can

Likewise most nominal uses of other phrasal constituents are right dominant:

(66) I spy, Simon says, odd man out

The kitchen sink: a potpourri of phrasal lefthand members. Here is as appropriate a place as any to note that in some informal styles, various phrasal categories can be freely used as prenominal modifiers, with an appropriately generic meaning. Verb and adjective phrases are particularly common. This usage permits free inclusion of pronouns, articles and other things that are usually forbidden in modifiers. Many such phrases—*top-of-the-line, hole-in-the-wall, turn-of-the-century*—are fixed expressions, but nonce formations do occur. Examples are extremely common in certain journalistic styles, from which the following examples are all taken.[10] Both left-dominant and right-dominant stress patterns occur in this group:

(67) an old-style white-shoe do-it-on-the-golf-course banker, the usual wait-until-next-year attitude, a wait-until-after-the-elections scenario, a kind of get-to-know-what's-going-on meeting place, the like-it-or-lump-it theory of public art, state-of-the-union address, a 24-hour-a-day job, a 1-percent-of-GNP guideline, a run-of-the-mill meeting, a sweep-it-under-the-rug amendment, a middle-of-the-road format, the state teacher-of-the-year title, a take-it-or-leave-it choice, the yet-to-be-written 1987 bill, a certain chip-on-the-shoulder attitude, make-it-from-scratch traditionalists, Speak-Mandarin-Not-Dialects Month, a rob-Peter-to-pay-Paul system, the nothing-left-to-chance approach, get-out-the-vote drives, the don't-trust-anybody-over-30 crowd, national clear-your-desk day

Such examples are quite consistent with our approach to predicting stress from structure in complex nominals, suggesting that both positions 1 and 2 may be occupied by elements projected from (nearly) any lexical category.

3.3 Right-dominant $[N\ N]$ Expressions

In the texts mentioned earlier in this paper, about 25% of the $[N\ N]$ phrases had main stress on the right, and essentially none of these had a plausible FCA account. We argue that these are instances of N^1.[11] In this section we outline some of the semantic relations which one finds in these cases[12]

Noun modifiers expressing composition. Some right-dominant $[N1\ N2]$ sequences are of a familiar type that means something like 'N2 made of N1', 'N2 made with N1', or 'N2 with N1 as a featured part':

(68) pattern $N1$ THING-MADE-OUT-OF-$N1$:
      rubber boots, steel plate, duck soup, gold medal, corduroy suit, brass

---

[10]Lieber (1988, 1992) also discusses examples of this kind, arguing that one needs to allow phrasal entities inside compounds in the general case.

[11]Again this is a traditional position: see Bauer 1983, pp. 104–108 for a discussion.

[12]See Fudge 1984 for a discussion of some of these classes.

bed, diamond ring, nylon rope, plaster cast, wax figure, asbestos tile, meat pie, chicken gumbo, wood floor, mushroom omelet, carrot halvah, rice pudding, apricot jam, corn tortillas, squash pie, beef burrito

In some cases of common words, 'made with N1' [*N1 N2*] sequences revert to lefthand stress, presumably due to lexicalization of the same type that is involved in (43); one may refer back to (25) for some examples, or consider:

(69)   banana bread, rye bread, peanut butter, corn chips, potato chips, butter cookies, oatmeal cookies, orange juice, coconut milk, aspirin tablet, chocolate bar, chocolate milk, cornstarch, silverware

As expected if lexicalization is at issue, there are many individual differences in this area; some people say *peanut bu' tter* in place of *pea' nut butter*, while others have *potato sa' lad* in place of *pota' to salad*, *chocolate mi' lk* in place of *cho' colate milk*, etc.

In (69), note the prevalence of left-dominance in the *cookie* and *bread*-head cases, even for new coinages like *zucchini bread* or *cinnamon cookies* (the latter for one of the authors only), and compare this pattern to the results of combining the same modifiers with the head *pie*. The left-dominance of bread terms even extends to some forms with adjective modifiers, such as *sticky bun* and *hard roll*. These cases, in which a particular head word has a more-or-less strong affinity for a particular stress pattern, are similar to the familiar case of *Street* versus *Avenue*, discussed below.

Time, place, class, etc. In other cases, N1 is a time or place, loosely defined:

(70)   a.   pattern PLACE-WHERE-N2-IS-FOUND N2:
            garage door, basement walls, attic roof, kitchen sink, cell window, pantry shelf, library curtains, bedroom furniture, cell membrane, mountain pass, valley floor, college president, city employee
       b.   pattern TIME-WHEN-N2-OCCURS N2:
            summer palace, fall weather, winter carnival, summer sausage, autumn leaves, spring flowers, winter cold, spring cleaning, September morning, January thaw, Christmas dinner

Proper name modifiers. Closely related are the cases in which a proper name is used as a modifier, to establish location, type, period, source, ownership, brand or whatever:

(71)   pattern PROPER-NAME THING
       Staten Island ferry, Connecticut Yankee, US ambassador, West Texas barbecue, Busch beer, Napoleon brandy, Pennsylvania crude, AT&T headquarters, India ink, Tiffany lamp, GB stronghold

Of course, full proper names go by the NSR, as do compound names for locations, other than those that end in *Street*, or *Land* such as those in (72c):

(72) a. George Washington, Barnacle Bill
      b. Newark Airport, Chesapeake Bay, Bryce Canyon, Park Drive, Baxter Estates, Niagara Falls, Strawberry Fields, Union Gap, Yosemite Lodge, Tuolumne Meadows, Adygei Autonomous Oblast, Abiathar Peak, Cat Mousam Road, Times Square, Sturbridge Village, Blue Jay Way
      c. Bank Street, Arnhem Land

Generally, names for institutions, organizations, and so forth, also go by the NSR, though there are exceptions (73b):

(73) a. Harvard College, Locksley Hall, Coolidge High, Bell Laboratories, Harvard Law, Widener Library, MIT Press, Bethlehem Steel, Stevens Tech, Yale University, Harvard Yard
      b. Dudley House

Measures, methods, media. Another case of right-dominant $[N\ N]$ phrases includes various sorts of measure-phrases in the N1 position:

(74) pattern MEASURE THING-MEASURED:
      mile run, pound note, gallon jug, pint jar, two-alarm chili, three dog night, four-man front, two-minute warning, eight-hour day, six-figure salary, fixed-length record, 12-gauge shotgun, three-day pass, three-minute egg

One apparent exception to this pattern is **minute** *steak*. However, the difference between the bulk of the examples in (74) and *minute steak* is that that the former are genuinely compositional instances of measure-phrase modification. That is, the lefthand material is measuring the head on an appropriate (if sometimes idiosyncratic) scale. So, a *mile run* is a run which is really a mile long, a *three-minute egg* takes three minutes to cook, *two-alarm chili* is placing the chili in question at a reasonably high point on a scale of potential gastric disturbance, and a *three dog night* gives a measure of the ambient temperature of the night in question using the number of dogs required to keep oneself warm as a metric. The term *minute steak*, however, does not mean that the steak in question takes one minute to cook, but merely that it cooks quickly.

Also, we have right-dominant $[N1\ N2]$ constructions with characteristic methods, media or energy-sources in the N1 position, although the behavior of this class is erratic; see left-dominant examples in (26) and (27):

(75) pattern METHOD-OR-MEDIA-FOR-N2 N2:
      bathtub gin, gas chromatograph, electron microscope, pinhole camera, gasoline engine, kerosene heater, propane torch, shotgun wedding, gunboat diplomacy, jet engine, steam radiator, microwave popcorn

Residual examples. Other examples of right-dominant [*N N*] phrases belong to patterns whose classification is not clear to us. We reproduce a list for illustrative purposes:

(76) fly ball, discount bookstore, dictionary definition, capital gains, weather helm, industry leader, color monitor, trial run, combination lock, sacrifice single, round-trip ticket, gospel truth, battleship grey, blood relative, tramp steamer, return ticket, precision tool, race suicide, eggshell china, fossil man, sex education, rogue elephant, touch football, ball bearing, fullback draw, championship series, party line, cash customer, child labor, chain reaction, touch typist, home run, string quartet, pony express, parcel post, police custody, polka-dot dress, box score, world bank, industry leader, crash course, crash landing, crack regiment, smash hit, snap judgment, bum rap, sponge rubber, college degree, shoestring tackle, bit part, barrier reef, toy gun

Some of these examples may follow the pattern *N2* IS-A-*N1*, which typically follow the NSR as discussed for (9b): *rogue elephant, fossil man, sponge rubber, toy gun.* Notice, incidentally, that *color monitor* is stressed one way if you mean 'monitor that shows color'—that is, the usual *Byte* magazine reading, and the other way if you mean 'device or circuit for monitoring colors'—say, a new improvement in TV set technology, also known as the *spectrum inspector.* In the second case, we have a clear argument-predicate compound.

Left-headed sequences. All of the examples of modified nominals (with the exception of *bahuvrihi* constructions) which we have discussed so far have had the nominal head on the right and the modifier(s) on the left, the normal ordering for English. However, there are some cases where it appears to be necessary to assume that the head of the construction is on the left and the modifier is on the right. We will assume that this is simply a marked option, though it is certainly true that adjectives in English may quite freely appear on the right of the noun they modify under appropriate conditions: *a man tall, dark and handsome* (see Bolinger 1967). In many of the examples we will see, the particular head in question is apparently marked to occur on the left. All of the leftheaded examples are stressed by the NSR, hence are N^1 under our analysis. For example, (77) below contains left-headed constructions where the righthand member is an identifying name or number:

(77) vitamin C, route 1, brand X, exit 14, peach Melba, steak diane, Cafe Beethoven, Club Med

So, while a *garage door* is a door, and a *company president* is a president, *vitamin C* is a vitamin, not a letter or a programming language, and *steak diane* is meat. The final examples in (77) are either borrowed from French, or at least modeled on French syntactic patterns, which are more single-mindedly left-headed than English ones. Note that food terms in particular are commonly (and productively) left-headed, and Romance influence is particularly likely in this domain: *beef Wellington, chicken cacciatori, lamb vindaloo, eggs benedict, bananas Foster*. Some of these may have questionable headedness: is *lamb vindaloo* a kind of vindaloo made with lamb, or is it a kind of lamb cooked with a vindaloo sauce?

As noted above, a number of these cases involve heads which seem simply to be marked to occur on the left: so if a new vitamin were discovered, and assigned the letter 'X', the vitamin would have to be called *vitamin X*, not **X vitamin*. Similarly, *exit 14* could not be called **14 exit*.

Further examples of constructions of that lean towards left-headedness, many of which instantiate productive patterns, are given below:

(78) pattern CLASSIFIER NAME:
Bayou Goula, Cape May, Chancellor Adenauer, Citizen Kane, Comrade Andropov, Dr. Smith, Fort Eustis, Key Largo, King George, Lake Erie, Lake Huron, Loch Ness, Mount Hood, planet Earth, widow Brown

The CLASSIFIER NAME pattern can be augmented as a class by the introduction of new titles borrowed from foreign languages, such as *Generalissimo Franco*, but it cannot be freely used for all classifiers, even for some that seem like minor variants of cases that work fine:

(79) *Pond Walden, *Hill Blue, *bride Smith

3.4 A Possible Reason for $N^1 [N\ N]$s: Is the nominal modifier an adjective?

Leaving the left-headed cases now, we now return to a possible explanation for the right-dominance of certain right-headed $[N\ N]$ compounds, namely the traditional notion that in such cases the lefthand noun is functioning as an adjective. For example, for the *N1* THING-MADE-OUT-OF-*N1* cases given in (68), we might postulate a null-affix derivational rule that makes adjectives out of nouns, since the usage usually generalizes to predicative patterns:

(80) The boots are rubber.
The plate is steel.
The medal is gold.
The suit is corduroy.
The bed is brass.

When the meaning is more like 'made with X as a relevant part', or whatever, the attributive noun cannot so felicitously be used in predicate position with its head as subject:

(81) ?The soup is duck.

And in the majority of the right-dominant $[N\ N]$ sequences we have surveyed, the predicative counterpart is totally implausible:

(82) *The ball is fly.
      *The jail is county.
      *The door is garage.
      *The membrane is cell.

All in all, the adjectival analysis of the lefthand noun in N^1 $[N\ N]$ constructions runs aground on the problem of limiting the distribution of the resulting adjectives. A more straightforward idea is simply to generate the nominal modifier in the same phrasal slot that an adjectival one would occupy; that is, in position 2 of (1), which we have identified as dominated by N^1. The stress and the meaning of the nominally modified phrase ought then to follow without further ado, if the rules of stress assignment and semantic interpretation are correctly arranged.

3.5   The Case of $[[A\ N]\ N]$

As is well known among aficionados of complex nominals, although occasionally ignored by other morphologists, one can combine an $[A\ N]$ unit with a nominal head in a semantic relation typical of a simple $[N\ N]$ compound with the same head. In such constructions, the main stress would typically fall on lefthand member, CSR style, as for most $[N\ N]$ compounds. Since the lefthand member itself is of the form $[A\ N]$, its internal stress pattern normally goes by the NSR, and the result is main stress on the middle word:

(83)   toxic waste cleanup, collective bargaining agreement, balanced budget amendment, civil rights bill, used car business, financial planning consultant, due process clause, floating underflow trap, systolic array machine, fresh fish shop

Both the existence of such examples and their normal stress pattern follow straightforwardly from our proposals.

4   The Structure of Premodified Nominals: A Summing Up of the Theoretical Issues

We have examined a wide range of modified noun phrases. In this section, we will summarize the structural analyses we have suggested for the various types of nominals that we have discussed. In addition, we will have a few things to say about some other nominal constructions in English and other languages.

We will then extend our arguments against what we have called FCA-only theories of nominal compound stress, by examining the approach of Ladd 1984. We will also discuss the distinction between morphology and syntax: should some of constructions we have been discussing be viewed as the product of a component of the grammar—the morphological component—that is crucially different from the component responsible for phrasal composition? Many writers have argued that this distinction should be made, Di Sciullo and Williams 1987 being perhaps the most vocal supporters of this view. We will evaluate some of their arguments in terms of the phenomena discussed in this paper, and suggest that the evidence for such a split is not strong.

4.1 A Summary of the Structure of the Modifying Phrase

We have seen examples of English premodified nominals with various sorts of supra-lexical constituents as their lefthand member. At least the patterns $[A \ N]$, and $[N \ PP]$ are fairly productive. This suggests that the lefthand constituent of premodified nominals is (maximally) an X^1, where X is commonly (though not necessarily) N^1:

(84) $[[_{N^1} A \ N] \ N]$ equal rights amendment
      $[[_{N^1} N \ PP] \ N]$ balance of payments problems

Again, there are certainly restrictions. For example, N-plus-comple-ment or A-plus-complement modifiers are somewhat restricted. There are stylistic issues, and common or lexicalized modifiers are preferred in these cases. Examples like these seem infelicitous:

(85) *Where's my [tree in the garden] clipper.
      *John is a [proud of his son] man.

Examples like those in (85) are generally taken to be ruled out by a Head-Final Filter (Fabb 1984, Di Sciullo and Williams 1987), which states that the head of a modifier must be adjacent to the modified word. However, the fact that more common phrases seem unproblematic as modifiers (*balance of payments problems*) suggests that the Head-Final Filter may actually not be a grammatical constraint, but rather a parsing constraint: as long as the lefthand component is recognizable as a unit in the context of use, its exact construction is not as limited as constraints such as the Head-Final Filter would suggest.

As exemplified in (11), the left member of a noun compound can ordi-narily not have its own independent article. The restriction against articles is pretty strong even for things that are clearly lexical items—thus we say *the Bronx Borough President*, not *the the Bronx Borough President*; see Fabb 1984 on these. Also excluded are noun phrases specified by a a *wh*-word, and any form of pronoun acting as the modifier on its own. Quan-tifiers, which are often taken to be specifiers of N^2 (see Abney 1987) are normally unacceptable. So, the following examples are all impossible:

(86) *an [every kitchen] table,*the [which dog] owner,*the [it] hater

However, note that modifiers containing numerals are not excluded:

(87) the four color theorem, the eight queens problem, three-mile mark,
      a $3 million offer

So, on the one hand we have clear evidence that in many cases the modifier must be phrasal, and we have equally clear evidence that the modifier cannot be a fully specified noun phrase. We can capture such restrictions quite neatly if we assume that prenominal nominal modifiers are maximally N^1. This will rule out modifiers such as *The Bronx, every kitchen, which dog*. To rule out pronouns such as *it* as modifiers, one could appeal to a suggestion of Paul Kiparsky (p.c.) that closed class items (at least in English) do not typically allow further morphological derivation. On this account, *it hater* would be bad for the same reason as a derived form such as *it-ishness* is bad. To be sure, other explanations are available: another line of thought says that projections of functional categories may not serve as modifiers. This rules out pronouns and also projections of D, such as *The Bronx*, as modifiers. Indeed, a similar set of restrictions holds of adjectival phrases: degree specifiers such as *so, that, how* are obligatorily absent from prenominal adjectival modifiers:

(88)   a. The houses are that large.
       *the that large houses
    b. How large are those houses?
       *Those how large houses are over there?
    c. The houses are so large.
       *the so large houses[13]

Abney (who discusses these facts) suggests, on analogy with his analysis of noun phrases, that full adjective phrases are really Degree Phrases (DegP) where the degree word is the head, just as a determiner is the head of DP, with the AP as a complement of the degree word; see Abney 1987, p. 321:

(89) $[_{DegP} \ [_{Deg} \ \text{so} \ ] \ [_{AP} \ [_A \ \text{nice} \ ]]]$

One can then rule out the examples in (88) by assuming that only APs— possibly, in fact, maximally A^1, can appear in prenominal position. This is essentially what Abney argues, although, his analysis makes the rather novel assumption that the adjective is the head in a construction like *big dog*, that this construction is therefore an AP, and that the NP *dog* is a complement of *big*. We have of course taken the more traditional view that canonical prenominal modifiers, namely the prenominal adjectives, are adjoined to N^1 in English.

So, it seems that for the canonical prenominal modifiers, namely projections of N and projections of A, there is some evidence that such modifiers are typically maximally single bar projections—X^1. If we look again at the examples of highly-complex modifiers in (67), we see that they are actu-

---

[13]One can say things like *how large a house, so large a house*. Such constructions are limited, in the sense that only an indefinite singular NP can follow the degree-marked adjective: *how large that house, *how large houses*. Abney argues that these are adjectival phrases (DegPs) where the head adjective takes a fully specified noun phrase as a complement.

ally consistent with this idea—they may be projected from non-traditional categories such as V, but may plausibly be analyzed as being of level X^1 or below.

4.2 More on the Distinction Between N^0 and N^1 Modifiers

Having argued that the modifier of a noun is maximally X^1, we now overview the arguments for our assumptions about the structural relationship between the modifier and the head. It is worthwhile to start out by placing this assumption about modifier-head relations in a broader context of current ideas about phrase structure.

We have maintained that modifiers are adjoined to either N^0 or N^1. The diagram in (90) illustrates the structure we have assumed for an N^1 modifier such as the adjective *red*:

(90) $[_{DP}$ $[_{D^0}$ the] $[_{N^2}$ $[_{N^1}$ $[_A$ red] $[_{N^1}$ $[_{N^0}$ book]]]]]]

We have assumed that most $[N\ N]$ compounds are instances of modifier-head constructions, in this case involving adjunction to N^0:

(91) $[_{N^0}$ $[_{N^0}$ dog] $[_{N^0}$ house]]

However, we have argued at length that not *all* instances of $[N\ N]$ modification are at the N^0 level; similarly, not all instances of $[A\ N]$ modification are N^1. Thus we have posited structures like these:[14]

(92) a. $[_{N^1}$ $[_{N^0}$ kitchen] $[_{N^1}$ $[_{N^0}$ sink]]]
     b. $[_{N^0}$ $[_{A^0}$ blind] $[_{N^0}$ spot]]

Our primary arguments involved default stress patterns and some informal consideration of semantic relations, but there is also evidence from sequence constraints among modifiers. Note that one does not find $[N\ N]$ constructions which we would argue on stress grounds to be of the type N^1, occurring as the righthand member of a construction whose parent node ought to be an N^0. So, one can say **coffee** *jar* (N^0), and *plastic* **jar** (N^1), but one cannot get ** coffee plastic **jar** (cf. *plastic* **coffee** *jar*) since the structure would have to be *$[_{N^0}$ N^0 $N^1]$, which is ruled out by X-bar considerations given that the rightmost member of a compound in English is generally the head (see (105) below).

On the other hand, complex expressions which look on the surface to be phrasal constructions, but which we have argued on stress grounds to be N^0, can occur in the righthand position of compound nouns. The complex

---

[14]It is worth noting that the structure in (92a) is vaguely related to the proposal in Selkirk 1984 (pp. 43–50) that right stressed compounds involve adjuncts, where the modifier is in some sense more external than modifiers in a left stressed compound, which are taken to be arguments. Selkirk, however, also seems to suggest that at least some compound-like constructions, such as *steel* **warehouse** (i.e., warehouse made of steel) might be viewed as phrasal collocations (p. 247) as opposed to compounds of the form *ADJUNCT-HEAD*. It is not clear from her discussion how one is supposed to distinguish these cases.

examples in the third column are all right-branching N^0s having primary stress on the penultimate member as predicted by the CSR:

(93) **user's** manual   **Unix** manual   [Unix [**user's** manual]]
      dry dock   **trawler** dock   [trawler [**dry** dock]]

Needless to say, prenominal noun modifiers that on our analysis are dominated by N^1, are generally reasonable candidates to stack outside adjectives that occur at the same level. Thus the right-dominant character of *plastic cup* is consistent with the possibility of *plastic disposable cup*, though the alternative ordering may be slightly preferred.

By giving a structural explanation for the unavailability of examples like *coffee plastic jar, we are claiming that such examples are ill-formed for the same kind of structural reason that *difficult the problems is ill-formed. It is worthwhile contrasting such rigid ordering restrictions with the much softer ordering restrictions on prenominal adjectival modifiers, which are all introduced at the same (N^1) level, but which nonetheless display well-known ordering preferences:

(94)   large red ball   ?red large ball
       oversize square table   ?square oversize table

One could, of course, ask whether these ordering restrictions should also be handled by assuming intermediate structural positions or levels? For example, measure adjectives like *large* could be placed in a slot "outside" color adjectives like *red*, since the former prefer to precede the latter. However, it has been observed in the literature on prenominal adjective ordering (see, most recently, Sproat and Shih 1990b) that these ordering restrictions are only preferences, operating in the absence of pragmatic reasons to choose a different order. It is perfectly possible to choose an alternative order, given appropriate context:

(95)   I want the *red* large ball, not the *blue* one.

So it seems best to agree with the traditional view that these ordering preferences reflect some sort of natural continuum of psychological affinity, even though it seems difficult to define such a scale in a non-circular way. In contrast, ordering restrictions on what we have argued to be modifiers at the N^0 and N^1 levels seem inviolable—like the ordering restrictions between specifiers and modifiers, suggesting that the structural analysis proposed for these modifiers is on the right track. Something seems definitely degraded about (96) as compared with (95):

(96)   ??I need the coffee plastic jar, not the tea plastic jar.

These considerations, as well as the stress and semantic considerations discussed throughout this paper have therefore led us to the conclusion that modifier-noun constructions can be either N^1 or N^0, no matter whether the modifier is adjectival or nominal. We now summarize the various classes of cases we have examined in this paper giving examples to fill out the structural possibilities. Non-lexicalized $[A\ N]$ combinations—instances of normal prenominal adjectival modification—are mostly phrasal. At least some of the productive cases of apparent N^0-level $[A\ N]$ combinations may really involve $[N\ N]$ modification at some level, as we argued in reference to (50), and as suggested by the discussion in Levi 1978. Lexicalized $[A\ N]$ forms—those forms that must be listed since they have more or less idiosyncratic or idiomatic meanings—may be either N^1 or N^0:

(97)

	Lexicalized	Non-Lexicalized
N^0	**yellow** pages	**dental** operation
N^1	red **herring**	red **paint**

With $[N\ N]$ modification we clearly get all possible combinations of Productive/Lexicalized and bar level. There is no sense that $[N\ N]\ N^0$ are more lexicalized than $[N\ N]$ phrasal combinations:

(98)

	Lexicalized	Non-Lexicalized
N^0	**eye**ball	**Capsicum** leaf
N^1	rice **pudding**	dingo **stew**

Finally, we have noted compound-like examples where the modifier is a possessive. These may be either N^1 or N^0. In both cases the expression tends to be lexicalized, though there are some productive subsystems, such as those left-stressed examples headed by *milk*:[15]

(99) N^1 Swainson's **thrush**
       N^0: **dog's** body

4.3 Some Other Compound-like Constructions in English and Elsewhere

We have discussed apparently left-headed nominals in English. On the basis of their stress behavior all such examples appear to be N^1. Many of these constructions have a questionable status in the minds of many speakers. Thus the prescribed plural *attorneys general*, which is what is expected given a left-headed structure, has already lost to the alternative *attorney generals*, suggesting that this form has been largely reanalyzed. Other examples, possibly because of their productivity, seem more solidly left headed: *Mounts Whitney and McKinley*. One can link these cases of post-nominal modification with the slightly marked, though still very productive class of post-nominal modifications with adjectives: *a man proud of his son, a river broad and long, a dragon fearsome to behold*.

Other compounds and compound-like words which do not fit so neatly into the discussion of most of this paper include exocentric bahuvrihi compounds. Bahuvrihi compounds have been analyzed (cf. Kiparsky 1982) as

---

[15]Note that some left stressed examples function as proper names and disallow preceding modifiers or specifiers in most cases, e.g., *Kayne's generalization*. There is nothing particularly surprising in this, and it seems reasonable to analyze such expressions as themselves being proper names, which typically lack articles in English.

modifiers to an empty headed noun (*redneck x*). Such an approach seems to solve the embarrassing problem that these constructions have no semantic head (a *redneck* is not in any sense a neck); however, we must assume in addition that these cases are all N^0, presumably a consequence of their having undergone at least the second stage of lexicalization outlined in Section 3.1

Examples like those of (35) are presumably nominalizations of phrasal fragments reminiscent of the Romance examples in (100):

(100) a. essuie-glace (wipe glass) 'windshield wiper'
   b. tocadiscos (play records) 'record player'
   c. guardaboschi (guard woods) 'forester'

Such examples are syntactic in appearance but have been transformed into nouns, suggesting a structure along the lines of that argued for in Di Sciullo and Williams 1987:

(101) $[_{N^0} [_{V?} [_V$ toca$] [_{N?}$ discos$]]]$

4.4 More on FCA-Only Theories: Ladd's Deaccenting Argument

We have taken the traditional generative view that syntax determines stress in the "normal" case—abstracting away from FCA effects. In adopting this view we are rejecting, among other approaches, Ladd's 1984 proposal that compound stress is a result of deaccenting the head. His idea is that the difference in representation between *steel warehouse* ('warehouse made of steel') and *steel warehouse* ('warehouse for storing steel') is purely metrical, the latter having the normal iambic phrasal structure *w s* and the latter the trochaic, deaccented structure *s w*. This deaccenting in compounds is explicitly claimed to be part of the more general phenomenon of phrasal deaccenting in examples like (102) (Ladd 1984, p. 255), where *books* is deaccented for pragmatic reasons:

(102) Has John read *Slaughterhouse Five*?
   No, John doesn't **read** books.

Ladd's basic claim is that in right-stressed modifier-head nominal constructions, the attribute (lefthand member) does not serve to *subcategorize*[16] the head. In the deaccented (CSR) cases the attribute does subcategorize the head, hence the head contributes only part of what is necessary to identify the new category. An obvious contrast is *green* **house** versus **green** *house*. In the former the attribute *green* does not produce a new type of entity, but merely serves to further specify the general category *house*; the accented head therefore provides the category. A **green** *house*, on the other hand, is a new category of entity, so *house* provides only part of the necessary information, which results in its being deaccented relative to *green*, which

---

[16]Ladd is not using the technical linguistic sense of *subcategorize*, but intends the sense of "making a subcategory out of" the head.

provides crucial additional information. The approach is argued to work not only in cases where semantic categorization is involved, but also in cases where this is much less clear, such as in the domain of place names. So, the contrast between *First* **Avenue** and **First** *Street* is argued to derive from the fact that *Street*, within the category of names for roads, is the more common or expected term, and also gives the least semantic information about what kind of road is involved (terms like *Avenue, Boulevard, Alley*, carry with them connotations which *Street* does not have). Thus *Street* is deaccented.

While there are surely areas in which notions of subcategorization-conditioned deaccenting plays a role, the idea is problematic as a general explanation for the stress patterns we have seen. For example, one pragmatic test proposed by Ladd to distinguish "flavors" from real "(sub)categories" in food terms falls far short of correlating with stress. Ladd's idea is that *cheese* **sandwich** is a sandwich flavored with cheese and *cheese* merely serves to further specify *sandwich*, not form a separate category: thus the stress is phrasal. In contrast, for **banana** *bread*, one clearly needs the information provided by the lefthand member to determine the category of food involved since banana bread is not really a kind of bread flavored with banana, but a new category of food similar to bread in some ways. Now, Ladd notes that while one can felicitously ask *do you want a sandwich?* and subsequently offer a cheese sandwich, one cannot felicitously ask *do you want some bread?* and offer banana bread. It is claimed that one can only felicitously offer *XY* if *XY* is merely a *Y* flavored with *X*, and not a different category of food. This test is then supposed to correlate with stress, righthand stress if the offer is felicitous, lefthand if it is not, for the reasons given above. However, this test makes the wrong predictions in whole categories of examples. For instance, most words headed with bread are left-stressed even when their referent is a canonical instance: one can felicitously offer a person bread and then give them any one of *wheat bread, rye bread, white bread* and a number of others. On the other hand, while *steak and kidney* **pie** follows the normal pattern of righthand stress for words headed by *pie*, it would come as quite a surprise to most Americans to get some after assenting to an offer of unmodified pie.[17].

Another problem with Ladd's reduction of compound stress to general mechanisms of phrasal deaccenting is that phrasal deaccenting can easily produce examples of right-branching structures where all the righthand material is deaccented:

(103) I don't [**like** [buckwheat [griddle cakes]]]

Ladd's theory therefore predicts that left dominance in right-branching compounds is possible, if the subcategories fall out right. This does not

---

[17]This point can be made even more strikingly with *shepherd's* **pie**, a concoction wherein ground lamb is topped with mashed potatoes and then baked.

seem to be true, even where one might expect such stressing given the behavior of binary compounds with identical heads and lefthand members:

(104) a. **buckwheat** cakes
   b. **griddle** cakes
   c. buckwheat **griddle** cakes
   d.***buckwheat** griddle cakes

Of course, (104d) is possible in FCA contexts, but it is not the default case for such compounds, contrary to what we might expect given Ladd's theory.[18]

4.5 Are N^0 Compounds Formed "in the Lexicon"?

In assuming, as we have been, that N^0 compounds are instances of modification constructions on a par with N^1 modification constructions, we have been at least implicitly assuming that such compounds are syntactic objects. Doing so, of course, runs counter to most theories of morphology, which assume that compounds are dealt with in the morphological component and that if compounds seem to share some properties with syntactic constructions this should nonetheless not be taken as evidence that they are syntactic (Selkirk 1982, Hoeksema 1984, Mohanan 1986, Di Sciullo and Williams 1987, among many others).

We would like to consider one recent attempt to justify this separation of compound formation from syntax, namely that of Di Sciullo and Williams 1987 (henceforth D&W), and consider whether the evidence they adduce for this separation is reasonable. D&W suggest an approach to morphology whereby words are constructed in a component of the grammar, the morphological component, which is in many ways similar to syntax, but is both (i) different in detail from syntax and (ii) separate from syntax. We discuss each of these points in turn.[19]

Differences of detail. A crucial difference of detail is that compounds are right headed in English, whereas phrases are left headed, at least at a very macroscopic level of analysis.

There are actually two issues relevant to comparing the headedness of phrases and compounds. One, D&W claim, is that one can always pick out the head in a phrase because it is "the item with one less bar level than the phrase" (p. 23) and which is generally of the same category as the phrase:

---

[18]Ladd's own examples involving the head noun *warehouse* might seem to be a contradiction to what we have just said since *warehouse* is, historically at least, a compound. However, it seems well within reason to assume that the analysis of *warehouse* as a compound is *only* of historical interest and that the word today lacks an internal word boundary. Certainly productively formed constructions with unequivocally complex heads do not seem to stress as Ladd ought to predict: a department store for electronics would be a *electronics* **department** *store*, except of course in clear FCA-contexts. Yet surely an electronics department store must be considered a subcategory of department store, at least if a steel warehouse is considered to be a subcategory of warehouse.

[19]See also Baker 1988 for a review of problems with D&W.

(105) $X^n \rightarrow \ldots YP \ldots X^{n-1} \ldots ZP \ldots$

They contrast this situation with the situation in a canonical compound where the two daughters of the N^0 are themselves N^0. They suggest that compounds follow a different, non-syntactic, morphological component rule for determining headedness, namely a modified version of the Righthand Head rule of Williams 1981, which states roughly that the head of a word is its rightmost morpheme. In compounds, it seems, the syntactic notion of head would not work.

Still, it is important to bear in mind that the ease with which one can apply the syntactic notion of head in phrases, and the seeming difficulty of using that notion in compounds derives from theoretical prejudice. To see this point, consider the structure of noun phrases in Welsh such as:

(106) meibion athrawon (sons teachers) 'teachers' sons'

This noun phrase consists of two plural nouns with no other markings, and yet there is no question that it is left-headed, as are all noun phrases in Welsh. In order to apply the syntactic notion of head, one would clearly want to argue that the righthand noun *athrawon* 'teachers' is really the sole member of a DP—hence could not count as the head under (105)— although there would be no way to ascertain the presence of the DP from the existence of *athrawon* alone. Returning to English compounds, there is no absolute reason why one cannot assert that all prenominal modifiers within N^0 are phrasal; we have already discussed examples which show that at least in some cases the prenominal modifier in the N^0 level must be an X^1. So, one might assume that *all* prenominal modifiers are X^1 just as we tend to assume that the noun *athrawon* in (106) is really a DP, despite the lack of direct evidence in the particular construction in (106). If we were to take that tack, we could clearly modify the syntactic notion of headedness to allow that the head of a construction must match the category of the parent and have a bar level not greater than that of the parent; something like this condition must be right more generally anyway if we are to define headedness correctly on adjunction structures under normal notions of adjunction. Then, the head of *dog house* would be clear: the prenominal modifier *dog* would be an N^1, whereas *house* would be an N^0, thus satisfying the conditions for headedness under the revised definition.

Still, we don't have to adopt this strategy. The other issue, raised by D&W's claim that English phrases are left headed is the question: left-headed at what level? Clearly, *modifiers*, whether phrasal or not, precede their heads in the typical case in English, and since we have assumed that N^0 compounds are merely a type of modification, we would expect that compounds are right-headed. Thus in order to determine the head, the syntax would merely need to take note of the kind of relationship—i.e., modification—holding between the members of the compound, and fix the head on the right. D&W, in claiming that English phrases are left headed,

have missed the locally more relevant point that in modifier-head constructions in English the head is on the right.

Of course, in deriving compound headedness in this way, we fail to link
the right-headedness of compounds with the right-headedness of words in
English: for example, many people (e.g., see Williams 1981, and also Lieber
1980) have argued that the head of, say, *grammaticality* is the suffix *-ity*
since that determines the category. Williams' Righthand Head Rule explicitly links compounds with affix right-headedness. We think, in contrast,
that the two should not be linked, at least synchronically. The fact that it
is typically suffixes and rarely prefixes that function as heads of words is
almost surely related to the cross-linguistic prevalence of suffixation, which
in turn may have psycholinguistic bases (see Cutler et al. 1985). Thus it
seems plausible to view the right-headedness of English compounds and the
right-headedness of English affixation as a coincidence, in the sense that
they are not diverse expressions of a single fact about English grammar.[20]

Indeed, we would expect languages with left-headed modification structures by and large to also show left-headed compounds if they have compounding, no matter what the headedness of affixation is. This appears
to be correct, as examples from French, discussed in Selkirk 1982, or from
Spanish, Breton "loose compounding" (Stump 1989) or Zhuang (Ramsey
1987).[21] For further discussion of this and related points see Lieber 1988,
1992, Baker 1988, and especially Clements 1989:

(107) a. timbres-poste (stamps post) 'postage stamps'

    b. los coches Chevrolet

    c. Breton: kaoc'h kezeg (dung horse) 'horse dung'

      (cf. paotr brav (boy fine) 'a fine boy')

---

[20]Of course, this is not to say that all other patterns would have been equally likely, or
that the two facts about English are not connected historically. As Cutler et al. 1985
show (see, e.g., pp. 727ff), there is a positive cross-linguistic correlation between suffixing
and *phrasal* right-headedness. In particular, right-headed languages—Object-Verb and
Postpositional languages—show an overwhelming preference to be exclusively suffixing.
Left-headed languages mostly have both prefixes and suffixes, and prefix-only languages
are very rare and are apparently always phrasally left-headed. English descends from
languages which were phrasally right-headed, as did Latin, from which half of English
affixational morphology comes. English prehead modification is likely to be a living fossil
of the former right-headed syntax. So right-headed compounding may be historically
related to right-headed affixation in English, by a history which makes crucial excursions
into the syntax.

[21]We should note that Welsh, which has left-headed modification structures, has a
number of frozen right-headed compounds: *ysgolfeistr* (school-master) 'school master';
rheilffordd orsaf (rail road station) 'railway station'. Some examples, such as the second
one, are clearly translation borrowings from English, and in any event this kind of
compounding is not productive in Welsh. Breton "strict compounds" (Stump 1989) are
also right-headed. Note that Welsh (and also Irish, Breton, French and Spanish) does
retain a few prenominal adjectival modifiers and so it may well be the case that Celtic and
Romance languages are only somewhat further along the transition to left-headedness
than is English.

    d. Zhuang: kai5-pou4 (chicken male) 'rooster'
      (cf., sai1 mo5 rau2 (book new our) 'our new book')

Concerning the French examples, D&W claim (p. 83) that "Selkirk misanal-ysed fixed phrases such as *timbres-poste* as 'left-headed compounds,' thus concluding that French morphology is a mixture of left- and right-headed structures (since affixation in French is clearly right-headed). This is a clear example of a generalization compromised by the failure to properly separate syntax and morphology."

This attack can easily be turned around, however: by insisting that mor-phological constructions, including compounds, must obey the Righthand Head Rule, D&W make it impossible both to recognize as compounds many constructions which any first-order description would classify as such, and to state the very clear generalization that compounds in a language gen-erally follow the ordering of modifier-head constructions in that language. In the other direction, relying on the Righthand Head Rule as a correlate of "morphological" constructions would prevent us from noting properties that left-headed examples in other languages may share with English com-pound nouns. Thus in cases like *carne de burro* (meat of donkey) 'donkey meat' in Spanish, it is essential that the complement phrase *de burro*, like the modifiers in English compounds, not be a full DP. With an article, the phrase *carne del burro* 'meat of the donkey' would not serve to refer to the generic substance donkey meat. *Carne de burro*, while having clear phrasal properties, equally clearly has properties commonly associated with compounds.

Separation from syntax. The other half of D&W's claim about the sta-tus of compounds is based upon the apparent *atomicity* of words from the point of view of syntax. In saying that compounds are atomic, D&W are buying into the familiar claims of lexical integrity (see, e.g., Mohanan 1986, pp. 24–25) which say that the syntax (or subsequent components) can have no access to the internals of words. To substantiate this claim, D&W present evidence that appears to show that various syntactic phenomena fail to make use of information internal to compounds. The strength of the evidence, however, fades rapidly on serious examination.

Consider, for example, the observation (D&W, p. 49) that rules of syn-tax cannot "discriminate among compounds whose nonhead members are plural or singular," so that *the parks commissioner* is treated by all rele-vant syntactic rules exactly the same way as *the park commissioner*. This seems simply to be an observation about headedness: in exactly the same way, relevant syntactic rules will not distinguish *the commissioner of meats* from *the commissioner of meat*. Since plurality is not being registered on the head of the noun phrase in either case, any syntactically relevant rule which cares about number (such as verb agreement) will register the gram-matical number of the head and not be affected by the plurality of modifiers or complements. In this respect there is absolutely nothing special about the compound case: one does not need to appeal to the existence of a separate morphological component to derive the relevant properties of *the parks commissioner*.

A second set of examples concerns cases like *it robber* (see D&W, p. 50) or *who killer*, which are argued to show that referential expressions, which are relevant to the syntax, may not occur within words. But, as we have already suggested (Section 4.1), there seems to be a constraint ruling out any kind of derivation from closed-class items; alternatively, one could claim that no projection of functional categories can serve as modifiers. In any case, we have argued that modifiers—whether at the N^0 or the N^1 level—are maximally X^1, thus ruling out a whole class of DP or DegP modifiers. These considerations subsume D&W's facts. Referential expressions are not in principle ruled out from occurring within words, but only those expressions which have the above mentioned forms. Proper names can certainly occur within compounds although D&W suggest that: (i) only famous names really allow this, since *Bill admirer* is supposedly unacceptable; and that (ii) even in such cases as *Nixon admirer*, *Nixon* doesn't really refer to Nixon. We briefly examine these claims.

With respect to the second claim, it has been argued extensively in Sproat and Ward 1987 and Ward et al. 1991, that names which are morphologically contained within compounds can indeed be used to refer to particular individuals, and this can be seen by the fact that such names can function as antecedents to pronouns:[22]

(108) a. There's a Thurber$_i$-story about his$_i$ maid...
   b. I was reading this Peggy Noonan$_i$ book on her$_i$ years at the White House...
   c. We went up to Constable$_i$ country; we stayed in the village he$_i$ was born in.

D&W's own evidence for their claim concerning the referentiality of *Nixon* in *Nixon admirer* is the assertion that in (109a), admiring Nixon is not an essential property of a *Nixon admirer*, since this example is not a contradiction, unlike (109b):

(109) a. John is a Nixon admirer in every sense except that he does not admire Nixon.
   b. John admires Nixon in every sense except that he does not admire Nixon.

Ward et al. (1991, footnote 16) have argued that (109a) is only non-contradictory under the interpretation of *Nixon admirer* as a person with a reliable set of traits (such as being clean-shaven, wearing a three-piece suit and always carrying an attaché case) which are independent of the

---

[22]Contrary to the predictions of the so-called *Anaphoric Island constraint* (Postal 1969).

property of admiring Nixon: in other words, *Nixon admirer* would have to have accreted additional meanings via institutionalization, along the lines of *Maoist*. In that case a person might be said to have those properties and thus qualify as being a *Nixon admirer*, even if he or she does not actually admire Nixon; hence (109a) would not be a contradiction. Needless to say, *Nixon admirer* has not achieved this institutionalized status in the minds of most speakers, and the contrast in (109) is therefore very hard to get.

More important for D&W's argument, however, is the observation that the putative accretion of such institutionalized meanings is largely orthogonal to the issue of whether *Nixon* in *Nixon admirer* can be used to refer to Nixon. Hence, even making the counterfactual assumption that the contrast in (109) were a clear one, that would not serve to support D&W's claim concerning the referential properties of compound-internal elements.

Returning to point (i), the obvious question which arises when confronted with an example like *Bill admirer* is: who is Bill? One might suppose that *Bill admirer* ought to be able to mean something like 'one who admires people with the name *Bill*', but there is really no reason to believe that it should have this reading: in its typical phrasal usage, a proper name like *Bill* is invariably used to refer to a specific individual. Therefore one would expect *Bill* in *Bill admirer* also to be used to refer to some specific individual, and if we do not know who that individual is, the example seems odd. The oddity is reinforced by the fact that, as is well-known, "agentive" nominals tend to have a "habitual" reading, and are typically used to refer to characteristic properties. To ascribe to someone the characteristic property of admiring some unspecified person named *Bill* seems odd indeed. Naturally, famous names do not have this problem, since there is no question about the intended referents of the names. And *Bill admirer* is, it seems to us, fine in a context where the interlocutors can assign a definite referent to *Bill*.

Still, there is no question that first names generally seem somewhat degraded over last names in such contexts: compare ?*Noam admirer* with *Chomsky admirer*. At least in part this seems to have to do with the fact *admirer* has an institutionalized connotation of 'admires in the professional sense', and this in turn requires that the admired individual be referred to using their normal professional designation, typically the last name.[23] But familiarity or conventional designation are clearly extragrammatical considerations, and there is no reason to suppose that there should be a statement in the *grammar* of English nominal compounds restricting the occurrence of proper names in that context.

---

[23] A similar constraint applies to cases of deferred reference (thanks to Mats Rooth for the second example):

    i. You'll find Chomsky on the top shelf.

    ii. ?#You'll find Noam on the top shelf.

In summary, we do not find any of the reasons adduced by D&W for separating compounding from phrasal constructions to be compelling. Therefore it seems possible to accept the assumption that English N^0 compounds are word-level objects that are formed in the syntax.

5   Two Approaches to Parsing and Stress Assignment

We turn now from the descriptive and theoretical issues which have occupied us for the bulk of this paper to the issue to which we would ultimately like to provide a solution, or at least a good approximation thereto, namely the correct parsing of and stress assignment to modified nominals as they occur in unrestricted text. We outline here some of the methods we have applied to solving this problem.

It is of practical concern that the correct stress pattern for a sequence $[N\ N]$ or $[A\ N]$ cannot be generally predicted from the preterminal sequence of categories alone. That is, if we know that we have a sequence of two nouns, we cannot be certain that we have an N^0 as opposed to an N^1 for a parent category, though if the preterminal sequence were all we could compute, guessing N^0 would more often lead to a correct stress assignment than guessing N^1. In general, some other type of analysis is necessary. In addition to the problem of deciding upon the appropriate stress assignment to a binary modified noun, there is the at least equally difficult problem of parsing more complex cases. As we shall see, the two problems, stress assignment and parsing, are related in the methodologies which one can apply to them. We shall first turn to the problem of stress assignment, and then consider parsing.

5.1   Stress Assignment in Binary Nominals

The phrase *safety board* has main stress on the left. As we have argued for other cases in the text, we might decide this because the phrase is an instance of a semantic pattern, informally stated as *N1 GROUP-WHOSE-CONCERN-IS-N1*. In Sproat and Liberman 1987 and Sproat 1990, we show that a rather crude implementation of such a method can improve considerably on the performance of an approach based purely on the syntactic categorization of the words in the text stream. However, as we noted in our discussion of the semantic patterns of argument-argument compounds, it is not at all clear on what basis a single, consistent, coherent set of such schemata can be defined.

Alternatively, we might depend on the fact that the words in the phrase *safety board* tend to yield a left-dominant stress pattern in other cases. So one might expect that the probability that the nominal will be stressed on the left given that the first word is *safety* and the second *board* is greater than the probability of righthand stress under those conditions, or in other words:

$$p(s_1|w_1{=}safety)\,p(s_1|w_2{=}board) > p(s_2|w_1{=}safety)\,p(s_2|w_2{=}board)$$

A survey of examples from a large corpus of naturally-occurring pre-modified nominals shows that this is indeed the case—*safety* as a noun modifier was always stress-dominant, while *board* when pre-modified by a noun was never stress-dominant. A representative sample:

(110) a. safety belt, safety binding, safety council, safety devices, safety equipment, safety feature, safety glasses, safety harness, safety margin, safety measure, safety net, safety nut, safety precautions, safety problem, safety procedure, safety razor, safety record, safety regulations, safety requirement, safety rule, safety school, safety shoes, safety standards

b. Federal Reserve board, advisory board, bulletin board, chalk board, chess board, circuit board, cutting board, dart board, draft board, drawing board, governing board, ironing board, memory board, particle board, planning board, promotion board, school board, score board, skate board, supervisory board, surf board, wall board, zoning board

Although most examples are not as clear-cut as this one, we believe that the method can work fairly well if properly trained. Its main drawback is that many words do not occur often enough in the needed constructions to generate useful statistics—it seems appropriate, in such cases, to depend on the observed behavior of "similar" words. The crux of the matter is then the similarity metric to be used.

5.2 Parsing Premodified Nominals

Again, we have explored two methods. One approach would use phrasal schemata of the kind used in assigning stress to decide upon a possible analysis for a modifier-head string; one might further extend such a method along the lines of Finin 1980 by adding scores for the various schemata, and pick the parse whose cumulative score is highest. This approach has the previously noted difficulties of creating a reasonable set of schemata, and, if scores are used, also the problem of juggling the interaction of possibly ad hoc scores, endemic to diagnostic systems of this type. Nevertheless, if the schemata are chosen so as to reflect the patterns found in a certain genre of text, the technique can work reasonably well.

A system of this kind currently under development in the context of Bell Labs ongoing text-to-speech effort is reported in Sproat 1990,[24] and is an extension of earlier work reported in Sproat and Liberman 1987. The program depends on semantic patterns of the kind described in this paper as well as large lists of common binary nominals to attempt to compute

---

[24]The scoring method alluded to above for picking among various possible semantic interpretations is not implemented in the system reported in Sproat 1990, though various ad hoc heuristics are used to pick one of several possible analyses.

a reasonable structure of multiply modified nominal phrases. As a simple example consider a semantic grammar which contains information that *table*, *chair* and some other items are HOUSEWAREs; that *kitchen*, *bathroom* and *living room* are ROOMs (and incidentally also N^0, this latter information being crucial for the binary cases); and that there is a pattern, which says that a ROOM word and a HOUSEWARE word may be combined into an N^1, which we will call a ROOM&THING. this rule can be thought of as an instance of the pattern PLACE-WHERE-N2-IS-FOUND N2 discussed in (70). In addition to semantic grammar rules and the rather large lexicon of binary cases, there are more traditional syntactic rules which handle syntactic aspects of noun phrase structure, such as the treatment of determiners. The system in its current form can assign appropriate structure and stress to noun phrases such as the following:

(111) $[_{DP}$ $[_{POSS}$ John's] $[_{NP}$ large $[_{\langle N^1, ROOM\&THING \rangle}$ $[_{\langle N^0, ROOM \rangle}$ living room] $[_{\langle N^0, HOUSEWARE \rangle}$ table]]]]

In this example, *living room* is correctly analyzed as a modifier of N^1. Another module of the program responsible for assigning stress can then take this assigned structure and determine that the main stress should be placed on the head noun in this case.

The second approach to parsing again relies on the statistical behavior of individual words, identifying the affinity of two adjacent words with the extent to which they occur together more often than one would predict based on how often they occur individually. One reasonable measure for such affinity might be MUTUAL INFORMATION, where the mutual information $I(a, b)$ between events A and B with probabilities $p(a)$ and $p(b)$ is defined as

(112) $I(a, b) = \log_2 \dfrac{p(a, b)}{p(a)p(b)}$

Mutual information measures have been used recently by Sproat and Shih (1990a)[25] in a domain rather similar to the current one, namely the problem of locating word boundaries in Chinese text. Chinese orthography, of course, traditionally does not indicate the location of word boundaries, but it turns out that considerations of the strengths of association between adjacent characters in a Chinese text, as measured by mutual information can achieve about 95% retrieval and precision for two-character words (which constitute the bulk of multicharacter words in Chinese text).

However, there is a problem with defining the association measure strictly in terms of mutual information as defined above. Instances of the sequence ABC in fact give us no information about the relative affinity of B for A as opposed to C, so if a significant fraction of (say) AB instances occur in ABC sequences, while BC is quite a bit more common outside

---

[25]See also Magerman and Marcus 1990 for more extensive use of mutual information in parsing.

A	B	C	AB			BC			ABC
F	F	F	F	I	IX	F	I	IX	F
interagency	*task*	*force(s)*							
35	756	6909	4	10.83	00	287	10.07	**10.06**	4
environmental	*impact*	*statement(s)*							
801	1110	4626	25	8.40	**7.50**	16	5.23	3.25	12
private	*arms*	*dealer(s)*							
3296	3822	1059	21	4.32	4.02	57	7.40	**7.30**	4
electoral	*college*	*system(s)*							
405	1949	4691	93	10.47	**9.29**	62	9.23	2.04	59

Table 1

these sequences, then a high value for I(A,B) will be misleading. It is better to compute a mutual-information-like affinity measure that excludes the useless ABC instances from the counts. If we use $-T$ to refer to the complement of the cases in which T is found, our affinity estimate for words A and B within the ternary unit T becomes:

$$(113) \quad IX_T(A, B) = \log_2 \frac{p(A, B \mid -T)}{p(A \mid -T) p(B \mid -T)}$$

Now, compare the right-branching ternary nominals *interagency task force* and *private arms dealer* with the left-branching ternary nominals *environmental impact statement* and *electoral college system*. In a 12-million-word sample of the *Associated Press* newswire, things work out as in Table 1.

In this example, the IX measure[26] gives the correct analyses, while the I measure fails for the case of *interagency task force*, which has the noted property in that the sequence *interagency task* never occurs other than in the larger frame. In general, the IX measure gives a stronger indication of affinity in the correct direction, even where the I measure is also correct.

Methods of this general type have a great deal of promise as aids to parsing in the all-too-common cases where structural indications are weak or lacking. However, it would be desirable to consider, in estimating the affinity between two words, the distribution of "similar" words.[27] Also, the generalization of the simple ternary case to more elaborate structures can be done in a variety of ways, and it is not trivial to find methods that are both tractable and correct. We believe that the analyses given in this paper will help to guide such explorations in sensible and productive directions.

---

[26]Note that we are using *00* to refer to the case where a pair does not occur other than in the triple.

[27]Indeed, one of the problems encountered in using this statistical measure as an additional option in the system reported in Sproat 1990 is that there is often not enough data about particular pairs of words in a given triple to estimate IX, even if one uses a moderately large corpus of about 10 million words.

References

Abney, Steven. 1987. *The English Noun Phrase in its Sentential Aspect*. Doctoral dissertation, Massachusetts Institute of Technology.

Baker, Mark. 1988. Morphological and Syntactic Objects: A review of Di Sciullo and Williams' *On the Definition of Word*. *Morphology Yearbook* 1:259-283.

Bauer, Lauri. 1983. *English Word-Formation*. New York: Cambridge University Press.

Blåberg, O. 1988. *A Study of Swedish Compounds*. Doctoral dissertation, Umeå University.

Bolinger, Dwight. 1967. Adjectives in English: Attribution and Predication. *Lingua* 18:1-34.

Bolinger, Dwight. 1972. Accent is Predictable (if you're a mind-reader). *Language* 48:633-644.

Chomsky, Noam. 1970. Remarks on Nominalization. In *Readings in English Transformational Grammar*, ed. Roderick A. Jacobs and Peter S. Rosenbaum, 184-221. Waltham, Massachusetts: Ginn and Company.

Chomsky, Noam, and Morris Halle. 1968. *The Sound Pattern of English*. New York: Harper and Row.

Clements, J. 1989. Lexical Category Hierarchy and Syntactic Headedness in Compounds. In *Proceedings of the 6th Annual Eastern States Conference on Linguistics*, 46-57.

Cutler, Anne, John Hawkins, and Gary Gilligan. 1985. The Suffixing Preference: A Processing Explanation. *Linguistics* 23:723-758.

Di Sciullo, Anne-Marie, and Edwin Williams. 1987. *On the Definition of Word*. Cambridge, Mass.: MIT Press.

Downing, Pamela A. 1977. On the Creation and Use of English Compound Nouns. *Language* 53:810-842.

Dowty, David. 1979. *Word Meaning and Montague Grammar*. Dordrecht: Reidel.

Fabb, Nigel. 1984. *Syntactic Affixation*. Doctoral dissertation, Massachusetts Institute of Technology.

Finin, Timothy W. 1980. *The Semantic Interpretation of Compound Nominals*. Doctoral dissertation, University of Illinois at Urbana-Champaign.

Fudge, Erik. 1984. *English Word-Stress*. London: George Allen and Unwin.

Hayes, Bruce. 1980. *A Metrical Theory of Stress Rules*. Doctoral dissertation, Massachusetts Institute of Technology (distributed by IULC).

Hirschberg, Julia. 1990. Using Discourse Context to Guide Pitch Accent Decisions in Synthetic Speech: The given/new distinction and deaccentability. In *Proceedings of AAAI-90*, 952-957.

Hoeksema, Jacob. 1985. *Categorial Morphology*. New York: Garland Publishers.

Jackendoff, Ray. 1977. *X-bar Syntax: a Study of Phrase Structure*. Cambridge, Mass.: MIT Press.

Kiparsky, Paul. 1982. Lexical Morphology and Phonology. In *Linguistics in the Morning Calm*, ed. I.-S. Yang, 3-91. Seoul: Hanshin.

Ladd, Robert. 1984. English Compound Stress. In *Intonation, Accent and Rhythm*, ed. Dafydd Gibbon and Helmut Richter, 253–266. Berlin: Mouton de Gruyter.

Lees, Robert B. 1960. The Grammar of English Nominalizations. *International Journal of American Linguistics, Publication 12*.

Levi, Judith N. 1978. *The Syntax and Semantics of Complex Nominals*. New York: Academic Press.

Levin, Beth, and Malka Rappaport. 1992. -*Er* Nominals: Implications for a Theory of Argument-structure. In *Syntax and Semantics 26: Syntax and the Lexicon*, ed. Eric Wehrli and Tim Stowell. New York: Academic Press.

Liberman, Mark, and Alan Prince. 1977. On Stress and Linguistic Rhythm. *Linguistic Inquiry* 8:249–336.

Lieber, Rochelle. 1981. *The Organization of the Lexicon*. Doctoral dissertation, Massachusetts Institute of Technology.

Lieber, Rochelle. 1983. Argument Linking and Compounds in English. *Linguistic Inquiry* 14:251–286.

Lieber, Rochelle. 1988. Phrasal Compounds in English and the Morphology-Syntax Interface. In *Papers from the 24th Regional Meeting of the Chicago Linguistic Society*, 398–405. University of Chicago.

Lieber, Rochelle. 1992. *Deconstructing Morphology: Word Formation in Syntactic Theory*. Chicago: University of Chicago Press.

Magerman, David, and Mitchell Marcus. 1990. Parsing a Natural Language Using Mutual Information Statistics. In *Proceedings of AAAI-90*, 984–989.

Maidment, J. A. 1989. On the Accentuation of Compounds in English. In *Speech, Hearing and Language: Work in Progress*, 181–188. University College, London.

Marantz, Alec. 1989. Projection vs. Percolation in the Syntax of Synthetic Compounds. Manuscript, University of North Carolina.

Marchand, Hans. 1969. *The Categories and Types of Present-Day English Word Formation*. München: C. H. Beck'sche Verlagsbuchhandlung.

Mohanan, K.P̃. 1986. *The Theory of Lexical Phonology*. Dordrecht: Reidel.

Postal, Paul. 1969. Anaphoric Islands. In *Papers from the 5th Regional Meeting of the Chicago Linguistic Society*, 205–239. University of Chicago.

Ramsey, S. Robert. 1987. *The Languages of China*. Princeton: Princeton University Press.

Roeper, Thomas, and Muffy Siegel. 1978. A Lexical Transformation for Verbal Compounds. *Linguistic Inquiry* 9:199–260.

Safir, Ken. 1987. The Syntactic Projection of Lexical Thematic Structure. *Natural Language and Linguistic Theory* 5:561–602.

Selkirk, Elizabeth. 1984. *Phonology and Syntax*. Cambridge, Mass.: MIT Press.

Selkirk, Elizabeth O. 1982. *The Syntax of Words*. Cambridge, Mass.: MIT Press.

Sproat, Richard. 1985. *On Deriving the Lexicon*. Doctoral dissertation, Massachusetts Institute of Technology.

Sproat, Richard. 1990. Stress Assignment in Complex Nominals for English Text-to-Speech. In *Proceedings of ESCA Workshop on Speech Synthesis*, 129–132.

Sproat, Richard, and Mark Liberman. 1987. Toward Treating English Nominals Correctly. In *Proceedings of the 25th Annual Meeting of the Association for Computational Linguistics*, 140–146. Association for Computational Linguistics.

Sproat, Richard, and Chi-lin Shih. 1990a. A Statistical Method for Finding Word Boundaries in Chinese Text. *Computer Processing of Chinese and Oriental Languages* 4:336–351.

Sproat, Richard, and Chi-lin Shih. 1990b. The Cross-linguistic Distribution of Adjective Ordering Restrictions. In *Interdisciplinary Approaches to Language*, ed. Carol Georgopoulos and Roberta Ishihara, 563–593. Dordrecht: Kluwer Academic Publishers.

Sproat, Richard, and Gregory Ward. 1987. Pragmatic Considerations in Anaphoric Island Phenomena. In *Papers from the 23rd Regional Meeting of the Chicago Linguistic Society*, 321–335. University of Chicago.

Stump, Greg. 1989. A Note on Breton Pluralization and the Elsewhere Condition. *Natural Language and Linguistic Theory* 7:261–273.

Thomason, Richard. 1985. Some Issues Concerning the Interpretation of Derived and Gerundive 'Nominals'. *Linguistics and Philosophy* 8:73–80.

Ward, Gregory, Richard Sproat, and Gail McKoon. 1991. A Pragmatic Analysis of So-called Anaphoric Islands. *Language* 67(3):439–474.

Williams, Edwin. 1981. On the Notions 'Lexically Related' and 'Head of a Word'. *Linguistic Inquiry* 12:245–274.

7

Hungarian Derivational Morphology, Semantic Complexity, and Semantic Markedness

FERENC KIEFER

1 Introduction

It is a well-known observation that the meaning of some words are more complex than others. In the simplest case the more complex meanings include simpler meanings plus other components.[1] For example, the meaning of the verb *sell* is semantically more complex than that of the verb *give* since it contains the semantic components of *give* plus some other semantic material. In general, the more semantic material the meaning of a word contains, the more complex it is semantically. The notion of semantic complexity is indispensable for any study of the organization of the lexicon and it can also be used to predict the order in which individual lexical items are acquired by children.

It has also been noticed that people divide things into categories, each of which is given a name. These categories are often hierarchically organized with several levels of abstraction. For example, *plant–tree–pine–Ponderosa pine–northern Ponderosa pine*. It has been argued that the third level (the generic level) is the most basic ("basic-level terms"). A basic-level term such as *pine, oak, elm* is more useful than any term on a higher or lower level of abstraction. Therefore, basic-level terms are acquired by children earlier than non-basic ones. Thus, in certain cases at least, the complexity

---

I am grateful to Wolfgang Dressler, Edith Moravcsik, and Anna Szabolcsi for detailed comments on earlier versions of this paper. I would also like to thank the audience of the Conference on Lexical Semantics at Stanford (1987) for many insightful comments and questions.

[1]In what follows I am going to draw heavily on Clark and Clark 1977, esp. pp. 337–342 and 487–501.

Lexical Matters. Ivan A. Sag and Anna Szabolcsi, eds.
Copyright © 1992, Stanford University.

hypothesis and the basic-level hypothesis make different predictions as to order of acquisition.

It has been suggested that it is possible that semantic complexity applies to verbs, adjectives and relational terms and basic-level predictions to category names. However, this proposal does not do justice to the facts since similar phenomena as with basic-level terms can also be encountered among verbs, which are clearly relational. This is one of the points which will be made in the present paper. As a consequence, a theory is called for which is able to reconcile the two hypotheses. The main aim of this paper is to sketch such a theory.

The meaning of a word can be more basic than the meaning of a related word in several ways, "basicness" is not restricted to levels of utility as stipulated for basic-level terms. In the present paper we will use the term 'semantic markedness' to describe phenomena which involve "basicness" or "naturalness," i.e., we will say that of two words w_i and w_j, which belong to the same semantic field, w_i is semantically more marked than w_j if w_i is less basic or natural than w_j. Semantic markedness is governed by various principles such as transparency of meaning, lexicalization patterns, restrictions imposed on the use of the words, etc. In this paper we will concentrate on the problem concerning restrictions on use.

We will see that whenever there is a conflict between the complexity and the markedness hypothesis, the latter takes precedence over the former.

Semantic complexity contrasts with formal complexity. Formal complexity may have to do with morphology or with syntax. In languages such as English morphological complexity is often explained in terms of irregularity. For example, the past tense in English is formally more complex than the expression of possession. The past tense is usually expressed by the suffix -ed, but there are numerous exceptions. The expression of possession, on the other hand, is quite regular. In the case of languages such as Hungarian, which is an agglutinating language, morphological complexity can be defined in terms of the number of morphemes which occur in a word. Consider, for example, the verb ír 'write' and the forms ír+at ('+' will be used to denote morpheme boundary throughout this paper) 'make write', ír+at+hat 'may make write', ír+at+hat+na 'could make write', ír+at+hat+nál 'you could make write' with increasing morphological complexity. In general, forms which contain more morphemes require a larger amount of processing time than forms with fewer morphemes.

Syntactic complexity may be defined in terms of predicate-argument structure, i.e., by the number of arguments required by a predicate and the various restrictions imposed on these arguments.

There are phenomena both in morphology and in syntax which cannot be explained by means of the notions of morphological or syntactic complexity. Some of these will be touched upon briefly in the present paper.

Though it will be proposed to use the terms 'morphological markedness' and 'syntactic markedness', respectively, for these cases, nothing substantial will be said about "formal" markedness in this paper.

There is a strong correlation between semantic complexity and syntactic complexity, on the one hand, and between semantic complexity and morphological complexity on the other. These correlations follow from the "coding principle" well-known in psycholinguistics which says that "complexity in thought tends to be reflected in complexity of expression." Such correlations do not seem to exist between the various types of markedness.

The observations to be presented in this paper are based on Hungarian. The semantic fields to be investigated are defined by the rules of derivational morphology. This means that we will leave out of consideration semantic fields whose members are not relatable to each other by such rules. Semantic fields of the former type make up a significant portion of lexical structure in Hungarian.

The reason why I think that it is worthwhile to restrict the examination of the interrelationship between complexity and markedness to semantic fields defined by derivational morphology is that in a language such as Hungarian the formal structure of words reflects complexity of content. Consequently, the feasibility and usefulness of the decomposition hypothesis cannot be questioned. It is hoped, however, that the basic ideas put forward here can be extended to the analysis of other types of lexical items as well.

The principles proposed are claimed to hold for languages which are typologically similar to Hungarian (roughly, for agglutinating languages), though most of them may turn out to be universal.

The main claim of the present paper can thus be summarized:

(i) Semantic complexity and semantic markedness are two different notions. Semantic complexity is based on the amount of the semantic material contained in the lexical items, semantic markedness, on the other hand, has to do with restrictions on use, but it is also related to such notions as productivity and semantic transparency.

(ii) Alongside of the distinction between semantic complexity and semantic markedness, a similar distinction between formal (morphological, syntactic) complexity and formal (morphological, syntactic) markedness has to be drawn.

(iii) Semantic complexity determines semantic markedness to a large extent, however, whenever there is a conflict between semantic complexity and semantic markedness, the latter takes precedence over the former.

(iv) It is markedness and not complexity that defines acquisition order.

(v) Markedness which is based on the notion of "level of utility" is not restricted to category names as suggested by earlier studies but has to be extended to relational terms as well. In this way the conflict between the two theories about acquisition order disappears.

2   Morphological, Syntactic, and Semantic Complexity

Let's first define the notions of morphological, syntactic and semantic complexity.

2.1   Morphological Complexity

For the description of Hungarian, Hungarian being an agglutinating language, morphological complexity can be defined easily. We may simply identify morphological complexity with the number of morphemes contained in a word.[2] More precisely,

(1)   A word w_i is morphologically more complex than another word w_j if w_i contains more morphemes than w_j.

According to this definition, (2a) is morphologically less complex than (2b), and (2b) is morphologically less complex than (2c). Furthermore, (2b,d,e) are all of equal complexity.

(2)   a. *olvas* 'read'
      b. *olvas+tat* 'make read' (causative)
      c. *el+olvas+tat* 'make read' (causative-perfective)
      d. *olvas+gat* 'read little by little' (frequentative)
      e. *el+olvas* 'read' (perfective)

Let's introduce the symbol '$<_m$' for the morphological complexity relation. We may thus represent the complexity relations at hand as in (3).

(3)   *olvas* $<_m$ *olvas+tat* $<_m$ *el+olvas+tat*

It goes without saying that the notion of morphological complexity has to be defined differently for each language type.

We know that complexity is not the only principle that determines the acquisition of morphology. Semantic transparency and productivity may even be more important principles than the complexity of form. In general, of two forms of equal morphological complexity the one which is more productive or which is more transparent in meaning is more basic or more natural.[3] Consider, for example,

(4)   a. *gereblyé+z* 'rake', *zongorá+z(ik)* 'play the piano'
      b. *hal+ász(ik)* 'fish', *vad+ász(ik)* 'hunt'

---

[2]Clearly, definition (1) is the simplest possible definition of morphological complexity which holds only for "pure" agglutinating languages of which Hungarian is not an example. In Hungarian, in addition to the number of morphemes, there are further aspects of morphological structure that may contribute to morphological complexity, e.g., stem alternations, "fused" morphemes, assimilation rules, etc. In the present paper we will neglect these additional complications, however.

[3]Naturalness phenomena constitute the main motivation for the introduction of the notion of markedness in morphology as well as in syntax and semantics. (See further below.) In most works complexity and markedness are not kept apart. See, however, the recent discussions of morphology (Dressler, Mayerthaler, Panagl and Wurzel 1988).

That transparency of meaning and productivity play an important role in the acquisition of derivational morphology has also been pointed out by Clark (1988).

Notice that both (4a) and (4b) are bimorphemic but whereas the suffix -z is fully productive and quite frequent, the suffix -ász is no longer productive in that it occurs in a small number of lexicalized items only. Consequently, the items in (4b) may be claimed to be less basic or less natural than the ones in (4a).

However, affix productivity is only one factor that determines basicness. In some cases a productive suffix can also be added to a phantom root, i.e., to a bound morpheme with no clear independent meaning. Consider, for example, the Hungarian suffix -int, which is used to derive instantaneous verbs: emel+int 'give it a lift', csavar+int 'give it a twist', sodor+int 'give it a twirl', etc., where the roots are full verbs with independent meanings (emel 'lift', csavar 'twist', sodor 'twine, twirl'). However, we may also encounter verbs such as köh+int 'give a little cough' or ból+int 'nod', where the bound morphemes köh- and ból- are semantically not transparent. (That they are nevertheless identifiable as morphemes is testified by the fact that they also occur with other derivational suffixes, e.g., köh+ög 'cough' and ból+ogat 'keep nodding'.) In view of the difference in semantic transparency one may argue that köh+int and ból+int are less basic than emel+int, csavar+int and sodor+int.

To mention yet another case where ease of perception may enter into play consider again the suffix -z (example (4a) above) together with its variant -zik:

(5)   a. bor+oz 'sit over one's wine', szem+ez 'ogle'

      b. tanyá+zik 'take shelter', zongorá+zik 'play the piano'

Notice that in the case of (5b) the morpheme boundary between the root and the suffix coincides with a syllable boundary, that is, syllabification does not affect morphemic structure. In the case of (5a), on the other hand, syllabification yields (6).

(6)   bo&roz, sze&mez

This means that the morpheme boundary between the root and the suffix does not coincide with a syllable boundary. In other words, the forms in (5b) are morphologically more transparent than those in (5a). Degrees of morphotactic transparency correlate with degrees of naturalness, hence the forms in (5b) are more natural or more basic than those in (5a).[4]

In sum, then, semantic transparency, morphotactic transparency and productivity are principles which may run counter morphological complexity. The effects of these principles may be subsumed under the term 'morphological markedness'. This means that, in addition to a theory of morphological complexity, a theory of morphological markedness is called for to explain morphological structure. In what follows I won't have anything more to say about morphological markedness.

---

[4]For the notion of morphotactic transparency see Schaner-Wolles and Dressler 1985.

2.2 Syntactic Complexity

For the purposes of the present discussion we will be content with a rather restricted notion of syntactic complexity. Consider

(7) a. *Ülök.*
'I'm sitting'
  b. *Írok (egy levelet).*
'I'm writing (a letter)'
  c. *Megírok *(egy levelet).*
Megírok egy levelet.
'I'm going to write up a letter'

The verb *ül* 'sit' requires just a subject, the verb *ír* 'write' a subject and optionally an object, the perfective verb *megír* 'write (up/down)' a subject and an obligatory object. In other words, *ül* is a one-place predicate, *ír* can be used either as a one-place predicate or as a two-place predicate, and *megír* is a two-place predicate. The verb *megír* will be said to be syntactically more complex than the verb *ír* which, in turn, will be said to be syntactically more complex than the verb *ül*.

To take another example, the verb *beszél* 'talk' and *beszél-get* 'converse' are alike except that the latter requires either the plurality of agent or a second agent represented by a *with*-phrase:

(8) a. *Péter és János beszélgetnek.*
'Peter and John are conversing'
  b. *Péter beszélget Jánossal.*
'Peter is conversing with John'

The verb *beszélget* has thus a more complex predicate-argument structure than the verb *beszél*, it is syntactically more complex.

On the basis of the above observations the following definition of syntactic complexity may be stipulated.[5]

(9) A predicate P_i is syntactically more complex than another predicate P_j if P_i contains more obligatory arguments than P_j and/or if the arguments required by P_i are syntactically more restricted than those required by P_j.

Again, there are good reasons to distinguish syntactic complexity from what may be termed syntactic markedness. In Hungarian a transitive verb may, in general, appear in sentence initial position, after the subject but before the object, and in sentence final position. For example,

---

[5]A note of caveat is in order here. Syntactic complexity should by no means be reduced to a simple count of the arguments. The definition proposed under (9) is, no doubt, over-simplified. The notion of syntactic complexity should be based on full-fledged syntactic representations.

(10) a. *János eszi az almát.*
      John eats the apple
      'John is eating the apple'
   b. *János az almát eszi.*
      'It is the apple that John is eating'
   c. *Eszi János az almát.*
      'John does eat apples'

It should be noted that the English translations are not the only possible interpretations of the corresponding Hungarian sentences. Now, any native speaker of Hungarian would readily admit that—quite independently of the meaning differences—only (10a) sounds quite neutral, (10b) and (10c) are somehow "marked." The details are, of course, anything but clear. But, again, we don't have to bother about this question in the present context.

2.3 Semantic Complexity

Semantic complexity can be defined on the basis of the amount of the semantic material contained in semantic representations. For example, causatives are semantically more complex than non-causatives since the former, but not the latter, contain the (elementary) predicate $CAUSE(x, y)$ in their semantic representations. In this sense, then, the causative *írat* 'make write' is semantically more complex than the non-causative *ír* 'write'. Similarly, the causative *olvastat* 'make read' is semantically more complex than the corresponding non-causative *olvas* 'read'. Or, to take another example, the perfective forms of telic predicates are semantically more complex than the corresponding imperfectives since they contain the components $BECOME(y, z)$ and $TERMINATED(z)$ in their semantic representations which are obviously lacking in the semantic representations of the corresponding imperfectives. Thus, the form *megír* 'finish writing' is semantically more complex than *ír* 'write' and the form *elolvas* 'finish reading' is semantically more complex than *olvas* 'read'. Yet another case can be illustrated by the frequentative. Frequentatives are semantically more complex than the corresponding non-frequentatives since the former, but not the latter, contain the semantic feature $REPEATEDLY(PRED(x, y))$. Thus the frequentative *írogat* 'write often' is semantically more complex than the corresponding non-frequentative *ír* 'write' and the frequentative *olvasgat* 'read little by little' is semantically more complex than the non-frequentative *olvas* 'read'.

So far we have been considering categories which had to do with aspect or *Aktionsart*. There are of course quite a few other things which contribute to semantic complexity. Remaining within the confines of derivational morphology, notice that there are pairs of verbs in Hungarian which differ from each other in presuppositional properties only. For example, *tagad* 'deny' is non-factive but *letagad* 'deny' with the prefix *le-* is factive. The verbs *titkol* 'hide, conceal' and *eltitkol* 'keep to oneself, withhold' represent a similar pair, where the latter verb is presupposition-inducing whereas the former is not. In general, the presupposition-inducing forms are semantically more complex than the corresponding non-inducers. Notice, furthermore, that verbal affixes do not only change the aspectual character or the *Aktionsart* of the verb to which they are attached but very often introduce further (in general, unpredictable) semantic material. This is particularly true of verbal prefixes except for the perfectivizing prefix *meg-*. Consequently, whereas forms such as *megír* 'write' with the perfective prefix have got a transparent meaning in the majority of cases, forms such as *leír* 'write down, register, copy, ...' or *felír* 'write down, prescribe, charge, ...' show unpredictable meanings. Both *felír* and *leír* are perfective but they contain further semantic material which is not present in the corresponding imperfective forms. Hence *felír* may be said to be semantically more complex than *megír* which, in turn, as we already saw above, can be said to be semantically more complex than *ír*.

By restricting ourselves to the semantic field defined by derivational morphology we need not take a stand on how the meaning of root words should be described and we don't have to bother about the question of how far down compositional meanings have to be looked for. By taking the meaning of the root word for granted we will simply ask the question of what the contribution of each derivational morpheme to that meaning is. If the semantic contribution of a derivational morpheme cannot be accounted for by general rule, the meaning of the derived word will be noncompositional or idiomatic.

The above examples may suffice to illustrate semantic complexity.[6]

To be sure, in order to be able to exactly define the notion of semantic complexity one would first have to develop a theory of semantic representations. Different theories may lead to different semantic representations of the very same item which entails that it may be characterized by different

---

[6]An interesting and in many ways illuminating way of approaching this can be found in Miller and Johnson-Laird 1976. Starting out with a set of core concepts (such as *TRAVEL, POSSESS, SEE, UTTER, SAY*) and a set of basic semantic operators (such as *HAPPEN, DO, ACT, POSSIBLE, CAUSE*), it is claimed that a core concept can be refined, modulated by means of these semantic operators in several ways. Each refinement or elaboration of a core concept makes it semantically (conceptually) more complex. A semantic field is defined by means of various ramifications brought about by these semantic operations. Thus, for example, the core concept $TRAVEL(x)$ can be refined by introducing a presuppositional $(LEAVE(x))$, or by specifying the manner $(LURCH(x))$, or by introducing a causal component $(CHASE(x,y))$, etc. (op. cit. pp. 666–67). Our discussion of Hungarian derivational morphology will be similar to the approach advocated by Miller and Johnson-Laird in one important aspect. Each derivational extension may be taken to correspond semantically to the application of a semantic operator (aspectual, directional or other) and may thus count as a further elaboration of the given meaning by rendering it more complex.

degrees of semantic complexity, depending on the semantic representation one wants to adopt. For the time being we have to be content with the following definition.

(11) A word w_i is semantically more complex than another word w_j if the semantic representation of w_i contains more semantic material than the semantic representation of w_j in terms of elementary semantic predicates, the types of these predicates and the operations performed on them.

It is worthwhile noticing that the definitions of morphological, syntactic and semantic complexity involve increasing levels of abstraction. The definition of morphological complexity is based on a straightforward count which depends merely on the definition of the notion of morpheme. The definition of syntactic complexity, on the other hand, presupposes a theory of syntactic representations. In general, however, the syntactic properties of predicates can be translated into these representations in a straightforward way. Finally, the definition of semantic complexity presupposes a theory of semantic representations. Such a theory involves questions such as (i) what are the primitives of the theory, (ii) how are meanings constructed out of these primitives, (iii) what kinds of aspects of meaning have to be reflected in semantic representations. In addition, definition (11) is committed to the view that semantic representations do consist of elementary predicates. If one is open-minded enough one has to admit, however, that the vast majority of lexical items are not amenable to a treatment presupposed by definition (11). For a large portion of the vocabulary one has to be content with a description as suggested by prototype semantics. But if one wants to make use of prototype semantics in the description of lexical items, the question immediately arises whether it is possible to correlate degrees of typicality or degrees of centrality and semantic complexity. I think this question should be answered in the negative. Why should there be any difference as to semantic complexity between, say, the word *sparrow* and the word *duck* or between the word *duck* and the word *penguin*? Consequently, it seems to make sense to talk about semantic complexity only in cases· in which it is meaningful to postulate (at least partial) semantic representations based on a set of elementary predicates.

We will see further below that—in whatever way we define semantic complexity—a notion of semantic markedness is called for in order to be able to describe certain phenomena which involve basicness or naturalness. But before embarking on the discussion of semantic markedness we will have a closer look at semantic complexity and the relationship between morphological complexity and semantic complexity, on the one hand, and between syntactic complexity and semantic complexity, on the other. Once again, in discussing these questions we will restrict ourselves to semantic fields defined by the rules of derivational morphology.

3 Semantic Complexity and its Relationship to Syntactic Complexity and Morphological Complexity

To begin with, let's take a common activity verb, say, *ír* 'write' and its derivational expansions. For simplicity's sake we will consider the aspectual prefixes as participating in the derivational processes, i.e., as being derivational prefixes.[7] Furthermore, we will take it for granted that suffixation precedes prefixation. It should be made clear, however, that the order of the two derivational processes is not quite obvious. In fact, in principle, there are three possibilities: (i) suffixation precedes prefixation, (ii) prefixation precedes suffixation and (iii) there is no general ordering relation between suffixation and prefixation. However, if we were to adopt (iii), we would have to give up any systematic account of derivational morphology. This alternative can thus be discarded. The decision between (i) and (ii) depends on various syntactic and semantic considerations but since this decision has no consequences for semantic complexity we will abstain from discussing these problems in more detail here.

Figure 1 shows a partial derivational expansion of the verb *ír* 'write'.

As can be gathered from Figure 1, the verb *ír* 'write' can be expanded by means of the perfectivizing suffix *meg-* to the perfective *megír* 'write down, finish writing' or by means of one of the prefixes *fel-* 'up', *ki-* 'out', *le-* 'down', etc., to the verbs *felír* 'write down, charge, ...' *kiír* 'copy out, write in full, ...' and *leír* 'write in, register, ...' which are perfective, on the one hand, and have often unpredictable meanings, on the other. Another expansion of *ír* produces the frequentative *írogat* (by means of the derivational suffix *-gat*) 'keep writing, write frequently' which in turn can be expanded by means of one of the prefixes *fel-*, *ki-*, *le-*, which yields *felírogat*, *kiírogat*, *leírogat*, which have the same meanings as *felír*, *kiír*, *leír* (see above) except that they are frequentative rather than perfective. Then, *ír* can also be expanded by means of the impersonal passive (reflexive) suffix *-ódik*, which yields *íródik* 'be/get written', which in turn can be perfectivized resulting in *megíródik* or in *felíródik*, *kiíródik*, which are the (impersonal) passive counterparts of *megír* and *felír*, *kiír*, *leír*, respectively. The passive suffix is *-atik*, which can be used to produce the passive form *íratik* 'be/get written', which again, can be perfectivized yielding *megíratik* or *felíratik*, *kiíratik*, *leíratik*. The causative suffix *-at*

---

[7]Traditionally, prefixation is not considered to belong to derivational morphology in Hungarian. First of all, prefixes, in contrast to suffixes, don't harmonize with the stem and are thus in this respect more like anterior constituents of compounds. On the other hand, they can be separated from the stem (just as, for example, the separable prefixes in German) which makes them dissimilar to anterior constituents of compounds. Semantically, they often resemble adverbials, esp. prefixes such as *ki-* 'out', *be-* 'in', *körül-* 'around', *vissza-* 'back'. The rather frequent prefix *meg-* is an aspectual operator in most cases. In other cases, prefixes behave like verbal suffixes: they are used to derive verbs from verbs. Prefixation seems thus to occupy an intermediate position between compounding and derivation.

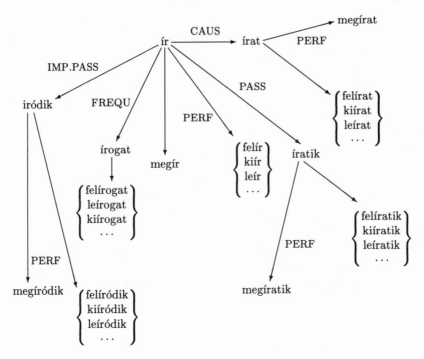

Figure 1

produces the causative *írat* 'make write', which can further be expanded by adding to it the perfectivizing prefix *meg-* resulting in *megírat* or one of the prefixes *fel-*, *ki-*, *le-* yielding *felírat*, *kiírat*, *leírat*.

It should also be noted that each form in Figure 1 can further be expanded by the possibility suffix -*hat* meaning 'may, can', e.g., *írhat* 'may be writing', *megírathat* 'may make write down', *kiíródhat* 'may get written/copied out', etc.

Notice that all the derivatives except for those with the prefixes *fel-*, *ki-*, *le-*, have got a transparent semantics, their meanings are fully predictable on the basis of the meanings of their constituent morphemes. In other words, the meanings of these derivatives are compositionally derivable. In contrast, the derivatives with the prefixes *fel-*, *ki-*, *le-* are, in general, semantically not transparent, their meanings cannot be predicted on the basis of the meaning of their constituent morphemes. That is, these meanings are not compositionally derivable.

It should be noted that the verbs with the prefixes *fel-* 'up', *ki-* 'out', *le-* 'down', *be-* 'in', *el-* 'away', etc., are semantically opaque just in case they don't denote mere direction. As long as they are used in their original meanings, they are completely transparent, e.g., *ki+megy* 'go out', *be+néz* 'look in', *fel+húz* 'draw up, hoist'.

Since we have been assuming that the more semantic material a form contains, the more complex it is semantically, in order to establish the semantic complexity relationship between two derivationally related forms it suffices to determine the relative amount of the semantic material contained in the two forms. As we saw above, perfective forms contain more semantic material than the corresponding imperfectives and some perfective forms (i.e., those with a prefix whose function is more than just perfectivization) are semantically richer than simple perfective forms, where the perfective prefix carries perfective meaning only. In what follows we will reserve the label 'perfective' to denote such simple perfective forms, the semantically more complex perfectives will be termed 'qualified perfective'. The above observations yield the following complexity relationships.[8]

(12) a. imperfective $<_{sem}$ perfective
      b. perfective $<_{sem}$ qualified perfective

It is also evident that causatives are semantically more complex than non-causatives. Furthermore, it would seem that passives are, in general, semantically more complex than the corresponding actives. That is, we get (13a)–(13b).[9]

(13) a. non-causative $<_{sem}$ causative
      b. active $<_{sem}$ passive

Frequentatives contain more semantic material than the corresponding duratives, as pointed out above, hence

(14) durative $<_{sem}$ frequentative

The impersonal passive and the passive do not seem to differ from each other with respect to semantic complexity, that is, the relationship (13b) is valid for both passives.

In sum, the operations denoted by PERF, CAUS, PASS, IMP.PASS, FREQU introduce additional semantic material which motivates the relationships (12a), (13a)–(13b) and (14). In Hungarian these operations are reflected in morphology as shown by Figure 1.

If we also take into account the possibility suffix -hat/-het, we may posit

(15) non-modal $<_{sem}$ modal

where 'modal' refers to a form expressing possibility and 'non-modal' to the corresponding "factual."

---

[8]We have already introduced the symbol '$<_m$' for the relation of morphological complexity (cf. example (3)). For syntactic complexity we may use the symbol '$<_{syn}$', for semantic complexity the symbol '$<_{sem}$' and for pragmatic complexity the symbol '$<_p$', respectively.

[9]Complexity relationships such as (12a) and (13a)–(13b) have been treated in earlier literature under the heading of markedness. See, for example, Lapointe 1986, or for structuralist treatments of the problem, Greenberg 1966 and Hjelmslev 1953. It has, however, not always been made clear whether these relationships refer to the "content plane" or to the "expression plane."

Informally, the active, the passive and the causative may be characterized by (16a)–(16c), respectively.

(16) a. x does y
   b. y is done by x
   c. x causes z to do y

It is therefore not at all surprising that on any analysis suggested so far the causative is considered to be semantically more complex than the passive and the passive semantically more complex than the active.[10] That is, we get

(17) active $<_{sem}$ passive $<_{sem}$ causative

For the lexical field of *ír* 'write' in Figure 1, the complexity relations formulated thus far yield, among other things, the following complexity orderings.

(18) a. *ír* $<_{sem}$ *írogat* $<_{sem}$ *felírogat* $<_{sem}$ *felírogathat*
   'write'   'write little   'write up little   'may write up
              by little'   by little'   little by little'

   b. *ír* $<_{sem}$ *megír* $<_{sem}$ *megírhat*
   'write'   'write down'   'may write down'

   c. *ír* $<_{sem}$ *írat* $<_{sem}$ *megírat* $<_{sem}$ *megírathat*
   'write'   'make write'   'make write   'may make
                              down'   write down'

   d. *ír* $<_{sem}$ *íródik* $<_{sem}$ *írat*
   'write'   'be/get written'   'make write'

   e. *felír* $<_{sem}$ *felíródik* $<_{sem}$ *felírat*
   'write down,   'be/get written   'make write down,
      prescribe'   down, be/get   make prescribe'
                   prescribed'

In the cases discussed thus far there is an interesting correlation between semantic complexity and morphological complexity. There are no two forms such that the semantically more complex form be morphologically less complex. In the case of (18d), on the other hand, the semantically more complex form does not always show an increase in morphological complexity. In particular, the forms *íródik* 'be/get written' and *írat* 'make write' are both bimorphemic. In sum, it would seem that the following rule holds.[11]

(19) By increasing semantic complexity, morphological complexity does not decrease.

---

[10]See Lapointe 1986 (p. 224).
[11]This holds within a semantic field defined by the rules of derivational morphology, of course. In view of the language-specific definition of morphological complexity, this correlation, too, has to be considered to be language-specific.

As to the syntactic properties, the situation is as follows: *ír* 'write' and *írogat* 'write little by little, write frequently' do not require an overt object in contrast to *írat* 'make write' , *megírat* 'make write down', *felírat* 'make write down, prescribe', *felírogat* 'write down repeatedly', *megír* 'write down', *felír* 'write down' which cannot occur without an overt object (except elliptically). The impersonal passive (reflexive) forms are used without an agent: *íródik* 'be /get written', *megíródik* 'be/get written down', *felíródik* 'be/get prescribed'. The passive forms *íratik, megíratik, felíratik* with the same meaning may be used with an agent, the agent is expressed by a *by*-phrase. That is, we have to do here with four degrees of syntactic complexity: the forms with an optional object are syntactically less complex than the forms that require an overt object which in turn are less complex than the passive forms. Furthermore, the impersonal passive is syntactically less complex than the agentive passive. For the forms of *ír*, then, it would seem that a similar correlation holds between semantic and syntactic complexity as between semantic and morphological complexity. The following rule seems to be valid:

(20) By increasing semantic complexity syntactic complexity does not decrease.[12]

The following example shows that the derivational expansions of a word may all be opaque. Figure 2 depicts the derivational expansions of the verb *beszél* 'talk'.

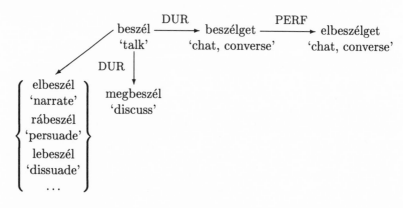

Figure 2

What may strike us at first glance is that, in general, the various derivational expansions of *beszél* 'talk' are not semantically transparent: *beszélget* 'chat, converse' is not simply the durative counterpart of *beszél*, similarly *megbeszél* 'discuss' is not the perfective variant of *beszél*. Nev-

---

[12]Since the definition of syntactic complexity given above, however restricted it may be, is not language-specific, (20) could, in principle, be a good candidate for being universal.

ertheless, the forms *beszélget* and *elbeszélget*, 'chat, converse' are durative and the prefixed variants of *beszél* are in a way perfective. Consequently, *megbeszél* 'discuss', in contrast to *beszél*, must contain a resultative component in its semantic representation. Furthermore, *beszélget*
'chat, converse' presupposes at least two participants, which *beszél* does
not. Consequently, it seems to be quite plausible to assume that *beszélget*
'chat, converse' is semantically more complex than *beszél* and *elbeszélget*
(at least if used transitively with the meaning 'pass time in conversation',
see below) semantically more complex than *beszélget*. Similarly, *megbeszél*
should be considered to be semantically more complex than *beszél* since
it demands that the topic be explicitly specified. The verb *elbeszél* 'narrate' is even more complex than *megbeszél* 'discuss' since (i) the topic must
be a story and (ii) the report must be rather detailed. Furthermore, it
is easy to see that the verbs *rábeszél* 'persuade' and *lebeszél* 'dissuade',
too, contain more semantic material than *megbeszél* 'discuss'. That is, the
complexity relations are not affected by the fact that all derivatives are
semantically opaque. This leads us to the formulation of the following
principle.

(21)   The semantic complexity relations among derivationally related lex-
       ical items which are semantically opaque are the same as if these
       lexical items were semantically transparent.

Principle (21) should be considered as a hypothesis about semantic complexity which must be tested on further material.[13]

As to the relationship between semantic and morphological complexity,
the derivational expansions, as can easily be seen, obey rule (19).

Syntactically, *beszélget* 'chat, converse' requires either a plural argument or two arguments but it is still intransitive. The verb *elbeszélget* has
two uses. On one of its uses it is synonymous with *beszélget* (i.e., it is neither transitive nor perfective). However, it may also be used transitively
with the object 'time': 'pass time in conversation'. *Megbeszél* 'discuss'
and *elbeszél* 'narrate' always require an overt object, *rábeszél* 'persuade'
and *lebeszél* 'dissuade' have three arguments. All this seems to indicate
that, in the case of the derivational expansions of the verb *beszél*, too,
the relationship between semantic and syntactic complexity is governed by
rule (20).

The next example which we will discuss is the basic verb of movement
mozog 'move' with the root *moz-*, whose derivational expansions are shown
in Figure 3.

The basic verb *mozog* is unspecified as to direction and it is intransitive
and durative. From the root *moz-* one can derive the punctual *mozdul*

---

[13]Principle (21) claims that the perfective operator makes the form more complex independently of whether the meaning arrived at is transparent or opaque. The same holds
true for the durative operator.

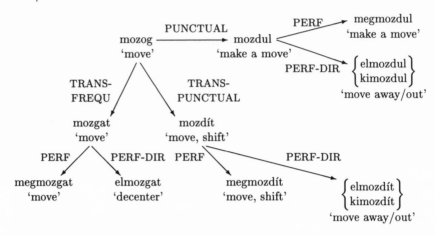

Figure 3

'make a move' which can receive the perfective prefix *meg-* yielding *megmozdul*. *Mozdul* can also be prefixed by a directional prefix, e.g., *ki-* 'out' or *el-* 'away' resulting in *kimozdul* 'move out' or *elmozdul* 'move away'. The intransitive *mozog* (more precisely, the root *moz-*) can be transitivized in two different ways. The frequentative suffix *-gat* yields *mozgat* 'move repeatedly' which is transitive and frequentative. This verb can be perfectivized by means of the perfective prefix *meg-* (*megmozgat*) or by means of the perfective-directional prefix *el-* (*elmozgat* 'move away'). The other transitive verb derived from *moz-* is the punctual *mozdít* to which either the perfective prefix *meg-* or one of the perfective-directional prefixes *el-* 'away', *ki-* 'out' can be added, which results in *megmozdít* 'move, shift' or in *elmozdít* 'move away', *kimozdít* 'move out'.

Notice that all the derivatives in Figure 3 are semantically transparent. Moreover, almost all of them can be rendered in English by the verb 'move' which is a clear indication of how different Hungarian and English can be with respect to lexical structure.

The complexity relations among the forms in Figure 3 are partly determined by directionality. In particular, the following complexity relation holds.

(22) unspecified $<_{sem}$ direction

where 'unspecified' should be read "unspecified with respect to direction." (22) does not only account for the complexity relation between, say, *megmozdít* 'shift' and *kimozdít* 'get out of place' (where both verbs are perfective) but also covers the complexity relationship between such verb pairs as *néz* 'look' and *benéz* 'look in' (where the first verb is imperfective and the second one has a perfective and an imperfective reading).

Punctual verbs are more complex than durative verbs (other things being equal), since only the latter, but not the former, are compatible with both durative and nondurative adverbials. Furthermore, punctual verbs can be used to express perfectivity even if they occur without a perfective prefix. The two sentences in (23a)–(23b) have identical meanings.

(23) a. *A kő mozdult egyet.*
          the stone move-Past one-Acc
          'The stone made a move'
      b. *A kő megmozdult.*
          'The stone made a move'

Consequently, we may posit

(24) durative $<_{sem}$ punctual

However, *mozdul* and *megmozdul* are not synonymous. Consider

(25) a. *Már mozdul a kő.*
          already move the stone
          'The stone starts moving'
      b.* *Már megmozdul a kő.*

As testified by (25a) *mozdul* 'start moving' has an inchoative meaning which is absent in *megmozdul*. In general, verbs with a perfective prefix cannot refer to on-going processes or activities, they don't have any present tense meaning. The verb *megmozdul* is semantically more complex than the verb *mozdul*.

4   Pragmatic Complexity

As we have seen above, each derivational morpheme contributes to the meaning of the "input." There are no derivational affixes (in Hungarian) without any content. Their contribution need not be semantic, however. Let's explore this question in some more detail.

The diminutive suffix *-i* is used to form nouns from nouns in two ways.

   (i) *-i* is added to the truncated form of the initial noun, e.g., *csok+i* (from *csokoládé* 'chocolate'), *dir+i* (from *direktor* 'director'), *ov+i* (from *óvoda* 'kindergarten'), *fagy+i* (from *fagylalt* 'ice cream').

  (ii) The suffix *-i* is added to the stem of the noun, e.g., *láb+i* (from *láb* 'foot'), *comb+i* (from *comb* 'thigh'), *has+i* (from *has* 'belly'), *husi* (from *hús* 'meat').

Words in group (i) belong to school slang. They presuppose a certain degree of intimacy and have often a jocular touch. The forms in (ii), on the other hand, belong to nursery talk: they are typically used in a discourse in which at least one small child participates. In neither case, however, does the suffix *-i* denote smallness. In fact, pairs such as *fagy+i* and *fagylalt* 'ice cream' or *has+i* and *has* 'belly' are truth-conditionally identical. What is then the contribution of the suffix *-i* to the meaning of the stem noun? It can determine the social setting of the speech situation (in the case of (i)). The second case can also be characterized by the label 'endearments'. Though these aspects of meaning are clearly conventional (they are not implicated "conversationally"), they are not truth-functional. Since, in principle, any conventional meaning can be accounted for in semantics, the suffix *-i* does not necessarily call for a pragmatic explanation.[14]

There are, however, cases which show that a derivational affix may introduce non-conventional meaning as well. The example we are going to consider comes from adjective morphology.[15] In addition to the positive, the comparative and the superlative, Hungarian has got an excessive. Consider

(26)   a. *nagy*   *nagy+obb*   *leg+nagy+obb*   *legesleg+nagy+obb*
           'big'   'bigger'   'biggest'   'very biggest'
       b. *okos*   *okos+abb*   *leg+okos+abb*   *legesleg+okos+abb*
           'clever' 'cleverer'   'cleverest'   'very cleverest'

The question immediately arises what the excessive means. The superlative already defines the highest degree of the property at hand, i.e., 'x is the biggest' means that from among the things considered x possesses the highest degree of the property at hand, that is, of being big. The excessive cannot change this state of affairs; what it does is to introduce a presupposition (and special discourse functions). Recall that what is biggest need not be big and who is cleverest need not be clever. In contrast, the thing that is the very biggest must be big and the person who is the very cleverest must be clever. That is, the excessive turns a relative property into an absolute one. The introduction of a (semantic) presupposition, as we saw above, leads to a higher degree of semantic complexity.

As to its discourse function, notice that the excessive can be considered as the emphatic variant of the superlative in a way. Emphasis is not neutral contextually. For example, in general, one cannot start a conversation by using the excessive. The excessive requires a context in which there is a discussion about the highest degree of a property (or at least such a discussion must be implicit in the context). The person who uses the excessive wants to emphasize *his* belief about the question: 'believe me, this is the very best solution' or the like.

---

[14]This problem and similar phenomena were treated under the heading of morphopragmatics in Dressler and Kiefer 1990.

[15]Comparison of adjectives is traditionally treated in inflectional morphology. In quite a few respects, however, it is more like derivation. First of all, the superlative prefix *leg-* can in no way be considered to be an inflectional affix since Hungarian inflectional affixes are suffixes. Second, the semantic properties of the superlative are not comparable to those of inflectional paradigms.

The excessive does not always introduce a presupposition, however.[16] Take, for example,

(27) a. *csúnya*   *csúnyá+bb*   *leg+csúnyá+bb*   *legesleg+csúnyá+bb*
         'ugly'   'uglier'   'ugliest'   'very ugliest'
      b. *buta*   *butá+bb*   *leg+butá+bb*   *legesleg+butá+bb*
         'stupid'   'more stupid' 'most stupid'   lit. 'very stupidest'

Adjectives which express negative evaluation are, in general, used in an absolute sense, i.e., 'uglier' induces the presupposition that the things compared are both ugly and 'more stupid' induces the presupposition that the things compared are both stupid. Similarly, if 'x is ugliest' then x must be ugly, and if 'x is most stupid' then x must be stupid. In such cases the excessive cannot induce a presupposition since this presupposition is already there. The contribution of the excessive to the meaning of the superlative is thus restricted to the special discourse functions. These discourse functions do not make the excessive semantically more complex than the superlative but they certainly make it pragmatically more complex in a way. This means that a definition of pragmatic complexity is called for.[17] If we use 'discourse function' as a cover term for any pragmatic restrictions or functions, then (28) holds.

(28) Of two forms x and y, which are semantically of equal complexity, y is pragmatically more complex than x if it differs from the latter by having specific discourse functions.

Since there are good reasons to assume that the comparative is semantically more complex than the positive and the superlative semantically more complex than the comparative, we get for the excessive one of the two complexity relations (29a) or (29b).[18]

(29) a. positive $<_{sem}$ comparative $<_{sem}$ superlative $<_{sem}$ excessive
      b. positive $<_{sem}$ comparative $<_{sem}$ superlative $<_p$ excessive

where $<_{sem}$ stands for "semantic complexity relation" and $<_p$ for "pragmatic complexity relation."

We are now in the position to reformulate principle (19) in the following fashion.

(30) Within a semantic field defined by the rules of derivational morphology, by increasing semantic or pragmatic complexity, morphological complexity does not decrease.

---

[16]I discussed the presuppositional properties of adjectives at considerable length in Kiefer 1977.

[17]It goes without saying that pragmatic complexity is also needed in order to account for the difference between other types of synonyms. Cf. *invite* versus *bid/come* or *roast/grill* as equivalents of *interrogate*. Cf. Verschueren 1985.

[18]For a detailed account of the semantics of dimensional adjectives and the semantic representations of the positive, the comparative, and the superlative, see Bierwisch 1987 and Lang 1987.

5 Semantic Markedness

Semantic complexity may explain a lot but it does not explain everything. In particular, there are certain phenomena which seem to run counter to the predictions of the complexity theory as developed thus far. In what follows we will discuss some such phenomena.

(i) Our first example is taken from the semantic field of verbs of movement. Recall that both *megmozgat* 'move' and *elmozgat* 'move away' were regular derivatives of the verb *mozgat* 'move' (see Figure 3). Though these verbs are not only morphologically regular but also semantically transparent, they have a rather restricted use. *Megmozgat* is not so much used in its literal sense, but it occurs quite frequently in idiomatic expressions, for example, *megmozgatja a képzeletet* 'quicken one's fantasy', *minden követ megmozgat* 'leave no stone unturned', *megmozgatja a tömegeket* 'rouse the masses'. *Elmozgat* 'move out/away' is a technical term ('decenter') and it is not part of our everyday vocabulary. Most often *megmozgat* is replaced by the transitive-punctual (and equally perfective) *megmozdít*, and in place of *elmozgat* the transitive-punctual-directional *elmozdít* is used. Notice furthermore that *megmozgat* need not imply durativity and iterativity, that is, *megmozgat* may be synonymous with *megmozdít*. Consequently they exhibit the same degree of semantic complexity. Similarly, *elmozgat* and *elmozdít* may also be semantically identical. Yet *megmozdít* is more useful than *megmozgat* because it can be employed in a larger number of situations. Its use is not collocationally restricted. In this sense *megmozdít* is more normal or more natural than *megmozgat*. Similar considerations hold for the pair *elmozgat* and *elmozdít*. Since *elmozgat* is only used as a technical term (in the sense of 'decenter'), it is not necessary to show that it has a more restricted use than *elmozdít*. Again, *elmozdít* is more normal or more natural than *elmozgat*.

(ii) The second example concerns the passive in Hungarian. Notice that the passive suffixes -*atik/-etik*, -*tatik/-tetik* are morphologically fully productive: *ad+atik* 'be given', *mond+atik* 'be said', *néz+etik* 'be looked at', *kér+etik* 'be asked', *tanít+tatik* 'be taught', *enged+tetik* 'be allowed', etc. However, the passive is hardly used in present-day Hungarian: it occurs almost exclusively in certain idiomatic expressions. In all other cases it is replaced by the corresponding active form. Compare

(31) a. *Nem adatott meg nekem.*
          'It was not granted to me'

      b. *Engedtessék meg, hogy ...*
          lit. 'let it be allowed that ...'

(31a) is rare and (31b) is stylistically marked. Normally, the passive (32a) would always be replaced by the (impersonal) active (32b).

(32) a. *Megtiltatott.*
'It was forbidden'

   b. *Megtiltották.*
'They have forbidden it'
(*meg-*: perfective prefix, *tilt*: verb stem 'forbid', -*at*: passive suffix, -*ott*: Past Tense, -*ák*: 3rd Person Plural)

Consequently, in spite of the morphological productivity of the passive, passive constructions are infrequent, unusual or even odd.

The impersonal passive -*ódik* is, no doubt, more often used than the agentive passive. Consider

(33) a. *Az ajtó jól csukódik.*
'The door closes properly'

   b. *A titok kitudódott.*
'The secret is out'
(*csuk*: verb stem 'close', -*ód*: impersonal passive, -*ik*: 3rd Person Singular, *tud*: verb stem 'know', *ki-*: prefix 'out', -*ód*: impersonal passive, -*ott*: Past Tense).

In general, the impersonal passive is more useful than the agentive passive in Hungarian. I argued above that the agentive passive is semantically more complex than the impersonal passive. One might thus conjecture that the degrees of complexity correlate with the levels of utility: the more complex a form is, the less useful it is. Although this may very often be the case, this correlation is not always valid. Recall that the causative was considered to be semantically more complex than the agentive passive. The causative, too, is morphologically fully productive in Hungarian. Consider

(34) a. *Péter taníttatja a gyerekeit.*
lit. Peter have taught the children-his
'Peter provides for the education of his children'

   b. *Anna ruhát csináltat.*
'Anna has a (new) dress made'

Sentences such as (34a)–(34b) are also widely used in Hungarian. In view of these facts the causative has to be considered more normal or more natural than the passive which seems to run counter the complexity hierarchy repeated here under (35).

(35) active $<_{sem}$ passive $<_{sem}$ causative

(iii) In some cases the perfective prefix *meg-* can be used to express single events. Notice that some verbs seem to express habitual or iterative meaning in virtue of their lexical potential. For example, *csókol* 'kiss', *látogat* 'visit', *dicsér* 'praise', *kóstol* 'taste', etc. As soon as these verbs are turned perfective, however, the habitual or iterative meaning disappears and what is left is the meaning referred to as 'single event'. Compare

(36) a. *Péter csókolja Katit.*
'Peter is kissing Kati' (iterative)

b. *Péter megcsókolja Katit.*
'Peter is going to kiss Kati' (single event)

(37) a. *Péter látogatja Katit.*
'Peter visits Kati' (iterative)

b. *Péter meglátogatja Katit.*
'Peter is going to visit Kati' (single event)

Even if the forms *megcsókol* and *meglátogat* are not perfective-resultative, i.e., they are not in the same way perfective as, for example, the verbs *megír* 'write down' (from *ír* 'write') or *megépít* 'build' (from *épít* 'build') implying a result (a letter or a house), they share two fundamental properties with them. First, their internal temporal structure has to be considered as an indivisible whole, hence perfectivity excludes iterativity. The 'single event' interpretation is a consequence of this property. Second, the verbs *megcsókol* 'kiss (once)' and *meglátogat* 'visit (once)', in general, cannot refer to the present, their potential time reference is non-present. There are thus good reasons to assume that the prefixed forms are semantically more complex than the corresponding forms without a prefix.

For some reason, however, sentences such as (36b) and (37b) express the preferred way of looking at the world. Of course, this has nothing to do with iterativity, sentences such as (38a)–(38b) sound quite normal.

(38) a. *Péter többször megcsókolta Katit.*
'Peter kissed Kati several times'

b. *Péter többször meglátogatta Katit.*
'Peter visited Kati several times'

Apparently, our preference goes for 'perfectivity', that is, for completed action, or terminated event in cases such as *csókol* 'kiss', *látogat* 'visit' and *kóstol* 'taste'. No wonder, then, that the perfective forms of these verbs are more frequent than the corresponding unprefixed verbs, as they sound more normal or more natural. And they do this in spite of the fact that they are semantically more complex.

(iv) A similar argument can be made for some other types of prefixed verbs. Thus, for example, verbs of movement are more often used with directional prefixes than without them. In general, we go in somewhere or come out from somewhere, we come down from somewhere or we go up somewhere. Direction is implicit in the case of verbs such as *come* and *go*, it has to be inferred on the basis of the respective positions of the speaker and the hearer and some other aspects of the speech situation. In certain contexts the utterances in (39a)–(39b) or the ones in (40a)–(40b) may be considered equivalent.

(39) a. *Pisti megy már.*
'Steve is already going'
b. *Pisti már elmegy.*
'Steve is already leaving'

(40) a. *Pisti jöjjön már!*
'Pisti should come'
b. *Pisti jöjjön már ide!*
'Pisti should come here'

In (39b) and (40b) the direction of the movement is made explicit: *el-* 'away' and *ide* 'here'. It is arguable that *elmegy* 'go away' is semantically more complex than *megy* 'go', but at the same time the former is more explicit about the direction of the movement, hence less marked, than the latter. The same holds true for the pair *idejön* 'come here' and *jön* 'come'.

Quite often a directional prefix of the verb also appears as a case suffix on the noun which denotes the goal of the movement. For example, *bemegy a terembe* 'go into the hall', *rálép a lábára* 'step on someone's foot'. The verbal prefix can be omitted under certain circumstances. One such case is if the directional noun is moved into focus position, i.e., in front of the verb: *a terembe megy, a lábára lép*. This is, no doubt, a syntactically more complex construction than the previous one. The situation is similar in the other cases in which the verbal prefix is omissible. This state-of-affairs leads to a higher frequency of the prefixed verbs in comparison with the unprefixed ones. That is, *bemegy* 'go in' is less marked than *megy* 'go' and *rálép* 'step on' can be claimed to be less marked than *lép* 'step'. Once again, higher semantic complexity means lesser degree of semantic markedness.

In the previous sections we have been discussing four cases which showed that two forms of equal semantic complexity need not be equally natural or normal or that semantically more complex forms may be more natural or normal than their semantically less complex equivalents. In these cases naturalness or normality has to do with restrictions on the use of the given form. That is, the more restricted its use is, the less natural or normal it will be. As a quasi-technical term 'natural' or 'normal' can be equated with 'unmarked', and 'unnatural' or 'unusual' with 'marked'. Naturalness is of course a matter of degree hence the markedness principle which covers the cases discussed above can be formulated as follows.

(41) Of two derivationally related forms x and y, y is semantically more marked than x if there are more restrictions imposed on the use of y than on that of x.

If there are no restrictions imposed on x and y, principle (41) does not apply.

Except in cases where markedness relations are derivable from (41), or from some markedness principle, obtain, markedness can be taken to be identical with complexity. This principle is formulated in (42).

(42)   In a semantic field defined by derivational morphology, the marked-
       ness relations are identical to the complexity relations, except in
       cases in which special markedness relations obtain.

Principle (42) holds true for semantic markedness and semantic complexity only. It is doubtful whether similar principles can be formulated for
morphological and syntactic markedness.

It would seem that it is markedness and not complexity (and this holds
for semantic, syntactic and morphological markedness alike) which should
be relatable to processing time and acquisition order.[19] Though no syntactic study has been undertaken so far with respect to the acquisition of
the derivational morphology of Hungarian, the preliminary data which we
have at our disposal seem to support this claim.[20]

6   Summary

To summarize, by examining some examples from Hungarian derivational
morphology definitions for morphological complexity, syntactic complexity
and semantic complexity were proposed. The definition of morphological
complexity was claimed to be language-specific (or language-type specific)
whereas the other two definitions should be considered to be universally
valid. It was pointed out, however, that the proposed definition of syntactic
complexity is too narrow as a general definition of syntactic complexity
since it is based solely on predicate-argument structure.

It was further claimed that markedness relations are different from
complexity relations on all levels considered. The principles which govern
markedness relations are thought to be universal but (some of) the particular markedness relations may be language-specific. In general, markedness has to do with naturalness phenomena. Some examples were given
for morphological markedness and syntactic markedness was discussed in
more detail. In general, there seems to be no direct relationship between
morphological markedness and morphological complexity, on the one hand,
and between syntactic markedness and syntactic complexity, on the other.
In contrast, semantic markedness seems to be identical with semantic complexity except where special markedness relations obtain.

Also, a few words were said about pragmatic complexity which can be
used to distinguish two forms of equal semantic complexity in terms of
discourse function.

---

[19] As for the hypothesis that semantic complexity determines acquisition order, see Clark
and Clark 1977 (pp. 498–500) and the references cited there. The hypothesis about
"basic level terms" is due to E. Rosch and her colleagues. (See, for example, Brown
1973 and Clark and Clark 1977 (pp. 500, 527–530) and the references cited there.)

[20] See, for example, Fazekas 1989. Some of the data on which the present study is based
are taken from a as yet unpublished material collected by Zita Réger from the Research
Institute for Linguistics of the Hungarian Academy of Sciences and by Csaba Pléh from
the Institute of Psychology at Budapest University and their collaborators.

Acquisition order is claimed to be determined by markedness rather than by complexity. If no special markedness relations obtain, however, semantic markedness is thought to be identical with semantic complexity.

A strong correlation was found between semantic and syntactic complexity: if semantic complexity increases, then in general, syntactic complexity cannot decrease. There is also a relationship between semantic complexity and morphological complexity. More precisely, it was shown that morphological complexity cannot decrease if semantic or pragmatic complexity is increased. Cross-linguistic studies should reveal to what extent these relationships are universal.

References

Bierwisch, Manfred. 1987. Semantik der Graduierung. *Studia Grammatica* 26–27:91–286.

Brown, Roger. 1973. *A First Language: The Early Stages*. Cambridge, Mass.: Harvard University Press.

Clark, Eve V. 1988. Acquisition Principles in Word-formation: Some Comparisons of English and Hebrew. Paper presented at the 3rd International Morphology Meeting in Krems, Austria.

Clark, Herbert H., and Eve V. Clark. 1977. *Psychology and Language*. New York: Harcourt, Brace, Jovanovich.

Dressler, Wolfgang U., and Ferenc Kiefer. 1990. Austro-Hungarian Morphopragmatics. In *Contemporary Morphology*, ed. Wolfgang U. Dressler, H. C. Luschïtzky, Oskar E. Pfeiffer, and John R. Rennison, 69–77. Berlin and New York: Mouton de Gruyter.

Dressler, Wolfgang U., Willi Mayerthaler, Oswald Panagl, and Wolfgang U. Wurzel. 1988. *Leitmotifs in Natural Morphology*. Amsterdam: John Benjamins.

Eckman, Frederick R., Edith A. Moravcsik, and Jessica R. (eds.) Wirth. 1986. *Markedness*. New York and London: Plenum Press.

Fazekas, Á. 1989. Az ige a gyermek beszédében (The Verb in Child Language). Manuscript, Institute of Psychology, Budapest University.

Greenberg, Joseph H. 1966. *Language Universals with Special Reference to Feature Hierarchies*. The Hague: Mouton.

Hjelmslev, Louis. 1953. *Prolegomena to a Theory of Language*. Baltimore: Waverly Press.

Kiefer, Ferenc. 1977. Adjectives and Presuppositions. *Theoretical Linguistics* 5:135–173.

Lang, Ewald. 1987. Semantik der Dimensionsauszeichnung. *Studia Grammatica* 26–27:287–458.

Lapointe, Steven G. 1986. Markedness: The Organization of Linguistic Information in Speech Production, and Language Acquisition. In *Markedness*, ed. Frederick R. Eckman, Edith A. Moravcsik, and Jessica R. Wirth, 219–239. New York and London: Plenum Press.

Miller, George A., and Philip N. Johnson-Laird. 1976. *Language and Perception.* Cambridge, Mass.: Harvard University Press.

Rosch, Elinor, C. B. Mervis, W. Gray, D. Johnson, and P. Boyes-Braem. 1976. Basic Objects in Natural Categories. *Cognitive Psychology* 8:382–439.

Schaner-Wolles, C., and Wolfgang U. Dressler. 1985. On the Acquisition of Agent/Instrument Nouns and Comparatives by Normal Children and Children with Down's Syndrome: A Contribution to Natural Morphology. *Acta Linguistica Academiae Scientiarum Hungaricae* 35:153–149.

Verschueren, Jef. 1985. *What People Say They Do with Words.* Norwood, NJ: Ablex Publishing Company.

8

Focus-Based Inferences in Sentence Comprehension
GYÖRGY GERGELY

1 Introduction

The aim of this paper is to investigate the nature of discourse inferential
processes in comprehending complex sentences. It will be argued that the
interpretational structure that the listener constructs for a sentence in discourse is a joint function of its abstract semantic content and its discourse
context (see e.g., Bierwisch 1981, Gergely and Bever 1986). The inferential processes involved in computing such a representation are constrained
by different sources of discourse information, such as (i) topic-focus (TF)
structure, (ii) interclausal semantic relations, and (iii) pragmatic knowledge
structures, like scripts. The present study will demonstrate that such discourse cues, when available, are employed *directly and interactively* in the
construction of a discourse interpretational representation for the sentence,
even before its full syntactic and semantic processing is complete.

The experimental studies to be discussed were carried out in Hungarian, a non-Indo-European, agglutinative, "free" word order language, where
the discourse functions (topic versus focus) of constituents are systematically related to surface structural positions in the sentence. Therefore,
Hungarian seems ideally suited for the investigation of discourse inferential

The experimental work reported in this paper forms part of my Ph.D. dissertation
(Columbia University, 1986). I am grateful to Tom Bever, Dave Townsend, Csaba
Pléh, Marylene Cloitre, Lou Ann Gerken, and Steve Dopkins for their intellectual and
personal support during the research. I thank Herb Clark, Dan Morrow, Richard Meier,
Anna Szabolcsi, and László Kálmán for their detailed comments on an earlier draft
of this paper. The experimental work was carried out at the Department of General
Psychology of the Eötvös Loránd University in Budapest; I wish to thank Sándor Illyés,
Ilona Barkóczi, and Csaba Pléh for making the research facilities of the University
available to me, András Varga for statistical, Károly Halmai, László Bernáth, Béla
Marián, and János Geier for technical help. During the writing of the final version of
this paper I was supported by a research grant from the MTA-Soros Foundation.

processes during sentence comprehension, since, apart from intonational cues, it also provides locally unambiguous *structural cues* for the on-line identification of TF structure.

The paper will be organized as follows. Section 2 will discuss some of the limitations of earlier approaches to discourse inferential processing, which used only off-line, post-sentence measures. In Section 3, I will argue that the sentence focus is directly accessed during on-line speech comprehension and plays a central role in the discourse interpretation of sentences. In Sections 4 and 5, I will develop some hypotheses about the role of focus-based inferences in the comprehension of adversative subordinate constructions. Section 6, will describe how the structural positions in the Hungarian sentence can act as cues for the on-line identification of the discourse roles of surface constituents. Then, Section 7 will summarize the results of an earlier study (Gergely 1986, 1991a, 1991b) which examined the role of focus-based inferences in establishing discourse antecedent relations during the processing of subordinate constructions. In Section 8, I will report a new study which investigates the role of focus-based predictive inferences in the processing of adversative subordinate constructions. Finally, in Section 9, I shall discuss the implications of the results for current models of speech comprehension.

2   The Role of Discourse Information in Sentence Comprehension

Early research on sentence comprehension (see Fodor, Bever, and Garrett 1974) was preoccupied with investigating how the listener employs grammatical cues in the surface sequence to assign underlying syntactic relations that are necessary to identify the semantic structure of the sentence. Typically, it was assumed that "... understanding a sentence requires the recovery of its semantic representation" (Fodor, Fodor, and Garrett 1975), which then serves as the input to the inferential processes that fix the interpretation of the sentence within its discourse context. The implication of this approach was that the processes integrating the sentence into the discourse structure take place only after its underlying linguistic structure has been fully assigned, i.e., not before the end of the sentence.

More recent approaches, however, (e.g., Marslen-Wilson, Tyler, and Seidenberg 1978, Marslen-Wilson and Tyler 1980, Riesbeck and Schank 1978, Johnson-Laird 1984, Crain and Steedman 1985) have tended to abandon this strictly modular view, and assume that as the listener proceeds in the sentence, he attempts to construct a discourse interpretational structure directly. These more interactive models pay increasing attention to the top-down influence of higher-order contextual variables on speech processing. As a result, researchers started to investigate the role of discourse informational cues in the inferential processes that are involved in com-

puting the contextual interpretation of sentences. However, until recently
the different types of discourse information (such as pragmatic knowledge,
TF tructure, or inter-propositional semantic relations) were typically studied in isolation, and their effects on comprehension were demonstrated
only indirectly, using off-line measures. As a result, the on-line nature
of the utilization of discourse cues in comprehension remained largely
unspecified.

For example, the construct of *scripts* (e.g., Schank 1975; Schank and
Abelson 1977; Bower, Black, and Turner 1979) provides a useful framework
for conceptualizing how pragmatic knowledge might bear on the interpretation of sentences in discourse. Scripts are characterized as complex memory
structures that represent our shared cultural knowledge about the typical
structure of events and situations in the world in terms of structured sets
of propositions. In discourse, speakers often make reference to information
that has not been explicitly introduced, but that they assume is available in
the listener's memory. Therefore, listeners often have to make linking inferences based on their pragmatic knowledge to establish coherent referential,
causal, and temporal relations between successive propositions. Scripts
constrain such inferential processes by providing the interpretational domain over which such relations are established (e.g., Sanford and Garrod
1981).

The relevance of scripts in sentence processing has been demonstrated
in a number of studies (e.g., Bower et al. 1979, Duffy 1983, Gibbs and
Tenney 1980, Townsend 1983). The typical finding is that after a script
has been activated by the previous text, a subsequent sentence is compre-
hended faster when its content is predictable from the script. These results
suggest that the processing of a sentence can be facilitated by script-based
expectations about its content. In fact, it has been proposed that sentence comprehension in normal discourse relies heavily on generating expectations through directly accessing contextual and pragmatic knowledge
(Riesbeck and Schank 1978).

The studies demonstrating such script-based effects, however, typically
examined overall reading times for *whole* sentences. As a result, they
cannot tell us whether the script-based expectations exert their influence
only *after* the syntactic and semantic processing of the sentence has been
completed, or whether they already affect the more immediate levels of
processing. In fact, it was not until relatively recently (see e.g., Sharkey
and Mitchell 1985, Gergely 1991a) that the on-line effects of higher-order
contextual constraints on such local aspects of speech processing as word
recognition have received systematic attention.

The situation was similar in studies (see Clark and Haviland 1977)
investigating another major source of discourse information that constrains
the construction of interpretational representations: what I shall call here
the *topic-focus* (TF) *structure* of sentences. Sentences provide cues that

allow the listener to identify two distinct parts of the expressed proposition: (i) what is variably called "topic," "old," or "given" information, that the sentence is "about," and that has typically been already established (or is readily inferable) in the listener's memory; and (ii) what is called "comment," or "new" information, that the speaker asserts about the topic, and that he believes to be not yet represented in the listener's memory (see Halliday 1967; Chafe 1970, 1976; Chomsky 1971; Jackendoff 1972; Reinhart 1981). The most prominent constituent, both semantically and phonologically, of the latter part of the proposition is the sentence "focus" which receives the primarys stress of the sentence (e.g., Chomsky 1971; Sgall, Hajicová, and Benesová 1973, Szabolcsi 1981).

In a series of experiments, Clark and Haviland (Clark and Haviland 1974, 1977; Haviland and Clark 1974) demonstrated that during comprehension the listener relies on TF structure to relate the new information in a propositional sequence to some previously established antecedent representation in the discourse. In particular, they hypothesized that the identification of the sentence *topic* leads to a *backward search* for a matching antecedent in the discourse structure. If no direct match is found, the listener has to infer an antecedent on the basis of his pragmatic knowledge.

But Clark and Haviland's data consisted of post-sentence measures of overall comprehension times. Clearly, while such studies do imply that listeners rely on the discourse functions (topic versus focus) of constituents for establishing discourse antecedent relations, they, nevertheless, fail to show how and when this process takes place during on-line processing. For example, is the backward search for a discourse antecedent initiated as soon as the topic of the sentence is identified? Or is the information provided by TF structure employed only after the full syntactic and semantic processing of the sentence is complete?

3 The On-Line Use of TF Structure in the Discourse Integrational Processing of Sentences

To answer such finer-grained questions about the processing of discourse informational cues, one needs to employ on-line measures, as exemplified by the studies of Cutler (1976) and Cutler and Fodor (1979). These authors demonstrated that listeners actively search for the focus while they process a sentence, as shown by shorter phoneme-monitoring latencies when the target word is focused than when it is not. Their results indicate that the focus is differentially processed already before the end of the sentence is reached (see also Crain and Steedman 1985). This finding, then, is consistent with the hypothesis that the on-line identification of TF structure directly initiates a backward search for a discourse antecedent.

In this paper I shall argue that TF structure, apart from triggering a backward search for antecedents, is also involved in generating *predictive inferential processes* that serve the discourse integration of complex sentences. In particular, I shall examine how during the on-line processing of subordinate constructions TF structure *interacts* in setting up interpretational representations with other major sources of discourse information, namely, interclausal semantic relations encoded by conjunctions (see Townsend and Bever 1978), and pragmatic knowledge stored in memory structures such as scripts (e.g., Schank and Abelson 1977, Bower et al. 1979) and lexical stereotypes (Gergely and Bever 1986).

4   The Interpretational Structure of Adversative Subordinate Constructions

As an example, let us first examine the structure of the inferential relations that the listener has to establish when comprehending an adversative subordinate construction. This analysis will be central for the empirical studies that follow, as the latter were designed to test different aspects of the processes through which listeners construct the interpretational structure for such constructions. Consider the initial 'though' clause in (1) and the two possible continuations (2a) and (2b):

(1)   Though yesterday John cleaned the bathroom,

(2)   a. Mrs. Jones is still convinced that it is Mary who does all the cleaning in the house.
        b. the tiles still looked a bit dirty.

The general interpretational schema for adversative constructions (see Figure 1) can be summarized as follows (see also Dakin 1970, Townsend and Bever 1978, Bever and Townsend 1979). The initial 'though' in (1) informs the listener that some expectable consequence of the first clause will be denied in the main clause. The particular consequence, however, is not explicitly specified: it has to be *inferred*. For example, the listener has to reconstruct different inferential paths leading from (1) to (2a) and (2b). For (2a) the implicit consequence of (1) is the expectation that because it was *John* who cleaned the bathroom, Mrs. Jones would change her belief about the unequal division of domestic labor between John and Mary. On the other hand, for (2b) the implicit effect is quite different: given that the bathroom has been *cleaned*, it is expected that the tiles would *not* look dirty.

How does the listener identify the inference that the speaker intends to deny, when there are always a number of typical consequences that follow from a given proposition? From the initial 'though' clause, he can generate a set of candidate consequences based on his knowledge of typical cause-effect relations (see Figure 1). However, the abstract propositional content of the clause does not indicate which of those is intended by the speaker.

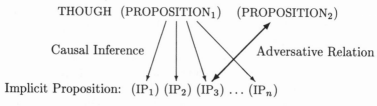

IP$_1$,..., IP$_n$ constitute the set of expectable consequences
based on the initial 'though' clause proposition.

Figure 1 Schematic Representation of the Interpretational Structure
of Adversative Subordinate Constructions

Does the listener have to wait until the main clause is processed, whose
content allows him to identify the denied consequence *retrospectively*?

Townsend and Bever (1978) reported evidence supporting this possibility (see also Bever and Townsend 1979, Townsend 1983). They used
on-line tests to assess the accessibility of (a) the meaning, and (b) the superficial aspects (such as the serial order of words) of the representation
of incomplete clauses. They found that the semantic content of an initial
'though' clause was less available than that of a corresponding main or
'if' clause, while the superficial aspects of the clausal representation were
more accessible in the initial 'though' clause. Townsend and Bever (1978)
hypothesized that the full semantic processing of an initial 'though' clause
is postponed and the clause is kept in a relatively superficial representational format, precisely because the listener "... cannot determine which
cause-effect relation the speaker is denying" before processing the second
clause.

5   The Role of TF Structure in Directing the Inferential Processing of Adversative Subordinate Clauses

In contrast, it can be argued (see Gergely 1986, 1991a, 1991b) that the TF
structure of an initial 'though' clause does provide information that can be
used by the listener on-line to restrict the set of expectable consequences
of the proposition to the one that is most likely to be intended by the
speaker. This is so because speakers, following a Gricean convention of
language use, tend to mark the inferential basis of the denied consequence
as the *informational focus* of the 'though' clause. Consider the sentence
pairs (3) and (4) below:

(3)   a. Though Daddy *praised* his daughter for the excellent dinner, she
         was still not happy.

      b.?Though Daddy praised his *daughter* for the excellent dinner, she
         was still not happy.

(4)   a.?Though Daddy *praised* his daughter for the excellent dinner, it was, in fact, his son who prepared it.

      b. Though Daddy praised his *daughter* for the excellent dinner, it was, in fact, his son who prepared it.

The initial subordinate clauses are identical in the four sentences in all respects save for one: in the placement of contrastive stress (indicated by italics), marking the *focus* of the clause. In (3a) and (4a) the focused element is the verb 'praised', while in (3b) and (4b) the object noun 'daughter' receives contrastive focus. In the case of (3a) and (3b) the final main clause contains the anaphoric pronoun 'she' whose antecedent is in both cases the object NP 'his daughter' from the initial clause. Notice, however, that this final clause is a perfectly natural continuation of the initial clause (3a), but sounds rather awkward following the first clause in (3b).

We can account for this difference in the following way. It can be hypothesized that when the listener identifies the *focus* of the initial 'though' clause, he will compute a *focus-based inference*, based on his pragmatic knowledge of typical cause-effect relations, about the implicit consequence that the speaker intends to deny. Furthermore, I shall assume (see Section 7) that this focus-based consequence will be "foregrounded" (i.e., become differentially activated) at the clause-boundary, because it contains the expectable antecedent argument for the next clause.

Thus, in (3a) the speaker focuses the fact that the daughter was *praised*. Since the typical effect of being praised is to feel happy, by hypothesis, the listener will compute the implicit consequence proposition 'the daughter is happy'. This proposition contains the *topic NP* of the initial subordinate clause, which, in (3a), serves as the antecedent for the anaphoric pronoun 'she' in the second clause. Therefore, on the assumption that the backward search for a coreferent during the processing of the second clause will first access the foregrounded (and, therefore, most available) consequence proposition, the focus-based inference in (3a) can be argued to facilitate the smooth integrational processing of the second clause.

Not so in (3b), however, where the antecedent NP 'his daughter' is *contrastively focused*. By contrastively focusing the object NP, the speaker makes implicit reference to a contrastive set of *entities other than the object* that could have been praised, but were not (see Jackendoff 1972, Chafe 1976). Therefore, the inferred focus-based proposition will contain the entities of the contrastive set, but not the focused object 'his daughter' which is, however, the antecedent for the pronoun 'she' of the second clause in (3b). Thus, in (3b) the speaker *misleads* the listener when, violating the Gricean cooperative convention, he denies in the main clause a consequence that is *not based on the focus* of the initial subordinate clause. As a result, the backward search for antecedent for the main clause pronoun 'she' will, at first, have to be aborted, as the foregrounded focus-based inference does *not* contain the right antecedent NP. For this reason, (3b) sounds awkward when compared to (3a).

In (4a) and (4b), however, the situation is reversed. Here the antecedent for the subject NP 'his son' of the second clause of (4b) is contained in the contrastive set of the inferred focus-based proposition, and so the backward search for antecedent is facilitated. In contrast, the foregrounded focus-based consequence in (4a) contains the topic NP 'the daughter' of the subordinate clause. Therefore, the backward search for a matching antecedent for 'his son' in the second clause will, at first, have to be aborted, since, by hypothesis, it will initially access the foregrounded consequence proposition. As a result, (4a) sounds awkward in contrast to (4b).

Therefore, if the above hypothesis is correct, we would expect a good deal of inferential processing to take place in an initial 'though' clause. This prediction, however, seems to contradict Townsend and Bever (1978) who found that the full semantic processing of an initial adversative clause is postponed until the second clause is reached. To resolve this contradiction, in an earlier study I replicated Townsend and Bever 1978 using Hungarian sentences (see Gergely 1986, 1991a). I argued that Townsend and Bever's subjects processed initial 'though' clauses only superficially because they could not identify the focus of the clause fragments used in the experiment. In English, information about TF structure is typically provided by (a) contextual cues, and (b) intonational cues such as focal stress, which normally falls on the last word of a simple clause (see e.g., Jackendoff 1972). The clause fragments used by Townsend and Bever, however, appeared in isolation, and were recorded with "normal intonation" with the last word of the clause cut out. As a result, none of the constituents was clearly marked as the focus of the clause. It is possible, therefore, that at the point of testing, subjects have not yet assigned focus role to any of the clausal constituents. Consequently, they could not carry out the hypothesized focus-based inferential processing of the initial 'though' clause.

In Hungarian, however, there are clear *structural cues* (see Section 6 below) that can help the listener identify the clausal focus long before the end of the clause. As a result, listeners should be able to assign discourse functions to constituents even when hearing isolated and incomplete clauses. In fact, the replication of Townsend and Bever (1978) in Hungarian showed no differences in either kind of on-line measure between initial 'though' clauses, on the one hand, and corresponding main or 'if' clauses, on the other (see Gergely 1986, 1991a). This indicates that the Hungarian initial 'though' clauses were as fully processed as the other clause types.

In sum, it seems that when cues for TF structure are available in an initial 'though' clause, listeners will compute focus-based inferences to anticipate the content of the main clause. The studies to be discussed below examine this hypothesis in more detail. Since the experimental work was carried out in Hungarian, in the next section I shall briefly describe how

the surface marking of the TF structure of Hungarian sentences differs
from English.

6 Structural Cues for the Identification of Discourse Functions in Hungarian

In English TF structure is often marked only by intonational cues. The
focused element receives the primary or "focal" stress, which in simple
declarative sentences falls on the final word (see Halliday 1967; Chafe 1970,
1976; Akmajian 1973; Chomsky 1971; Jackendoff 1972). Other elements
can also be marked as the focus, if they receive contrastive stress (e.g.,
Jackendoff 1972). Thus, though there are certain syntactic constructions,
such as cleft sentences, which mark the discourse functions of constituents
explicitly, in general, syntactic structural positions do not provide cues for
the identification of TF structure during processing.

In contrast, Hungarian—a non-Indo-European, agglutinative language
with a rich inflectional system and so-called "free" word order—marks
grammatical relations and discourse functions by clearly distinct *structural cues* (see e.g., É. Kiss 1981, 1987; Horvath 1981; Pléh 1982; Szabolcsi
1981). Grammatical relations, such as subject, object, indirect object, etc.,
are encoded by *local cues* in the form of case-marker suffixes attached to
the nouns. This allows the surface order of the major constituents to be
relatively free: practically any permutation of subject, verb, object, and
adverbial yields a grammatical sequence.[1] The resulting versions of a sentence, however, are not interchangeable, they receive different discourse
interpretations. In fact, in Hungarian, discourse functions are related to
particular surface structure positions in a systematic manner. Therefore,
the structural positions of the Hungarian sentence can function as *configurational cues* of high cue validity for the identification of the discourse
roles (topic versus focus) of constituents.

The basic structural positions of the Hungarian sentence can be schematic-ally depicted as follows (see É. Kiss 1981, 1987):

$$[T_1, T_2, \ldots]\ [F]\ V\ [X_1, X_2, \ldots]^2$$

---

[1]However, word order *within* a major constituent (e.g., Det Adj N) is fixed, and some
further restrictions, such as obligatory OV order for indefinite objects, apply. In fact,
constituent order is really free only with respect to grammatical functions and cases, the
position of question words, negated complements, or quantified phrases cannot be freely
varied (see e.g., É. Kiss 1987).

[2]The syntactic characterization of Hungarian sentence structure is controversial at
present. Working within the framework of generative grammar, some linguists (e.g.,
Dezső 1965, Kiefer 1967, Horvath 1981) propose a fully configurational base structure
for the Hungarian sentence of the form [$_S$NP[$_{VP}$V NP]]. The different permutations of
the verb and its complements are derived by various reordering rules such as subject
postposing and focus movement (see Horvath 1981). In contrast, É. Kiss (1981, 1987)
developed within the GB framework (Chomsky 1981) a partially non-configurational
approach in which the underlying structure of the Hungarian sentence has the V in initial

The sentence focus always appears in the immediately preverbal position (i.e., the "focus slot": [F]) and carries the focal stress of the sentence (when there is one).[3] This position can be occupied only by a single element. The element(s) (if any) in the position *preceding* the focus (i.e., the "topic slot": [$T_1, T_2, \ldots$]) is/are the topic(s) of the sentence. The verb can optionally be followed by further complements ([$X_1, X_2, \ldots$]) which, when conveying new information, receive secondary stress, or, if they are known, remain unstressed.

The verb in its stem form can itself become the focus in which case it carries the primary stress of the sentence. However, the experiments to be reported below rely heavily on a special feature of Hungarian grammar: namely, that verbs often form complex predicates when combined with a class of aspect-marking adverbial particles, called verbal modifiers or converbs (e.g., *be* /='in'/, or *el* /='away'/) (see É. Kiss 1981, 1987; Ackerman and Komlósy 1983; Szabolcsi 1986) which indicate the perfectivity of the action.[4] Complex verbs of this type can appear in two forms. On the one hand, the verbal modifier can occupy the F slot, in which case it is *prefixed* to the verb (e.g., '*el*mosta' in (5a) below). Alternatively, the focus slot may be filled by some other constituent. In that case, the modifier has to appear in a *postverbal* position as a separate element (e.g., 'mosta *el*' in (5b) below).

---

position followed by its complements (including the subject) generated in an arbitrary order as sisters to the V. The different surface permutations are generated by movement rules (such as topicalization and focusing) which move the postverbal complements into the syntactic Topic and Focus positions in front of the verb. For a critical discussion of these positions, see Abraham and de Mey 1986, the papers by Kálmán, Prószéky, and Varga in Kenesei 1987.

[3] As pointed out recently by Kálmán (1985) (see also the papers by Prószéky and Varga in Kenesei 1987), there is a class of Hungarian sentences, the so-called "level-prosody" sentences, in which no element receives focal stress. Such neutral sentences have several main stresses one of which falls on the element appearing in the syntactic focus position. In such "flat" sentences the syntactic focus slot is not interpreted as the communicative focus of the sentence. What is important for our present purposes, however, is that when the sentence *does* have a communicative focus (as in so-called "corrective" sentences, see Kálmán 1985) it will always occupy the syntactic focus position. Therefore, this structural position acts as a configurational cue of high cue validity for the listener who attempts to identify the focus of the sentence. For further details on the treatment of the syntactic focus position in generative grammar, see Selkirk 1984, Schmerling 1980, Farkas 1986, Abraham and de Mey 1986, and Rochemont 1988.

[4] The verbal modifier is, in fact, only one kind of constituent which can be incorporated into the Hungarian verb to form a complex predicate. Other incorporated constituents include a bare N of object, subject, adverbial, or predicate function, or an Adj of predicate function. Incorporated constituents are not referring expressions, they add semantic features to the verb and together they form a single semantic unit. However, they are affected by syntactic operations: e.g., if another complement is moved into F position, they surface postverbally. Their correct grammatical (syntactic versus lexical) treatment is presently subject of a controversy (see É. Kiss 1987, Horvath 1981, Ackerman and Komlósy 1983, Kenesei 1983, Szabolcsi 1986, Farkas 1986, Abraham and de Mey 1986).

(5) a.
TOPIC   FOCUS

Nagymama *el*mosta a tányérokat a tegnapi házibuli után, ...

/[T: Grandmother (=nom)] [F: away (=V-mod)] + washed the plates +t (=acc) yesterday +i (=adj) party after, .../

('Grandmother has *washed* the plates after yesterday's party')

b.
TOPIC   FOCUS

Nagymama a *tányérokat* mosta el a tegnapi házibuli után, ...

/[T: Grandmother (=nom)] [F: the plates +t (=acc)] washed away (=V-mod) yesterday +i (=adj) party after, .../

('It was the *plates* that Grandmother has washed after yesterday's party')

These examples illustrate two important points about the difference between the encoding of TF structure in Hungarian and English. First, in Hungarian *the placement of the verbal modifier around the verb* provides a clear structural cue for the assignment of discourse functions to constituents, even when contextual and suprasegmental cues are not present. Secondly, this structural cue can appear long before the end of the sentence or clause is reached. With these points in mind let us return to the role of TF structure in sentence comprehension.

7 The Role of Focus-Based Inferences in Discourse Antecedent Matching

The hypothesized *focus-based inferential processes* (see Section 5 above) involved in establishing across-clause antecedent relations in subordinate constructions, such as (3) and (4), were tested in a previous study (Gergely 1986, 1991a, 1991b) whose main results I shall now summarize. The analysis of (3) and (4) above suggests that an object NP of an initial subordinate clause can be expected to resurface as an argument of the following main clause with higher likelihood when it is topic in the initial clause than when it is contrastively focused. By hypothesis, it can be predicted that *an object NP, that is topic, will be foregrounded from an initial subordinate clause at the clause-boundary*, while a corresponding object NP, that receives contrastive focus, will not.

To test this hypothesis the experiment examined the on-line accessibility of initial clause object nouns in complex Hungarian sentences using an on-line word recognition task. Word probes were presented either *before the end of the initial clause* (see (6a) and (6b)), or *following the first constituent of the final clause* (see (7a) and (7b)). The initial clauses tested were either *subordinate* ('if' and 'though') or *main* clauses. In the critical cases, the tested object noun (indicated by italics) always appeared in a serially identical, preverbal position in the clause, however, it was either the *topic* of the clause (as in (6a) and (7a)), or it was contrastively *focused* (as in (6b) and (7b)).

             TOPIC   TOPIC   FOCUS   W.S.

(6)   a. Ugyan | az estélyen| a *herceget*| bemutatta| a báró a ... | ******|

        PROBE

        HERCEGET|

        /Though | [T_1: at the party | T_2: the *prince*+t (=acc)] | [F: in-(=V-mod 'be-')] showed \=introduced\ | the baron (=nom) \to\ the ... | /

        ('Though at the party the prince was introduced by the baron to the ...')

             TOPIC   TOPIC   W.S.

   b. Ugyan | az estélyen| a *herceget*| mutatta be | a báró a ... | *******|

        PROBE

        HERCEGET|

        /Though | [T: at the party] | [F: the *prince* +t (=acc)] | showed in /=introduced/ | the baron (=nom) /to/ the ... | /

        ('Though at the party it was the prince whom the baron introduced to the ...')

             TOPIC   TOPIC   FOCUS   W.S.

(7)   a. Ugyan | a gerillák| a *herceget*| elrabolták,| az őrnagy a ... | ******|

        PROBE

        HERCEGET|

        /Though | [T_1: the guerrillas (=nom) | T_2: the *prince* +t (=acc)] | [F: away- (=V-mod 'el-')] robbed \=kidnapped\, | the major (=nom) the ... | /

        ('Though the guerrillas have kidnapped the prince, the major the ...')

             TOPIC   FOCUS

   b. Ugyan | a gerillák| a *herceget*| rabolták el, | az őrnagy a ... |

        W.S.   PROBE

        ********| *HERCEGET*|

        /Though | [T: the guerrillas (=nom)] | [F: the *prince* +t (=acc)] | robbed away, (=V-mod 'el') \=kidnapped\ | the major (=nom) the ... | /

        ('Though it was the prince that the guerrillas have kidnapped, the major the ...')

    The sentences were presented to the subjects visually constituent-by-constituent (indicated by vertical lines in (6)–(7)) in a subject-paced reading paradigm. The last constituent was followed by a warning signal (W.S.)

shown for .5 sec. Then the word probe was presented and the subjects had to decide by pushing a '*YES*' or a '*NO*' button whether the probe was from the sentence just read or not. (For further details, see Gergely 1986, 1991a, 1991b). The main results of the experiment are summarized in Figures 2 and 3 below:

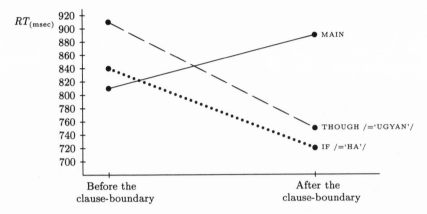

Figure 2 The Accessibility of Initial Clause *Topic* Objects
as a Function of Clause Type and Clause Completeness:
Mean Probe Recognition Times

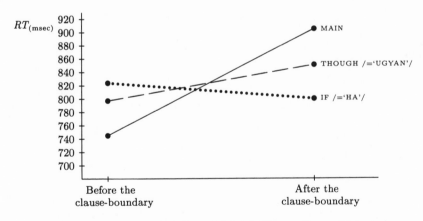

Figure 3 The Accessibility of Initial Clause *Focus* Objects
as a Function of Clause Type and Clause Completeness:
Mean Probe Recognition Times

Figure 2 shows that, as predicted, the *topic* objects from initial *subordinate* clauses (both 'if' and 'though') were *more* accessible when tested during the second clause than before the end of the initial clause ($F(1, 92) =$ 12.62, $p < .01$). In contrast, when the corresponding object nouns were contrastively focused, no increase in target accessibility was observed as a function of the clause-boundary (see Figure 3). These findings support the hypothesis that *topic objects from initial subordinate clauses are foregrounded at the clause-boundary* as likely candidates for second clause antecedent matching.

The results also indicate that the selective foregrounding of an initial clause constituent is a joint function of (i) the discourse role (topic versus focus) of the constituent, and (ii) the sentence-initial conjunctions ('if' and 'though') marking the particular semantic relation between the two clausal propositions. Thus, when no information is available about the interclausal semantic relation, as in initial main clauses, the listener has no sufficient basis to compute predictive inferences about the expectable content of the next clause. As a result, neither topic nor focus targets get foregrounded at the clause-boundary (see Figures 2 and 3). In fact, irrespective of their discourse role in the initial main clause, constituents became less accessible after the clause-boundary than before it ($F(1, 92) = 14.04$, $p < .01$). This can be interpreted as being due to a process of recoding at the end of the clause, which discards the clausal representation from working memory when no predictive hypothesis about its likely involvement in the processing of the next clause can be generated.

To sum up: the results of the experiment support the hypothesis that the assignment of discourse functions to constituents, apart from initiating a backward search for antecedent, also starts a complementary *predictive* process. As a result, the initial clause constituent, that can be expected to serve as the discourse antecedent for the next clause, is foregrounded (i.e., differentially activated) at the clause-boundary. The discourse integrational function of the hypothesized process is that of feeding the backward search for an antecedent in the upcoming clause by making the most likely candidate from the initial clause more accessible for efficient antecedent matching.

8 Focus-Based Predictive Inferences in Clausal Processing

8.1 Introduction

In this section I shall report an experiment to test the hypothesis that during the comprehension of an initial 'though' clause (see Figure 1) the listener computes focus-based inferences to *predict* the propositional content of the upcoming clause. The hypothesized function of computing such a predictive inferential structure is to facilitate the processing of the main clause by anticipating its content.

I assume (see also Crain and Steedman 1985, Johnson-Laird 1984, Marslen-Wilson et al. 1978) that as the listener proceeds in the sentence, he attempts to directly construct an interpretational model of the speaker's intended meaning. In doing so, he accesses his general pragmatic knowledge represented in memory structures such as scripts. The activated script structure (together with the overall discourse structure) serves as the interpretational domain for the constructed representation. I assume that TF structure guides the construction of such a representation by *foregrounding* the focus-related parts of the interpretational domain. I hypothesize that the foregrounded parts receive a higher level of temporary activation than the remaining (backgrounded) aspects of the constructed representation.

Consider the contribution of TF structure to the interpretation of initial main clauses such as (5a) and (5b) above repeated here as (8a) and (8b):

TOPIC   FOCUS

(8)   a. Nagymama *el*mosta a tányérokat a tegnapi házibuli után, ...

/[T: Grandmother (=nom)] [F: away (=V-mod)] + washed the plates +t (=acc) yesterday +i (=adj) party after, ... /

('Grandmother has *washed* the plates after yesterday's party')

TOPIC   FOCUS

b. Nagymama a *tányérokat* mosta el a tegnapi házibuli után, ...

/[T: Grandmother (=nom)] [F: the plates +t (=acc)] washed away (=V-mod) yesterday +i (=adj) party after, ... /

('It was the *plates* that Grandmother has washed after yesterday's party')

When hearing these clauses, the listener accesses the corresponding 'dishwashing' script in his memory. The script specifies that the typical input state of the object (*DIRTY*) is transformed into its characteristic output state (*CLEAN*) as a result of washing. In (8a) the focus position is filled by the verbal modifier *el* (*elmosta* = 'has washed') which expresses the perfectivity of the washing event. By hypothesis, then, the representation of the object ('the plates') will be foregrounded with its *output* state property, i.e., *CLEAN*.

The situation is different, however, in (8b). Here the fact that Grandmother has washed something is not in focus, and so it will be in the backgrounded part of the representation. The contrastive focus on the object 'the plates' implies a set of other things which also *could* have become washed, but were *not*. Therefore, it is hypothesized that in the constructed representation for (8b) this implicit contrastive set will be foregrounded. Since this set contains *potential* objects of washing, it is predicted that they will be represented with the foregrounded property of their characteristic *input* state, i.e., *DIRTY*.

The present study tested these predictions in an on-line probe naming task. Subjects were presented with a word probe describing either the foregrounded, or the backgrounded part of the constructed representation. I assume that if foregrounding results in higher level of activation, then a related word probe will be relatively more accessible (see e.g., Morton 1969, Marslen-Wilson and Welsh 1978) due to spreading activation (e.g., Collins and Loftus 1975) from the foregrounded aspects of the interpretational structure. Thus, the word probe 'dirty', which describes the typical input state of the potential objects of a washing-event, should be primed in (8b), where *DIRTY* is hypothesized to be a foregrounded property of the representation. It should be less accessible, however, in (8a), where the foregrounded object property is *CLEAN*.

Similar predictions can be developed for corresponding initial 'though' (='ugyan' in Hungarian) clauses, as in (9a) and (9b) below:

(9) a. Ugyan Nagymama *el*mosta a tányérokat a tegnapi házibuli után,
...

     b. Ugyan Nagymama a *tányérokat* mosta el a tegnapi házibuli után,
...

In Section 4 I argued that the sentence-initial 'though' cues the listener to generate predictive inferences about the content of the upcoming clause. Let us consider (9a). For the corresponding *main* clause in (8a) it was predicted that focusing the perfective verbal modifier 'el' would foreground the representation of the object of washing with its typical *output* state property, *CLEAN*. The initial 'though', however, indicates that the next clause will contain the *denial* of the focus-based consequence of the initial clause (see Figure 1). As a result, in (9a) the construction of the predictive structure involves a further, adversative inferential step that transforms the foregrounded representation of the output state of the object into its *opposite*, i.e., *DIRTY*. Therefore, in contrast to (8a), the word probe 'dirty' should become relatively more accessible in (9a).

For (9b), however, no corresponding facilitation of 'dirty' is predicted. Here the predicate is not focused, and so the consequence of washing (*CLEAN*) will be in the backgrounded part of the representation. The foregrounded focus-based consequence, that is expected to be denied in the next clause, has to do with the *contrastive choice* as a result of which 'the plates' became the object of washing rather than the other potential objects in the implied contrastive set. Therefore, the listener's hypothesis about the content of the speaker's denial will not involve the opposite (*DIRTY*) of the typical consequence of washing (*CLEAN*). By hypothesis, then, in (9b) the word probe "dirty" should not be primed.

For initial 'though' clauses the hypothesized predictive inferences are jointly determined by the TF structure of the clause and by the semantic value of 'though'. This suggests that, in general, the content of the constructed representation for an initial subordinate clause varies as a function of the kind of interclausal semantic relation. To test this hypothesis, the

experiment also examines 'while' (= *mialatt* in Hungarian) clauses such as
(10a) and (10b) below:

(10) a. Mialatt Nagymama *el*mosta a tányérokat a tegnapi házibuli után,
...

 b. Mialatt Nagymama a *tányérokat* mosta el a tegnapi házibuli után,
...

The initial 'while' in (10) instructs the listener that the event in the up-coming main clause takes place simultaneously with the event expressed in the initial clause. This predictive cue does not imply adversative content for the main clause. For 'while' clauses, therefore, the projected expectations about the simultaneous event should not contain the meaning of 'dirty' as a foregrounded element in either the verb-focus or the object-focus version of (10). Thus, no facilitation of the word probe 'dirty' is predicted in either (10a) or (10b).

Finally, the experiment also examined the temporal characteristics of the hypothesized priming effects. Are the inferential processes initiated as soon as their basis in the clause (i.e., the element in the focus position) is identified, or are they delayed until the full clause has been processed? To find out, the word probes were presented in two serial positions: either (i) before the end of the clause (but following the focus position), or (ii) after the clause-boundary.

Another question concerns the difference in the *processing functions* of the hypothesized inferences in initial subordinate clauses, on the one hand, and in corresponding main clauses, on the other. I argued that in initial 'though' clauses the focus-based inferences are *predictive*: their function is to facilitate the processing of the main clause by anticipating its content. Therefore, the priming effect in (9a) should be present at (or carry over to) the beginning of the main clause.

In initial *main* clauses, however, the hypothesized focus-based infer-ences have no predictive function. The results of the previous study (Gergely 1986, 1991a, 1991b), discussed in Section 7 above, indicate that an initial clause representation is discarded from working memory due to recoding at the clause-boundary, unless the presence of an initial sub-ordinate conjunction overrides this process. In (8b), therefore, the hy-pothesized priming effect is predicted to disappear following the clause-boundary.

8.2 Method

The experiment examined naming times for visually presented word probes at different points in the sentence. Subjects heard three kinds of Hungarian initial clause (main, 'though', and 'while'), each in two focus versions: (i) with a perfective verbal modifier in focus position prefixed to the verb, and (ii) with a contrastively focused object noun in focus position. The verbs always expressed causative events (e.g., 'wash'), which imply pragmatically (but not necessarily) a typical change of state in their object (e.g., from *DIRTY* to *CLEAN*). Probes were presented either (i) before the end of the clause, or (ii) after it. The critical probes always expressed the state (e.g., *DIRTY*) that is the *opposite* of the typical output state of the object (e.g., *CLEAN*) implied by the clausal predicate (e.g., 'wash').

Subjects

Forty eight subjects (28 females and 20 males, with a mean age of 24 years) participated in the experiment. They were all students at the Eötvös Lóránd University in Budapest; their mother tongue was Hungarian.

Materials

Twelve lists were created, each containing 12 experimental and 16 filler sentence fragments. A given experimental fragment appeared in a list in one of two Discourse Type versions: (i) the focus position being filled by the verbal modifier prefixed to the verb (the "verb-focus" version) as in (11a), or (ii) with the object in focus ("object-focus" version) as in (11b) below:

TOPIC   FOCUS

(11) a. Ugyan Nagymama *el*mosta a tányérokat a tegnapi házibuli * után,
      ... **

    /Though [T: Grandmother (=nom)] [F: away- (=V-mod 'el-')] + washed the plates +t (=acc) yesterday +i (=adj) party * after, ... **/

    ('Though Grandmother has *washed* the plates after yesterday's party')

TOPIC   FOCUS

  b. Ugyan Nagymama a *tányérokat* mosta el a tegnapi házibuli * után,
      ... **

    /Though [T: Grandmother (=nom)] [F: the plates +t (=acc)] washed away (=V-mod 'el') yesterday +i (=adj) party * after, ... **/

    ('Though it was the *plates* that Grandmother has washed after yesterday's party')

The verb-focus fragments always had an 'S V-mod +V O Adv Phrase' constituent order. The object-focus versions were always 'S O V V-mod Adv Phrase'. That is, the object-focus fragments were identical with the verb-focus versions, except for the change in word order: the object NP appearing in the preverbal focus position, and the verbal modifier surfacing in a postverbal position. All experimental fragments contained equal number of words. Across subjects each fragment appeared equally often in the three Clause Types: either as an initial main, 'though', or 'while' clause. Thus, an experimental fragment was tested in six Clause Type/Discourse Type versions. The sixteen fillers varied in length, and were either initial main or subordinate clauses introduced by conjunctions other than 'though' or 'while'.

Each fragment was paired with two kinds of probes: "related" or "unrelated." The "related" probes were always state-descriptive terms expressing the opposite of the typical output state of the object implied by the verb. Thus, the "related" probe for (11a) and (11b) was 'dirty'. The "unrelated" probes, however, described a state that was not related to the state of the object (either before or after the causative event has occurred). For example, the "unrelated" probe for (11a) and (11b) was 'torn'. Each "relevant" probe of a fragment also appeared as an "unrelated" probe for another fragment, and *vice versa*. The two kinds of probes appeared with equal frequency throughout the lists in a random order. The fillers were followed by probes that either could or could not be part of a typical, "good" second clause continuation of the fragment.

Across subjects, an experimental fragment appeared in each of the 12 combinations of the three Clause Types, two Discourse Types, and two Probe Types. Accordingly, 12 lists were created and a fragment appeared once in each list as a token of one of the 12 combinations. The 12 fragment types appeared in an identical randomized order in each list, randomly intermixed with the 16 fillers. The order of the 12 experimental types was randomized so that the three clause types appeared with equal frequency over the list. Across lists the 12 experimental fragments were rotated so that a fragment appeared once in each of the 12 experimental positions. Each list was presented to two subjects.

The lists were recorded in two completeness versions with normal intonation. In the Incomplete Clause version the experimental (but not the filler) fragments were recorded so that the last word of the clause was not heard by the subjects. Instead, they heard a 50 msec 1000 Hz warning tone in both ears at the point where the experimental fragment was interrupted (as indicated by the single asterisk '*' in (11a) and (11b)). The filler fragments were fully complete even in the Incomplete Clause condition so that subjects would not develop strategies to cope with truncated, incomplete fragments only.

In the Complete Clause condition, both the experimental and the filler fragments were complete initial clauses. Just after the end of the clause (indicated by two asterisks '**' in (11a) and (11b)) subjects heard a 50 msec 1000 Hz warning tone in both ears. In normal speech there is a short pause between the end of the first clause and the beginning of the second clause. To allow for clause-boundary bound processes to take effect before the on-line test, the probe word in this condition followed the warning tone by a 250 msec delay. The lists were preceded by 8 practice trials that varied in length and structural type similarly to the fillers.

Procedure

Subjects sat in an armchair in a dimly lit room facing a screen placed approximately 12 feet in front of them. A microphone was placed at the level of the subject's head slightly to his right in such a way that it would not block his view. The lists were presented through headphones to both ears. Subjects heard a 50 msec 1000 Hz warning tone in both ears two sec before the presentation of a fragment.

The subjects were instructed to listen to the clause fragments trying to fully comprehend their meaning. They were told that the sentences would be interrupted at some (unspecified) point by a warning tone followed by the presentation of the probe on the screen. In the Incomplete Clause condition the warning tone immediately started the timer, stopped the tape-recorder, and opened the shutter of the slide projector. In the Complete Clause condition, there was a 250 msec delay between the warning tone and the appearance of the probe. There were 24 subjects in both completeness conditions.

Subjects had to perform two tasks. First, they had to name the probe word as fast as they could. Naming times from the appearance of the probe until the subject's verbal response were recorded automatically by a timer (BP 2045982) located in the other room. To insure that subjects fully understood the fragments, a second task was introduced. After they had named the probe, subjects had to judge whether or not it "would fit into a good, typical, well-sounding continuation of the interrupted sentence." Their response was recorded by the experimenter. Following the completion of the second task, the experimenter restarted the tape-recorder to present the next sentence. Each list was preceded by 8 practice trials. Overall, the experiment lasted for approximately 45 minutes.

8.3 Results

Scores that were more than two standard deviations above each subject's mean on a given condition were excluded from the data analysis. Such scores constituted less than 3% of the responses. The results were analyzed by a three-way analysis of variance with one grouping factor and two within-subject variables. The grouping factor had two levels: the Incomplete Clause and the Complete Clause conditions. The two within-subject variables were: (i) Clause Type with three levels (main, 'though', and 'while'), and (ii) Discourse Type with two levels ("verb-focus" and "object-focus"). Since both sentence fragments and subjects were fully crossed with experimental types, separate subject-based and item-based ANOVAs were performed.

Overall, Clause Completeness did not show a main effect (Subjects: $F(1, 46) = .63$, $p > .6$; Items: $F(1, 22) = 2.07$, $p < .2$). There was no main effect of Clause Type in the item-based analysis ($F(2, 44) = 1.57$, $p < .25$), however, the subject-based analysis showed a slight effect ($F(2, 92) = 2.81$,

$p < .07$). The subject analysis also showed a marginal interaction between Clause Type and Clause Completeness ($F(2, 92) = 2.42$, $p < .1$), but no such interaction was apparent in the item-based analysis ($F(2, 44) = 1.07$, $p < .4$).

There was a significant main effect of Discourse Type in both the subject ($F(1, 46) = 5.15$, $p < .03$) and the item ($F(1, 22) = 4.48$, $p < .04$) analysis. Furthermore, Discourse Type and Clause Type showed a significant interaction (Subjects: $F(2, 92) = 6.09$, $p < .005$; Items: $F(2, 44) = 3.71$, $p < .04$). Clause Completeness, however, did not interact significantly with either Discourse Type or Clause Type.

Figures 4 and 5 illustrate the pattern of "related" probe naming times[5] for the 'incomplete clause', and for the Complete Clause conditions, respectively.

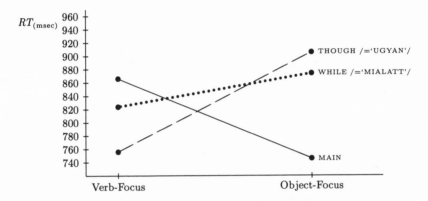

Figure 4 Mean "Related" Probe Recognition Times
in the Incomplete Clause Condition

Overall, the results supported the tested hypotheses. As predicted, Discourse Type had a clear effect on probe recognition in both initial main and initial 'though' clauses in the Incomplete Clause Condition (see Figure 4). Furthermore, for 'though' clauses this effect carried over to the Complete Clause Condition as well (Figure 5).

The significant Clause Type × Discourse Type interaction is largely due to the opposite effect of Discourse Type on main versus 'though' in the Incomplete Clause condition. Figure 4 shows that the verb-focus version of initial 'though' clauses resulted in significantly faster probe naming times than the corresponding object-focus version (Subjects: $F(1, 92) = 8.90$,

---

[5]The relatively long mean probe naming times are due to the fact that the probes were often rather long (ranging from 2 to 5 syllables, with a mean syllable length of 2.95), morphologically complex word-formations (e.g., 'megsavanyodott' /= [it] turned sour/, 'kiszáradtak' /= [they] dried out/).

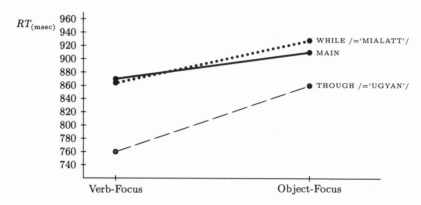

Figure 5 Mean "Related" Probe Recognition Times
in the Complete Clause Condition

$p < .001$; Items: $F(1,44) = 11.94$, $p < .001$). The opposite prediction for
initial main clauses was also borne out by the data (Subjects: $F(1,92) = 6.18$, $p < .01$; Items: $F(1,44) = 7.37$, $p < 0.01$) (see Figure 4).

Figure 5 illustrates that for the object-focus version of initial main
clauses, the probe facilitation, present in the "incomplete clause" condition, disappeared after the clause-boundary. In contrast, for initial 'though'
clauses the probe facilitation effect observed in the verb-focus version of the
Incomplete Clause condition was present in the Complete Clause condition
as well (Subjects: $F(1,92) = 5.32$, $p < 0.01$; Items: $F(1,44) = 6.34$,
$p < 0.01$). Finally, as expected, the different discourse versions of initial
'while' clauses showed no priming effect in either completeness condition.

8.4 Discussion

The results of the experiment make it possible to evaluate three alternative hypotheses about how the listener identifies the implicit consequence
of an initial 'though' clause that is denied by the speaker in the final main
clause. First, Townsend and Bever (1978) proposed that the listener cannot anticipate from an initial 'though' clause which cause-effect relation
the speaker is denying. As a result, he computes no inferences based on
the adversative clause until the main clause is reached. In this view, the
identification of the particular consequence denied by the sentence takes
place only *retrospectively*, during the processing of the final main clause.

Alternatively, the listener, when processing the initial 'though' clause,
could immediately compute from his pragmatic knowledge the exhaustive
set of typical consequences based on all parts of the clausal proposition. He
would select the intended one only later, on the basis of the second clause.

Finally, according to the present hypothesis, the listener could rely on
the TF structure of the initial 'though' clause to restrict the set of ex-

pectable consequences to only those that follow from the *focused* part of the clause. This way he could anticipate the adversative content of the final clause *even before* the clause-boundary.

The results support the final hypothesis. First, naming times for a word probe, whose meaning is in adversative relation to the focus-based consequence of the initial 'though' clause, were significantly decreased both when tested before the end of the clause (Figure 4) and following the clause-boundary (Figure 5). This indicates that by the time the main clause is reached, subjects have generated a predictive hypothesis about its adversative content, resulting in the observed probe facilitation. This rules out the first hypothesis that listeners postpone the inferential processing of an initial 'though' clause.

The result demonstrates that when the TF structure of an initial adversative clause is clearly marked (as in the case of the tested Hungarian sentences), the listener accesses his knowledge of typical cause-effect relations to compute focus-based predictive inferences about the content of the final clause. This is also in line with the results of the replication of Townsend and Bever (1978) using Hungarian sentences (Gergely 1986, 1991a), where, in contrast to the English results, no evidence was found for a relatively shallow processing of initial 'though' clauses (see Section 5 above). Furthermore, the fact that probe facilitation was present already *before* the end of the clause (Figure 4) indicates that the focus-based inference is generated even before the full clause has been processed.

This finding, however, is not sufficient to rule out the second hypothesis that the *whole set* of typical consequences, based on *all* parts of the initial clause, would be computed from pragmatic knowledge. But the fact that the word probes were primed only in the verb-focus version of the initial 'though' clause, rules out the latter alternative as well. The selective nature of the facilitation effect demonstrates that subjects inferred only those consequences that were based on the *focused part* of the clause.

The results indicate that the sentence-initial 'though' modifies the processing of the first clause by invoking a focus-based adversative inference whose function is to predict the content of the upcoming clause. This is also supported by the finding that when *no* initial conjunction is present, as in the corresponding main clauses (see Figures 4 and 5), the verb-focus version does *not* result in probe facilitation.

Furthermore, the priming effect present in the initial 'though' clauses, was absent in the corresponding 'while' clauses in both completeness conditions. This can be attributed to the different semantic value of 'while' whose dominant interpretation is temporal rather than adversative. As such, it is likely to cue the listener to develop predictive hypotheses about a *simultaneous* event in the upcoming main clause. Since there was no specific contextual information to suggest that this next clause event would have an adversative content, the predictive structure computed did not contain the *opposite* of the output state of the object in either the verb-focus or the object-focus version of the initial 'while' clause. As a result, no probe facilitation was observed in either of these conditions (see Figures 4 and 5).

It seems, however, that some predictive inference of a *different* content was, nevertheless, computed during the initial 'while' clause as well. This is suggested by the fact that the 'while' clause data do *not* show the object-focus probe facilitation that was present in corresponding initial main clauses. It seems, therefore, that the sentence-initial 'while' also modifies the processing of the initial clause, but in a manner different from 'though'.

These findings are in line with the general hypothesis that the focus-based inferential structures computed for initial *subordinate* clauses serve a *different processing function* than those generated for corresponding *main* clauses. I argued that sentence-initial conjunctions, cueing the listener about the interclausal semantic organization of the sentence, invoke focus-based inferences to *predict* the content of the second clause. In initial main clauses, however, no such predictive cues are available, and so the observed focus-based inferences have no interclausal predictive relevance.

This interpretation is also supported by the temporal characteristics of the priming effects. On the assumption that the focus-based inferences in the initial 'though' clause serve to facilitate the processing of the *upcoming* clause, it was predicted that the resulting probe facilitation would be present at the beginning of the final clause. The fact that the priming effect in the verb-focus version was present *after* the clause-boundary in the case of initial 'though' clauses (Figure 5) clearly supports this hypothesis. In contrast, since the focus-based inferential structure constructed for an initial *main* clause serves no predictive function, it becomes discarded from working memory at the end of the clause. This is shown by the fact that the priming effect, present in the object-focus version before the end of the main clause (Figure 4), disappears in the after-clause condition (Figure 5). This finding is also in line with the results of my earlier study (Gergely 1986, 1991a, 1991b) discussed in Section 7, where targets from an initial main clause were found to be less accessible after the clause-boundary than before it.

The relatively early presence of the priming effects in *both* the main and the adversative clauses indicates that the focus-based inferences tested are computed more or less *directly*, certainly *before* the full syntactic and semantic processing of the clause is completed. This supports the *interactive* models of speech comprehension (e.g., Marslen-Wilson and Tyler 1980, Johnson-Laird 1984, Crain and Steedman 1985), which hold that the different sources of discourse-relevant information are employed as they become available to constrain the direct construction of a discourse representation of the sentence.

The results also support the assumption that the focus-based inferences directly access pragmatic knowledge of the typical structure of events. The critical verbs in the experiment (e.g., 'wash') always expressed a typical (but not necessary) change of state in their object (e.g., from *DIRTY* to *CLEAN*).[6] It was hypothesized that when the object is contrastively focused, the listener constructs a representation of the implied set of *potential* objects. In doing so, he accesses his pragmatic knowledge in which the typical *input* state of the predicate event is specified, and so the objects in the contrastive set will be represented with the input state property foregrounded. The finding that the object-focus version of the main clause primed the adjective probe that described this input state, clearly supports the hypothesis. Thus, it can be concluded that the on-line construction of an interpretational representation during sentence comprehension has *direct access to pragmatic knowledge structures* such as (e.g., Schank and Abelson 1977, Bower et al. 1979, Sharkey and Mitchell 1985) and lexical stereotypes (Gergely and Bever 1986).

Finally, let us compare the focus-based inferential priming effects demonstrated in the present study to other cases of contextual facilitory effects on word recognition such as lexical priming (e.g., Becker 1979; Fischler and Goodman 1978; Meyer and Schvaneveldt 1971; 1975) or script-based priming (see Sharkey and Mitchell 1985). In lexical priming the presence of a prior context word (e.g., *DOCTOR*) that is semantically or associatively related to a target word (e.g., *NURSE*) results in faster recognition of the latter. Current theories of word recognition (e.g., Morton 1969, Marslen-Wilson and Welsh 1978) assume that such priming effects are due to the temporal lowering of the recognition threshold of the target word as a result of spreading activation coming through the semantic/associative links from the context word that has just been activated (see Collins and Loftus 1975).

At first, one might think that the probe facilitation in the present experiment is a further case of lexical priming. For example, spreading activation propagating through the associative link from the focused predicate 'wash' could prime the word probe 'dirty'. However, there are two aspects of the results suggesting that the priming effect brought about by focus-based inferences is a qualitatively different kind of contextual facilitory effect than associative lexical priming.

The first concerns the *selective nature* of the observed priming effects. Focus-based priming of e.g., the probe 'dirty' (with the perfective verbal modifier 'el' of the complex predicate 'elmosta' (='has washed') in focus position) occurred only when the clause was introduced by 'though'. Had

---

[6]Note that 'wash' is only a "quasi-causative" verb in so far as it is possible to wash clean things, as well as to wash something without succeeding in making it clean. All the critical verbs were quasi-causatives of this kind.

this effect been due to automatic activation through associative lexical connections, one would have expected comparable probe facilitation in the corresponding verb-focus versions of initial 'while' and main clauses as well. However, no such effects were observed.

Secondly, focus-based inferential priming seems to have a *different time course* than lexical associative priming. Previous studies indicate that lexical priming is both very short lived (e.g., Warren 1972, Neely 1977, Loftus 1973) and can be easily disrupted by even one single unrelated intervening item (e.g., Meyer and Schvaneveldt 1971; Gough, Alford, and Holley-Wilcox 1981; Foss 1982). However, in this study there were always five or six intervening words between the focused item and the word probe (see (11a) and (11b)). In addition, the priming effect in the 'though' clause condition survived even an intervening clause-boundary.

These considerations indicate that the observed facilitory effect is not a case of simple lexical priming, as the latter is more localized and subject to rapid automatic decay. Focus-based inferential priming seems to be a more robust, higher-order contextual facilitation effect. It disappears only when the representational structure underlying the effect is discarded from working memory. In main clauses, this takes place at the clause-boundary as shown by the lack of priming in the after-clause condition. In initial 'though' clauses, however, where the function of the focus-based inferential structure is predictive, the probe facilitation is present even after the clause-boundary.

Inferential priming seems more similar, therefore, to the robust higher-order contextual facilitation of script-associated words demonstrated by Sharkey and Mitchell (1985). These authors found that the facilitation of words associated with a script that was activated by the previous text, is not subject to automatic decay, but is *deactivated* by discourse-relevant control cues indicating script-switch in the text.

However, it seems that the priming effects in the present study cannot be accounted for solely in terms of script activation either. Rather, the observed probe facilitation is the result of an *interactive inferential process* that is a joint function of (i) script-based knowledge, (ii) TF structure, and (iii) interclausal semantic relation. The respective contribution of these factors to the construction of the inferential structure underlying the priming effect can be characterized as follows:

The predicate expression of the initial subordinate clause (e.g., 'washing the plates') activates the corresponding script structure in memory (e.g., the "dishwashing" script) which acts as the interpretational domain over which the inferential structure is computed. The semantic value of the particular subordinate conjunction restricts the size of the active interpretational domain by identifying those parts of the script that are relevant for the computed inference. For example, the initial 'though' indicates that the next clause will relate to an implicit *consequence* of the adversative clause.

This information restricts the active interpretational domain to that part of the script which specifies typical cause-effect relations. Then TF structure further restricts the active script domain to only those cause-effect relations that are based on the *focus* of the clause.[7] Finally, the conjunction 'though', which cues the listener that the next clause will deny the implicit consequence, specifies a further *adversative inferential step* in constructing the predictive structure, which transforms the focus-based consequence in the active script domain into its *opposite*.

9 Conclusions

To sum up: the studies discussed in this paper examined the role of three sources of discourse information in the on-line processing of complex sentences: (i) TF structure, (ii) interclausal semantic relations, and (iii) pragmatic knowledge. The results indicate that listeners employ these cues *interactively*, as they become available in the clause, to constrain the construction of an interpretational model of the speaker's intended meaning.

Overall, the reported experiments support recent *interactive models* of speech processing (e.g., Marslen-Wilson et al. 1978, Marslen-Wilson and Tyler 1980, Johnson-Laird 1984, Crain and Steedman 1985), which argue that the listener accesses the available contextual information directly, and starts to construct a discourse interpretational representation for a sentence even before its full syntactic and semantic structure has been identified. The present studies demonstrate that in this process a central role is played by *focus-based inferences* that have direct access to pragmatic knowledge represented in script-like memory structures. Focus-based inferences serve several different processing functions during clausal processing: they are involved in establishing implicit discourse antecedent relations as well as in setting up implicit inferential structures linking clausal propositions in discourse.[8]

---

[7]Discourse context typically provides even more information helping the listener to further constrain the set of expectable consequences that the speaker's choice of focus implies. Consider the sentence 'Though it was the *plates* that John has washed, Mother was still not satisfied' in a context where it is known that (i) Mother had asked John to wash the dishes, and (ii) the bulk of the dirty dishes consisted of plates. Clearly, the listener could anticipate from the initial 'though' clause that the main clause will deny John's expectation that his choice to do the plates would be sufficient to satisfy mother.

[8]It should be pointed out that the discourse inferential processes demonstrated in the present experiments seem to fit well the more recent discourse-oriented approaches to lexical semantics, such as the one proposed by Kálmán and Szabó (1990). Kálmán and Szabó distinguish a part of the discourse representation, called an "enclosure," that contains implicit pragmatic information associated with predicates, which, however, doesn't belong to the propositional content to which the speaker has committed himself truth-conditionally, called the "rigid" part of the discourse representation. Under certain conditions (e.g., for recovering implicit antecedents), enclosures can be "unpacked," i.e., their contents can be raised into the rigid part of the discourse representation. Within this framework, the demonstrated focus-based inferences can be interpreted as

The observed priming effects indicate that focus-based inferences result in the *foregrounding* of certain parts of the constructed representation making them more accessible for on-line processes of discourse integration. The temporal pattern of this selective activation process is related to the particular processing function that the focus-based inference serves. For example, in an initial main clause, where the inference which contributes to the construction of the clausal representation is nonpredictive, the foregrounded inferential structure becomes deactivated at the clause-boundary due to recoding at the end of the clause. On the other hand, when sentence-initial conjunctions provide predictive cues about the likely content of the next clause, as in initial subordinate clauses, focus-based inferences generate interclausal *predictive* hypotheses to facilitate the integrational processing of the upcoming clause. In such cases, the presence of the sentence initial subordinate conjunction acts as a cue to block the process of recoding at the end of the clause, and so the predictive inferential structure does not get deactivated at the clause-boundary.

References

Abraham, Werner, and Sjaak de Meij. 1986. *Topic, Focus, and Configurationality.* Amsterdam: John Benjamins.

Ackerman, Farrell, and András Komlósy. 1983. Néhány lépés a magyar szórend megértése felé. Manuscript, Linguistic Institute, Academy of Sciences, Budapest.

Akmajian, Adrian. 1973. The Role of Focus in the Interpretation of Anaphoric Expressions. In *A Festshrift for Morris Halle*, ed. Stephen R. Anderson and Paul Kiparsky. New York: Holt, Rinehart, and Winston.

Becker, Curtis A. 1979. Semantic Context and Word Frequency Effects in Visual Word Recognition. *Journal of Experimental Psychology: Human Perception and Performance* 5:252–259.

Bever, Thomas G., and David J. Townsend. 1979. Perceptual Mechanisms and Formal Properties of Main and Subordinate Clauses. In *Sentence Processing: Psycholinguistic Studies Presented to Merrill Garrett*, ed. William E. Cooper and Edward C. T. Walker. Hillsdale: Erlbaum.

Bierwisch, Manfred. 1981. Basic Issues in the Development of Word Meanings. In *The Child's Construction of Language*, ed. Werner Deutsch. London: Academic Press.

Bower, Gordon H., J. B. Black, and T. J. Turner. 1979. Scripts in Memory for Text. *Cognitive Psychology* 11:177–220.

Chafe, Wallace L. 1970. *Meaning and the Structure of Language.* Chicago: University of Chicago Press.

Chafe, Wallace L. 1976. Givenness, Contrastiveness, Definiteness, Subjects, Topics, and Point of View. In *Subject and Topic*, ed. Charles N. Li, 26–55. New York: Academic Press.

---

one kind of processing operation which accesses the encyclopedic knowledge represented in enclosures during discourse processing.

Chomsky, Noam. 1971. Deep Structure, Surface Structure, and Semantic Interpretation. In *Semantics: An Interdisciplinary Reader in Philosophy, Linguistics, and Psychology*, ed. Danny D. Steinberg and Leon A. Jakobovits. New York: Cambridge University Press.

Chomsky, Noam. 1981. *Lectures on Government and Binding*. Dordrecht: Foris.

Clark, Herbert H., and Susan E. Haviland. 1974. Psychological Processes as Linguistic Explanation. In *Explaining Linguistic Phenomena*, ed. David Cohen, 512–521. New York: Halsted Press.

Clark, Herbert H., and Susan E. Haviland. 1977. Comprehension and the Given-New Contract. In *Discourse Production and Comprehension*, ed. Roy O. Freedle. Norwood, NJ: Ablex.

Collins, Allan M., and Elizabeth F. Loftus. 1975. A Spreading Activation Theory of Semantic Processing. *Psychological Review* 82:407–428.

Crain, Steven, and Mark Steedman. 1985. On Not Being Led Up the Garden Path: The Use of Context by the Psychological Parser. In *Natural Language Processing*, ed. David Dowty, Lauri Kartunnen, and Arnold Zwicky. New York: Cambridge University Press.

Cutler, Anne. 1976. Phoneme-Monitoring Reaction Times as a Function of Preceding Intonation Contour. *Perception and Psychophysics* 20:55–60.

Cutler, Anne, and Jerry A. Fodor. 1979. Semantic Focus and Sentence Comprehension. *Cognition* 7:49–59.

Dakin, Julian. 1970. Explanations. *Journal of Linguistics* 6:199–214.

Dezső, László. 1965. Notes on the Word Order of Simple Sentences in Hungarian. *Computational Linguistics* 4:3–60.

Duffy, S. 1983. Predicative Processing in Story Comprehension. Technical report. Eastern Psychological Association.

Farkas, Donka. 1986. On the Syntactic Position of Focus in Hungarian. *Natural Language and Linguistic Theory* 4:77–96.

Fischler, Ira, and George O. Goodman. 1978. Latency of Associative Activation in Memory. *Journal of Experimental Psychology: Human Perception and Performance* 4:455–470.

Fodor, Janet D., Jerry A. Fodor, and Merrill F. Garrett. 1975. The Psychological Unreality of Semantic Representations. *Linguistic Inquiry* 6(4):515–531.

Fodor, Jerry A., Thomas G. Bever, and Merrill F. Garrett. 1974. *The Psychology of Language*. New York: McGraw-Hill.

Foss, Donald J. 1982. A Discourse on Semantic Priming. *Cognitive Psychology* 14:590–607.

Gergely, György. 1986. *Discourse Integrational Processes in Sentence Comprehension: A Study in Comparative Psycholinguistics*. Doctoral dissertation, Columbia University.

Gergely, György. 1991a. *Free Word Order and Discourse Interpretation: Experimental Studies on Hungarian Sentence Processing*. Budapest: Academic Press.

Gergely, György. 1991b. The Role of Foucs-based Inferences in Antecedent Matching: Topic Foregrounding at the Clause-boundary. Submitted for publication to *Language and Cognitive Processes*.

Gergely, György, and Thomas G. Bever. 1986. Relatedness Intuitions and the Mental Representation of Causative Verbs in Adults and Children. *Cognition* 23:211–277.

Gibbs, Ray W., and Yvette J. Tenney. 1980. The Concept of Scripts in Understanding Stories. *Journal of Psycholinguistic Research* 9:275–284.

Gough, Philip B., Jack A. Alford, Jr., and Pamela Holley-Wilcox. 1981. Words and Contexts. In *Perception of Print: Reading Research in Experimental Psychology*, ed. Ovid J. L. Tzeng and Harry Singer. Hillsdale: Erlbaum.

Halliday, Michael A. K. 1967. Notes on Transitivity and Theme in English: II. *Journal of Linguistics* 3:199–244.

Haviland, Susan E., and Herbert H. Clark. 1974. What's New? Acquiring New Information as a Process in Comprehension. *Journal of Verbal Learning and Verbal Behavior* 13.

Horvath, Julia. 1981. *Aspects of Hungarian Syntax and the Theory of Grammar*. Doctoral dissertation, University of California at Los Angeles.

Jackendoff, Ray S. 1972. *Semantic Interpretation in Generative Grammar*. Cambridge, Mass.: MIT Press.

Johnson-Laird, Philip N. 1984. *Mental Models*. Cambridge, Mass.: Harvard University Press.

Kálmán, László. 1985. Word Order in Neutral Sentences. In *Approaches to Hungarian, Vol. 1: Data and Descriptions*, ed. István Kenesei. Szeged: JATE.

Kálmán, László, and Zoltán Szabó. 1990. D.I.R.T.: An Overview. In *Proceedings of the 7th Amsterdam Colloquium*, Part 1, ed. Martin Stokhof and Leen Torenvliet, 253–277. Institute for Language, Logic, and Information, Amsterdam University.

Kenesei, István. 1983. A hatókör és a szórend összefüggései a magyar nyelvben. Manuscript, József Attila University, Szeged.

Kenesei, István. 1987. *Approaches to Hungarian, Vol. 2: Theories and Analyses*. Szeged: JATE.

Kiefer, Ferenc. 1967. *On Emphasis and Word Order in Hungarian*. The Hague: Mouton.

Kiss, Katalin É. 1981. Structural Relations in Hungarian, a "Free" Word Order Language. *Linguistic Inquiry* 12(2):185–213.

Kiss, Katalin É. 1987. *Configurationality in Hungarian*. Budapest: Academic Press and D. Reidel Publishing Company.

Loftus, Elizabeth F. 1973. Activation of Semantic Memory. *American Journal of Psychology* 86:331–337.

Marslen-Wilson, William D., and Lorraine K. Tyler. 1980. The Temporal Structure of Spoken Language Understanding. *Cognition* 8:1–71.

Marslen-Wilson, William D., Lorraine K. Tyler, and Mark Seidenberg. 1978. Sentence Processing and the Clause-boundary. In *Studies in the Perception of Language*, ed. Willem J. M. Levelt and Giovanni B. Flores d'Arcais. Chichester: Wiley.

Marslen-Wilson, William D., and A. Welsh. 1978. Processing Interactions and Lexical Access During Word Recognition in Continuous Speech. *Cognitive Psychology* 10:227–234.

Meyer, David E., and Roger W. Schvaneveldt. 1971. Facilitation in Recognizing Pairs of Words: Evidence of a Dependence Between Retrieval Operations. *Journal of Experimental Psychology* 10:227–234.

Meyer, David E., Roger W. Schvaneveldt, and Margaret G. Ruddy. 1975. Loci of Contextual Effects on Word Recognition. In *Attention and Performance V*, ed. P. M. A. Rabbitt and S. Dornic. New York: Academic Press.

Morton, J. 1969. The Interaction of Information in Word Recognition. *Psychological Review* 76:165–178.

Neely, James H. 1977. Semantic Priming and Retrieval from Lexical Memory: Roles of Inhibitionless Spreading Activation and Limited-capacity Attention. *Journal of Experimental Psychology: General* 106:226–254.

Pléh, Csaba. 1982. Subject or Topic in Hungarian. In *Hungarian Linguistics*, ed. Ferenc Kiefer. Amsterdam: John Benjamins.

Reinhart, Tanya. 1981. Pragmatics and Linguistics: An Analysis of Sentence Topics. *Philosophica* 27(1):53–94.

Riesbeck, Christopher K., and Roger C. Schank. 1978. Comprehension by Computer: Expectation-based Analysis of Sentences in Context. In *Studies in the Perception of Language*, ed. Willem J. M. Levelt and Giovanni B. Flores d'Arcais. Chichester: Wiley.

Rochemont, Michael. 1988. *FOCUS in Generative Grammar*. Amsterdam: John Benjamins.

Sanford, Anthony J., and Simon C. Garrod. 1981. *Understanding Written Language: Exploration of Comprehension Beyond the Sentence*. New York: Wiley.

Schank, Roger C. 1975. A Story Understander. Technical Report 3. Yale University. AI Project Research Report.

Schank, Roger C., and Robert P. Abelson. 1977. *Scripts, Plans, Goals, and Understanding*. Hillsdale: Erlbaum.

Schmerling, Susan. 1980. The Proper Treatment of the Relationship between Syntax and Phonology. Paper presented at the 55th annual meeting of the LSA, December 1980, San Antonio, TX.

Selkirk, Elizabeth. 1984. *Phonology and Syntax*. Cambridge, Mass.: MIT Press.

Sgall, Petr, Eva Hajicová, and Eva Benešová. 1973. *Topic/Focus and Generative Semantics*. Kronberg Taunus: Scriptor Verlag.

Sharkey, Noel E., and D. C. Mitchell. 1985. Word Recognition in a Functional Context: The Use of Scripts in Reading. *Journal of Memory and Language* 24:253–270.

Szabolcsi, Anna. 1981. The Semantics of Topic-focus Articulation. In *Formal Methods in the Study of Language*, ed. Jeroen Groenendijk, Theo Janssen, and Martin Stokhof. Amsterdam: Mathematisch Centrum.

Szabolcsi, Anna. 1986. From the Definiteness Effect to Lexical Integrity. In *Topic, Focus, and Configurationality*, ed. Werner Abraham and Sjaak de Meij. Amsterdam: John Benjamins.

Townsend, David J. 1983. Thematic Processing in Sentences and Texts. *Cognition* 13:223–61.

Townsend, David J., and Thomas G. Bever. 1978. Interclause Relations and Clausal Processing. *Journal of Verbal Learning and Verbal Behavior* 17:509–21.

Warren, R. E. 1972. Stimulus Encoding and Memory. *Journal of Experimental Psychology* 94:90–100.

9

Combinatory Grammar and Projection from the Lexicon

Anna Szabolcsi

Objective

This paper addresses the relation between the lexicon and syntax, and suggests that projection from the lexicon should be the constitutive principle of grammar. The argument will consist of a general part in Section 1 and a specific part in Section 2.

In Section 1, I will ask to what extent the assumptions concerning the nature of lexical items determine the form of syntactic representations in various theories. As an illustration, I will briefly examine the treatments of unbounded dependencies in Government and Binding theory, Head-driven Phrase Structure Grammar, and Combinatory Categorial Grammar. I will argue that the concept of lexical items as functions underlies all three of them. However, only CCG recognizes this within its theoretical frames, and therefore only CCG can use it as an explanatory principle.

In Section 2, I present a case study on anaphora as a specific example of the connection between the lexicon and syntax within this theory. I will show that a simple lexical distinction between duplicators and free variables interacts with the independently motivated machinery of CCG to derive what is commonly stipulated in Binding Theory in syntax. Section 2.1 will be concerned with reflexives, and Section 2.2 with pronouns. After showing that the combinatory approach inescapably leads to a theory *à la* Reinhart, in Section 2.3 I will extend the proposal to VP-ellipsis, and elim-

The research reported in this paper was supported by a fellowship from IREX at the 1987 Linguistic Institute at Stanford University, and one from the British Council in the Centre for Cognitive Science in Edinburgh in 1988. I wish to thank the members of those communities, as well as of MIT, for insightful objections and suggestions. I am furthermore indebted to Jeff Goldberg, László Kálmán, Katalin E. Kiss, Edith Moravcsik, Stanley Peters, and Mark Steedman for recent discussions.

Lexical Matters. Ivan A. Sag and Anna Szabolcsi, eds.

inate an apparent problem caused by strict readings with non-referential antecedents.

1 The Projection Principle: One Filter or the Whole Story?

In current theories of grammar the relation of the lexicon to syntax is regulated by some form of the Projection Principle:

(1)   Syntactic representations are projected from the lexicon in that they observe the pertinent properties of lexical items (where "pertinent" and "observe" are defined theory-internally)

This principle is used to impose a necessary, but not sufficient, condition on well-formed syntactic representations; they must not contradict the properties of the lexical items they contain (subcategorization properties in the first place). That granted, however, they may be subject to any kind of further conditions (pertaining to empty elements and binding, for instance). Given that nothing constrains the nature of such conditions with reference to the nature of lexical items, the extent to which the lexicon eventually determines the form of syntactic representations need not be overwhelming.

This conclusion, while perfectly compatible with the technical status of the Projection Principle, is in conflict with the constraining power many linguists attribute to it. Intuitively, what we want may be stated as *make as much of the lexicon as possible*, or, more strongly, *take lexical items to be axioms and derive sentences as theorems*. This intuition would require that projection from the lexicon be the constitutive principle of grammar.

One obvious part of this program is to develop a sophisticated empirical theory of the lexicon that explains, for instance, why certain argument structures are attested and others are not. All "interesting" issues about grammar should belong here, and I will not be concerned with it in this paper. The other part of the program, on which I will focus, is to show how "uninteresting" our beloved syntax actually is. This involves making specific assumptions about the general nature of lexical items that, so to say, "predict syntax." I believe that the crucial reason why syntactic representations tend to be underdetermined by the lexicon is that most theories are extremely neutral as to what kind of objects lexical items are. Given this neutrality, the choice of syntactic tools is extremely free, so the "laws" of syntax turn out to be rather independent of "lexical substance".

1.1 Government-Binding Theory and Head-Driven Phrase Structure Grammar

To illustrate this independence, let us consider two examples, one from GB as in Kayne 1983[1] and another from HPSG as in Pollard 1984, 1988

---

[1]The insights of Kayne 1983 are also featured in versions of GB, based on Chomsky 1986a. See Koster 1987 as well.

and Pollard and Sag 1987. GB is a theory in which there is no prevalent specific mathematical commitment as to what kind of entities linguistic objects, lexical items among them, are. HPSG is a theory that makes a very general but mathematically precise commitment: it takes linguistic objects, including lexical items, to be feature structures in a strict technical sense. In this section I will first briefly review their treatments of "extraction" and "parasitic gaps". I will then point out that in neither theory does the nature of the generalizations concerning the well-formedness of syntactic structures follow naturally from the view of lexical items that the theory adopts.

Consider the following examples:

(2)   (a gangster) who Mary said relatives of ___ thought Kim eliminated ___.

(3)   (a gangster) who Mary said the police thought Kim eliminated ___.

(4)   *(a gangster) who Mary said relatives of ___ thought Kim died.

For (2) to be well-formed in Kayne's theory, it must be possible to assign a structure to it that conforms to the X-bar theory of phrase structure and the theta theory of subcategorization in the first place. I assume that the reader can imagine how this would work. Secondly, given that gaps are filled by an empty category, (2) must satisfy the Empty Category Principle (ECP) that Kayne defines as follows:

(5)   **Empty Category Principle:**
       An empty category e must have an antecedent a such that

       a. a governs e, or
          a c-commands e and there exists a lexical category X such that X governs e, and a is contained in some g(overnment)-projection of X, and
       b. the union of the g-projection sets of all the empty categories $e_1, \ldots, e_n$ bound by the same antecedent a must constitute a subtree.

(6) Y is a *g-projection* of X iff

       a. Y is an X-bar projection of X or of a g-projection of X, or
       b. X is a structural governor, and Y immediately dominates W and Z, where Z is a governed (Longobardi's amendment) maximal projection of a g-projection of X, and W and Z are in a canonical government configuration. (English being a VO language, the canonical government configuration is WZ.)

(7)   The *g-projection set* of e contains

       a. every p that is a g-projection of X, the governor of e, and
       b. e itself.

Now consider (2). Note that Kayne takes S and S' to be projections of V. In diagram (8) below only branching nodes are given. Nodes are labelled with the numbers of the relevant clauses of the definition.

(8)

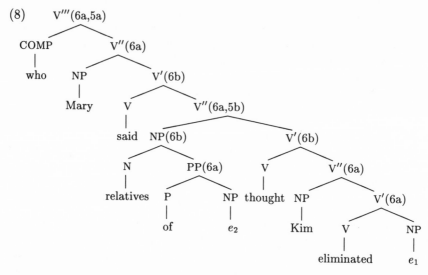

Let us first see whether e_1 is legitimate in view of the ECP (5). e_1's antecedent *who* c-commands e_1 but it is too far up in the tree to govern it. On the other hand, there exists a lexical category, *eliminate*, that governs e_1. So the question is whether *who* is contained in a *g*-projection of *eliminate*. We check this against definition (6), proceeding from bottom to top. V′ and V″ are X-bar projections, and hence *g*-projections, of *eliminate*. V″ is in a canonical government configuration with its sister *thought*, hence the next V′ is a *g*-projection of *eliminate*. The V″ on top of it is an X-bar projection of V′ and hence a *g*-projection of *eliminate*. With similar steps we get as far as the topmost V‴ (= S-bar). It indeed contains the c-commanding binder *who*. The relation between *who* and the "real gap" e_1 is therefore legitimate, as is also attested by the grammaticality of (3).

Now take the relation between *who* and e_2. *Of* governs e_2. PP is an X-bar projection, hence a *g*-projection, of *of*. PP is in a canonical government configuration with *relatives*; hence NP is a *g*-projection of *of*. V″ is not an X-bar projection of this NP, nor is NP in a canonical government configuration with its sister. Hence V″ is not a *g*-projection of *of*. Therefore, if e_2 were the only gap, it could not be connected to *who*, as is also attested by the ungrammaticality of (4). However, the *g*-projection of *of* that reaches NP forms a subtree with that of *eliminate*. Hence, in view of the second clause of ECP, e_2 is saved; it can be "parasitic" on e_1.

Consider now the treatment of the same example in Pollard 1984 and 1988. For (2) to be well-formed in HPSG, it must be obtainable by unifying the feature structures corresponding to its lexical items. *Eliminate* has, for instance, alongside with features specifying its part of speech and morphological properties, a feature SUBCAT, whose value is $\langle NP, NP \rangle$, and an empty category e has a feature SLASH with value $\langle NP \rangle$. It is an important property of the grammar that it contains, in addition to the general principles of unification, principles specifically pertaining to such particular features. The informal summary of the principles that govern the behavior of SUBCAT and SLASH is modeled after that of Pollard (1988):

(9)   Remove symbols from the front of the SUBCAT list one by one, observing the *Subcategorization Principle* (SCP):

      Match the symbols with a complement.

(10)   *Binding Inheritance Principle* (BIP):

      a. For each binding feature B, the value of B on the mother is obtained by starting with the value on the head daughter and appending (host dependency) or merging (parasitic dependency) into it the values on the other daughters, in the order more-oblique to less-oblique.

      b. Binding features are not passed up if they are specifically discharged in the construction.

(11)   *Head Feature Principle* (HFP):

      For other features, the value on mother is obtained from the head daughter.

(12)   SLASH and REL are binding features.

Caution: only the relevant portion of feature structures is given in (13).

We start from e_1 again. Unification of *eliminated* with the trace e_1 yields the feature structure V[SUBCAT $\langle NP \rangle$, SLASH $\langle NP \rangle$]. Unification of this with *Kim* yields V with [SUBCAT $\langle \; \rangle$] by the SCP and [SLASH $\langle NP \rangle$]] by the BIP. [SLASH $\langle NP \rangle$] will propagate up by the BIP. At the node dominating *relatives of e_2 thought Kim eliminated e_1* we have merger since another SLASH value turns up, coming from e_2. Note, incidentally, that nothing in (10) would prevent this latter SLASH from propagating even in the absence of e_1, in which case (4) needs to be excluded by an extra constraint on the BIP (Pollard 1984, p. 175). At the top we find *who* with another binding feature, REL, of value NP, and *Mary said relatives of thought Kim eliminated* with [SUBCAT $\langle \; \rangle$, SLASH $\langle NP \rangle$]. Finally, a topicalization rule allows these to unify, emptying SLASH and retaining NP in the REL-stack.

Let us return to Kayne's proposal now. The first thing to notice is that the presence of *who* needs to be guaranteed by the ECP, for the principles pertaining to subcategorization are already satisfied by the empty categories e_1 and e_2. Second, the g-projection mechanism seems entirely stipulative in the sense that there is no independent reason in the grammar to make us expect that "pathbuilding" between the governor of the gap and its antecedent will play a role in the grammaticality of sentences. Viewed

(13)

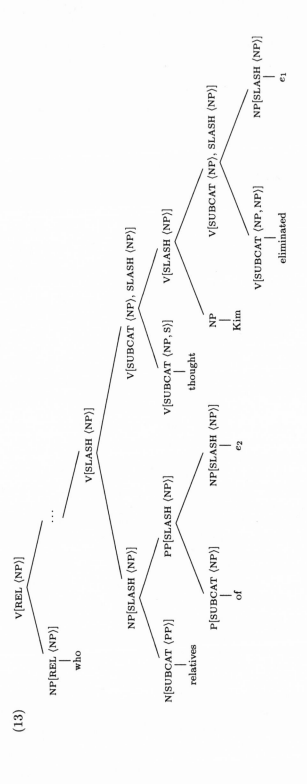

from another angle, Kayne's proposal is not arbitrary, however. Suppose that heads are not merely said to "subcategorize for" specifiers and complements but are admitted as functions of these. Then, using the notation $f : a \rightarrow b$, viz., *function: domain $\rightarrow$ co-domain*, (6a,b) can be said to be about the following constellation (assume association to the right): X is a function from e (and possibly other arguments) to $X^{\max}$, and W is a function from $X^{\max}$ (and possibly other arguments) to $W^{\max}$:

(14) a. $X: \ldots \rightarrow e \rightarrow \ldots \rightarrow X^{\max}$
      b. $W: \ldots \rightarrow X^{\max} \rightarrow \ldots \rightarrow W^{\max}$

To say now that a path is definable between e and $W^{\max}$ is to notice that X and W as given above are composible functions. The path-forming operation can be schematized as a general version of *function composition*:

(15) $\lambda e[W \ldots (X \ldots (e) \ldots) \ldots]$

Furthermore, the subtree condition suggests an extension of this operation which, in addition to composing W and X, identifies one argument of W with an argument of X. Let us say that W and X are *connected* in this case:

(16) $\lambda e[W \ldots (e) \ldots (X \ldots (e) \ldots) \ldots]$

Now we can say that Kayne's definition of g-projection is nothing other than an algorithm that specifies how the items intervening between the empty categori(es) and the antecedent can be assembled into one big function by composition and connection (plus application to pick up other arguments on the way). This is an interesting result because we may now feel we understand the rationale behind this rather complex mechanism. First, we understand what a g-projection path is: the result of application, composition and connection. Second, we understand why g-projection, as opposed to any arbitrary graph-theoretic notion, may play a distinguished role in grammar: because heads are function-like and it is in the nature of functions to apply, compose and connect. Third, we even understand why g-projection is specifically relevant for structures with gaps: because composition and connection allow a function to extend itself and thus combine with a distant argument. The presence of *who* on top will now be directly related to the subcategorization of the governor(s) at the root(s) of the path. Note, though, that while these considerations provide glorious justification for Kayne's ECP, they remain external to his theory since GB does not explicitly identify lexical items with subcategorization frames as functions.

The situation is even more striking in the case of HPSG. Pollard (1988) demonstrates, for example, with exemplary clarity, that the Subcategorization Principle could be paraphrased as "Combine signs as if heads were functions applying to complements as arguments", and the use of SLASH plus Binding Inheritance can be paraphrased as "Propagate information as if you were composing (connecting) functions". It remains a fact, though, that HPSG's lexical items are not even uncommitted entities but are entities committed specifically not to be functions. SUBCAT and SLASH are just features on a par with, say, suppletion features. Therefore every bit of their functional behavior needs to be imposed by brute force (by means of the SCP and the BIP). That is to say, the recognition of their functional behavior is not merely external but rather orthogonal to the theory they are part of.

1.2 Combinatory Categorial Grammar

We have seen that the "function metaphor" appears insightful in connection with important properties of syntactic representations. It may thus be interesting to consider a grammar that elevates this metaphor to the status of a theoretical claim and thereby lets the kind of operations found in syntax be a natural consequence of the kind of entities it takes lexical items to be.

Categorial grammar is known for adopting the view that lexical items with subcategorization frames are to be conceived of as functions/functors. One respect in which versions of categorial grammar differ quite significantly has to do with what abilities of functions they make use of in syntax. For extensive discussion, see the contributions in Oehrle et al. 1988. The version that I will explore below began to take shape in Ades and Steedman 1982 and Szabolcsi 1983, and has come to bear the name "combinatory categorial grammar" (CCG), for reasons that will become clear shortly. Its main strategy can be summarized as follows.

(17) a. No appeal is made to a phonetically empty placeholder or some equivalent instance of hidden application to satisfy the subcategorization requirements of the head when it does not combine immediately with its intended argument.

b. The observations concerning functional behavior that are built into GB/HPSG in the form of constraints are turned into operations that construct the well-formed representations, and only those, directly.

For an expression to be well-formed in this theory, it must be possible to assemble its lexical items in a strictly monotonic fashion by rules that are applicable whenever they meet categories they are defined for, and whose output is not subjected to further constraints. Rules (18)–(21) constitute a representative portion of the grammar. Their input ought to be more restricted, but I will adhere to these overly general formulations to let the reader see what can be achieved without fixes.

The rules in (18)–(21) are given in the same format as derivations will be. For example, (18a) can be spelled out as follows: Let a be an expression of category Y/X, the category of functors that look for an X on their right and return a Y, and let b be an expression of category X. They can be concatenated in this order to yield ab of category Y. In (18b) we have a of $Y\backslash X$, a leftward-looking functor from X to Y, hence b of X must precede a. (Notice that it is the orientation of the slash that indicates the directionality of the functor; the domain category is always to the right of the co-domain category.) In both cases the result of concatenation is interpreted by applying a', the function interpreting a, to b', the argument interpreting b. Underlines bear an index that has no status in the theory but merely indicates, for the sake of transparency, what semantic operation is performed, and which version of concatenation is used.[2]

The output of each semantic operation is spelled out in lambda terms for convenience. Notice that we use exactly application, composition and connection—the operations noted in the preceding section. (The fourth rule, lifting, is a kind of auxiliary device that is necessary but is of no particular theoretical interest in the present context.)

(18)   Concatenation interpreted as application: $a'(b')$

   i. a b ii. b a

       Y/X X X $Y\backslash X$

       —————$\mathbf{A}_i$ —————$\mathbf{A}_{ii}$

         Y Y

(19)   Concatenation interpreted as composition: $\lambda x[a'(b'(x))]$

   i. a b ii. b a

       Z/Y Y/X Y/X $Z\backslash Y$

       —————$\mathbf{B}_i$ —————$\mathbf{B}_{ii}$

        Z/X Z/X

(20)   Concatenation interpreted as connection:[3] $\lambda x[a'(x)(b'(x))]$

   i. a b ii. b a

       $(Z/Y)/X$ Y/X Y/X $(Z\backslash Y)/X$

       ——————————$\mathbf{S}_i$ ——————————$\mathbf{S}_{ii}$

          Z/X Z/X

(21)   Category lifting interpreted as: $\lambda f[f(a')]$

   i. a ii. a

            Z Z

       ————————$\mathbf{T}_i$ ————————$\mathbf{T}_{ii}$

       $Y/(Y\backslash Z)$ $Y\backslash(Y/Z)$

The derivation of (2) will proceed as follows:

---

[2] For the choice of index letters, see (23) below.

[3] The connection operation, introduced in Szabolcsi 1983, is renamed as substitution in Steedman 1987, 1988.

(22)

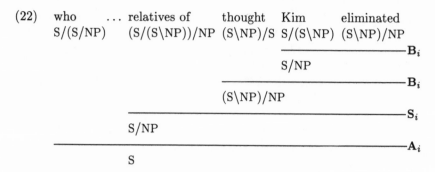

The (S\NP)/NP category of *eliminated* specifies that it is a functor with two NP arguments, of which the first (object) is expected from the right and the second (subject) is expected from the left. In this sentence there is nothing in the position where *eliminated* expects its object to be, and it is a remarkable feature of the grammar that it does not insert a phonetically empty element, either. So *eliminated* combines directly with *Kim*. This cannot be by application, though, since the subject NP is not the first argument of the transitive verb (and there is nothing in the grammar to change argument order). The subject and the transitive verb can combine via composition, which is possible iff the subject also bears an appropriate functor category, cf. the input conditions of (19i). (Whether a noun phrase in the nominative comes with the functor category S/(S\NP) from the lexicon, or (21i) lifts NP to S/(S\NP), is immaterial for our present concerns.) The composed functor *Kim eliminated* is exactly like *eliminated* in that it expects an NP from its right. The same holds for *thought Kim eliminated* that we compose in the next step.

Now comes *relatives of*. Its internal structure can be ignored; the important point is that, once more, it has nothing in the position of the prepositional object and is therefore a functor. *Relatives of* and *thought Kim eliminated* match the input conditions in (20i), so they can be connected into a big "forked" functor that is looking for one NP (*who*) which, when found, will satisfy both prongs. (This grammar, just like that of Pollard (1988), would require an extra restriction to rule (4) out. As things stand now, S\NP can be lifted to S\(S/(S\NP)), whence *thought that Kim died* can compose with *relatives of* of (S/(S\NP))/NP.) The trivial composition steps that take care of *said* and *Mary* are omitted to save space. Finally, accusative *who* must bring its S/(S/NP) category from the lexicon. The reason is partly semantic (*who* does not denote an entity, hence cannot be just NP), and partly syntactic (lifting as in (21) preserves the order of combination and hence cannot be responsible for the "left-extracting" property of *who*). *Who* combines with *(Mary said) relatives of thought Kim eliminated* by application.

Now, do the lack of traces and the use of complex operations, as in

(17ab), represent two arbitrarily juxtaposed grammatical strategies, or are they logically coherent? It seems they are, since as Steedman (1987, 1988) observes, there exists a system of logic that has essentially these features as its defining properties. This is combinatory logic, initiated by Schönfinkel (1924), developed, among others, by Curry and Feys (1958), and expanded in a most enjoyable fashion by Smullyan (1985). Combinatory logic is a system with the same potential expressive power as the lambda calculus. But while the lambda calculus uses abstraction and bound variables, combinatory logic appeals solely to functional operations (combinators), to achieve the same results. That is, it differs from the lambda calculus in precisely the same way as the grammar just sketched differs from GB and HPSG.

For a fast-and-easy introduction to combinators, note the following. In (15)–(16) and (19)–(21) we were dealing with "composed functions", "connected functions", and "lifted objects". The combinators "compositor" (**B**), "connector" (**S**) and "lifter" (**T**) are the operations themselves that we get by abstracting from those functions/objects. In (23) I define them both in usual lambda terms and in standard combinatory notation. The latter should be read as follows: **B** is that operation which, when applied to f, g, and x in this order, returns $f(gx)$, etc. Left-associativity is assumed, i.e., $(ab)c = abc$.

(23) a. Compositor: $\mathbf{B} = \lambda f \lambda g \lambda x [f(gx)]$
$\qquad\qquad\qquad\quad \mathbf{B}fgx = f(gx)$

  b. Connector: $\mathbf{S} = \lambda h \lambda g \lambda x [h(x)(gx)]$
$\qquad\qquad\qquad\quad \mathbf{S}hgx = hx(gx)$

  c. Lifter: $\mathbf{T} = \lambda x \lambda g [g(x)]$
$\qquad\qquad\qquad\quad \mathbf{T}xg = gx$

Application is not a combinator; it is the interpretation of the concatenation of any two combinatory terms. However, it is possible to define a combinator **A** that does exactly this, $\lambda g \lambda x [g(x)]$.

The fact that combinatory logic has the same potential expressive power as the lambda calculus entails that variable binding can be dispensed with. To illustrate what sameness of expressive power means in more complex cases, consider two examples in (24), which will also be useful below:

(24) a. **ST** expresses the same as $\lambda f \lambda x [f(x)(x)]$ because
$\qquad\qquad \mathbf{ST}fx = \mathbf{T}x(fx) = fxx$

  b. **BB(ST)** expresses the same as $\lambda f \lambda g \lambda x [f(gx)(gx)]$ because
$\qquad\qquad \mathbf{BB(ST)}fgx = \mathbf{B(ST}f)gx = \mathbf{ST}f(gx) = \mathbf{T}(gx)(f(gx)) = f(gx)(gx)$

It may be interesting to point out that the operations we found useful in devising a grammar of English are not merely definable in combinatory terms but actually all correspond to rather fundamental combinators. **B**, **S** and **T** represent those independent operation types which, were they supplemented with an identificator or a cancellator and allowed to apply recursively, would actually yield the power of the full lambda calculus.

Since that power is neither necessary nor desirable in our syntax, I will continue to restrict my attention to combinators with specific linguistic motivation. Another important assumption that I make is that combinators are typed (cf. Hindley et al. 1972 and Morrill and Carpenter 1987. For instance, in (23a,b,c), f is to have a type of the form $P \to R$, g of $Q \to P$, x of Q, and h of $Q \to (P \to R)$. Typing will be assumed but not notated throughout the discussion.

In sum, the pursuit of the "function metaphor" appears to have led us to the "combinator metaphor". Again, the question is whether we should leave it as a metaphor, or we should assign it the status of a theoretical claim. The latter possibility would mean that we try to devise a restrictive theory of grammar by letting the spirit and techniques of combinatory logic delimit our analytic options.

In what follows I will make one move in this direction. I will present a case study of anaphors and pronouns, and argue that, in view of both its positive and negative results, combinatory logic can serve as a guideline for their study.

Caveat: In the rest of the paper I will continue to use lambda terms alongside with, and sometimes even instead of, combinatory terms. I wish to point out that this is only because combinators are unfamiliar to many readers. Lambda terms will merely serve the purpose of exposition; they have the same status as a paraphrase in ordinary English would.

2   Anaphora—Lexical Semantics and Syntax

The suggestion that natural language syntax implements combinators, rather than explicit variable binding, was motivated above by a specific kind of example in which the variable would be phonetically empty. In those cases it is easy to argue that we only need to account for the placement and interpretation of overt words, and thus the use of variables is a mere artifact of some theories. Consider the phenomenon of anaphora, however. The items *himself* and *him* below can be looked upon as bound variables, but both they and their binders are in every respect normal arguments of the verb, so they cannot be dispensed with:

(25)   a. *Everyone* loves *himself*.
        b. *Everyone* thinks that Mary loves *him*.

Modulo technical details, standard theories of anaphors and pronouns have two components. The lexical component is rather meager; these items are assigned a so-to-say minimal interpretation, namely, that of a free variable. The syntactic component is rather rich: it consists of a mechanism for binding those variables plus a set of constraints on what they can, or must, be bound to. See Chomsky 1981, 1986b; Chierchia 1988; Pollard 1984; among others.

The crucial binding component of these theories is not reproducible in our grammar. The reason is that combinatory logic does not merely allow us to handle specifically extraction and parasitic gap structures without bound variables: it has no variable binding at all.[4]

Alongside with the above theories of binding, a number of proposals have been put forth to the effect that (sentences containing) a reflexive can be interpreted as (containing) a kind of argument reducer, in lambda terms, $\lambda f \lambda x[fxx]$. Applied to a two-place function, say, $\lambda z \lambda y[SEE(z)(y)]$ it returns a one-place function obtained by identifying SEE's arguments, viz., $\lambda x[SEE(x)(x)]$. See, for example, Quine 1960, Geach 1972, von Stechow 1979, Keenan 1987, and Kański 1987.

Given that combinatory logic has the same expressive power as the lambda calculus, this proposal does have a straightforward equivalent in our grammar. The requisite combinator is known as **W**, the duplicator in Curry and Feys 1958.

(26) Duplicator: $\mathbf{W} = \lambda f \lambda x[fxx]$
$\mathbf{W}fx = fxx$
where f is of $P \to (P \to Q)$, x of P

Notice that **W** is the combinator that we defined as **ST** in (24a).

The argument reducer proposals in literature have been essentially semantic in nature. They were not intended to account for the syntactic constraints that binding theories are preoccupied with. Keenan 1987 even argues that semantics is all that there should be to it: matters of interpretation are independent of matters of form like constituency.

The question that is interesting to us is this: What happens if we incorporate the duplicator account of anaphors into the grammar outlined in 1.2? In the rest of the paper I will focus on three aspects of this question. In 2.1, I will examine how the duplicator account of reflexives interacts with the syntax of CCG as in (18)–(21) to make predictions concerning "Principle A" properties. In 2.2, I will examine what the theory entails for pronouns, free and bound, and point out that it practically derives Reinhart's (1983) results. In 2.3, I will extend the proposal to VP-ellipsis to resolve a problem facing any Reinhart-like theory of anaphora.

2.1 Reflexives

Standard binding theories attribute three primitive properties to anaphors: the necessity for there to be a binder, the prominence condition on the binder, and the locality condition on the binder. I suggest that the simplest possible account of the first of these is *to interpret reflexives as duplicators in the lexicon*. Given that reflexives are lexical items in need of some

---

[4]That is, we have combinatory terms with the same meaning as $f(x)$ and combinatory terms with the same meaning as $\lambda x[f(x)]$, but the latter is not obtained from the former.

meaning in any case, any other treatment would involve that we assign the "wrong" lexical meaning to them, and go on to put it "right" in syntax.

Note a problem now: **W** is an operation over functions, whereas *himself* is an argument of the verb. But notice that turning a two-place function into a one-place function is essentially the same as providing one of its arguments. The conceptual gap is bridged by function-argument structure reversal, viz., lifting. This tells us what kind of a noun phrase a reflexive is: nothing but a lifted kind.

Lifting has ample syntactic motivation in our grammar (see especially Steedman 1986 and Dowty 1988), so reflexives are by no means exceptional in having lifted kind of categories. The only peculiarity is that while an entity-denoting item like *Mary* may come from the lexicon with the category NP and get lifted in syntax, the same categories are assigned to reflexives directly in the lexicon, matching their meaning. In this regard the treatment of reflexives is like that of quantifiers. See (27), in which items in the first row are annotated with a category and an interpretation that suit the subject position, and those in the second, the object position. I continue to use lambda terms for the reader's convenience:

(27) everyone   Mary   *sheself
      $S/(S\backslash NP)$ $S/(S\backslash NP)$ $S/(S\backslash NP)$
      $\lambda f \forall y[fy]$ $\lambda f[fm]$

      everyone   Mary   herself
      $(S\backslash NP)\backslash((S\backslash NP)/NP)$ $(S\backslash NP)\backslash((S\backslash NP)/NP)$ $(S\backslash NP)\backslash((S\backslash NP)/NP)$
      $\lambda g \lambda y \forall x[gxy]$ $\lambda g \lambda y[gmy]$ $\lambda g \lambda x[gxx]$

A simple example is then derived as below. *Herself* is a leftward-looking functor with the duplicator interpretation $\lambda g \lambda x[gxx]$. It applies to the transitive verb *sees* to yield a verb phrase $S\backslash NP$ with the interpretation $\lambda x[SEE(x)(x)]$. The subject quantifier *everyone* is a rightward-looking functor with interpretation $\lambda f \forall y[fy]$. It applies to the verb phrase and yields a sentence with the desired interpretation $\forall y[SEE(y)(y)]$.

(28) Everyone   sees   herself
      $S/(S\backslash NP)$ $(S\backslash NP)/NP$ $(S\backslash NP)\backslash((S\backslash NP)/NP)$
      ——$\mathbf{A}_{ii}$
                          $S\backslash NP$
      ——$\mathbf{A}_{i}$
                          S

Now consider how this proposal accounts for the ungrammaticality of (29a,b):[5]

---

[5] (29a,b) cannot be ruled out with reference to a morphological gap. They are equally ungrammatical in Hungarian, a language that has nominative anaphors in the subject position of NP. (On the clause-like structure of the Hungarian noun phrase, see Szabolcsi 1984.)

(29) a.*Sheself left.

    b.*_Sheself_ sees _everyone_.

As for (29a), the non-existence of _sheself_ of category S/(S\NP) is due to the fact that the duplicator is by definition a two-place function, which cannot be the interpretation of a one-place functor. No such simple semantic explanation can be given for (29b), however. To wit, _sheself_ might also be expected to bear the lexical category (S/NP)/((S\NP)/NP), which may well be interpreted as a duplicator and bind the subject to the object. This is essentially what Keenan points out when he invokes his Nominative Reference Condition to eliminate (29b).

The situation in our grammar is slightly different, however. Notice that the dangerous category above cannot be obtained by lifting NP but only by applying the compositor **B** to S/(S\NP) unarily. To make this more transparent, in (30) let us use the ad hoc labels _subj_ and _obj_, and ignore directionality:

(30) a. (S/NP)/((S\NP)/NP) is (S|_obj_)|((S|_subj_)|_obj_)

      S/(S\NP) is S|(S|_subj_)

    b. **T** of _subj_ may be (S|_obj_)|((S|_obj_)|_subj_)

      T of _obj_ may be (S|_subj_)|((S|_subj_)|_obj_)

    c. **B** of S|(S|_subj_) may be (S|_obj_)|((S|_subj_)|_obj_)

Now, in distinction to Lambek calculi, for instance, the syntax in (18)–(21) does not include unary **B** (division). We only used **B** to interpret concatenation. This is not accidental. There are various kinds of disasters, some but not all mentioned in (the revised version of) Szabolcsi 1987, that unary **B** may cause in syntax. Hence the problematic category is not a standard category for noun phrases in English: even _Mary_ will never acquire it. So all we need to assume in order to exclude (29b) is that reflexives may not have lexical categories that are not available in syntax to normal noun phrases. Which, in fact, is the null hypothesis.

It may be concluded that by lexically interpreting reflexives as duplicators, plus assigning them to categories in conformity to independently motivated syntactic assumptions, we predict that they "are bound by a more prominent argument". But no binding mechanism and c-command condition need to be stipulated. Further details of this proposal, including the treatment of two-complement verb cases, pied piping, and interaction with extraction and coordination are developed in Szabolcsi 1987.

That said about the requirement of a more prominent binder, let us turn to the locality condition on anaphors. It is to be observed that locality cannot appear as a natural condition in a system that includes composition. Consider, for instance:

(31) a.*Mary believes that John loves herself.

    b. Who does Mary believe that John loves?

The extraction structure (31b) shows that _believe that John loves_ of category (S\NP)/NP can be obtained by composition. If *herself* in (31a) applies to such a composed transitive verb, it will "get bound" by the subject *Mary*. So, in case the treatment of anaphors is to be part of this system, we must resort to brute force to capture the locality condition. The brute force method is, basically, to require that the duplicator only apply to functors that are lexical in some sense. (Cf. Chomsky's 1986b minimal complete functional complex.)

Without going into details regarding the precise definition of lexicality, let us ask how sad one should be about this. Is the locality condition part and parcel of the notion anaphor, where by "anaphor" we mean an item that must be bound by a c-commanding argument, i.e., which is interpreted as a duplicator?

The existence of long-distance anaphors has been widely recognized for quite some time. Most of them reside within NPs and are exclusively subject oriented, that is, they appear to have rather peculiar restrictions. A very interesting case from Modern Greek is reported by Iatridou 1986, however. Greek has two anaphors in our sense, of which *ton eafton tou* is bound within, and *ton idhio* outside, its governing category. The data Iatridou presents also indicate that this latter, long-distance anaphor has no funny restrictions:

(32) O Yanis$_i$ ipe   ston Costa$_j$ oti i Maria$_k$ aghapa ton idhio$_{i/j/*k}$
            said to   that   loves   himself

A plethora of further relevant data can be found in Keenan 1988.

This indicates that locality can in general be divorced from the core notion of anaphor, contrary to what binding theories suggest. The locality condition (lexicality requirement) may really be a brute force device employed by natural language to facilitate processing. Clearly, it is very useful for the hearer if binding ambiguities are reduced by having different forms for the duplicator; but there may be nothing more to it. While my proposal (as it stands, at least) is unrevealing with respect to what locality conditions different languages may impose on their anaphors, it may be taken to be revealing in the sense that it predicts locality to be a more or less ad hoc matter.

2.2 Pronouns

There is another phenomenon that the present theory makes predictions about, namely, bound versus free pronouns.

If the local binding condition on reflexives is a more or less ad hoc matter, there is in principle no obstacle to extending the class of anaphors—i.e., lexical duplicators—to include items which only differ from reflexives in that they are subject to no, or different, locality conditions. This is good news because, given that our combinatory logic has no variable binding (assignment switching) mechanism, having a duplicator kind of meaning is the only chance for an item to get interpreted as a bound variable in the usual sense. Besides this, combinatory logic only offers free variables. But those are like any name: they start out free and remain free. They may only co-refer with other referential expressions on independent grounds.

These considerations imply that pronouns must be multiply ambiguous.

(33) a. *He*[bound] is a member of the class of anaphors. As a first approximation, it may be assigned the same lexical meaning(s) as reflexives, whence it is subject to the same prominence/constituency requirements, and to possibly different locality conditions.

   b. *He*[free] is basically deictic. It represents arbitrarily many different free variables, each having its value fixed once and for all.

Consider now the anti-locality condition on pronouns ("free in its governing category"). The main point to note is this. The relation between *he*[bound] and its antecedent is recognizable within the combinatory theory, but the relation between *he*[free] and the item it happens to co-refer with is not. Hence we may hope to be able to impose an anti-locality condition only on the former, but not on the latter.

Anti-locality for *he*[bound] can be captured by something like the opposite of the lexicality requirement for reflexives or, more interestingly, by utilizing a combinator that is independently necessary for standard cases of pied piping. The combinatory equivalent of having a feature inherited by mother from daughter is discussed in Szabolcsi 1987, following Steedman (p.c.):[6]

(34) If a noun phrase is interpreted as a, its pied piper version is interpreted as $\mathbf{C}(\mathbf{B}(\mathbf{B}a)\mathbf{B})$ or $\mathbf{B}(\mathbf{B}a)\mathbf{B}$, and has a matching category. For example: $X\backslash(X/\mathrm{NP})$—its pied piper version: $(X\backslash(X/Y))\backslash(Y/\mathrm{NP})$.

For instance, if a is $\mathbf{W}$ and Y is PP, the use of the pied piper category will allow *to himself* to inherit anaphorhood from *himself*.[7] But notice now that the "feature" that "percolates" from NP to Y is necessarily "inert" within Y. Thus, by making pronouns obligatory S-pied pipers, we let S inherit anaphorhood from *he* and *him* and, at the same time, we guarantee that *him* has no antecedent within its minimal S. So let us assume that *he*[bound] has no simple $\mathbf{W}$ interpretation but is at least $\mathbf{C}(\mathbf{B}(\mathbf{BW})\mathbf{B})$ or $\mathbf{B}(\mathbf{BW})\mathbf{B}$, viz., $\lambda g\lambda f\lambda x[f(gx)(x)]$.

(35) a.

Everyone	thinks	he[bound]	likes John
S/VP	VP/S	$(\mathrm{VP}\backslash(\mathrm{VP}/\mathrm{S}))/(\mathrm{S}\backslash\mathrm{NP})$	S\NP

$$\underline{\hspace{6cm}}\mathbf{A}_i$$

$\mathrm{VP}\backslash(\mathrm{VP}/\mathrm{S})$
$\lambda f\lambda x[f(likes(j)(x))(x)]$

---

[6]$\mathbf{C}$ is the permutator, $\mathbf{B}(\mathbf{T}(\mathbf{BBT}))(\mathbf{BBT})$ or $\lambda f\lambda x\lambda y[fyx]$.

[7]*Pace* Pollard's "Evidently, there is no principled analysis of pied piping in an extended categorial framework like Steedman's without the addition of a feature-passing mechanism for unbounded dependencies" (1988, 421).

b. Everyone   thinks   John   likes   him[bound].
   S/VP   VP/S   S/VP   VP/NP (VP\(VP/S))\(S/NP)
                                    ————————————————*

c. Everyone   thinks   John   likes   him[bound]
   S/VP   VP/S   S/VP   VP/NP (VP\(VP/S))\(S/NP)
                          ————————$\mathbf{B}_i$
                          S/NP
                          ————————————————————$\mathbf{A}_{ii}$
                          VP\(VP/S)
                          $\lambda f \lambda x[f(likes(x)(j))(x)]$

He/him[bound], the S-pied piper, can only combine with S/NP or S\NP, whence it cannot be bound to anything within its own clause. As was pointed out above, anti-locality for *he/him*[free] cannot be accommodated in this way and must therefore be attributed to independent mechanisms.

The picture emerging here is not only technically but also conceptually different from that of standard binding theory, which specifies only that pronouns are free in their governing category. However, it squares rather well with an alternative theory proposed in Reinhart 1983. Reinhart argues that the conflation of coreference and bound variable interpretation leads to enormous complications because the two are empirically different. A pronoun may be coreferential with another referential expression even if the latter does not c-command it; moreover, their (non-)coreference is affected by pragmatic factors. On the other hand, a pronoun can only be bound by a quantifier that c-commands it from a distance at s-structure: i.e., bound variable interpretation is as strictly syntactic as reflexivization. In conclusion, she proposes to distinguish the syntactic theory of bound anaphora from the pragmatic theory of coreference. See also Partee 1978.

It is extremely interesting to note here that acquisition studies by Wexler and Chien from 1988 provide evidence in support of Reinhart's distinctions. In previous experiments they had found that English-speaking children's performance on locality properties of reflexives increases steadily from age 2;6 to almost perfect performance at 5;6. On the other hand, children in the age range 5;6 to 6;6 still do not show that they have the knowledge that a pronoun may not have a local c-commanding antecedent. However, in the study reported in this paper they tested the hypothesis that, in line with Reinhart's proposal, principle B really applies to bound, and not coreferential, pronouns. They found that children at age 6 violate principle B approximately 50% of the time with coreference, but less than 15% of the time in the case of a bound variable pronoun.[8]

---

[8]The significance of Chien and Wexler's earlier results has been challenged by Grimshaw and Rosen 1988: they argue that children know, although they may not obey, principle B. The 1988 study involving bound variables is not subjected to criticism in Grimshaw and

These results, if correct, are especially important for combinatory grammar. As was pointed out, the above treatment of reflexives and bound versus free pronouns is the only kind of treatment the logical foundations make available. Therefore it makes a much stronger case than Reinhart's theory, which formulates empirical observations within a grammar explicitly incorporating the lambda-calculus.

Despite its acknowledged appeal, Reinhart's theory has been criticized in the literature from various angles. In this paper I will not be concerned with the problem raised by the possibility of a pronoun being bound by a quantifier that does not c-command it at s-structure. (See a suggestion in the revised version of Szabolcsi 1987.) Rather, I will turn directly to a third crucial binding phenomenon in Reinhart's theory, viz., VP-ellipsis.

2.3 VP-Ellipsis

It is well-known that elliptical VPs may be ambiguous between the "strict" and the "sloppy" readings in the following kind of context:

(36) *Felix* hates *his* neighbors and so does Max.

    a. sloppy reading: "and Max hates Max's neighbors"

    b. strict reading: "and Max hates Felix's neighbors"

Reinhart (1983, 150–51) points out that the sloppy reading is obtained if *Felix* binds *his* in the antecedent clause, and the strict reading is obtained if *his* is merely coreferential with *Felix*. Reinhart is primarily interested in the sloppy case, and her pertinent claim is generally accepted. On the other hand, her claim concerning the strict reading faces a serious problem. If the strict reading is contingent on accidental coreference, then it is predicted to be available only if the antecedent itself is referential. But this prediction is refuted by quantificational antecedents, which also support the strict reading in a slightly different context, viz., when we are not dealing with coordination:

(37) *Every man* mentioned *his* merits before Mary did.

    a. sloppy: "before Mary mentioned her merits"

    b. strict: "before Mary mentioned his merits"

Gawron and Peters (1990) discuss this point extensively and take it to be one important piece of evidence against the correctness of Reinhart-like theories of pronominal anaphora. They propose a system whose innovations include the postulation of three, rather than two, kinds of anaphoric relations: co-variation (cf. co-reference), role-linking (cf. binding) and, crucially, co-parametrization for cases like (37b). The reader is referred to their book for details.

Rosen's paper, however, and it appears to me that Grimshaw and Rosen's findings are perfectly compatible with the results concerning the differential acquisition of conditions on binding and coreference.

Let us see what the combinatory theory of anaphora has to say about example (37). At first glance, it appears to be impossible to give an account of (37b). The reasoning, along the lines of Gawron and Peters, goes as follows. We have binding in the first clause, so its VP must be interpreted as $\lambda x[mentioned(x\text{'s } merits)(x)]$. If the ellipted VP echoes this, we get the sloppy reading; fine. In order to get the strict reading, we should start out with an antecedent VP meaning containing a free variable, echo this, and then bind both occurrences of that variable. But we cannot get free variables bound. Hence (37b) seems disastrous. In a sense, it is even more disastrous for this theory than for Reinhart's since, as I noted above, what is stipulated in her theory is a matter of logical necessity here.

This reasoning has an important presupposition, namely, that strict readings with non-referential antecedents need to be accounted for specifically by the machinery for pronominal anaphora and, therefore, if the pronominal anaphora machinery has nothing to say about it, the availability of this reading is evidence against the machinery.

In what follows I will suggest that this presupposition is false, and hence the reasoning is wrong. First, I will observe that strict readings with non-referential antecedents arise even in contexts without any overt anaphora. Therefore the existence of (37b) does not directly reflect on the viability of proposals concerning pronouns. Second, I will ask whether the treatment of the natural class of phenomena to which (37b) belongs really requires that we go beyond the tools of combinatory grammar and introduce a novel device like co-parametrization. I will argue that it does not. I will outline an account in CCG, and point out that it requires only a minimal extension of what we already have, because good old composition plus duplication will do "co-parametrization" for us. In this paper I will not investigate how other theories that do not have these would derive the critical examples.

The first step is entirely theory-independent. The consideration of two examples will suffice to show that the problem and, consequently, the treatment of (37b) is independent of the specific abilities of pronouns. One is (38):

(38) *Every man* mentioned *himself* before Mary did.

      a. sloppy: "before Mary mentioned herself"
      b. strict: "before Mary mentioned him"

Given that (38) contains a reflexive, it shows that we must be able to produce the strict reading with a non-referential antecedent even under the canonically syntactic conditions reflexive binding is subject to. Second, consider (39):

(39) Who did you mention before Mary did?
      "Which x, you mentioned x before Mary mentioned x"

As the interpretation makes clear, (39) presents precisely the same problem as (37b) and (38b). But it is a simple extraction structure, so the problem must be independent of the treatment of overt anaphoric elements on the whole.

With these observations in mind we may now proceed and see how the phenomenon can be handled in CCG. It is to be emphasized that in this paper I will not develop a detailed account of VP-ellipsis but concentrate only on the points relevant for the argument as sketched above. The first task is to accommodate the simplest case of VP-ellipsis, with which we start:

(40)   John left before Mary did.

Observe that the interpretation of (40) involves duplication, namely: *before*(*left*(*Mary*))(*left*). One way to capture this would be to say that *did* is a duplicator, i.e., it has the same meaning as items like *himself*, but its typing is different: the function whose arguments it identifies has VP, rather than NP, arguments. This proposal encounters two kinds of difficulty. One is the fact that many of the pertinent examples work also in the absence of *did* (*John left before Mary*, etc.). The second is that this proposal would extend easily to (39) but, for rather technical reasons, not to (38b). Therefore I will largely ignore the contribution of *did* and use the same **W** as the interpretation of a syntactic operation. Technically, **W** can be implemented as a new interpretation for concatenation, see (41a), or as a unary (type-change) rule that applies to the material in the second clause, as in (41b). Given that here the use of **W** is followed by application, the choice makes no difference. I sketch both options because binary **W** may be more intuitive, but subsequent steps will have to utilize the unary one.

(41) a.

left	*before*		*Mary did*
S\NP	((S\NP)\(S\NP))/S		S/(S\NP)

$$\frac{}{((S\backslash NP)\backslash(S\backslash NP))/(S\backslash NP)}\mathbf{B}_i$$

$$\frac{}{S\backslash NP}\mathbf{W}_{ii}$$

b.

left	*before*		*Mary did*
S\NP	((S\NP)\(S\NP))/S		S/(S\NP)

$$\frac{}{((S\backslash NP)\backslash(S\backslash NP))/(S\backslash NP)}\mathbf{B}_i$$

$$\frac{}{(S\backslash NP)\backslash(S\backslash NP)}\mathbf{W}$$

$$\frac{}{S\backslash NP}\mathbf{A}_{ii}$$

For the reader's convenience, in what follows I will spell out the interpretation of each line in lambda terms. Intermediate steps will be omitted if given in a previous example:

(41′) a. **B**(before)(Mary did)
$= \lambda a \lambda b \lambda c[a(bc)](\lambda p \lambda g \lambda x[\text{before}(p)(g)(x)])(\lambda f[f(m)])$
$= \lambda b \lambda c[\lambda p \lambda g \lambda x[\text{before}(p)(g)(x)](bc)](\lambda f[f(m)])$
$= \lambda b \lambda c \lambda g \lambda x[\text{before}(bc)(g)(x)](\lambda f[f(m)])$
$= \lambda c \lambda g \lambda x[\text{before}(\lambda f[f(m)](c))(g)(x)]$
$= \lambda c \lambda g \lambda x[\text{before}(cm)(g)(x)]$

W(**B**(before)(Mary-did))(left)
$= \lambda a \lambda b[abb](\lambda c \lambda g \lambda x[\text{before}(cm)(g)(x)])(\text{left})$
$= \lambda b[\lambda c \lambda g \lambda x[\text{before}(cm)(g)(x)](b)(b)](\text{left})$
$= \lambda b \lambda x[\text{before}(bm)(b)(x)](\text{left})$
$= \lambda x[\text{before}(\text{left}(m))(\text{left})(x)]$

  b. **B**(before)(Mary-did) $= \lambda c \lambda g \lambda x[\text{before}(cm)(g)(x)]$

W(**B**(before)(Mary-did))
$= \lambda a \lambda b[abb](\lambda c \lambda g \lambda x[\text{before}(cm)(g)(x)])$
$= \lambda b \lambda x[\text{before}(bm)(b)(x)]$

W(**B**(before)(Mary-did))(left)
$= \lambda b \lambda x[\text{before}(bm)(b)(x)](\text{left})$
$= \lambda x[\text{before}(\text{left}(m))(\text{left})(x)]$

This accommodates the simplest case of VP-ellipsis. Now consider (39):

(39) Who did you mention before Mary did?

Sentence (39) presents a problem on its own right. **W** echoes a VP-meaning but,. the direct object being extracted, there is no VP in the antecedent clause. Recall that our grammar has no traces.

The problem of (39) is in fact easy to solve with the tools our grammar has had all along. In (41b) the segment **W**(**B**(before Mary)) is combined with *left* by application. But it can equally well combine with *mention* by composition—and that is all we need. A straightforward execution of this idea is given in (42a). Once more, (42b) presents an alternative that makes no difference here but will underlie the next derivation. In (42b) a unary combinator **BBW** is used, followed by application. **BBW** is obtained by composing the above motivated steps **W** and **B**, and serves no other end than lumping these two together in the said order. For its expression in lambda terms, recall (24b).

(42) a.

mention	before	Mary did
(S\NP)/NP	((S\NP)\(S\NP))/S	S/(S\NP)

$$\overline{\rule{0pt}{0pt}\hspace{5cm}}\text{B}_i$$

((S\NP)\(S\NP))/(S\NP)

$$\overline{\rule{0pt}{0pt}\hspace{5cm}}\text{W}$$

(S\NP)\(S\NP)

$$\overline{\rule{0pt}{0pt}\hspace{5cm}}\text{B}_{ii}$$

(S\NP)/NP

b. mention   before   Mary did
    $(S\backslash NP)/NP$ $((S\backslash NP)\backslash(S\backslash NP))/S$ $S/(S\backslash NP)$

$$\frac{\qquad\qquad\qquad\qquad\qquad\qquad\qquad}{((S\backslash NP)\backslash(S\backslash NP))/(S\backslash NP)}\mathbf{B}_i$$

$$\frac{\qquad\qquad\qquad\qquad\qquad\qquad\qquad}{((S\backslash NP)/NP)\backslash((S\backslash NP)/NP)}\mathbf{BBW}$$

$$\frac{\qquad\qquad\qquad\qquad\qquad\qquad\qquad}{(S\backslash NP)/NP}\mathbf{A}_{ii}$$

Note the replacement of the two occurrences of b in (42′a) with cd: this has the effect of "co-parametrization".

(42′) a. $\mathbf{W}(\mathbf{B}(\text{before})(\text{Mary-did})) = \lambda b\lambda x[\text{before}(bm)(b)(x)]$

$\mathbf{B}((\mathbf{W}(\text{before})(\text{Mary-did})))(\text{mention})$
$= \lambda a\lambda c\lambda d[a(cd)](\lambda b\lambda x[\text{before}(bm)(b)(x)])(\text{mention})$
$= \lambda c\lambda d[\lambda b\lambda x[\text{before}(bm)(b)(x)](cd)](\text{mention})$
$= \lambda c\lambda d\lambda x[\text{before}(cdm)(cd)(x)](\text{mention})$
$= \lambda d\lambda x[\text{before}(\text{mention}(d)(m))(\text{mention}(d))(x)]$

b. $\mathbf{B}(\text{before})(\text{Mary-did}) = \lambda c\lambda g\lambda x[\text{before}(cm)(g)(x)]$

$\mathbf{BBW} = \lambda f\lambda h\lambda y[f(hy)(hy)]$

$\mathbf{BBW}(\mathbf{B}(\text{before})(\text{Mary-did}))$
$= \lambda f\lambda h\lambda y[f(hy)(hy)](\lambda c\lambda g\lambda x[\text{before}(cm)(g)(x)])$
$= \lambda h\lambda y\lambda x[\text{before}(hym)(hy)(x)]$

$\mathbf{BBW}(\mathbf{B}(\text{before})(\text{Mary-did}))(\text{mention})$
$= \lambda y\lambda x[\text{before}(\text{mention}(y)(m))(\text{mention}(y))(x)]$

In view of the informal suggestion made at the outset, with these we must have everything ready to cater to the ambiguity with anaphors. To avoid the treatment of possessive pronouns, I will only consider (38) here.

The sloppy reading is derivable by mimicking (41b). For compactness, $S\backslash NP$ will be abbreviated as VP whenever this does not affect intelligibility.

(43) mention   himself   before Mary did
      VP/NP   VP\(VP/NP) $\frac{\qquad\qquad\qquad}{}\mathbf{B}_i$
      $\frac{\qquad\qquad\qquad\qquad\qquad}{\text{VP}}\mathbf{A}_{ii}$ $\frac{\qquad\qquad\qquad}{(S\backslash NP)\backslash VP}\mathbf{W}$

$$\frac{\qquad\qquad\qquad\qquad\qquad\qquad\qquad}{S\backslash NP}\mathbf{A}_{ii}$$

(43′) $\mathbf{W}(\mathbf{B}(\text{before})(\text{Mary-did})) = \lambda b\lambda x[\text{before}(bm)(b)(x)]$

$himself = \mathbf{W} = \lambda f\lambda y[fyy]$

$\mathbf{W}(\text{mention}) = \lambda f\lambda y[fyy](\text{mention}) = \lambda y[\text{mention}(y)(y)]$

$\mathbf{W}(\mathbf{B}(\text{before})(\text{Mary-did}))(\mathbf{W}(\text{mention}))$
$= \lambda b\lambda x[\text{before}(bm)(b)(x)](\lambda y[\text{mention}(y)(y)])$
$= \lambda x[\text{before}(\text{mention}(m)(m))(\text{mention}(x)(x))]$

Consider now the strict reading. The correct semantic result obtains if we apply *himself*, the duplicator to the interpretation of *mention before Mary did* derived in (42):

(44) $\mathbf{W}(\mathbf{BBW}(\mathbf{B}(\text{before})(\text{Mary-did}))(\text{mention}))$
$= \lambda f \lambda z [f z z](\lambda y \lambda x [\text{before}(\text{mention}(y)(m))(\text{mention}(y))(x)])$
$= \lambda z [\lambda y \lambda x [\text{before}(\text{mention}(y)(m))(\text{mention}(y))(x)](z)(z)]$
$= \lambda z [\text{before}(\text{mention}(z)(m))(\text{mention}(z))(z)]$

We could indeed do this and thus derive the strict reading by simply mimicking (42) if we had a wrap operation in syntax:

(45)   mention himself before Mary did

himself   mention before Mary did

As a matter of fact, the grammar I am working with does not have wrap. This is not the only case for which wrap would be needed, however. An account of VP-internal anaphora presupposes that the neutral linear order of complements in English is the reverse of their semantic order. Therefore in Szabolcsi 1987, a simulation of wrap is developed, using forward mixing composition (i.e., disharmonic composition with the direct object acting as principal functor). Since that is an operation we otherwise do not want to set free in syntax, it is pushed back into the lexicon in the form of unary **B** with idiosyncratic slashing. Using this lexically derived category, wrap can be broken into two concatenation steps.[9]

With these technicalities in mind, consider (46). Notice that it utilizes, and thus provides the ultimate motivation for, the composite combinator **BBW** developed in (42b):

(46) $\mathbf{B}_{lex}(\text{himself})$
$(\text{VP} \backslash (\text{VP/NP})) / ((\text{VP/NP}) \backslash (\text{VP/NP}))$

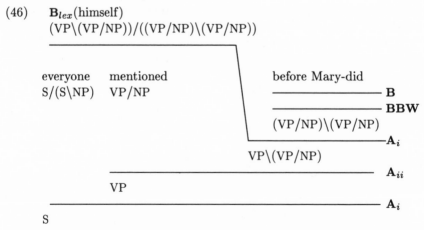

---

[9]This is not the only, or even the best, imaginable simulation of wrap in CCG. It is possible that a nicer solution will also allow us to dispense with **BBW** and, hence, **W** as the interpretation of a syntactic rule in general.

(46′) $\mathbf{BBW}(\mathbf{B}(\text{before})(\text{Mary-did})) = \lambda h\lambda y\lambda x[\text{before}(hym)(hy)(x)]$

$\mathbf{B}_{\text{lex}}(himself) = \mathbf{BW} = \lambda f\lambda g\lambda v[f(gv)](\lambda k\lambda z[kzz]) = \lambda g\lambda v\lambda z[gvzz]$

$\mathbf{BW}(\mathbf{BBW}(\mathbf{B}(\text{before})(\text{Mary-did})))$
$= \lambda g\lambda v\lambda z[gvzz](\lambda h\lambda y\lambda x[\text{before}(hym)(hy)(x)])$
$= \lambda v\lambda z[\lambda h\lambda y\lambda x[\text{before}(hym)(hy)(x)](v)(z)(z)]$
$= \lambda v\lambda z[\text{before}(vzm)(vz)(z)]$

$\mathbf{BW}(\mathbf{BBW}(\mathbf{B}(\text{before})(\text{Mary-did})))(\text{mention})$
$= \lambda z[\text{before}(\text{mention}(z)(m))(\text{mention}(z))(z)]$

$\lambda f\forall x[fx](\lambda z[\text{before}(\text{mention}(z)(m))(\text{mention}(z))(z)])$
$= \forall x[\text{before}(\text{mention}(x)(m))(\text{mention}(x))(x)]$

Finally, note that this treatment does not carry over to VP-ellipsis in coordination or in discourse. But that makes just the right prediction. In contradistinction to (36) with referential *Felix*, (47a) and (47b) have no strict readings:[10]

(47) a. Every man corrected himself, and so did Mary.

     b. Every man corrected himself. So did Mary.

Let me summarize what we have done as follows. We need some new tool to account for the simplest case of VP-ellipsis, viz., *John left before Mary did*. We choose this tool to be the rule **W**. Once we add that, the tools we have always had in the grammar, composition (**B**) in particular, will allow us to derive *Who did you mention before Mary did?*. This latter, in conjunction with the apparatus necessary for pure reflexivization, will derive the sloppy as well as the strict readings of *Everyone mentioned himself before Mary did*. In this way, the existence of the strict reading of VP-ellipsis with non-referential antecedents ceases to constitute an argument against Reinhart-like theories of pronominal anaphora in general and against the combinatory theory in particular.

3 Conclusion

In Section 1 a specific problem was raised concerning the implementation of the Projection Principle. It was pointed out that in various theories of grammar the nature of syntactic representations is underdetermined by the nature of lexical items. An examination of accounts of extraction and parasitic gaps suggested that taking lexical items to be functions allows us to establish a significant link between the two. The "function

---

[10]I tentatively assume that in coordination and in discourse *do* has the interpretation of a free variable and co-refers with the antecedent VP. The fact that VP-variables cannot be deictic need not rule out this analysis; it may be due to an independent requirement that the referents of VP-variables be linguistically individuated. I am grateful to Frederic Evans, Jorge Hankamer and Ivan Sag for discussion of this point.

metaphor" was then shown to lead to the "combinator metaphor" in a natural way.

In Section 2 the combinatory proposal was confronted with a new phenomenon, namely, anaphora. A selection of specific problems concerning reflexives, pronouns, and VP-ellipsis was examined. At the technical level it was argued that combinatory logic offers a simple lexical-based treatment of anaphora which, in conjunction with the grammar independently motivated in Section 1, factors out and derives a set of coherent properties of anaphora without any specific stipulation. At the intuitive level I hope to have shown that the use of combinators in grammar has its own heuristic value and offers genuine insights.

References

Ades, Anthony, and Mark J. Steedman. 1982. On the Order of Words. *Linguistics and Philosophy* 4(4):517–558.

Chierchia, Gennaro. 1988. Aspects of a Categorial Theory of Binding. In *Categorial Grammars and Natural Language Structures*, ed. Richard Oehrle, Emmon Bach, and Deirdre Wheeler. Dordrecht: Reidel.

Chomsky, Noam. 1981. *Lectures on Government and Binding*. Dordrecht: Foris.

Chomsky, Noam. 1986a. *Barriers*. Cambridge, Mass.: MIT Press.

Chomsky, Noam. 1986b. *Knowledge of Language*. New York: Praeger.

Curry, Haskell B., and Robert Feys. 1958. *Combinatory Logic I*. Amsterdam: North-Holland.

Dowty, David R. 1988. Type Raising, Functional Composition, and Non-Constituent Conjunction. In *Categorial Grammars and Natural Language Structures*, ed. Richard Oehrle, Emmon Bach, and Deirdre Wheeler. Dordrecht: Reidel.

Gawron, Jean Mark, and Stanley Peters. 1990. *Anaphora and Quantification in Situation Semantics*. CSLI Lecture Notes No. 19. Stanford: CSLI Publications.

Geach, Peter T. 1972. A Program for Syntax. In *Semantics of Natural Language*, ed. Gilbert Harman and Donald Davidson. Dordrecht: Reidel.

Grimshaw, Jane, and Sarah T. Rosen. 1990. The Developmental Status of the Binding Theory or Knowledge and Obedience. *Linguistic Inquiry* 21(2):187–222.

Groenendijk, Jeroen, Disk de Jongh, and Martin J. B. Stokhof (eds.). 1987. *Proceedings of the 6th Amsterdam Colloquium*. Amsterdam University: Institute for Language, Logic, and Information.

Hankamer, Jorge, and Ivan A. Sag. 1976. Deep and Surface Anaphora. *Linguistic Inquiry* 7:391–426.

Hindley, J. Roger, B. Lercher, and Jonathan P. Seldin. 1972. *Introduction to Combinatory Logic*. New York: Cambridge University Press.

Iatridou, Sabina. 1986. An Anaphor Not Bound in its Governing Category. *Linguistic Inquiry* 17(4):766–772.

Kański, Zbigniew. 1987. Logical Symmetry and Natural Language Reciprocals. In *Proceedings of the 1987 Debrecen Symposium on Logic and Language*, ed. Imre Ruzsa and Anna Szabolcsi. Budapest: Akadémiai Kiadó.

Kayne, Richard. 1983. Connectedness. *Linguistic Inquiry* 14(2):223–249.

Keenan, Edward L. 1987. Semantic Case Theory. In *Proceedings of the 6th Amsterdam Colloquium*, ed. Jeroen Groenendijk, Disk de Jongh, and Martin J. B. Stokhof, 109–133. Amsterdam University: Institute for Language, Logic, and Information.

Keenan, Edward L. 1988. Complex Anaphors and Bind α. In *Papers from the 24th Regional Meeting of the Chicago Linguistic Society*. University of Chicago.

Koster, Jan. 1987. *Domains and Dynasties*. Dordrecht: Foris.

Lambek, Joachim. 1958. The Mathematics of Sentence Structure. *American Mathematical Monthly* 65:154–170.

Morrill, Glyn, and Bob Carpenter. 1987. Compositionality, Implicational Logics, and Theories of Grammar. Manuscript, Edinburgh University.

Oehrle, Richard, Emmon Bach, and Deirdre Wheeler (eds.). 1988. *Categorial Grammars and Natural Language Structures*. Dordrecht: Reidel.

Partee, Barbara. 1978. Bound Variables and Other Anaphors. In *Proceedings of TINLAP 2*, ed. David L. Waltz. University of Illinois, Urbana.

Pollard, Carl. 1984. *Generalized Phrase Structure Grammars, Head Grammars and Natural Languages*. Doctoral dissertation, Stanford Universtiy.

Pollard, Carl. 1988. Categorial Grammar and Phrase Structure Grammar: An Excursion on the Syntax-Semantics Frontier. In *Categorial Grammars and Natural Language Structures*, ed. Richard Oehrle, Emmon Bach, and Deirdre Wheeler. Dordrecht: Reidel.

Pollard, Carl, and Ivan A. Sag. 1987. *Information-Based Syntax and Semantics, Vol. I: Fundamentals*. CSLI Lecture Notes No. 13. Stanford: CSLI Publications.

Quine, Willard V. O. 1960. Variables Explained Away. *Proceedings of the American Philosophical Society* 104(3):343–347.

Reinhart, Tanya. 1983. *Anaphora and Semantic Interpretation*. London: Croom Helm.

Schönfinkel, M. 1924. Über die Bausteine der mathematischen Logik. *Mathematische Annalen* 92:305–316.

Smullyan, Raymond. 1985. *To Mock a Mockingbird*. New York: Knopf.

Steedman, Mark J. 1985. Dependency and Coordination in the Grammar of Dutch and English. *Language* 61:523–568.

Steedman, Mark J. 1987. Combinatory Grammars and Parasitic Gaps. *Natural Language and Linguistic Theory* 5(3):403–349.

Steedman, Mark J. 1988. Combinators and Grammars. In *Categorial Grammars and Natural Language Structures*, ed. Richard Oehrle, Emmon Bach, and Deirdre Wheeler. Dordrecht: Reidel.

Szabolcsi, Anna. 1983. ECP in Categorial Grammar. Manuscript, Max Planck Institute for Psycholinguistics, Nijmegen.

Szabolcsi, Anna. 1984. The Possessor That Ran Away From Home. *The Linguistic Review* 3:89–102.

Szabolcsi, Anna. 1987. Bound Variables in Syntax (Are There Any?). In *Proceedings of the 6th Amsterdam Colloquium*, ed. Jeroen Groenendijk, Disk de Jongh, and Martin J. B. Stokhof. Amsterdam University: Institute for Language, Logic, and Information. Revised version in *Semantics and Contextual Expression*, ed. Renate Bartsch et al. (Dordrecht: Foris, 1989).

Szabolcsi, Anna. 1990. Across-the-Board Binding Meets Verb Second. In *Grammar in Progress: GLOW Essays for Henk van Riemsdijk*, ed. Joan Mascaró and Marina Nespor, 409–418. Dordrecht: Foris.

Szabolcsi, Anna. 1991. Antecedent-Contained VP-Deletion: A Misnomer. Manuscript, University of California at Los Angeles.

von Stechow, Arnim. 1979. Deutsche Worstellung und Montague Grammatik. In *Linear Order and Generative Theory*, ed. Jürgen Meisel and Martin D. Pam, 319–488. Amsterdam: John Benjamins.

Wexler, Ken, and Yu-Chin Chien. 1988. The Acquisition of Locality Principles in Binding Theory. *GLOW Newsletter* 20.

10

The Lexical Entailment Theory of Control and the *Tough*-Construction

PAULINE JACOBSON

For well over a decade, research on a variety of fronts has indicated that the role of the lexicon in the statement of various grammatical phenomena had been very much underestimated in earlier work within Generative Grammar. A serious look at lexical items—their subcategorization possibilities, their meaning, and the relationship among items—has shown that phenomena once thought to necessitate complex syntactic apparatus can instead be accounted for by independently motivated properties of lexical items. This is not to say that relegating some process to the lexicon necessarily results in an overall simplification of the grammar—it does so, of course, only when the process can be handled by independently motivated apparatus. But one of the most successful applications of the lexical program has been what I will refer to as the *lexical entailment theory of control*, as put forth in, e.g., Chierchia 1984, Dowty 1985 and others. The central claim here is that control is nothing more than a fact about lexical meaning.

The bulk of research on the lexical entailment theory of control has dealt with cases of the "understood subject" relation. Yet there are also cases in which a higher NP is the "understood object" of some embedded constituent; the paradigmatic case of this being the *tough* construction, as exemplified in (1):[1]

---

*This paper owes a considerable debt to David Dowty, both for his work on control and for numerous discussions of much of the material herein. Moreover, part of this paper is based on our joint work in Dowty and Jacobson 1988. I would also like to thank Bob Levine for much useful discussion. This research was supported by NSF grant #BNS9014676.

[1]I will not deal here with the closely related construction exemplified in (i):

i. The rock is too heavy for me to move.

For the most part, the analysis proposed here extends straightforwardly to this construction, although there are some differences between this and the *tough* construction. For

Lexical Matters. Ivan A. Sag and Anna Szabolcsi, eds.
Copyright © 1992, Stanford University.

(1)   That rock is hard for me to move.

The purpose of this paper is to show that the lexical entailment theory of control extends straightforwardly to this construction. In particular, I will argue that there is no syntactic relationship between the subject of the *tough* adjective and the "gap," and this then raises the question of how it is that the subject is understood as filling the gap position. I will suggest that this can be handled purely by lexical meaning, exactly as in the case of control of a "missing" subject. A thorough treatment of either the syntax or the semantics of this construction is far beyond the scope of this paper, but it is hoped that the analysis here can be fine-tuned in a more complete account.

The *tough* construction exhibits a seemingly baffling array of properties. As discussed in Chomsky 1977, the "gap" following *move* behaves in many respects like a gap in a *wh*-construction; most notably, it can be embedded indefinitely far down from the *tough* adjective (although these do decay more quickly than the corresponding *wh*-movement gaps; I have no explanation for this):

(2)   a. That rock is hard for me to try to move.
       b. That house is pretty hard to imagine Bill buying.
       c. That house is pretty hard to imagine Bill thinking Mary would
          buy.

And, as originally pointed out in unpublished work by Maling and Zaenen, parasitic gaps are possible here:

(3)   ?John is hard to convince friends of to invite.

But unlike run-of-the-mill *wh*-constructions, the apparent "binder" for the gap is in an "A-position" rather than an "Ā-position," and in this respect, the *tough* construction more closely resembles a control or raising construction. And of these two, *tough* sentences are again somewhat schizophrenic. As is typical in raising but not in run-of-the-mill control cases, the *tough* adjective imposes no selectional restrictions on the subject position; this property is often taken as a diagnostic for raising rather than control. Along these lines, some of the adjectives in the *tough* class at least arguably assign no θ-role to the subject. Indeed, there has been some controversy in the literature over just this point (see, e.g., Lasnik and Fiengo 1974 and Hukari and Levine 1990), and the notion "assigning a θ-role" is notoriously difficult to pin down. Nonetheless, we can at least note that sentences like (4a) and (4b) have the same truth conditions:

---

example, in the *too-Adj* construction it is much more difficult to get a deeply embedded gap. Thus compare (ii) and (iii):

    ii. ?John is hard for me to imagine Mary wanting to meet.

    iii. ?*John is too obnoxious for me to imagine Mary wanting to meet.

I return to this very briefly in Section 4.1.

(4)   a. That rock is impossible for me to move.

         b. It's impossible for me to move that rock.

Moreover (*pace* Lasnik and Fiengo 1974) at least certain idiom chunks can appear here (Berman 1973), and even a case like (6) is surprisingly good on the idiomatic reading:

(5)   Careful attention was very hard to pay to that boring lecture.

(6)   ?The cat would be quite easy to let out of the bag.

It is presumably these kinds of facts which first led Postal (1971) to analyze this construction in a fashion parallel to raising, and a more recent version of the raising analysis is developed in Bayer 1990. But in other respects *tough* adjectives behave more like run-of-the-mill control verbs and adjectives than like raising adjectives. I postpone the demonstration of this point until Section 2, as one of the central claims of this paper is that the lexical entailment theory of control extends to this construction.

Of course the above discussion presupposes a sharp distinction between raising and control; a distinction which has been maintained in most work since Rosenbaum 1967 and which is further argued for in Jacobson (1990, to appear). However, Dowty (1985) proposes that a raising verb or adjective is nothing more than a control verb or adjective which simply fails to assign selectional restrictions or a θ-role to the controller argument position. Although I have argued in the works cited above that this analysis is incorrect for the usual raising cases and that these instead involve syntactic function composition, I will be claiming here that Dowty's basic analysis *is* correct for the *tough* construction.

Thus my analysis of the *tough* construction combines the syntactic analysis defended in detail in Fodor 1983 and Jacobson 1984 with a semantic analysis based on the lexical entailment theory of control. A related analysis is developed in Pollard and Sag 1992. The gist of the analysis of this. *Tough* adjectives subcategorize for a VP which contains a gap of the same (or at least similar) sort found in *wh*-constructions. This was originally proposed in Gazdar 1980, and Gazdar's analysis itself is quite similar in spirit to the analysis of Chomsky 1977. This general kind of analysis is also adopted in Gazdar, Klein, Pullum, and Sag 1985, but in their version an elaborate set of conventions are developed to ensure feature matching between the subject of the *tough* adjective and the gap. In Jacobson 1984 and Dowty and Jacobson 1988 it was argued that there is no such matching, and arguments for this will be reviewed here. In other words, the subject of the *tough* construction in no way syntactically "links" to the position of the gap; the linkage is purely one of lexical entailments.

The organization of this paper, then, is as follows. Section 1 reviews the basic premises of the lexical entailment theory of control, both to flesh out this theory and to lay out some background assumptions used in the analysis here. Section 2 turns to several issues regarding the *tough* construction, and in particular argues against any analysis which posits syntactic connectivity between the subject and the gap. Section 3 turns to the semantics, and extends the lexical entailment theory of control to this construction. Section 4 outlines some of the remaining problems and peculiarities with the *tough* construction, and suggests some directions towards solutions. The basic remarks will be developed using the apparatus of Categorial Grammar, but most of the material contained here does not crucially rely on the premises of Categorial Grammar. For this reason, I will keep the categorial apparatus to a minimum.

1 The Lexical Entailment Theory of Control

Let us first turn to an ordinary control case such as (7):

(7)   John wants to win.

The lexical entailment theory of control, as discussed in, e.g., Chierchia 1984 and Dowty 1985, embodies two main premises regarding (7). The first is that syntactically the complement here is a bare VP with no subject. The second premise is parallel: semantically this complement denotes not a proposition, but a property (that is, it denotes the same kind of object that VPs in general do).[2] Thus *want* denotes not—as conventional wisdom has it—a relation between individuals and propositions but rather a relation between individuals and properties. Of course more needs to be said; some explanation must be given for the fact that *John* in (7) is the "understood subject" of *to win*. Under this view, the explanation for this resides completely in the meaning of *want*—the "control" relation is merely one of entailments associated with a lexical item. A subject control verb, for example, is one which entails something about the individual denoted by its subject having the property denoted by its VP complement; call this a *control entailment*. Of course this is not to say that the verb or adjective entails that the individual denoted by the subject actually has the property denoted by the VP complement, and the particular control entailment will vary according to the verb in question. In the case of *want*, for example, we might say roughly the following: *want* denotes a relation between individuals and properties, such that for any individual x which stands in the **want'**-relation to a property P then in the "want-world" of x, x has the property P.

A variety of evidence for this view is adduced in Chierchia 1984, Dowty 1985, Chierchia and Jacobson 1985 and others; we will briefly review just some of this here. Perhaps the most compelling argument for this view is

---

[2]These two premises are logically independent, and so all four possible combinations of these have been proposed at various times. For example, Klein and Sag (1985) propose an analysis of control constructions whereby the complement is syntactically a VP but denotes a proposition; the semantics thus supplies the subject argument. And Chierchia (n.d.) explores an analysis whereby the complement is a syntactic S with a PRO subject which denotes a property. We will not consider either of these analyses here.

one discussed in detail in Dowty 1985, which is that this is the null hypothesis. By this I mean that this view of control requires no additional apparatus in grammatical theory which is not independently motivated. As a consequence, extra principles would in fact be needed to rule out the existence of a verb whose meaning contained a control entailment. Thus on the syntactic side, nothing extra is needed to allow for a verb or adjective which takes a VP complement; indeed, something extra is needed to rule out such a lexical item.[3] To be sure, many theories do provide such extra principles: in many theories it is assumed either implicitly or explicitly that all VPs must contain overt syntactic subjects, and hence a bare VP could not serve as complement to some verb. But this requires an extra stipulation, and does not follow from any independently motivated principle of grammar. The reasoning on the semantic side is parallel: there is no reason not to expect a verb or adjective which denotes a relation between individuals and properties. Moreover, in any theory, the meaning of a lexical item will have certain entailments associated with it, and so there is no reason not to expect lexical meanings to have associated control entailments.

To pursue this point further, consider the standard alternative theory of the control relation, according to which *want* takes a sentential complement and denotes a relation between individuals and propositions. Such a theory requires a co-indexing mechanism, but in addition it too must contain a statement quite similar to the one above regarding the meaning of *want*. Here *want* denotes some relation between individuals and propositions such that an individual x stands in the **want'**-relation to a proposition p just in case p is true in the "want world" of x. While the meaning postulate given above under the lexical entailment theory is, perhaps, slightly more complex than this meaning postulate, the important point is that the lexical entailment theory makes use only of apparatus which is required in any theory.

Note moreover that under the lexical entailment view of control, we would expect to find a verb or adjective taking a property-denoting complement, but where the meaning of that verb or adjective did not have an associated control entailment. And, in fact, there are such cases; the so-called "pro-arb" cases as in (8) can be viewed in just this way (see Chierchia and Jacobson 1985):

(8)   Polluting the atmosphere is harmful to the children.

Nor is there any reason not to expect some verb which takes a property-denoting complement and two individual-denoting arguments and which entails something about its two arguments jointly having the property denoted by the VP Complement. While such cases of split controllers are rare, they do seem to exist, and have been discussed by Postal (1970), Jackendoff (1972), and more recently Dowty and Jacobson (1988):

---

[3]Although it is true that nothing subcategorizes for a tensed VP complement, and so this remains to be explained under the view here.

(9)   ?John argued with Mary about buying themselves a new house.

Control entailments are, of course, not the only sorts of entailments associated with lexical items. I will assume that "selectional restrictions," when not purely pragmatic in nature, are also facts about lexical meaning— the meaning of *frighten*, for example, is such that if x stands in the **frighten'** relation to y, then y is a sentient being. Ladusaw and Dowty 1988 and Dowty 1988 analyze θ-roles in a similar way; to say that a verb or adjective assigns a particular θ-role to one of its arguments is to say that part of its meaning includes a particular entailment or a clustering of entailments of relevance to that argument. Under this view of θ-roles and selectional restrictions, there is no reason to expect that every verb or adjective will have a θ-role or a selectional restriction entailment associated with each of its argument positions (the θ-Criterion notwithstanding). This point is discussed in detail in Dowty 1985; I will be suggesting that some *tough* adjectives may be just such a case.

Before leaving this, it should be noted that there are, of course, well-known arguments to the effect that a controlled VP contains a syntactic subject. The familiar arguments generally center on agreement facts of the type shown in (10):

(10)   The woman persuaded the man to shave himself/*herself.

If the embedded VP contains a subject, then agreement between this subject and the reflexive reduces to normal agreement; without a subject some other conventions are needed to ensure that the reflexive agrees in features with its "understood subject." However, it has often been proposed that this kind of agreement is also non-syntactic and should be accounted for in the semantics. While open questions remain concerning how best to treat agreement in languages with "syntactic gender," the important point is that agreement is found in a variety of cases where it would be difficult, if not impossible, to provide a syntactic account. Space precludes a discussion of this issue here, but see Pollard and Sag 1988 and Dowty and Jacobson 1988 for two recent discussions of this point and for two different although closely related non-syntactic accounts of agreement, including agreement in languages with syntactic gender.

2   Syntax of the Tough-Construction

2.1   Preliminaries

Before turning to the syntactic analysis, a few preliminary remarks are in order. The first concerns the status of the material *for me* in (11):

(11)   That rock is hard for me to move.

Following Bresnan 1971, Lasnik and Fiengo 1974, and others, I will assume here that this is a PP within the matrix VP. While the fundamental points of this paper do not crucially hinge on this, it is nonetheless worth considering some evidence for it in view of recent work which claims instead that *for* is a complementizer where *me* is in subject position (see, e.g., Gazdar, Klein, Pullum, and Sag 1985; Hukari and Levine 1990). Thus first, as discussed in Chomsky 1973, the PP here can both front and extract, and it can appear in other PP positions:

(12) a. For whom is the rock easy to move?
        b. For Bill, the rock is easy to move.
        c. The rock is easy to move for Bill.

As is well-known, the sequence *Comp–Subj* normally cannot occur in these positions:

(13) a. It's unlikely for John to win.
        b.*For whom is it unlikely to win?
        c.*For Bill, it's unlikely to win.
        d.*It's unlikely to win for Bill.

Nonetheless, Hukari and Levine (1990) challenge this argument, and claim that the PPs in (12) are not "displaced" PPs. Their evidence for this is based on an observation of Samuel Bayer's (cited in Hukari and Levine 1990) which centers on the behavior of the adjective *worth*. Like a typical *tough* adjective, *worth* selects a VP complement with a gap, and it can also have a PP in the positions shown in (12):

(14) a. For whom is the book worth reading?
        b. For Bill, the book is worth reading.
        c. The book is worth reading for Bill.

However, here the PP cannot precede the complement; in view of this Hukari and Levine conclude that there is no evidence that the PPs in (12) are "displaced" PPs:

(15) *The book is worth for Bill reading.

But while the behavior of *worth* is quite interesting, it seems to have little relevance to the question at hand. For the hypothesis that *me* in (11) is in subject position explains neither the existence of sentences like (12) nor the peculiar behavior of *worth*. On the other hand, the hypothesis that *for* NP is in all cases a matrix PP—combined with one principle concerning linear order—can account for the full range of facts. Thus assume that *worth* is like other *tough* adjectives in taking both a PP argument and a VP with a gap; the difference being that here the VP must be a gerund. Moreover, there appears to simply be some principle regarding linear order to the effect that the gerundive VP cannot be separated from the adjective while infinitive VPs show no such restriction. Some independent confirmation for such a principle comes from the following contrast:

(16) a. That book was easier than pie to read.
        b.*That book is worth more than you think reading.

Additional evidence for the PP hypothesis is the fact discussed in Bresnan 1971 that dummies do not occur in this position; under all accounts of the distribution of dummies that I am aware of this fact follows immediately under the PP analysis but not under the subject analysis:

(17) a. ?*This park would be easy for there to be a riot in.

   b.*John would be easy for it to be obvious that Bill likes.[4]

Related to this is the fact that the *tough* adjective imposes selectional restrictions on the constituent following *for*; roughly, it must be something with certain abilities. This is not surprising, as the meaning of the construction is such that some claim is being made about the ability of this NP. (18), then, is decidedly strange, and we also find contrasts such as (19):

(18) ?*John would be easy for that picture to frighten.

(19) a. John is easy for Mary to show that picture to.

   b.*John is easy for that picture to be shown to by Mary.

Again, Hukari and Levine (1990) argue that these facts do not give evidence regarding the *syntactic* structure; they show only that the NP following *for* is in some sense a semantic argument of the *tough* adjective. They propose, therefore, that there is a mismatch here between the semantic and the syntactic structure, and that there is a meaning postulate which ensures that the lower subject is a semantic argument of the adjective. However, I know of no way to state such a meaning postulate. Leaving aside for the moment the status of *John* in the above examples, the claim that *for Mary* is in subject position in (19a) means that **easy′** takes as one argument the denotation of *for Mary to show that picture to*. But note that the constituent *that picture to be shown to by Mary* in (19b) has exactly this same denotation. A meaning postulate could impose certain constraints regarding the set of possible denotations for this argument position, but there is no way that it could access the syntactic structure of this argument.[5]

---

[4] *Tough* gaps are generally somewhat bad in tensed Ss, as in (i):

   i. ??John is hard for me to believe that Bill likes.

Nonetheless, (17b) is robustly worse than (i).

[5] However, Hukari and Levine (1990) construct an ingenious argument which seems to show that the material following *for* can indeed be in subject position. This centers on (i), where a parasitic gap occurs within this constituent:

   i. John would be hard for friends of to admire.

If *for friends of* were a matrix PP, then the appearance of this gap would be quite surprising. The reason is that under the sort of analysis here, this PP is not within what we might call the gap domain. If, on the other hand, a *tough* adjective subcategorizes for a subject with a gap and *friends of* is in subject position, then it is not surprising that the gap can occur here.

I have no explanation for the appearance of the parasitic gap in (i). Nonetheless, the fact that the *tough* adjective imposes selectional restrictions on the NP following *for* seems almost impossible to explain if this NP can be in subject position. And note thateven when this NP contains a parasitic gap the same selectional restrictions hold;

The second preliminary remark concerns the nature of the gap in the complement VP. Following the general line first put forth in Chomsky 1977 I assume that this is much like the gap in a *wh*-construction. For convenience, I will here follow the basic line on extraction developed in Steedman 1987. Under this view, an extraction gap is nothing more than the failure of some argument to be introduced at the expected time. In other words, to use the usual notation of Categorial Grammar, the constituent *to move* in (11) is a VP/NP. I will ignore here the question of whether or not slashes should indicate the direction in which they want their argument, and thus a category of the form A/B should be interpreted as an item which wants a B to give an A and does not specify whether it wants the B to the left or to the right. It should, however, be noted that a number of researchers have suggested that extraction "gaps" are not the same as arguments which have not been introduced in the normal way and have therefore proposed that there is a distinction between an ordinary VP/NP and a VP with an extraction gap (see, e.g., Jacobson 1987b, 1989; Oehrle 1990). Such proposals have suggested that an extraction gap be treated more along the lines developed within GPSG, and have thus notated a VP with an extraction gap as VP[SLASH NP]. Should this turn out to be correct it will not affect the basic premises of this paper; we need only say that *to move* in (11) is a VP[SLASH NP] rather than VP/NP. I will briefly return to the status of the gap in Section 4.1.

The third preliminary concerns the status of Adjective Phrases and verbs like *be*. Consider, for example, an ordinary sentence with an adjective like (20):

(20)   The ball is red.

It is clear that *the ball* is an argument of the adjective here, even though it is not the actual subject of the adjective but rather of the verb *be*. Following the analysis laid out in Jacobson 1990, we will therefore assume that an adjective like *red* is of category A/NP; in general the term "AP" can be understood as an abbreviation for an item of category A/X (for X any category). What is peculiar about the category A, however, is that it rarely surfaces; adjectives rarely directly take subjects.[6] Rather, APs generally occur as arguments of verbs like *be*, and any syntactic restrictions imposed by the adjective on the subject are inherited by *be*. In Categorial Grammar terms, this can easily be stated by assuming that *be* is of the category $(S/\alpha)/(A/\alpha)$; α here is a variable over categories which is contained within the lexical specification of *be*; this means that *be* is marked so as to inherit

---

thus (ii) is quite bad:

    ii.*John would be hard for pictures of to frighten.

[6]Although adjectives do directly take subjects in a case like (i), discussed in Akmajian 1984:

    i. With Barbara angry, you'll never settle out of court.

the subject selection properties of the adjective. We will call such an item a *lexical inheritor*. I will assume further that the meaning of *be* is the identity function on properties.[7]

2.2 The Syntactic Analysis

The syntactic analysis of (1) is now straightforward. *Hard* is of category $((A/NP)/(VP/NP))/PP$[8] and so it combines first with the PP *for me* and then with the VP/NP *to move* to give the A/NP *hard for me to move*. This in turn is the argument of *be*, and the result is the S/NP *is hard for me to move*. Note that although NP occurs twice in the category of *hard* this is an accident; I am claiming that *hard* is not a lexical inheritor, and thus its category is not $((A/\alpha)/(VP/\alpha))/PP$. (In fact, the above category for *hard* will be revised slightly below so that the subject position need not be an NP.)

Consider now a case like (2b):

(2) b. That house is pretty hard to imagine Bill buying.

The analysis of extraction in Steedman 1987 allows for a constituent like *to imagine Bill buying* to compose to form a complex transitive verb; that is, it too has the category VP/NP. Consequently, this too can serve as argument of *hard*. This, then, is much like the analyses in Chomsky 1977, Gazdar 1980, Fodor 1983, Jacobson 1984, Pollard and Sag 1992 and others whereby a *tough* adjective subcategorizes for a constituent with a *wh*-type of gap. The fact that the gap can be embedded indefinitely far down and the fact that parasitic gaps are possible here follows immediately in all of these analyses.

Of course there are some well-known differences between gaps in the *tough* construction and gaps in *wh*-constructions; a discussion of many of these can be found in Hukari and Levine 1987; 1991). I do not have a solution to all of these differences, but I will briefly return to this one of these in Section 4.1.

2.3 The Lack of Syntactic Connection Between the Subject and the Gap

Although the basic analysis is quite familiar, there are two alternatives in the literature. The first analysis is similar, but proposes that there must

---

[7]Alternatively, following the general line of Chierchia (1984), an AP might denote what Chierchia refers to as a nominalized property, where the meaning of *be* maps a nominalized property (the individual correlate of some function) into its corresponding function.

[8]Or perhaps its category is $((A/NP)/(VP/NP[ACC]))/PP$. This is an adaptation of the proposal in Gazdar, Klein, Pullum, and Sag 1985; they point out that restricting the gap to accusative positions accounts for the fact (discussed originally in Schachter 1981) that *tough* gaps are impossible in subject position:

i.*John is hard for me to believe likes Mary.

be category matching between the subject position and the gap position (Gazdar, Klein, Pullum, and Sag 1985). The motivation for this stems from agreement facts of the type shown in (21)

(21)   That man is hard for me to persuade to shave himself/*herself.

Suppose that agreement is indeed a matter of syntactic feature matching. Then there must be some set of conventions to ensure that the features on the "missing" NP following *persuade* match those of the reflexive, and there must thus be additional conventions to ensure that the features on the subject match those on the missing position. But as discussed earlier, there are proposals to treat agreement semantically, and if it is correct that agreement is non-syntactic then no such feature-matching conventions are needed for (21). (For additional discussion of this point, see Jacobson 1987b and Dowty and Jacobson 1988.) Put somewhat differently, I will below review some evidence which suggests that the *tough* construction does not in fact impose any syntactic matching between the subject and the gap. Given this, this construction provides further support that the kind of "matching" in (21) is a semantic matter.

The second proposal derives originally from Postal 1971 (see also Postal and Ross 1971), and claims that the *tough* construction is a species of raising. A more recent version of this, based on my analysis of raising in Jacobson 1990 is developed in Bayer 1990. In the raising analysis of Jacobson 1990, a raising verb like *seem* is (roughly) of category S/S and concomitantly denotes a function from propositions to propositions. This, then, is much like the conventional analysis of raising verbs, which derives originally from Rosenbaum (1967). There is, however, no movement of the "raised" NP. Rather, such a verb must function compose with its complement; we will thus notate the category of *seem* as $S/^oS$. Thus in a sentence like *John seems to be tall*, *seems* does not take its sentential argument in the normal way. Instead, it function composes with the S/NP *to be tall* to give a new S/NP *seems to be tall*, and this takes *John* as subject. By the definition of function composition, any category requirements imposed by the embedded VP will be inherited by the composed expression. Thus in general *seem* will compose with a complement of category S/X to give an expression of category S/X. The semantics is similar; **seem′** function composes with **be-tall′** and the resulting VP has the meaning $\lambda P[\textbf{seem}'(\textbf{be-tall}'(P))]$. Thus in this case the fact that *John* is the understood subject of *be-tall* is not a matter of lexical entailments; it follows directly from the compositional semantics.

Bayer (1990) suggests that the *tough* construction should be analyzed similarly. In his analysis, *hard* is (to use the present notation) of category $(A/^oVP)/PP$. In (1), it first combines with the argument *for me*. At the next step, however, it does not take an ordinary VP argument, but rather function composes with a VP/NP to give an A/NP, and this will then occur as argument of *be*.[9] Thus if this or some other version of the Raising analysis were correct, then the *tough* construction would provide no evidence for the lexical entailment theory of control. Under any kind of Raising analysis (by which I mean either movement or function composition), the fact that *the rock* is the "understood object" of *to move* in (1) would follow directly from the compositional semantics. Note further that, as in the analysis of Gazdar, Klein, Pullum, and Sag 1985, any kind of Raising analysis predicts that there will be syntactic matching between the category requirements of the gap position and the subject of the *tough* construction. In the function composition analysis, for example, a phrase like *hard for me* will function compose with a VP/X to become an A/X, and so the category which the AP wants as subject is inherited from the position of the gap. Moreover, since *be* is a lexical inheritor (see Jacobson 1990 for motivation for this claim), the category restriction will again be passed up to the subject position. We turn then first to some evidence specifically against any kind of Raising analysis (whether via function composition or via movement), and then more generally to evidence against any analysis which requires syntactic matching between the gap and the *tough* subject.

2.3.1 Tough versus Raising

Perhaps the strongest piece of evidence against any sort of Raising analysis is a point which is actually noted in Bayer 1990 and centers on the phenomenon termed Null Complement Anaphora by Hankamer and Sag (1976). By way of background, Jacobson (1990; to appear) demonstrates that raising and control verbs and adjectives exhibit very different behavior with respect to this process and that this follows as a consequence of the fact that these have very different argument structures. Thus many control verbs allow their VP complement to be missing:

(22)   John tried.

(23)   John hopes.

A diagnostic for the phenomena under discussion here is that the "missing" complement is not understood as an existentially quantified property; rather, it is understood anaphorically and refers to some property which is salient in the discourse context. Note, then, that all of the following are possible, and the "missing" complement is most naturally understood as the meaning of *to climb a mountain*:[10]

(24)   John tried to climb the mountain, and Bill also tried.

---

[9]This is not quite Bayer's analysis; in his analysis *be* is of category S/°NP, and so function composes with the A/NP. For evidence that *be* is not a function composer but takes APs as arguments, see Jacobson 1990.

[10]The missing complement can also be understood as any other property salient in the discourse context; this is an instance of what Hankamer and Sag (1976) called deep anaphora.

(25) I $\left\{\begin{array}{l}\text{persuaded}\\\text{ordered}\\\text{taught}\end{array}\right\}$ John to climb the mountain, but I haven't

yet $\left\{\begin{array}{l}\text{persuaded}\\\text{ordered}\\\text{taught}\end{array}\right\}$ Bill.

I assume, then, that there is a lexical argument drop process. In the present terms, this lexical rule can be stated as in (26) (this will be generalized later):

(26) A lexical item α_1 of category $X/(S/NP)$ maps into a homophonous item α_2 of category X (for X a variable over categories)

$$\alpha_2' = \alpha_1'(P)$$

P here is a free variable over properties, and so its value is contextually supplied. This is not an entirely productive lexical process; while most or all object control verbs allow it, some subject control verbs do not:

(27) *John $\left\{\begin{array}{l}\text{wants}\\\text{attempted}\end{array}\right\}$ to climb the mountain, and Bill

also $\left\{\begin{array}{l}\text{wants}\\\text{attempted}\end{array}\right\}$.

That this process exhibits a certain amount of lexical idiosyncrasy is not surprising under the analysis here; like many lexical rules, the rule in (26) is only semi-productive.

Control adjectives also generally allow this process, although one caveat is perhaps in order. Some such adjectives appear to have pure intransitive homophonous variants, where there is no anaphorically understood property. Take, for example, a case like (28):

(28) Sam is happy.

Surely the most natural interpretation of this does not involve an understood property as complement of *happy*; whether *happy* ever allows the Null Complement Anaphora reading is unclear to me. Nonetheless, many control adjectives do have a reading in which a property salient in the discourse context is understood as the argument of the adjective. This becomes clear in a case like (29):

(29) a. John is very eager to leave, but Bill is much less eager.
      b. John is willing to serve on committees but Bill is not particularly willing.

But now let us turn to the situation with raising verbs and adjectives. As discussed in detail in Jacobson (1990; to appear), these do not work in this way. Thus note that none of the following are possible on the relevant reading:

(30) *John seems to be tall, and Sam also seems.

(31) *I expect Mary to win, but I don't expect Bill.

(32) *John is certain to win, but Mary is not certain.

As mentioned above, the lexical rule in (26) does not apply with all control verbs, and so one might think that (30)–(32) are simply accidental gaps, just like (27). However, the contrast between raising verbs/adjectives and control verbs/adjectives is far too systematic to be a case of lexical idiosyncrasy; see Jacobson (1990, to appear) for a detailed demonstration of this point.

Moreover, the fact that raising verbs and adjectives do not allow the VP complement to be missing follows immediately under either the classical account of raising or on the function composition analysis. To illustrate with the latter approach: I claimed that (as conventional wisdom has it) a Raising verb or adjective syntactically selects for an S rather than a VP complement. As discussed earlier, then, *seem* is of category S/^{o}S, *expect* is of category (S/NP)/^{o}S, and *certain* is of category A/^{o}S. The raising effect is the result of syntactic function composition of such an item with an S/NP (i.e., a VP). This means that the VP "complement" is not a lexical argument of the raising verb or adjective, and so it obviously could not be missing due to a lexical process which removes an argument position. A lexical argument drop process could, of course, remove the S argument position (as in *I expect*), but then there could be no "raised" NP. The reason is that the slot for this NP in the upper clause is created only when the verb or adjective function composes with an S/NP; the "raised" NP slot is the slot which is inherited from the complement as a result of function composition. A movement analysis of raising makes exactly the same prediction; if the S argument is removed by a lexical argument drop process there will be no embedded S from which an NP can raise.

Thus if the *tough* construction involved either movement from the position of the gap or function composition with a VP/NP, we would predict that this complement cannot be missing. But (as noted in Bayer 1990), it indeed can be, and in this respect a *tough* adjective behaves like a typical control adjective. This is demonstrated by the following, which are good on the anaphoric reading:

(33) a.?This rock is impossible for me to move, and that one is impossible for John.

  b.?This rock is hard for me to move, but that one is easy for John.

(34) a. This rock is impossible for me to move, and that one is equally impossible.

  b. This rock is hard for me to move, but that one is quite easy.

For reasons that I do not understand, these are most natural if the PP complement is also missing (as in (34)); but this does not affect the point at hand. The grammaticality of (33) and (34) is completely mysterious under a raising analysis, but is not at all surprising under the sort of analysis proposed here.[11] Under the present analysis the subject, the PP, and the VP/NP are all arguments of the *tough* adjective, and so the VP/NP argument position may be removed by a generalized version of the lexical rule in (26) (the generalized version is given below in (62)) . Note, incidentally, that the rule in (26) should be generalized in any case since S complement positions may also be deleted (see Grimshaw 1976). In view of the fact that both S and VP complement positions may be deleted, it is not surprising to find that VP/NP complement positions may also be.[12]

2.3.2   The Lack of Connectivity Effects

Further evidence against a Raising analysis comes from the fact discussed in detail in Jacobson 1982, 1984 and Dowty and Jacobson 1988 that the category of the subject is not inherited from the category allowed in the position of the gap. Such facts also argue against analyses like that of Gazdar, Klein, Pullum, and Sag 1985 which require feature matching between these two positions. We will thus consider here two ways in which the category requirements in the gap position need not match the category of the subject.[13] The first is major category mismatch. By way of background,

---

[11]Jacobson (1990) discusses two other lexical processes which apply to control verbs and/or adjectives but not to raising verbs and/or adjectives. As it turns out, *tough* adjectives also do not undergo these processes, and so Bayer (1990) uses this in support of the raising analysis. However, Levine (1991) points out that an adjective like *ready* in (i) also does not undergo these lexical processes:

    i. The beans are ready for me to cook.

Since the raising analysis cannot plausibly be extended to (i), the failure of *tough* adjectives to undergo these processes provides no evidence in support of the raising analysis for the *tough* construction. Rather, it would appear that the failure of *tough* adjectives and adjectives like *ready* to undergo these processes is due to the fact that these take VP/NP complements rather than full VP complements. See also Jacobson (1990, fn. 29) for discussion of this point.

[12]Another possible difference between typical raising cases and the *tough* construction centers on scope facts. It has sometimes been noted that in a sentence like (i) the subject NP has only wide scope with respect to the adjective:

    i. Every book is hard for me to read.

I am, however, not convinced that the narrow scope reading is always impossible; this seems to emerge in (ii) and in (iii), where it is clearest in (iii) with stress on *every*:

    ii. A whole book would be hard for me to read.

    iii. Every book would be hard for me to read.

If the narrow scope reading is possible here, then this does not jeopardize the account of control to be developed in Section 3; Chierchia (1984) and Dowty (1985) demonstrate that control verbs can be assigned a meaning such as to allow for the narrow scope reading.

[13]Actually, the most obvious case of this kind of mismatch is discussed in detail in Jacobson 1984; this concerns the fact that a subject pronoun will be nominative while the gap is in a position normally marked accusative:

    i. He/Him is hard for me to please.

However, both Hukari and Levine 1987 and Bayer 1990 provide mechanisms to account for this mismatch under the assumption that matching is, in general, required, and so I will not deal with case mismatch here.

it is well-known that there are verbs like *hope* which allow $\bar{S}$ objects and not NP objects (Rosenbaum 1967):

(35) a. I hope that Bill will win.
   b.*I hope that outcome.

But the reverse case also exists; Grimshaw (1982) points out that there is a class of verbs like *express*, *reflect*, and *capture* which allow NP and not $\bar{S}$ complements despite the fact that their meaning is compatible with a propositional object:

(36) a. This principle expresses the fact that languages are learnable.
   b.*This principle expresses that languages are learnable.

(37) a. This theory captures the fact that languages are learnable.
   b.*This theory captures that languages are learnable.

That there is no semantic problem here is evidenced by the following pairs of sentences:

(38) This principle expresses something. It's that languages are learnable.

(39) This theory captures something. It's that languages are learnable.

Taken together, the two sentences in (38) (under the relevant understanding of *it*) entail that **this-principle'** stands in the **express'** relation to the proposition **that-languages-are-learnable**, and this is a perfectly coherent discourse. Thus the problem cannot be a semantic one; rather, *express* subcategorizes for an NP and not for an $\bar{S}$ object.

A similar phenomenon occurs with infinitive complements. For many speakers, the verb *dislike* (in contrast to *like*) surprisingly takes only NP objects:

(40) a. I like to play poker.
   b.*I dislike to play poker.

Again (38) shows that the problem is not a semantic one:

(41) I dislike something. It's to play poker.

Grimshaw further observes that while a verb can choose the major category of its object, selection for subject position in English is much more limited. Why this is so is not clear, but it does indeed appear to be the case that any verb or adjective which can take an $\bar{S}$ subject can also take an NP, provided, of course, that the NP has the appropriate kind of meaning. For example, we have pairs like (42) and (43):

(42) a. That Bill will leave is likely.
   b. That outcome is likely.

(43) a. That Bill will leave is obvious.
   b. That fact is obvious.

On the other side of the coin, any verb or adjective which takes a propositional NP as subject can also take an S. Counterexamples to this claim have occasionally been adduced; thus Pollard and Sag (1992) cite examples like the following of an adjective which appears to take only an NP subject:

(44) a. ??That images are waterproof is incoherent.
      b. That idea/claim/proposition that images are waterproof is incoherent.

I find (44a), and Pollard and Sag's other examples, only marginally deviant. But in any case the problem here seems to be semantic, as the following pair of sentences shows little improvement:

(45) ??Something is incoherent. It's that images are waterproof.

Similar remarks hold for VPs in subject position; if a verb allows a VP it also allows an NP, and if it allows an NP with the appropriate meaning it also allows a VP.

As further evidence that there is no selection for NP versus $\bar{S}$ in subject position Grimshaw points out that passives corresponding to (36b) and (37b) are fine:

(46) That language is learnable is expressed by that theory.

(47) That language is learnable is captured by that theory.

This follows under the assumption that passive is a lexical process (or a phrasal one in the sense of Bach 1979)). Assuming that passive maps a verb (or, in Bach's terminology, a TVP) which subcategorizes for an NP object into an intransitive verb, and assuming there is no selection for NP versus $\bar{S}$ in subject position, then it follows immediately that the passive of *express* can take an $\bar{S}$ subject.[14]

It is unclear how best to capture the lack of category selection in subject position. One possibility, which is discussed in Jacobson 1987a and which I adopt here for convenience, is to assume that there are actually no lexical items of the form S/NP, S/$\bar{S}$, A/NP, etc. in English. Rather, assume that English grammar contains a super-category SUB, and that most verbs and adjectives actually have the category S/SUB. A further rule specifies that SUB can be NP, $\bar{S}$, or VP. (Another possibility is that there is a lexical redundancy rule.) This is not to say that there is never selection for subject position. I assume that in sentences like (48a) and (48b) the VPs have the category S/there and S/it respectively:

(48) a. There was a riot.
      b. It is obvious that John came.

---

[14](40b) does not have a corresponding passive, or the passive is at least marginal:

   i. ?*To play poker is disliked by everyone.

This, however, has nothing to do with the fact that a VP cannot occur in subject position but is probably due to some constraint requiring the controller to be in an argument position. Note that the passive of (40a) is equally marginal:

   ii. ?*To play poker is liked by everyone.

I assume further that *there* and *it* cannot instantiate SUB; this means simply that they are not allowed in the default case but must be specifically selected.

Now consider the following *tough* sentences, which are discussed in Dowty and Jacobson 1988:

(49)   That language is learnable is hard for any theory to capture/express.

(50)   ?To win the lottery is hard to imagine anyone disliking.

There is indeed some awkwardness in (50), but this does not seem to be due to any problem with category mismatching; (51) is equally awkward:

(51)   ?To lose one's money is hard to imagine anyone liking.

The interesting point is that (49) has an $\bar{S}$ subject, but the gap is in a position in which only NPs are allowed. Similarly, (50) contains a VP subject and an NP gap.[15]

Under both the raising analysis and the analysis which posits matching between the *tough* subject and the gap, this is quite surprising. However, it follows immediately under the non-matching analysis proposed here. Since there is no selection for major category in subject position, *hard* is not actually of the category shown earlier, but is, rather, of the category $((A/SUB)/(VP/NP))/PP$. The gap must be an NP, but the subject position can be anything which can instantiate SUB. Moreover, any other way (that I can see) to capture the fact that subject selection is free will make the same prediction. Note further that pairs like (52) do not provide evidence for a requirement that the category of the subject match that of the gap:

(52)   a.*It's hard for me to imagine anyone hoping that outcome.

      b.*That outcome is hard for me to imagine anyone hoping.

(52b) is bad simply because the *hard* requires that its VP complement contain an NP gap, while *hope* allows only $\bar{S}$ as complement. Thus (contra a claim made in Hukari and Levine 1991), the analysis here does not predict that an NP subject should be allowed when the gap is in a position permitting only $\bar{S}$s.

In the case of (49), we find that a complement type which is barred in the gap position is nonetheless allowed in subject position, since subject

---

[15]Larry Horn (among others) has pointed out to me that category mismatch of the kind found in (46) is also found in topicalization:

i. ?That language is learnable, no theory can capture.

I am not sure what conclusion should be drawn from this. First, it does not seem quite as good as (46), although the judgments are delicate. Moreover, there are other ways in which there can be mismatch in the topicalization construction. For example, some speakers allow sentences like (ii):

ii. Him, I think likes Bill.

(Heavy stress is required on *him* as is always the case with topicalized pronouns.) The topicalization construction, then, might simply turn out to be another construction without connectivity.

position is generally free. But we also find the opposite sort of situation with regard to dummies. Thus dummies are in general not allowed in subject position—they are allowed there only if explicitly sanctioned by the verb or adjective in question. Moreover, while there have been attempts to reduce all co-occurrence restrictions centering on dummies to semantic restrictions (e.g., Sag 1982), it would appear that the ability of a verb or adjective to require a dummy in subject position and to select among dummies is a syntactic fact. Consider, for example, the analysis of dummies in Gazdar, Klein, Pullum, and Sag 1985 and Dowty 1985. Here the meaning of the VPs in (53) involve vacuous λ-abstraction; their meanings are as represented in (54):

(53) a. It is obvious that John left.

     b. There was snow in New Hampshire.

(54) a. **obvious-that-John-left$'$** $= \lambda P[\textbf{obvious}'(\textbf{left}'(\textbf{John}'))]$

     b. **was-snow-in-New-Hampshire$'$** $=$
$$\lambda P[\textbf{in}'(\textbf{New-Hampshire}')(\textbf{snow}')]$$

But under this kind of analysis, the subject makes no contribution to the meaning and hence nothing in the semantics would ensure that the subject is a dummy, let alone that it is the correct dummy. In other words, if this general kind of analysis is correct, then there is nothing semantically deviant about sentences like the following:

(55) a.*Bill is obvious that John left.

     b.*There is obvious that John left.

Presumably, then, dummy selection is at least in part a syntactic matter; I assume that *obvious* in (53a) is of category $(A/it)/\bar{S}$, while the verb *be* in (53b) is of category $((S/there)/PP)/NP$.

Given that dummies are allowed only where specifically sanctioned by a given verb, we predict that if a dummy is sanctioned in the position of the gap, it nonetheless cannot occur in subject position since the subject category is not "inherited " from the position of the gap. And indeed this prediction is borne out:

(56) a. It's hard for me to imagine John ever being nice.

     b.?John is hard for me to imagine ever being nice.

(57) a. It's hard for me to imagine there ever being enough snow in New England.

     b.*There is hard for me to imagine ever being enough snow in New England.

(58) a. It's hard for me to imagine it ever being obvious that there's a level of LF.

     b.*It's hard for me to imagine ever being obvious that there's a level of LF.

As is well-known, a gap in the position following *imagine* in (56b) is far from impeccable. Nonetheless, there is a robust contrast between this and the sentences in (57b) and (58b). This is completely unexpected both under a Raising analysis and under an analysis positing feature matching.

The *tough* construction is thus quite interesting, in that it appears to provide a good diagnostic for syntactic versus semantic co-occurrence restrictions. Whether a given co-occurrence restriction is a syntactic or a semantic one is not an easy question to answer in any given case, but those co-occurrence restrictions which are preserved in the *tough* construction are just those which are plausibly analyzed as semantic, while those which are not are just those which appear to be syntactic. Thus, as noted in the introductory section, we find separable idiom chunks as in (5) and (6); but many researchers have concluded on quite independent grounds that such idiom dependencies are a semantic matter (see, e.g., Wasow, Sag, and Nunberg 1983). Moreover, as shown in (21), there is agreement in person, gender, and number between the subject and the gap. But this too has a semantic account, and there is a good deal of independent evidence that such matching cannot be handled in the syntax (for discussion see, among others, Pollard and Sag 1988, Dowty and Jacobson 1988). And while there are indeed cases where the *tough* subject seems to inherit a major category requirement from the position of the gap, such cases can be shown independently to be cases where the matching requirement is semantic. Consider, for example (59), which is cited by Hukari and Levine as evidence for the claim that there is category connectivity in the *tough* construction:

(59) a. I demand that you be/*are there on time.
      b. That you be/*are there on time is hard for me to demand.

But the fact that *demand* requires a subjunctive complement is a semantic one; this can be demonstrated by the fact that this co-occurrence restriction is preserved across sentences:

(60) I'm demanding something. It's that you be/*are there on time.

On the other side of the coin, (49) and (50) show a mismatch in major category; but (38), (39) and (41) demonstrate independently that here the category selection is not a semantic phenomenon. And the distribution of dummies is also a likely candidate for a syntactic treatment, and dummy selection is also not preserved in the *tough* construction. It seems quite reasonable to conclude, then, that there is no syntactic matching required in this construction—the only matching requirements will be those imposed by the fact that the gap is subject is "understood" in the gap position. We thus turn now to the semantic analysis.

3   The Control Relation

Since I am claiming that there is no sense in which the *tough* subject is in the position of the gap at some syntactic level, the question arises as to how it is interpreted as the "missing object." Earlier versions of this kind of syntactic analysis within the general framework assumed here made use of a distinguished variable in order to capture the semantic linkage. For example, consider again (1) *That rock is hard for me to move.* Jacobson (1984), following the general line in Gazdar 1980, took the meaning of the VP/NP to be **move'**(P_1) where P_1 is a distinguished variable. *Hard for me* combines with this argument, and the associated semantics both applies **hard'(me')** to the meaning of the complement and at the same time λ-abstracts over this variable. The result, then, is that *(is) hard for me to move* translates as $\lambda P_1[\textbf{hard'}(\textbf{me'})(\textbf{move'}(P_1))]$, and this ultimately applies to the subject argument. But in addition to whatever theoretical and/or aesthetic objections that one might level against the use of distinguished variables, this kind of solution—and, perhaps more importantly, any similar solution involving the binding of a variable in the complement—does not appear to be viable.

Thus consider the Null Complement Anaphora case (33b) which was discussed earlier:

(33) b.?This rock is hard for me to move, but that one is easy for John.

(For ease of exposition, I will demonstrate the point here with respect to (33b) where the PP is present; the same point could be made for the slightly more natural sentences in (34).) The "missing" material in the second conjunct can be understood as *to move*, and on this interpretation *that rock* is understood as the object of *move*. Under the distinguished variable analysis, however, the semantic linkage between the subject and the gap is accomplished only when the complement combines with the *tough* adjective. If the complement position were removed by a lexical argument drop process, then there would be no complement here, no distinguished variable, and hence no way for *that rock* to bind the gap position in the understood complement. As mentioned above, this problem is probably not unique to the distinguished variable analysis. Any similar attempt to establish semantic connectivity via a variable which is somehow bound by the subject will most likely face the same difficulty, as will any account of control which relies on a co-indexing mechanism between the subject and the gap. For the second conjunct contains no syntactic complement, and thus there is no position to be co-indexed with the controller.

The lexical entailment theory of control, on the other hand, extends straightforwardly to this construction. In fact, the *tough* construction is especially interesting because two arguments of the *tough* adjective are controllers. The subject is understood as the object of the VP/NP, while the PP is the understood subject of this complement. (Notice, incidentally, that this fact is especially problematic for any theory of control which must designate a single argument as a "controller.") Thus a *tough* adjective has three arguments: the subject, the PP, and the VP/NP. Under the view of extraction assumed here, any VP/NP—whether complex or simple—denotes a two-place relation R. (This follows both under the account of extraction developed in, e.g., Steedman 1987 and in the account within GPSG.) For simplicity, let us take this relation to be one between two individuals (rather than a relation between two generalized quantifiers). The claim, then, is that each *tough* adjective entails something about the individual denoted by the PP standing in the R relation to the individual denoted by the subject.

The point is most easily illustrated with respect to an adjective like *impossible*, as its meaning is less complex than most other *tough* adjectives. *Impossible* denotes a three-place relation holding among an individual x (the denotation of the subject argument), a two-place relation R, and an individual y (the denotation of the PP argument). Moreover, it contains a meaning postulate to the effect that if x, y, and R stand in the **impossible'** relation, then there is no possible world out of some suitably defined set in which y stands in the R relation to x. Of course some of the most interesting questions center on just what is the relevant set of possible worlds; presumably these are worlds in which x and y have the same properties in this world, and other things may also have to be held constant. The meaning of adjectives like *hard* and *easy* are much more complex and would probably require considerably more apparatus, but the essential point with respect to the control relation remains the same. In each case, the claim is that the control relation arises because the adjective entails something about the denotation of the PP argument and the denotation of the subject argument standing in the relation which is the denotation of the VP/NP.

Viewed in this way, the fact that at least some *tough* adjectives impose no selectional restrictions on the subject is not particularly problematic. As noted earlier, selectional restrictions can be seen simply as further constraints on an argument position which arise from the lexical meaning of the adjective; these adjectives thus seem to have few or no other associated entailments of relevance to the subject position. (They do, however, impose selectional restrictions on the PP argument, which simply means that they do have additional entailments associated with this position.) Similar remarks apply to θ-roles. If we follow the basic line of Ladusaw and Dowty 1988 and Dowty 1991 that a θ-role is just a label for one or a clustering of entailments associated with a given argument position, then an adjective like *impossible* seems to simply lack any such entailment with respect to the subject position.

It is, incidentally, an open question as to just what if any entailments the *tough* adjectives do impose on the subject position. Some of these adjectives (and nouns) in this class appear to have a more robust relationship to the subject (see especially Lasnik and Fiengo 1974 and Hukari and Levine 1990 for discussion). This can be seen in cases like (61a) and particularly (61b) where, as has often been noted, it appears that the difficulty of performing the action is being ascribed to some property of the subject NP:

(61) a. Those new bindings are really hard for me to fasten.

b. Those new bindings are a bitch for me to fasten.

Impossible, on the other hand, seems to have minimal entailments associated with the subject position beyond, of course, the control entailment. But the key point here is simply that if indeed some *tough* adjectives assign no θ-role to the subject position, then this is not a particularly problematic state of affairs for the lexical entailment theory of control.

Note that the Null Complement Anaphora case exemplified in (33b) is also handled easily under this analysis:

(33) b.?This rock is hard for me to move, but that one is easy for John.

To demonstrate this, we need to first generalize the lexical rule given earlier in (26). Two modifications are needed. First, since $\bar{S}$, VP, and VP/NP complement positions all can delete, the rule needs to be generalized accordingly . Second, since we have been assuming that a *tough* adjective first combines with its PP argument and then with the VP/NP, the rule needs to be generalized so that it is not only the outermost argument position which can delete.[16] Therefore, we will revise (26) as (62):

(62) A lexical item α_1 of category $(X/Y)/Z$ (for $Y = \bar{S}$, VP, or VP/NP) maps into a homophonous α_2 of category X/Z (for Z any or no category)

$$\alpha_2' = \lambda Z[\alpha_1'(Z)(Y)]$$

where Z is a variable of the semantic type of Z, and Y is a free variable of the semantic type of Y (hence, a free variable over propositions is supplied if $Y = \bar{S}$; a free variable over properties is supplied if $Y = $ VP; and a free variable over 2-place relations is supplied if $Y = $ VP/NP).

This means that the lexical item *easy*$_1$ of category $((A/SUB)/(VP/NP))/PP$ maps into the homophonous item *easy*$_2$ of category $(A/SUB)/PP$. Using R as a free variable over 2-place relations, the meaning of *easy*$_2$ is $\lambda x[\mathbf{easy}_l'(x)(R)]$, and this is the item which occurs in the second conjunct in (33b). Since R is free, its value is contextually supplied, and it can, therefore, pick up the relation **move**$'$ which is the meaning of the VP/NP in the first conjunct. Hence when **move**$'$ is supplied as the understood relation, the meaning of the sentence is such that **the-rock**$'$ and **John**$'$

---

[16]However, the assumption that the PP is the first argument is one which I have made for convenience only; it could be that a *tough* adjective is actually of the category $((A/SUB)/PP)/(VP/NP)$ where the PP complement wraps in. If this is the case, then the rule could perhaps be stated so as to delete only the outermost argument position.

stand in the **easy$'_1$**-relation to the **move'** relation. This in turn entails something about **John'** standing in the **move'**-relation to **the-rock'**, and consequently *the rock* is the understood object of the missing complement in the second conjunct. Thus the fact that the subject is understood as the object of a non-overt complement follows quite easily under this view of control.

More complex cases of control as in (63) are equally straightforward:

(63)   John is hard for Sam to persuade to run for office.

Following the basic line in, e.g., Bach 1979, let us assume that *persuade* first combines with its VP argument, then with its object argument, and finally with its subject. This means that *persuade to run for office* is a complex transitive verb, and so it denotes the relation which can be represented as **persuade'(run-for-office')**. The meaning of *hard* is such that it entails something about this relation holding for the pair (**Sam'**, **John'**). However, the **persuade'** relation in turn is such that if this relation holds among two individuals x (the subject argument), y and some property P, then something else is entailed about y having the property P. Thus by the transitivity of entailments, (63) entails something about **John'** having the **to-run-for-office'** property. Under the sort of account of agreement discussed in Dowty and Jacobson 1988, it is also predicted that there is a semantic mismatch in (21). There we suggested that the meaning of a VP like *to shave herself* is a function which is undefined for certain objects, and in particular it is undefined for the denotation of *that man*. Since (21) ultimately entails something about the denotation of *that man* having the property denoted by the lowest VP (*to shave himself*) there is a semantic mismatch.

4   Remaining Questions

The above analysis is by no means definitive; there remain a number of peculiarities associated with the *tough* construction which are not accounted for here. To deal with all of these is far beyond the scope of this paper, but I will conclude with a brief look at two of these.

4.1   Island Effects

The first remaining question concerns one of the major differences between the *tough* construction and the *wh*-construction: *wh*-constructions are islands, while *tough* sentences (often) are not. Thus, as pointed out in Chomsky 1977, *wh*-constructions not only preclude other *wh*-gaps, but a *tough* gap is also disallowed in a *wh*-construction:

(64)   a.*Which book did you decide who to give to?
       b.*That book is hard for me to decide who to give to.

However, the *tough* construction itself is (in some cases) not an island; both *wh*-gaps and other *tough* gaps are possible here. Thus sentences like

(65a) are well-known; note that (65b) which contains two *tough* gaps is also possible:[17]

(65) a. Which violin are sonatas easy to play on?

     b. That violin is hard to imagine any sonata being easy to play on.

Broadly speaking, there are two main approaches to island effects. On one, the fact that *wh*-constructions are islands is attributed to the fact that these contain a gap. While the details of course vary according to the particular theory, the idea in all of these accounts is that two gaps are not permitted in the same domain. The other locates the island effect to the *wh*-construction itself: some principle simply precludes certain types of constituents (including relative clauses and questions) from containing gaps. An example of this approach can be found in Gazdar, Klein, Pullum, and Sag 1985, where island effects are the result of a feature co-occurrence restriction according to which a slash cannot occur on a *wh*-node. (This of course assumes that "slash" is a feature; but this basic kind of account could be translated into a theory with the view of extraction assumed here.) Each of these approaches has certain advantages. The first accounts for the fact that extraction gaps are, in general, possible in *wh*-constructions containing resumptive pronouns rather than gaps. The second, however, generalizes to *wh*-constructions without gaps. Thus *whether* clauses are also islands, even though these contain no gaps. Moreover, the italicized constituent in (66a) is also an island, but there is little reason to assume here that the embedded constituent *who saw the woman* contains any kind of "gap" in subject position (see, e.g., Gazdar, Klein, Pullum, and Sag 1985):

(66) a. I wonder *who saw the woman*.

     b.*Which woman do you wonder who saw?

Since we are assuming that a *tough* gap is much like a *wh*-gap, the island differences shown in (64) and (65) are problematic only under an account

---

[17]Hukari and Levine (1991) (following earlier work within GPSG) claim that island effects are due to a principle precluding two "slashes" of the same type on a single node. To account for the fact that a *tough* gap and a *wh*-gap are possible in the same domain (as in (65a)) they propose that there are two separate features here: SLASH (for *wh*-gaps) and GAP (for *tough* gaps). But this does not account for the ungrammaticality of (64b) (which contains one gap of each type), and it also incorrectly predicts that (65b) should be ungrammatical. In fact they do claim that sentences of the general form in (65b) are bad, but I find (65b) as good as any other *tough* sentence where a gap is deeply embedded. In support of the claim that two *tough* gaps are impossible, Hukari and Levine cite the following sentence from Brame 1979:

    i.*This violin would be hard for these sonatas to be easy to play on.

But the problem with (i) has nothing to do with the existence of two *tough* gaps, as the following is equally bad:

    ii.*It would be hard for these sonatas to be easy to play on this violin.

The deviance of both of these is predicted by the fact that the PP does not denote something with abilities, and thus the selectional restrictions on this PP position are violated.

of extraction which attributes the island effect to the presence of two gaps within the same domain. If instead the effect is due to the fact that a gap cannot be located in certain kinds of constituents (those which I am calling "*wh*-constituents") then there is little reason to expect the *tough* construction to be an island.

But the situation is considerably more complex than it would appear at first glance. Notice that in, for example, (65a), the *tough* gap is immediately within the VP complement of the *tough* adjective. This, then, raises the following question: If a *tough* gap is more deeply embedded, does the complement remain amenable to a *wh*- (or, another *tough*) gap? Interestingly, the answer is no: if the *tough* gap is more deeply embedded, then the *tough* construction becomes an island. This is evidenced by the contrasts in (67):

(67) a. Which violin is it hard to imagine John being able to play this sonata on?
      b. This sonata is hard to imagine John being able to play on that violin.
      c.*Which violin is this sonata hard to imagine John being able to play on?

(67c) is quite strikingly ungrammatical, and is just as bad as a run-of-the-mill island violation as in (68):

(68) *Which violin do you know which sonata John is able to play on?

This suggests several things, although the remarks here should be taken as quite tentative. First, it may well be that some distinction is needed between gaps which occur locally within the domain in which they are sanctioned and gaps which can be embedded indefinitely far down. One might, for example, assume that there is a distinction between the ordinary VP/NP of Categorial Grammar and a VP with an extraction gap ; we will notate the latter as a VP[SLASH NP] (see, e.g., Jacobson 1987b, 1989; Oehrle 1990). If such a distinction is correct, this will not affect the semantic analysis developed above; a VP/NP and a VP[SLASH NP] can be given the same semantic treatment, where both denote 2-place relations. Second, this suggests that a *tough* adjective selects for either a VP/NP or a VP[SLASH NP], while a *wh*-word takes as its complement an S[SLASH NP]. Third, categories of the form X[SLASH Y] are "islands"—they cannot contain additional slash features, while categories of the form X/Y can. Thus in (65) the complement contains a local gap, and is therefore of the category VP/NP; hence it can have an additional SLASH feature. In (67c), on the other hand, as in a *wh*-extraction case, the complement is a VP[SLASH NP] and so cannot contain another SLASH. Moreover, some confirmation for a distinction between local and non-local gaps comes from the fact noted in fn. 1 that (for some speakers at least) missing object constructions of the kind in (69) do not allow embedded gaps:

(69) a. The rock is too heavy for me to move.

b.*The rock is too heavy for me to imagine Bill moving.

It may be, then, that *too heavy* selects only for a VP/NP and not a VP[SLASH NP].

4.2 Missing PPs

In the discussion above, I have dealt only with cases in which the *tough* adjective contains an overt PP complement. However, this complement can quite easily be absent, as in (70):

(70) The rock is impossible to move.

There are two issues surrounding this construction: just how is the missing PP argument interpreted, and how is it that this understood argument is also the understood subject of *to move*? The second question can be answered straightforwardly under the lexical entailment theory of control. As a point of departure, take the analysis proposed in Chierchia 1984. Chierchia suggests that the lexical item *impossible* in (70) is derived from the corresponding item which deletes the PP argument slot as follows: (I am taking slight liberties here with Chierchia's actual proposal, but none which affect the point at hand):

(71) α_1 of category $((A/SUB)/(VP/NP))/PP$ maps into an item α_2 of category $(A/SUB)/(VP/NP)$

$$\alpha_2' = \lambda R[\lambda y[\exists x[\alpha_1'(x)(R)(y)]]]$$

What this means is that if some individual y (the denotation of the subject argument) stands in the α_2' relation to the relation R denoted by the VP/NP complement, then there is some individual x such that y, x, and R stand in the α_1' relation. Now this is not quite right, since the missing PP complement is not understood as existentially quantified. The most natural reading for (70) is one where the missing PP is understood generically, or has an interpretation much like the NP *one*. Thus let us reformulate the semantic part of Chierchia's proposal as in (72):

(72) $\alpha_2' = \lambda R[\lambda y[\alpha_1'(one')(R)(y)]]$

The key point is that it follows that **one'** is also the understood subject of the VP; this basic point is discussed in detail in Chierchia 1984. Take the case where this rule applies to a lexical item like *impossible*. The lexical item derived by the rule (71–72) is such that if a sentence like (70) is true, then **the-rock'** and **one'** stand in what we will now call the **impossible$_1'$**-relation to **move'**. Note, though, that **impossible$_1'$** is simply the relation discussed earlier, and it therefore entails something about **one'** and **the-rock'** standing in the **move'**-relation. It follows, then, that the understood argument of *impossible* is also the understood subject of the complement.

But this is not a full account, for the missing argument of *impossible* need not be understood as **one'**. As detailed in Kimball 1971, it can also be understood as the meaning of some NP in a higher clause, as in (73):

(73) a. John thought that the rock would be impossible to move.
    b. John thought that the movie would be hard to convince himself to like.

Just how to account for this second reading is unclear. It is tempting to posit another lexical rule here by which a free variable is supplied in the relevant argument position, where the value of that variable will be contextually supplied. However, this predicts that the value for this variable can be any individual salient in the discourse. Yet it seems difficult, if not impossible, to get the relevant reading in a case like (74):

(74) John is always procrastinating. ?*This last homework assignment was particularly difficult to convince himself to do on time.

Compare (74) to (75), where the PP is overt:

(75) John is always procrastinating. This last homework assignment was particularly difficult for him to convince himself to do on time.

Thus the problem of how to establish the control relation between *John* and the "missing PP" in (73) remains an unsolved problem.

There are, then, several peculiarities of the *tough* construction which remain unexplained. Nonetheless, I hope to have established two main points. First, there is no syntactic linkage between the *tough* subject and the gap. Second, the semantic linkage can be handled straightforwardly under the lexical entailment theory of control. Thus this construction provides additional evidence for the hypothesis that control is only a matter of entailments associated with lexical items.

References

Akmajian, Adrian. 1984. Sentence Types and the Form-Function Fit. *Natural Language and Linguistic Theory* 2:1–23.

Bach, Emmon. 1979. Control in Montague Grammar. *Linguistic Inquiry* 10:515–532.

Bayer, Samuel. 1990. Tough Movement as Function Composition. In *Proceedings of the 9th Annual West Coast Conference on Formal Linguistics*, ed. Peter Sells. Stanford: CSLI Publications.

Berman, Arlene. 1973. *Adjectives and Adjective Complement Constructions in English*. Doctoral dissertation, Harvard University.

Brame, Michael. 1979. *Essays Toward Realistic Syntax*. Seattle: Noit Amrofer.

Bresnan, Joan. 1971. Sentence Stress and Syntactic Transformation. *Language* 47:257–281.

Chierchia, Gennaro. 1984. *Topics in the Syntax and Semantics of Infinitives and Gerunds*. Doctoral dissertation, University of Massachusetts. Distributed by the Graduate Linguistics Student Association, University of Massachusetts.

Chierchia, Gennaro. To appear. Anaphora and Attitudes *De Se*. In *Language in Action*, ed. Renate Bartsch et al. Dordrecht: Foris.

Chierchia, Gennaro, and Pauline Jacobson. 1985. Local and Long Distance Control. In *Proceedings of NELS 16*, 57–74. Amherst: Univeristy of Massachusetts, GLSA.

Chomsky, Noam. 1973. Conditions on Transformations. In *A Festschrift for Morris Halle*, ed. Stephen R. Anderson and Paul Kiparsky, 232–286. New York: Holt, Rinehart and Winston.

Chomsky, Noam. 1977. On Wh-movement. In *Formal Syntax*, ed. Peter Culicover, Thomas Wasow, and Adrian Akmajian. New York: Academic Press.

Dowty, David. 1985. On Recent Analyses of the Semantics of Control. *Linguistics and Philosophy* 8:291–331.

Dowty, David. 1991. Thematic Proto-Roles and Argument Selection. *Language* 67(3):547–619.

Dowty, David, and Pauline Jacobson. 1988. Agreement as a Semantic Phenomenon. In *Proceedings of the 5th Annual Eastern States Conference on Linguistics*, ed. Joyce Powers and Ken de Jong. Columbus: Ohio State University.

Fodor, Janet D. 1983. Phrase Structure Parsing and the Island Constraints. *Linguistics and Philosophy* 6:163–223.

Gazdar, Gerald. 1980. English as a Context-free Language. Manuscript, University of Sussex.

Gazdar, Gerald, Ewan Klein, Geoffrey K. Pullum, and Ivan A. Sag. 1985. *Generalized Phrase Structure Grammar*. Cambridge, Mass.: Harvard University Press, and Oxford: Basil Blackwell.

Grimshaw, Jane. 1976. *Wh-Constructions and the Theory of Grammar*. Doctoral dissertation, University of Massachusetts.

Grimshaw, Jane. 1982. Grammatical Relations and Subcategorization. In *Subjects and Other Subjects: Proceedings of the Harvard Conference on Grammatical Relations*, ed. Annie Zaenen, 35–55. Bloomington: Indiana University Linguistics Club.

Hankamer, Jorge, and Ivan A. Sag. 1976. Deep and Surface Anaphora. *Linguistic Inquiry* 7:391–426.

Hukari, Thomas, and Robert Levine. 1987. Rethinking Connectivity in Unbounded Dependency Constructions. In *Proceedings of the 6th Annual West Coast Conference on Formal Linguistics*, ed. Megan Crowhurst, 91–102. Stanford University: Stanford Linguistics Association.

Hukari, Thomas, and Robert Levine. 1990. The Complement Structure of *Tough* Constructions. In *Proceedings of the 7th Annual Eastern States Conference on Linguistics*. Columbus: Ohio State University.

Hukari, Thomas, and Robert Levine. 1991. On the Disunity of Unbounded Dependency Constructions. *Natural Language and Linguistic Theory* 9(1):97–144.

Jackendoff, Ray. 1972. *Semantic Interpretation in Generative Grammar*. Cambridge, Mass.: MIT Press.

Jacobson, Pauline. 1982. Evidence for Gaps. In *The Nature of Syntactic Representation*, ed. Pauline Jacobson and Geoffrey K. Pullum, 187–228. Dordrecht: Reidel.

Jacobson, Pauline. 1984. Connectivity in Phrase Structure Grammar. *Natural Language and Linguistic Theory* 1:535–581.

Jacobson, Pauline. 1987a. Generalized Phrase Structure Grammar (review article). *Linguistics and Philosophy* 10:389–426.

Jacobson, Pauline. 1987b. Phrase Structure, Grammatical Relations and Discontinuous Constituents. In *Syntax and Semantics 20: Discontinuous Constituency*, ed. Geoffrey Huck and Almerindo Ojeda, 27–69. New York: Academic Press.

Jacobson, Pauline. 1989. A(nother) Categorial Grammar Account of Extraction. Paper presented at the Conference on Categorial Grammar at the LSA Summer Linguistic Institute, Tucson.

Jacobson, Pauline. 1990. Raising as Function Composition. *Linguistics and Philosophy* 13:423–475.

Jacobson, Pauline. To appear. Raising Without Movement. In *Control and Grammatical Theory*, ed. Richard Larson et al. Dordrecht: Kluwer.

Kimball, John. 1971. Super-Equi-NP-Deletion as Dative Deletion. In *Papers from the 7th Regional Meeting of the Chicago Linguistic Society*, ed. D. Adams et al. University of Chicago.

Klein, Ewan, and Ivan A. Sag. 1985. Type-driven Translation. *Linguistics and Philosophy* 8:163–202.

Ladusaw, William, and David Dowty. 1988. Toward a Nongrammatical Account of Thematic Roles. In *Syntax and Semantics: Thematic Relations*, ed. Wendy Wilkins, 61–73. New York: Academic Press.

Lasnik, Howard, and Robert Fiengo. 1974. Complement Object Deletion. *Linguistic Inquiry* 5:535–571.

Levine, Robert. 1991. On Missing Object Constructions and the Function-composition Analysis of Raising. Manuscript, Ohio State University.

Oehrle, Richard. 1990. Categorial Frameworks, Coordination, and Extraction. In *Proceedings of the 9th Annual West Coast Conference on Formal Linguistics*, ed. Peter Sells. Stanford: CSLI Publications.

Pollard, Carl, and Ivan A. Sag. 1987. *Information-Based Syntax and Semantics, Vol. I: Fundamentals*. CSLI Lecture Notes No. 13. Stanford: CSLI Publications.

Pollard, Carl, and Ivan A. Sag. 1988. An Information-based Theory of Agreement. In *Proceedings of the Parasession on Agreement*, ed. Diane Brentari, Gary Larson, and Lynn McCleod, 236–257. Chicago: Chicago Linguistic Society.

Pollard, Carl, and Ivan A. Sag. 1992. *Head-Driven Phrase Structure Grammar*. Chicago: University of Chicago Press, and Stanford: CSLI Publications.

Postal, Paul. 1970. On Coreferential Complement Subject Deletion. *Linguistic Inquiry* 1:439–500.

Postal, Paul. 1971. *Cross-Over Phenomena*. New York: Holt, Rinehart, and Winston.

Postal, Paul, and John R. Ross. 1971. Tough Movement Si, Tough Deletion No! *Linguistic Inquiry* 2:544–546.

Rosenbaum, Peter. 1967. *The Grammar of English Predicate Complement Constructions*. Cambridge, Mass.: MIT Press.

Sag, Ivan A. 1982. A Semantic Theory of NP-movement Dependencies. In *The Nature of Syntactic Representation*, ed. Pauline Jacobson and Geoffrey K. Pullum, 427–466. Dordrecht: Reidel.

Schachter, Paul. 1981. Lovely to Look At. *Linguistic Analysis* 8:431–448.

Steedman, Mark J. 1987. Combinatory Grammars and Parasitic Gaps. *Natural Language and Linguistic Theory* 5(3):403–349.

Wasow, Thomas, Ivan A. Sag, and Geoffrey Nunberg. 1983. Idioms: An Interim Report. In *Proceedings of the XIIIth International Congress of Linguists*, ed. Shiro Hattori and Kazuko Inoue, 102–115. Tokyo: CIPL.

11

A Lexical Analysis of Icelandic Case

IVAN SAG, LAURI KARTTUNEN, AND JEFFREY GOLDBERG

1 Introduction

The facts of performance have much to tell us about our knowledge of language. In performance—that is, in real-time language use—our knowledge of language is deployed in wondrous harmony with knowledge of the world, knowledge of the utterance situation, knowledge of our fellow interlocutors, and so forth. Given the extent to which interpretation depends on such factors, i.e. the extent to which linguistic knowledge alone fails to determine interpretation, it remains quite mysterious how we humans are able to use language to communicate determinate messages accurately and efficiently.

One fundamental problem that will occupy the study of language in the decades to come is one we will refer to here as the *Resolution Problem*: the problem of how diverse kinds of knowledge—linguistic and otherwise—are efficiently integrated in real-time language processing. From a linguistic perspective, taking this problem seriously means that we must ask our linguistic descriptions to do more for us than they have in the past. It is not enough that grammars express linguistic generalizations. If our grammars are ultimately to help us address the Resolution Problem (and explain other properties of performance), then they should be designed in accordance with certain criteria that emerge from basic observations about the nature of performance. Some of the relevant observations about human language processing are these:

(1) *Partiality*: In real-time, partial descriptions of linguistic structure are accessed incrementally.

 Flexibility: The partial information from these descriptions may be

We would like to thank Avery Andrews, Joan Maling, and Annie Zaenen for their help. This research was supported in part by a gift to Stanford University from The System Development Foundation, and in part by a grant from the National Science Foundation (BNS-8511687).

Lexical Matters. Ivan A. Sag and Anna Szabolcsi, eds.

flexibly integrated with non-linguistic information in real-time processing.

Order-Independence: Linguistic information is not consulted in any fixed order; there may be task-specific variations in the order in which relevant information is accessed.

Reversibility: In general, linguistic knowledge is consulted equally well by diverse kinds of processors, e.g., those that perform comprehension and those that perform production.

While such observations about language use could in theory be explained in a variety of ways, and perhaps made consistent with a number of architectures for the design of grammar, it is evident that certain existing grammatical architectures—and not others—begin to make sense of these facts of performance.

We are in a better position to begin to explain the observations in (1) if we render linguistic knowledge declaratively, i.e., as a static system of constraints, as is the case, for example, within work in the traditions of phrase structure and categorial grammar. These systems of grammar employ no destructive rules whose order of application with respect to other rules must be crucially fixed. Hence these systems of grammar are appropriately unbiased with respect to comprehension and production. Lexical entries and grammar rules in phrase structure and categorial systems can be interpretd as nothing more than constraints on structures that provide reliable partial information about linguistic structures, rather than information that is true of a structure only at some point in its derivation. And because the information involved is highly restricted, the data structures to be computed in incremental processing of substrings are highly constrained. It thus becomes possible to formulate precise models of processing that attempt to reflect the observed properties of partiality, flexibility, and order-independence.

By contrast, transformational models (including GB models where 'Move α' is interpreted literally) provide little help in explaining the performance properties listed above. Rules perform mappings from total representations of a sentence at a particular "level of representation" to other total representations, and these mappings have typically involved deletions, permutations, insertions, and the like. Moreover such mappings are not in general reversible; nor are their computational properties in general well understood. There is no clear way to model flexible, integrative processing of partial transformational descriptions, though one can imagine that a performance model based on transformational grammars would require some mechanism for mapping transformational descriptions onto some set of constraints that either are otiose or else closely resemble those posited within phrase structure and categorial theories.

These considerations strongly suggest that constraint-based linguistic descriptions like phrase structure grammars and categorial grammars hold greater promise for reconciling the theory of linguistic knowledge (or "competence") with the facts of language processing (performance). However, the fact remains that many complex and well-studied sets of language data constitute a serious challenge for purely constraint-based, non-derivational linguistic theories such as these.[1] In this paper, we discuss one of these challenges, namely the problem of "quirky" case in Icelandic, which has been analyzed by Thráinsson (1979), Andrews (1976, 1982, 1990) and Yip et al. (1987), among others. The data we discuss appear to warrant an analysis that employs transformational rules, constraining equations (Kaplan and Bresnan 1982), or some other non-monotonic syntactic device. The analysis we propose, however, functions in a purely monotonic, order-independent, process-neutral fashion, and hence constitutes a performance-compatible description of this troublesome set of facts. This description involves only lexical entries and schematic phrase structure rules, which together specify a set of constraints that the well-formed structures of Icelandic must satisfy.

Constraint-based analyses in general, and ours in particular, rely heavily on lexical information. The complexity of this information raises new questions about how lexical information is structured and how lexical generalizations are expressed. In light of these concerns, we also discuss the implications of our analysis for the organization of the Icelandic lexicon.

2 The Problem of "Quirky" Case

Icelandic verbs, in the default circumstance, take subjects whose case must be nominative:

(2)   Drengurinn   kyssti   stúlkuna   í   bílnum
      the-boy.NOM kissed the-girl.ACC in the-car.DAT
      'The boy kissed the girl in the car.'

But Icelandic has a number of verbs that assign quirky (i.e., non-nominative) case to their subjects. In (3)–(6) we see examples with accusative subjects.[2]

(3)   Mig   langar að fara   til   Íslands.
      me.ACC longs   to to-go to(LOC) Iceland
      'I long to go to Iceland.'

(4)   Hana   dreymdi um   hafið.
      she.ACC dreamed about the-sea
      'She dreamed about the sea.'

---

[1]For some discussion, see Kay 1986, Sag et al. 1985, and Sag 1991.

[2]All of the data we will discuss here are taken from Andrews 1982.

(5)   Mig   velgir   við setningafræði.
      me.ACC is-nauseated at   syntax
      'Syntax turns my stomach.'

(6)   Drengina   vantar mat.
      the-boys.ACC lack   food.ACC
      'The boys lack food.'

In (7)–(10) we see examples with dative subjects.

(7)   Honum mæltist vel í kirkjunni.
      He.DAT spoke   well in the-church
      'He spoke well in church.'

(8)   Henni   áskotnaðist bíll.
      her.DAT lucked-onto car.NOM
      'She got possession of a car by luck.'

(9)   Stúlkunni svelgdist   á   súpunni.
      girl.DAT   mis-swallowed on the-soup
      'The girl swallowed the soup wrong.'

(10) Barninu   batnaði   veikin.
      the-child.DAT recovered-from the-disease.NOM
      'The child recovered from the disease.'

And we also find verbs that take genitive subjects as shown in (11)–(12).

(11) Verkjanna   gætir   ekki.
      the-pains.GEN is-noticeable not
      'The pains are not noticeable'

(12) Konungs   var þamgað von.
      the-king.GEN was thither   expectation.NOM
      'The king was expected there.'

In all three instances, the quirky case is the only possible one for the subject in question.

Raising verbs are what makes Icelandic case assignment intriguing. If the infinitival complement's verbal head does not assign quirky case, then the "raised" subject of a finite form of a subject raising verb must be nominative in case:

(13) Hann   virðist elska   hana.
      he.NOM seems to-love her.ACC
      'He seems to love her.'

This is what one might expect. But in examples like the following, the raised subject takes the quirky case assigned by the verb that is the head of the infinitival complement:

(14) Hana   virðist vanta   peninga.
      her.ACC seems to-lack money
      'She seems to lack money.'

(15) Barninu   virðist hafa   batnað   veikin.
    the-child.DAT seems to-have recovered-from the-disease
    'The child seems to have recovered from the disease.'

(16) Verkjanna   virðist ekki gæta.
    the-pains.GEN seems not to-be-noticeable
    'The pains don't seem to be noticeable.'

Note that in (15), the quirky case NP is separated from its case assigner by two subject raising verbs (*virðist* and *hafa*).

Similar facts may be observed in the case of object raising constructions. If the head of the infinitival complement is a quirky case assigner, then the raised object NP must bear the appropriate quirky case:

(17) Hann   telur   mig   vanta   peninga.
    he.NOM believes me.ACC to-lack money
    'He believes that I lack money.'

(18) Hann telur   barninu   hafa   batnað   veikin.
    he   believes the-child.DAT to-have recovered-from the disease
    'He believes the child to have recovered from the disease.'

(19) Hann telur   verkjanna   ekki gæta.
    he   believes the-pains.GEN not to-be-noticeable
    'He believes the pains to be no noticeable.'

But if the infinitival complement's verbal head is not a quirky case assigner, then the raised NP must be accusative in case as shown in (20).

(20) þeir telja   Maríu   hafa   skrifað ritgerðina.
    they believe Mary.ACC to-have written the-thesis
    'They believe Mary to have written her thesis.'

In short, Icelandic exhibits what appears to be a syntactic non-monotonic case assignment system. It is one that could be described in transformational terms by assuming (1) that quirky verbs assign case to their subjects prior to the application of raising rules (or, if one prefers, 'Move α'), (2) that finite subject raising verbs optionally assign nominative case to their subjects, (3) that object raising verbs optionally assign accusative case to their objects, and that (4) all NP's must be assigned case somehow (the "Case Filter").[3]

But the derivational (movement transformations) and non-monotonic (filtering conditions) character of such an analyses is inconsistent with the performance-based design considerations we discussed at the outset. Perhaps there is a version of this analysis that can be made to provide answers to the puzzles posed by performance, but it is certainly not any analysis based on the Case Filter that has been discussed in the literature we are

---

[3]Chomsky 1981 and elsewhere.

familiar with. All such analyses presume derivational mappings between fully specified syntactic representations, with the Case Filter functioning as a non-monotonic constraint that must be checked *only after all transformational rules have had an opportunity to apply*.

In another influential analysis of Icelandic case dependencies, Yip et al. (1987) explain an impressive array of complex facts by adapting certain ideas from non-linear phonology (Goldsmith 1976, 1990). The essence of their analysis is a factoring of the case assignment patterns into the interaction between a basic nominative—accusative tier and a restricted set of lexical and semantically based exceptions. Their analysis also relies on a principle filtering derivations where an NP receives no case. Moreover, their approach clearly employs cyclic application of syntactic rules (p. 241ff.) whose effect is to destructively modify the initial (lowest cycle) case value assigned to a given NP. Although their analysis expresses generalizations about Icelandic case not captured by previous approaches, it fails to do so in a way that is compatible with the declarative, constraint-satisfaction architecture for the design of grammar.

There are alternatives that one can imagine. Following the style of Neidle's (1982) LFG analysis of Russian, one might employ constraining equations (Kaplan and Bresnan 1982) to ensure that case is assigned to every NP in a syntactic structure. Like the transformational analysis, this approach would have quirky verbs obligatorily assign case to their subjects, while raising verbs assigned the appropriate default case optionally. A raised NP is identified with the subject of the appropriate complement, hence if nouns are lexically specified with constraining equations requiring that the appropriate case must get assigned to them, then this analysis accomplishes the same effect as the transformational one, without transformational rules.

But such an analysis is also potentially objectionable on performance grounds, for the constraint that it relies on functions in a non-monotonic fashion. Constraining equations are defined as conditions that must be met by functional descriptions, that is, they are not just constraints on functional structures. Rather, they are crucially defined as filters on the *process* that maps constituent structures to functional structures.[4] Perhaps models of language processing could be devised to deal with limited non-monotonicity of this sort,[5] but this remains an open issue.[6]

The question of how to reconcile limited non-monotonicity with the facts of performance is one that need not arise. Appearances to the contrary

---

[4] An analysis essentially equivalent to this can be formulated using Kay's ANY variable, one which must receive a value in a complete linguistic description.

[5] See, for example, Johnson's (1988) discussion of completeness and consistency constraints in LFG.

[6] We will not discuss here the alternate LFG analysis of Icelandic case proposed by Andrews (1990).

notwithstanding, the generalizations of Icelandic quirky case assignment can be elegantly expressed within an analysis that involves no destructive operations, no non-monotonic constraints, and no transformational derivations. It is to this analysis that we turn directly.

3   A Lexical Solution

In any adequate lexical theory, verbs must be provided with some mechanism for selecting for their various dependents, including subjects, objects, oblique NP's or PP's, and complements of various sorts. We will assume, following a long-standing tradition of research in Categorial Grammar,[7] that the syntactic arguments of a verb are hierarchically arranged according to a more or less traditional notion of "obliqueness". This notion has also played a role in Relational Grammar analyses of grammatical relations, in Keenan and Comrie's (1977) cross-linguistic work on relative clause formation, and in the LFG theory of default controller assignment (Bresnan 1982).

To implement this idea, we will assume a simplified version of the notion of SUBCAT list, developed independently by Pollard and Sag within Head-Driven Phrase Structure Grammar (Pollard and Sag 1987, 1992) and by researchers developing the PATR-II system at SRI International (Shieber et al. 1983). The order of elements on the SUBCAT list corresponds not to surface order (i.e., the linear order in which the phonological realizations of the elements occur), but rather to the order of obliqueness, with more oblique elements appearing later than (i.e., to the right of) less oblique elements. Following long-standing tradition, PP (or VP or S) complements are treated as more oblique than direct objects when both occur, and direct objects in turn are more oblique than subjects. Thus the SUBCAT list for an intransitive verb contains exactly one NP, corresponding to the verb's subject; and the SUBCAT list for a (strict) transitive verb contains exactly two NP signs, the first corresponding to the verb's subject and the second to its direct object. Verbs of higher valence have appropriately specified longer SUBCAT lists.

Thus the lexical representation of each verb specifies partial information about the number and kind of syntactic dependents that that verb can combine with. Each element on the SUBCAT list is a partial specification of information about a particular syntactic dependent of the verb, and the actual complements the verb combines with must be consistent with the partial information the verb selects for. Verbs may thus select (for any of their dependents): grammatical category, agreement features, case, valence, and so forth.

A typical finite, transitive verb form like *kyssti* ('kissed') would be specified as follows:

---

[7]See, for example, Dowty 1982a,b.

(21)
$$\text{SUBCAT} \left\langle \begin{bmatrix} \text{CAT} & \text{np} \\ \text{CASE} & \text{nom} \\ \text{PERS} & \text{3rd} \\ \text{NUM} & \text{sing} \end{bmatrix}, \begin{bmatrix} \text{CAT} & \text{np} \\ \text{CASE} & \text{acc} \end{bmatrix} \right\rangle$$

From this lexical specification, it follows that *kyssti* can combine only with an accusative object NP, and a 3rd person singular subject NP.[8]

And we have already introduced sufficient machinery to provide an analysis of the *finite* forms of quirky subject verbs in Icelandic. These forms simply specify different information about their subjects' case, as illustrated in (22)–(24).

(22) langar:
$$\text{SUBCAT} \left\langle \begin{bmatrix} \text{CAT} & \text{np} \\ \text{CASE} & \text{acc} \end{bmatrix}, \begin{bmatrix} \text{CAT} & \text{vp} \\ \text{FORM} & \text{inf} \end{bmatrix} \right\rangle$$

(23) áskotnaðist:
$$\text{SUBCAT} \left\langle \begin{bmatrix} \text{CAT} & \text{np} \\ \text{CASE} & \text{dat} \end{bmatrix}, \begin{bmatrix} \text{CAT} & \text{np} \\ \text{CASE} & \text{nom} \end{bmatrix} \right\rangle$$

(24) gætir:
$$\text{SUBCAT} \left\langle \begin{bmatrix} \text{CAT} & \text{np} \\ \text{CASE} & \text{gen} \end{bmatrix} \right\rangle$$

But this simple method of imposing case restrictions on verbal dependents is insufficient for the raising constructions discussed earlier, as we will now show.

The most straightforward treatment of raising constructions in lexically-based theories of grammar (e.g., Bresnan 1982, Pollard and Sag 1987, 1992) involves identifying the raised element with the unexpressed subject of the VP complement. Under the assumptions we are making here, VP complements are phrases whose SUBCAT value contains exactly one element, corresponding to the unexpressed subject of the "downstairs" verb. Raising is thus accomplished by positing SUBCAT lists like the following for raising verbs.

(25) Simple subject raising verb:
$$\text{SUBCAT} \left\langle \boxed{1}[\text{CAT} \quad \text{np}], \begin{bmatrix} \text{CAT} & \text{vp} \\ \text{FORM} & \text{inf} \\ \text{SUBCAT} & \langle \boxed{1} \rangle \end{bmatrix} \right\rangle$$

Simple object raising verb:
$$\text{SUBCAT} \left\langle \boxed{1}[\text{CAT} \quad \text{np}], [\text{CAT} \quad \text{np}], \begin{bmatrix} \text{CAT} & \text{vp} \\ \text{FORM} & \text{inf} \\ \text{SUBCAT} & \langle \boxed{1} \rangle \end{bmatrix} \right\rangle$$

---

[8]We use the attribute CAT here as an expository convenience. In the theory of grammar developed in Pollard and Sag 1987, 1992, category information is analyzed partially in terms of values for the feature HEAD. In virtue of the Head Feature Principle, category information is projected from verbs to VPs and Ss, from nouns to 'N̄'s and NPs, and so forth. Nothing hinges on this in the present discussion.

Here the tags (e.g., ①) indicate identity (or structure-sharing) between the VP complement's unexpressed subject (the one element on its SUBCAT list) and the appropriate other dependent of the verb.

This lexical approach to raising phenomena would appear to give the right result for complements headed by quirky verbs. Assuming the SUBCAT specifications given above hold for both finite and non-finite verbal forms, the infinitive form of an accusative subject verb (e.g., *vanta*) would give rise to a VP specified as [SUBCAT ⟨NP[acc]⟩]. The subject raising verb *virðist*, specified as in (25), would then combine with the VP *vanta peninga* to form a VP that is also specified as [SUBCAT ⟨NP[acc]⟩], as shown in (26).

(26)

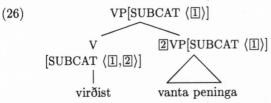

And this VP can combine only with an accusative subject to form such sentences as *Hana.ACC virðist vanta peninga*.

Similarly, the lexical analysis of raising correctly predicts that quirky case selections will be inherited in object raising:

(27)

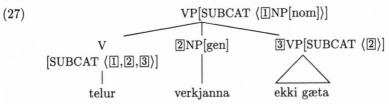

The object of *telur* ('believe') must appear in whatever case the VP complement requires of its (unexpressed) subject.

The problem that now arises concerns non-quirky verbs. If we assume that non-finite forms of non-quirky verbs select for nominative subjects (like their finite counterparts), then the lexical raising analysis works fine for simple subject raising cases, but incorrectly predicts that the object of *telur* will also be nominative when the VP complement is headed by a non-quirky verb. As we saw earlier, such raised objects must be accusative in case. If, on the other hand, we were to assume that the non-finite forms of non-quirky verbs selected for accusative case subjects, then we would have no account of the fact that in subject raising, the matrix subject (e.g., of *virðist* must be nominative if the VP complement is headed by a non-quirky verb. Nor can we allow such verbs to make disjunctive case selections (nominative *or* accusative) for their subjects, because this is not sufficient to block the incorrect choice of case in either raising construction.

The problem here is that the notion of default case assignment is not being expressed. The default case for subjects of finite verb forms is nominative; the default case for direct objects is accusative. The non-quirky verbs obey these defaults; the quirky verbs do not. This is the fundamental intuition of the solution we now propose.

Let us assume that there are two distinct features that nominals bear: CASE and DCASE, where CASE, as before, corresponds to the actual case that the NP in question will bear and DCASE corresponds to the default case that a nominal bears in a given syntactic position. Nominals have no inherent DCASE value, but verbs may subcategorize for subjects or objects that have particular CASE values or particular DCASE values. The difference between quirky and non-quirky verbs can now be analyzed as follows:

(28) Non-quirky verbs require that the DCASE and CASE values of their subjects be identified (structure-shared).

Quirky verbs impose no such identity, and select a particular CASE value for their subject.

Thus the SUBCAT lists for all forms of quirky verbs are just as before (see (19) above). They specify CASE values for their subjects, but say nothing about the subjects' DCASE values. The lexical entries for non-quirky verbs, on the other hand, will all contain the following information:

(29)
$$\text{SUBCAT} \left\langle \begin{bmatrix} \text{CAT} & \text{np} \\ \text{CASE} & \boxed{1} \\ \text{DCASE} & \boxed{1} \end{bmatrix}, \ldots \right\rangle$$

Note that no particular value for either CASE or DCASE is assigned to the subject in (29). The only information specified is that the two features have the same value, however that may be determined.

We may now articulate the rest of our analysis and illustrate its consequences. First, it is a general fact about realized subjects in Icelandic (in finite and non-finite contexts alike), that their default case value is nominative. This information is presumably to be associated with the grammar rule that introduces subjects. The fact that a realized subject[9] must bear the specification [DCASE nom] has important consequences for non-quirky verbs. Since the CASE and DCASE values of the realized subject of a non-quirky verb are identified, it follows that the actual case (determined by the CASE value) of such a subject must be nominative. This is true not only for the subjects of finite forms of non-quirky verbs, as we saw earlier (e.g., (2)), but also for examples like (30), where the subject of a non-finite form is realized.

(30) Mér   virðist hun   elska   hann.
      me.DAT   seems   she.NOM to-love him.ACC
      'It seems to me that she loves him.'

---

[9]Given the range of modifiers that exhibit default nominative case (Andrews 1990), this analysis may have interesting consequences for the treatment of the unexpressed subjects in such modifiers.

For quirky verbs, on the other hand, the constraint that realized subjects are specified as [DCASE nom] has no particular consequence. The actual case of the subject (determined by the CASE value) is assigned by the individual quirky verb, and nothing requires the CASE and DCASE values of the subject to be the same.

Second, the SUBCAT specifications for object raising verbs will no longer be as in (25) above, but rather will be as shown in (31).

(31) Simple object raising verbs:

$$\text{SUBCAT} \left\langle \begin{bmatrix} \text{CAT} & \text{np} \end{bmatrix}, \boxed{1}\begin{bmatrix} \text{CAT} & \text{np} \\ \text{DCASE} & \text{acc} \end{bmatrix}, \begin{bmatrix} \text{CAT} & \text{vp} \\ \text{FORM} & \text{inf} \\ \text{SUBCAT} & \langle\boxed{1}\rangle \end{bmatrix} \right\rangle$$

Again, this will have important consequences when the VP complement of an object raising verb is headed by a non-quirky verb. In that event, since the complement's subject's DCASE and CASE values are identified and since the complement's subject is identified with the direct object of the object raising verb, it follows that the object must be accusative. If the VP complement is headed by a quirky verb, again nothing of consequence follows—the case of the raised object will be determined by the CASE value assigned by the downstairs quirky verb.

These observations are illustrated in figures (32)–(35).

(32) Finite non-quirky verb:

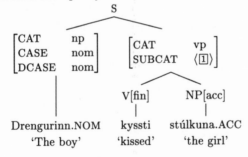

(33) Finite quirky verb:

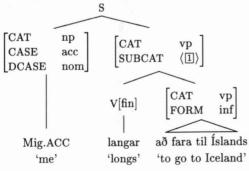

(34) Object raising verb with non-quirky VP complement:

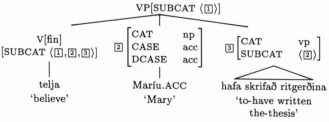

(35) Object raising verb with quirky VP complement:

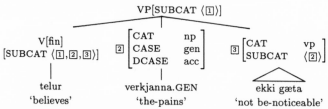

In our analysis, subject raising verbs are exceptional only in not specifying that their subject's CASE and DCASE values are identified. Finite forms of subject raising verbs, e.g., *virðist*, like all finite verb forms, select for subjects that are [DCASE NOM]. Again, this has consequences when the VP complement is headed by a non-quirky verb, but not when the VP contains a quirky head. This is illustrated in (36) and (37).

(36) Subject raising verb with non-quirky VP complement:

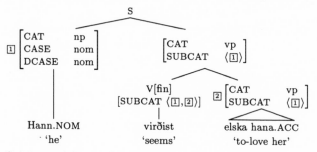

(37) Subject raising verb with quirky VP complement:

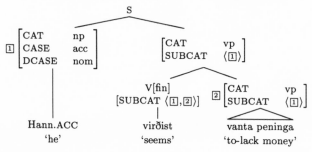

The lexical entries we have proposed, together with general principles that directly constrain syntactic information in phrase structure all provide partial information that must be satisfied by the phrase structures of Icelandic. But the constraints need not be satisfied in any particular order. Our analysis thus accounts for the puzzles of quirky case in Icelandic in a purely monotonic fashion, i.e., in terms of constraints that may be satisfied in any order and which provide flexible, process-neutral, partial information about the structures of the language.

4   Expressing Lexical Generalizations

Although fully specified attribute-value matrices for individual verbs in our analysis of Icelandic may appear to be somewhat complex, their lexical entries may be stated very concisely by generalizing over classes of similar lexical items. A set of features common to a class of words can be defined just once so that the definition is shared by all the entries which have that property. In the PATR-II notation, such named properties are called *templates*.[10] A simple template definition consists of path equations that describe an attribute-value matrix. Templates can also be defined in terms of other templates; in this way a lexicographer may construct inheritance hierarchies of generalizations. In the PATR-II formalism, such definitions are not necessarily monotonic because the information in a higher ranked template may override some specification that is inherited from a template with a lower rank. However, our analysis of Icelandic verbs can be stated under the simpler assumption that templates are composed by unification without overriding.

In this section we show how the complex feature structures for Icelandic verbs can be decomposed to a small number of simple lexical properties. The only technical problem in converting from the semi-formal notation we have used so far to explicit attribute-value structures is the representation of a list—the value of the SUBCAT feature. In a manner reminiscent of CAR and CDR in Lisp, we use the attributes FIRST and REST for the head and the tail of a list, respectively. A special atom, *none*, marks the end of a list. For example, a list of two elements, (A B), would be designated as in (38).

(38) $\langle$FIRST$\rangle$ = A
       $\langle$REST FIRST$\rangle$ = B
       $\langle$REST REST$\rangle$ = none

In defining our first template, *Verb*, we leave the REST argument unspecified so that this basic definition can be shared by all types of verbs that have at least one argument—a subject—on their SUBCAT list:

---

[10] A very similar device is incorporated into the theory of the "hierarchical lexicon" presented in Flickinger 1987 and Pollard and Sag 1987, Chapter 8.

(39) *Verb*: ⟨CAT⟩ = verb
       ⟨SUBCAT FIRST CAT⟩ = np

In terms of the semi-formal notation we have used so far, the definition of *Verb* in (39) is equivalent to (40), where '...' means that the number of elements on the list is unspecified.

(40) SUBCAT ⟨[CAT np] ... ⟩

The next two definitions are straightforward:

(41) *Finite*: ⟨FORM⟩ = fin
       Infinitive: ⟨FORM⟩ = inf

And the following set of templates serve to subcategorize verbs on the basis of the number and type of their non-subject arguments:

(42) *Strict-Intransitive*: ⟨SUBCAT REST⟩ = none

(43) *Transitive*:   ⟨SUBCAT REST FIRST CAT⟩ = np
                           ⟨SUBCAT REST FIRST DCASE⟩ = acc

(44) *Strict-Transitive*: ⟨SUBCAT REST REST⟩ = none

The effect of (42) is to limit the SUBCAT list of the verb to a subject. Note that (43) makes the *default* case of an object be accusative irrespective of whether the verb is finite or non-finite.

The two types of complementizable verbs we have discussed are characterized by the templates (45)–(46). The subject raising verbs merge the subject role of the complement with the subject role of the matrix verb, the object raising verbs equate the object of the matrix with the subject of the complement clause.

(45) *Subject-Raising*:
       ⟨SUBCAT REST FIRST CAT⟩ = vp
       ⟨SUBCAT REST FIRST FORM⟩ = inf
       ⟨SUBCAT REST FIRST SUBCAT FIRST⟩ = ⟨SUBCAT FIRST⟩
       ⟨SUBCAT REST REST⟩ = none

(46) *Object-Raising*:
       ⟨SUBCAT REST REST FIRST CAT⟩ = vp
       ⟨SUBCAT REST REST FIRST FORM⟩ = inf
       ⟨SUBCAT REST REST FIRST SUBCAT FIRST⟩ =
            ⟨SUBCAT REST FIRST⟩
       ⟨SUBCAT REST REST REST⟩ = none

The next two templates characterize non-quirky intransitive and transitive verbs.

(47) *Normal-Subject*:
       ⟨SUBCAT FIRST CASE⟩ = ⟨SUBCAT FIRST DCASE⟩

(48) *Normal-Object*:
       ⟨SUBCAT REST FIRST CASE⟩ = ⟨SUBCAT REST FIRST DCASE⟩

Templates (49) and (50) define two types of quirky verbs.[11]

(49) *Accusative-Subject*: ⟨SUBCAT FIRST CASE⟩ = acc

(50) *Genitive-Subject*: ⟨SUBCAT FIRST CASE⟩ = gen

Using the definitions in (45)–(50), we can now define useful composite templates:

(51) *Intransitive Verb*:   Verb ∧ Strict-Intransitive
      Transitive Verb: Verb ∧ Transitive ∧ Strict-Transitive
      Subject-Raising-Verb: Verb ∧ Subject-Raising
      Object-Raising-Verb: Verb ∧ Transitive ∧ Object-Raising.

Because the definitions of individual templates do not introduce any conflicts, the interpretation of these composite definitions is straightforward: the definition of an object raising verb, for example, is a simple union of the path equations that define the templates *Verb*, *Transitive*, and *Object-Raising*. It describes the attribute-value matrix in (52).

(52) Object raising verb:

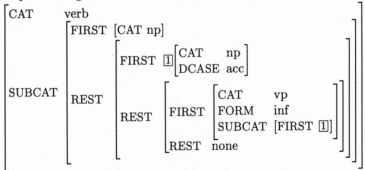

Note that this is a notational variant of (31) above.

We now have all the general properties needed for the entries of individual verbs. For example:

(53) a. kyssti:
         Finite ∧ Transitive-Verb ∧ Normal-Subject ∧ Normal-Object
      b. langar:
         Finite ∧ Equi-Verb ∧ Accusative-Subject
      c. telja:
         Infinitive ∧ Normal-Subject ∧ Object-Raising-Verb
      d. gæta:
         Infinitive ∧ Intransitive-Verb ∧ Genitive-Subject
      e. virðist:
         Finite ∧ Subject-Raising-Verb

---

[11]We leave open here the possibility, suggested by Yip et al. (1987), that there are semantic regularities underlying some of the quirky case assignments we assume here.

As a consequence of the definitions we have given for the various lexical classes, the syntactic behavior and case assignment properties of these verbs are correctly and completely specified by the simple lexical entries in (53).

5 Conclusion

At first glance, The problem of "quirky" case in Icelandic seems to involve non-monotonic (overriding) behavior of default and exceptional case assignment principles. However, as we have shown in this paper, the relevant information, reified in terms of the attributes CASE and DCASE, can be treated quite naturally in terms of simultaneous constraint satisfaction.

An interesting feature of the analysis we have proposed is that it crucially depends on partial information. For example, the subject raising verbs assign case to their subject by letting it be determined by the verb in the complement clause. When a subject is overtly realized, the relevant grammar rule also requires that subjects be specified as [DCASE nom]. And the lexical entry for object raising verbs require their objects to be specified as [DCASE acc]. These specifications, together with a set of identities specified by the constraints of the grammar interacting with those of the lexicon, are what account for the realization of case when the complement's verb is non-quirky.

And because the CASE and DCASE values of the subjects of quirky verbs are distinct, it follows that when a quirky verb appears within the complement of a raising verb, the DCASE specifications just mentioned have no effect on the case of the raised element, which is determined entirely by the quirky verb within the complement. It seems to us that the use of partial information, together with the distinction between default case and actual case, provides a much simpler and more satisfactory account of Icelandic case than earlier descriptions.

One shortcoming of the analysis presented here is that it provides no account of the nominative-accusative template effect whose utility is demonstrated by Yip et al. (1987). We believe, however, that their generalizations can be introduced into our analysis, once rules of case association are seen to apply not to ordered phrase structures (as Yip et al. assume), but rather to hierarchical syntactic argument structures of the sort provided by our SUBCAT feature. In this way, we can incorporate the central insight of the Yip et al. analysis into an analysis that avoids the destructive rule application (cyclical reassignment of non-lexical case) that their analysis employs.

Finally, our analysis embodies a lexical architecture that we believe to be of considerable value in the context of the increasing trend within grammatical theory to locate crucial syntactic information within more complex lexical entries. The lexicon need not be just a list of forms and meanings, coupled with idiosyncratic grammatical information. Rather, in virtue of the organization provided by templates of the sort we have used here, the lexicon can be viewed as an elegant hierarchical (or even heterarchical) database, where every significant generalization about classes of words may be expressed in compact terms. As complexity of syntactic rules is continually eliminated in favor of more complex lexical entries, the development of such methods for achieving lexical compaction is not just a desideratum, it is a necessity.

References

Andrews, Avery. 1976. The VP Complement Analysis in Modern Icelandic. In *Proceedings of NELS 6* (Montreal Working Papers in Linguistics), 1–22. Amherst: University of Massachusetts, GLSA.

Andrews, Avery. 1982. The Representation of Case in Modern Icelandic. In *The Mental Representation of Grammatical Relations*, ed. Joan Bresnan. Cambridge, Mass.: MIT Press.

Andrews, Avery. 1990. Case Structures and Control in Modern Icelandic. In *Syntax and Semantics 24: Modern Icelandic Syntax*, ed. Joan Maling and Annie Zaenen, 187–234. San Diego: Academic Press.

Bresnan, Joan. 1982. Control and Complementation. In *The Mental Representation of Grammatical Relations*, ed. Joan Bresnan. Cambridge, Mass.: MIT Press.

Chomsky, Noam. 1981. *Lectures on Government and Binding.* Dordrecht: Foris.

Dowty, David. 1982a. Grammatical Relations and Montague Grammar. In *The Nature of Syntactic Representation*, ed. Pauline Jacobson and Geoffrey Pullum, 79–130. Dordrecht: Reidel.

Dowty, David. 1982b. More on the Categorial Analysis of Grammatical Relations. In *Subjects and Other Subjects*, ed. Annie Zaenen, 115–153. Bloomington: Indiana University Linguistics Club.

Flickinger, Daniel. 1987. *Lexical Fules in the Hierarchical Lexicon.* Doctoral dissertation, Stanford University.

Goldsmith, John. 1976. An Overview of Autosegmental Phonology. *Linguistic Analysis* 2:231–68.

Goldsmith, John. 1990. *Autosegmental and Metrical Phonology.* Oxford: Basil Blackwell.

Johnson, Mark. 1988. *Attribute-Value Logic and the Theory of Grammar.* CSLI Lecture Notes No. 16. Stanford: CSLI Publications.

Kaplan, Ronald, and Joan Bresnan. 1982. Lexical-Functional Grammar: A Formal System for Grammatical Representation. In *The Mental Representation of Grammatical Relations*, ed. Joan Bresnan. Cambridge, Mass.: MIT Press.

Kay, Martin. 1986. Parsing in Functional Unification Grammar. In *Natural Language Parsing*, ed. David Dowty, Lauri Karttunen, and Arnold Zwicky. New York: Cambridge University Press.

Keenan, Edward, and Bernard Comrie. 1977. Noun Phrase Accessibility and Universal Grammar. *Linguistic Inquiry* 8:63–99.

Maling, Joan, and Annie Zaenen (eds.). 1990. *Syntax and Semantics 24: Modern Icelandic Syntax.* San Diego: Academic Press.

Neidle, Carol. 1982. Case Agreement in Russian. In *The Mental Representation of Grammatical Relations,* ed. Joan Bresnan. Cambridge, Mass.: MIT Press.

Pollard, Carl, and Ivan A. Sag. 1987. *Information-Based Syntax and Semantics, Vol. I: Fundamentals.* CSLI Lecture Notes No. 13. Stanford: CSLI Publications.

Pollard, Carl, and Ivan A. Sag. 1992. *Head-Driven Phrase Structure Grammar.* Chicago: University of Chicago Press, and Stanford: CSLI Publications.

Sag, Ivan A. 1991. Linguistic Theory and Natural Language Processing. In *Natural Language and Speech,* ed. Ewan Klein and Frank Veltman. Berlin: Springer-Verlag. Symposium Proceedings. Brussels, November 1991.

Sag, Ivan A., Ronald Kaplan, Lauri Karttunen, Martin Kay, Carl Pollard, Stuart Shieber, and Annie Zaenen. 1985. Unification and Grammatical Theory. In *Proceedings of the 5th West Coast Conference on Formal Linguistics,* ed. Mary Dalrymple, Jeffrey Goldberg, Kristin Hanson, Michael Inman, Christopher Piñon, and Stephen Wechsler. Stanford University: Stanford Linguistics Association.

Shieber, Stuart, Hans Uszkoreit, Fernando Pereira, Jane Robinson, and Mabry Tyson. 1983. The Formalism and Implementation of PATR-II. In *Research on Interactive Acquisition and User of Knowledge,* ed. Barbara Grosz and Mark Stickel. Menlo Park, CA: SRI International. (SRI Final Report 1984).

Thráinsson, Höskuldur. 1979. *On Complementation in Icelandic.* New York: Garland.

Yip, Moira, Joan Maling, and Ray Jackendoff. 1987. Case in Tiers. *Language* 63:217–250.

Author Index

Abelson, Robert P., 211, 213, 233
Abney, Steven, 133, 162, 163
Abraham, Werner, 218
Ackerman, Farrell, x, 55, 58, 75, 218
Ades, Anthony, 248
Akmajian, Adrian, 277
Alford, Jack A., Jr., 234
Allen, Margaret R., 111
Alsina, Alex, 62
Anderson, Mona, 8
Anderson, Stephen R., 14, 55, 111
Andrews, Avery, 303, 306, 310
Aronoff, Mark, 94, 111

Bach, Emmon, 31, 47, 285, 292
Baker, Mark, 2, 169, 171
Barwise, Jon, 96
Bauer, Lauri, 156
Bayer, Samuel, 271, 275, 279, 280,
    282, 283
Becker, Curtis A., 233
Belletti, Adriana, 17
Benešová, Eva, 212
Bennett, Michael, 47
Berman, Arlene, 271
Bever, Thomas G., 209, 210, 213,
    216, 230, 231, 233
Bierwisch, Manfred, 201, 209
Blåberg, O., 146
Black, J. B., 211
Bolinger, Dwight, 133, 135, 159
Bouchard, Denis, 85, 90, 107
Bower, Gordon H., 211, 213, 233
Brame, Michael, 293

Bresnan, Joan, 56, 58, 61, 62, 71,
    76, 274, 276, 303, 306–308
Brown, Roger, 206
Burzio, Luigi, 11

Carlson, Greg, 44
Carpenter, Bob, 252
Chafe, William L., 212, 215
Chien, Yu-Chin, 258
Chierchia, Gennara, xvi, 252, 269,
    272, 273, 278, 283, 295
Chomsky, Noam, xi, xvi, 132, 139,
    147, 212, 252, 256, 270,
    271, 275, 277, 278, 292
Clark, Eve, 111, 183, 186, 206
Clark, Herb, 111, 183, 206, 211, 212
Clements, J., 171
Collins, Allan M., 224, 233
Comorovski, Ileana, 95
Comrie, Bernard, 307
Crain, Steven, 210, 212, 222, 235
Culicover, Peter, 62
Curry, Haskell B., 251, 253
Cutler, Anne, 171, 212

Dakin, Julian, 213
de Meij, Sjaak, 218
Dezső, László, 217
Di Sciullo, Anna Maria, 123, 124,
    133, 150, 162, 167, 169
Downing, Pamela A., 141, 143
Dowty, David, viii, x, xvi, 5, 7, 13,
    21, 22, 30, 31, 44, 57, 60,
    62, 63, 142, 254, 269, 272,

273, 279, 283, 286–288, 290, 292

Dressler, Wolfgang U., 186, 187

Duffy, S., 211

Esau, Helmut, 111

Fabb, Nigel, 138, 162

Farkas, Donka, xi, xv, xvii, 88, 95, 218

Fauconnier, Gilles, 99

Fazekas, Á., 206

Fellbaum, Christiane, 8

Feys, Robert, 251, 253

Fiengo, Robert, 270, 271, 274

Filip, Hana, 49

Fillmore, Charles, 55, 63, 128

Finin, Timothy W., 176

Fischler, Ira, 233

Flickinger, Daniel, 313

Fodor, Janet D., 210, 271, 278

Fodor, Jerry A., 210, 212

François, Jean, 30

Fudge, Erik, 143, 156

Garrett, Merrill F., 210

Garrod, Simon C., 211

Gawron, Jean Mark, 63, 259, 260

Gazdar, Gerald, 271, 275, 278–280, 283, 287, 289, 293

Geach, Peter T., 253

Gergely, György, xiv, 209, 210, 211, 213, 214, 221, 225, 231, 233

Gibbs, Ray W., 211

Gleitman, Lila, 23

Goldberg, Jeffrey, 23

Goldsmith, John, 306

Goodman, George O., 233

Gough, Phillip B., 234

Greenberg, Joseph H., 194

Grimshaw, Jane, 11, 113, 258, 283–285

Gropen, Jess, 23

Gruber, Jeffrey S., 7

Hajicová, Eva, 212

Hale, Kenneth, 8

Halle, Morris, 132, 147

Halliday, Michael A. K., 212

Hankamer, Jorge, 280

Hasegawa, Nobuko, 113, 114

Haviland, Susan E., 211, 212

Hayes, Bruce, 132, 147

Heinämäki, Orvokki, 46

Hindley, J. Roger, 252

Hinrichs, Erhard, 7, 31

Hirschberg, Julia, 134

Hjelmslev, Louis, 194

Hoeksema, Jacob, 169

Hoepelman, Jakob, 31

Holley-Wilcox, Pamela, 234

Horn, Laurence R., x, 94, 106, 286

Horvath, Julia, 217

Householder, Frederick W., x, 123

Hualde, José Ignacio, 122

Hukari, Thomas, 270, 275, 276, 278, 283, 286, 288, 290, 293

Inoue, Kazuko, 113

Jackendoff, Ray, 7, 56, 131, 132, 212, 215, 216, 273

Jacobson, Pauline, xvi, xvii, 271–274, 277–283, 285, 286, 288, 289, 292, 294

Johnson, Mark, 306

Johnson-Laird, Phillip N., 190, 210, 222, 235

Joseph, Brian, 95

Kageyama, Taroo, 113, 116

Kálmán, László, 218, 235

Kanerva, Jonni M., 61, 62

Kański, Zbigniew, 253

Kaplan, Ronald, 303, 306

Kawakami, Shin, 115

Kay, Martin, 128, 303

Kayne, Richard, 242, 243, 245, 247

Keenan, Edward L., 253, 255, 256, 307

Kempchinsky, Paula, 85, 89

Kenesei, István, 218

Keyser, S. Jay, 8

Kiefer, Ferenc, 201, 217

Kimball, John, 296

Kiparsky, Paul, 85, 94, 111, 163, 167
Kiss, Katalin É., 217
Klein, Ewan, 271, 275, 278–280, 283, 287, 293
Komlósy, András, 218
Koster, Jan, 242
Krifka, Manfred, viii–x, 7, 31, 36, 38

Laczkó, Tibor, 55, 75
Ladd, Robert, 133, 135, 161, 167
Ladusaw, William, 62, 274, 290
Landau, Barbara, 23
Lang, Ewald, 201
Lapointe, Steven G., 194, 195
Lasnik, Howard, 270, 271, 274
Lees, Robert B., 137
Leisi, Ernst, 31
Levi, Judith N., 137, 141, 142, 151, 166
Levin, Beth, 14, 55, 56, 71, 72, 76, 137
Levine, Robert, 270, 275, 276, 278, 283, 286, 288, 290, 293
Levinson, Stephen, x
Liberman, Mark, xii, 132, 147, 175, 176
Lieber, Rochelle, 137, 156, 171
Link, Godehard, 31, 45
Loftus, Elizabeth F., 224, 233, 234

Magerman, David, 177
Maidment, J. A., 135
Maling, Joan, 270
Marantz, Alec, 137
Marchand, Hans, 145
Marcus, Mitchell, 177
Marslen-Wilson, William D., 210, 222, 224, 233, 235
Mayerthaler, Willi, 186
McCawley, James, x, 94, 106, 123
Mchombo, Sam, 62
Meireles, J., 85, 87
Mester, Armin, 113
Meyer, David E., 233, 234
Miller, George A., 190
Mitchell, D. C., 211, 233, 234
Miyagawa, Shigeru, 111, 113
Mohanan, K. P., 169, 172

Moravcsik, Edith, 46
Morton, J., 224, 233

Neely, James H., 234
Neidle, Carol, 306
Nunberg, Geoffrey, 288

O'Connor, Mary Catherine, 128
Oehrle, Richard, 248, 277

Padilla-Rivera, J., 87, 103
Panagl, Oswald, 186
Partee, Barbara, 47, 258
Paul, Hermann, 111
Perlmutter, David, 1, 11
Perry, John, 96
Peters, Stanley, 259, 260
Picallo, Carme, 85, 87
Pinker, Steven, 23, 55
Platzack, Christer, 31
Pléh, Csaba, 206, 217
Pollard, Carl, 242–244, 247, 252, 271, 274, 278, 285, 288, 307, 308, 313
Poser, William J., 113
Postal, Paul, 1, 11, 173, 271, 273, 279
Prince, Alan, 132, 147
Pullum, Geoffrey K., 271, 275, 278–280, 283, 287, 293
Pustejovsky, James, 7

Quine, Willard van Orman, 30, 253

Ramsey, S. Robert, 171
Raposo, Eduardo, 85, 87
Rappaport, Malka, 14, 55, 56, 71, 72, 76, 137
Réger, Zita, 206
Reinhart, Tanya, 107, 212, 258–260
Riesbeck, Christopher K., 210, 211
Rizzi, Luigi, 17
Roberts, Ian, 8
Rochemont, Michael, 218
Roeper, Thomas, 137
Rohrer, Christian, 31
Rooth, Mats, 174
Rosch, Elinor, 206

Rosen, Carol, 258
Rosenbaum, Peter, 271, 279, 284
Ross, John R., 279
Ruddy, Margaret G., 233
Ruwet, Nicolas, 88, 89, 103

Safir, Ken, 139
Sag, Ivan A., 243, 272, 274, 275, 278–280, 283, 285, 288, 293, 303, 307, 308, 313
Saiki, Mariko, 116
Salamanca, D., 87
Salkoff, Morris, 55
Sanford, Anthony J., 211
Scha, Remko, 43
Schachter, Paul, 278
Schaner-Wolles, C., 187
Schank, Roger C., 210, 211, 213, 233
Schmerling, Susan, 218
Schönfinkel, M., 251
Schvaneveldt, Roger W., 233, 234
Schwartz-Norman, Linda, 14
Seidenberg, Mark, 210
Selkirk, Elizabeth, 137, 145, 164, 169, 171, 218
Sgall, Petr, 212
Sharkey, Noel E., 211, 233, 234
Shih, Chi-lin, 165, 177
Siegel, Muffy, 137
Simpson, Jane, 56
Sproat, Richard, xii, 137, 139, 165, 173, 175–178
Steedman, Mark, 210, 212, 222, 235, 248, 249, 251, 254, 257, 277, 278, 290
Stump, Greg, 171
Suñer, Margarita, 87, 103
Szabó, Zoltán, 235

Szabolcsi, Anna, xv, xvii, 55, 92, 212, 217, 218, 248, 249, 254, 257, 259, 264

Tenney, Yvette J., 211
Tenny, Carol, viii, x, 19
ter Meulen, Alice, 31
Thomason, Richard, 139
Thráinsson, Höskuldur, 303
Tomán, Jindrich, 111
Townsend, David J., 211, 213, 216, 230, 231
Turner, T. J., 211
Tyler, Lorraine K., 210, 235

Van Valin, Robert, 11, 13
Vendler, Zeno, 30, 60
Verkuyl, Henk J., 7, 31, 46
Verschueren, Jef, 201
von Stechow, Arnim, 253

Ward, Gregory, 173
Warren, R. E., 234
Wasow, Thomas, 71, 288
Welsh, A., 224, 233
Wexler, Ken, 258
Wierzbicka, Anna, 49
Williams, Edwin, 4, 123, 124, 133, 150, 162, 167, 169–171
Wurzel, Wolfgang U., 186

Yip, Moira, 303, 315, 316

Zaenen, Annie, x, 11, 56, 58, 60–64, 76, 270
Zaring, L., 87, 103
Zec, Draga, 93
Zubizarreta, Maria-Luisa, 57
Zwanenberg, Weicher, 111

Subject Index

Accomplishment, 29, 30
acquisition, 23
    order, xiii, xiv, 206
activities, 29
adjective
    comparative, 120
    superlative, 120
adjective-noun compounds, xii, 148, 151
adverbial
    aspect-marking, 218
    directional, 51
    durative, 30, 51
    locative, 51
    time-span, 30, 51
adversative, xiv
    inference, 231
    subordinate clauses, 213, 214
affected arguments, 9, 10
affectedness, viii, 8, 10, 23
agentive-headed compounds, 137
    pseudo-object lefthand members, 138
    restrictions on lefthand members, 138
agglutinative language, 209, 217
agreement, 274, 288, 292
aktionsart, 29, 189
    frequentative 51
anaphora, xvi, 241, 252, 253, 255–260, 265, 266
    deep, 280
    null complement, xvi, 280, 281, 289, 291

anaphoric island constraint, 173
antecedent matching, 222
argument structure, viii, x, xiii, 2, 3, 21, 23
argument-argument compounds, 137, 140, 143
argument-predicate compounds, 137, 140
aspect, ix, x, 2, 4, 10, 11, 13, 16–18, 20, 21, 23, 29, 31, 38, 60, 189, 192
aspect-marking adverbial, 218
atelic predicate, viii, 30, 34, 35
atomic reference, ix, 32
atomicity of word, 172

Backward search for discourse antecedent, 212, 213, 216
basic lexical entry, 64
basic-level term, 183
Basque, xi, 122
binding, xi, xv, xvi, 251–253, 255, 256, 258–260
blocking, viii, x–xiii, 94, 111
Brazilian Portuguese, 87
Breton, 171

Case, xv, xvii, 303, 305
    filter, 305, 306
case-marker suffixes, 217
categorial grammar, xv, 241, 248, 272, 277, 294, 302, 303, 307
causativization, xiii, 56

cause-effect relation, xiv, 213, 230, 235
change, 3, 6, 8, 19–21
    of location, 79
Chinese, 177
closed class items, 163
collective readings, 44
combinator, xv, 241, 248, 251–253, 256, 257, 259, 260, 262, 264–266
competence, 303
complex predicate, 55, 58, 65, 70, 218
complexity, formal, xiii, 184
compound
    bahuvrihi, 148, 166
    derived-nominal headed, 139
    English
        orthographic conventions, 136
    modifiers, 132
    stress rule, 146
    with possessive modifiers, 153
        implicit contrast theories, 155
conjunction, 232
constraining equations, 303, 306
constraint, xvii, 302, 303, 306, 313, 316
construction grammar, 128
control, xi, xv, xvi, 269–272, 280, 289, 291, 295, 296
controller choice, 88, 103
count nouns, 29
cumulative
    readings, 43
    reference, ix, 30, 32
Czech, 46, 49

Deep anaphora, 280
default case, 307, 309, 310, 314, 316
deferred reference, 174
definiteness, 49
degree of agentivity, 88
delimitedness, 5, 7, 11, 19, 24
derivational morphology, xiii, 185, 192
derived-nominal headed compound, 139

direct internal argument, 4, 6–8, 10, 15, 23
directional adverbial, 51
discourse
    functions in Hungarian, 217
    informational cues, 210
    representation, 232
disjoint reference, 85
dummy, 276, 287, 288
durative adverbial, 30, 51

Effected objects, 41
elementary predicates, 191
elsewhere principle, x, xi, 90, 107, 111
English, xii, xiv, 120
    compound, 136, 169
    noun phrases, 131
epithets, 149
event, 4, 5, 12
    tokens, 34
    types, 34
external argument, 4, 11, 17, 18, 24
extraction, xvi, 243, 253, 255, 261, 262, 265
    gap, 277

Finnish, ix, 46
"flat" sentences, 218
focus, 212, 214, 217, 218
    movement, 217
focus-based inference, xv, 209, 210, 215, 231–236
    in discourse antecedent matching, 219
    predictive, 210, 231
        clausal processing, 222
    priming, 233
    processes, 219
foregrounding, 222, 223, 236
formal complexity, 184
"free" word order, 209, 217
French, 86–89, 167, 171
frequentative
    verb form, xiii
    aktionsart, 51

function composition, xvi, 247–249, 251, 260, 271, 279, 280, 282

Gap, xv, xvi, 247
    extraction, 277
    parasitic, 243, 244, 270, 278
German, 46
gerund-headed compounds, 139
    pseudo-object lefthand members, 139
given information, 212
goal, 14, 15, 19
government-binding theory, xv, 4, 85, 241–243, 247, 248, 302
graduality, 42
Gricean convention, 214, 215

Head-driven phrase structure grammar, xv, 241–244, 247, 248, 307
head feature principle, 308
head-final filter, 162
headedness
    of affixed words, 171
    of compounds and phrases in English, 169
hierarchical lexicon, 313
Hindi, 51
Hungarian, ix–xi, xiii, xiv, xviii, 55, 58, 64, 71, 72, 81, 90–92, 95, 96, 184, 185, 209, 217, 254
    discourse functions, 217
    sentence structure, 217
    topic-focus structure 219

Icelandic, xvii, 301–317
idiom chunks, 288
incremental theme, viii, 7, 22, 62–63
indirect internal argument, 4, 7
inference
    adversative 231
    focus-based, xv, 209, 210, 215, 231–236
    predictive, 213, 222, 224
information
    cues, 210

given, 212
new, 212
mutual, 177
inheritance hierarchy, 313
interactive model, 232, 235
interclausal semantic relations, xiv, 209, 213, 232, 235
internal argument, ix, 3, 4, 10, 11, 13, 17–20
    indirect, 4, 7
island, 292–294
Italian, 167
iterativity, 39, 40

Japanese, 112

Language processing, 301, 303
lattice, ix, 31, 32
left-headed modified nominals, 166
    stress pattern in, 159
lexical
    aspect 60
    entry, vii, 3
    form, 69
    integrity, 172
    item, xiii, 241–244, 248, 253, 265
    mapping theory, x, 55–81
    priming, 233
    semantics, x, xiii, 1, 18, 21, 60, 252–256
    versus syntactic analysis, xv, 241–244
lexicalization, xiii, 150
lexicon, vii–xv, 241, 242, 254, 264
locative
    adverbial, 51
    alternation, ix, 14, 15, 23, 55, 56, 58, 64
    inversion, 57

Manner of motion, 79
mass nouns, 29
measure constructions, 29, 51
measuring out the event, ix, 2–7, 12–20, 23
middle, 10, 11
monotonicity, xvii, 57, 68, 248, 303

morpholexical operation, x, 55, 56, 80

morphological
  complexity, xiii, 184–187, 191, 192, 194–197, 201, 206, 207
  component, 133, 169
  construction, 125
  markedness, 187

morphosyntactic operation, x, 56, 80

morphotactic transparency, 187

motion, 3, 21

move α, 302, 305

mutual information, 177

Names as modifiers, 173

negation, 51

new information, 212

nominal reference, 30
  with possessive modifiers, 154

non-binary premodified nominal, 146, 161

nondelimited event, 5, 7

nonstative verb, 3

noun phrase, xii, 131

noun-noun compound, xii, 156, 160

noun-PP expressions
  left-stressed cases, 155

nuclear stress rule, xii, 146

null complement anaphora, xvi, 280, 281, 289, 291

O-ellipsis, 116

obliqueness, 307

observed object, 31

obviative complement, 85

overlap, 32

overriding, 313, 316

Parasitic gap, 243, 244, 270, 278

partitive, ix, 46

passive, xiii, 8, 11, 57, 285

path equations, 313, 315

PATR-II, 307, 313

perfective, ix, x, xiii, 49

performance, 301–306

periphrastic verb, xi, xii, 112, 122

phrasal modifiers, 132

plural, 29

Polish, 49

possessives, distributional properties of, 154

pragmatic complexity, 201, 206, 207

predicate-argument structure, 188

predictive inference, 213, 222, 224

premodified nominal
  N^0 versus N^1 cases, 164
  automatic parsing
    statistical methods, 177
    and stress assignment, 175
  basic stress-pattern, 148
    exceptions, 148
    "implicit contrast", 152
    interspeaker variation, 149, 157
    Ladd's "subcategorization" theory, 167
  deaccenting in, 168
  determiners in, 162
  non-binary, 146, 161
  pronouns in, 162
  quantifiers in, 162
  semantics of
    classificatory schemes, 141
    'connected-with' theory, 142
  structure of, 162
  syntactic restrictions on lefthand member, 162
  with phrasal modifier, 156, 161

prenominal adjective ordering restrictions, 165

presuppositional properties, 189

pro-arb, 273

process nominals in compounds, 139

processing time, xiv, 206

productivity, 186

progressive, ix, 46

proto-agent, 21, 22, 63

proto-patient, viii, 7, 21, 22, 63, 78

proto-role, viii, x, 63

prototype semantics, 191

psych verb, 16

Quantification, 51

quantized reference, ix, 30, 32

quirky case, xvii, 303–316

Raising, 304–316
  construction, xvii, 270, 271, 279–
    282, 286, 288
  function composition analysis
    of, 279, 280
recoding
  at clause-boundary, 225
  at end of clause, 222, 236
reference
  atomic, ix, 32
  cumulative, ix, 30, 32
  deferred, 174
  disjoint, 85
  nominal, 30
    with possessive modifiers, 154
  quantized, 30, 32
  singular, 32
referential expressions within com-
    pounds, 173
relational grammar, 307
resolution problem, 301
result nominal, 139
resultative preverb, x, 18, 59
Romance, xi, 85, 87, 96
  compounds, 167
Romanian, xi, 88, 89, 95

Scenario, 45
script, xiv, 211, 233, 234
selectional restriction, 270, 271, 274,
    276, 290, 293
self as lefthand member of compound,
    140
semantic
  complexity, xiii, xiv, 183–186,
    189–192, 194–197, 200–202,
    206, 207
  fields, 185
  markedness, xiii, 184, 185, 191,
    205–207
  representations, 189
  transparency, 186
semantics
  lexical x, xiii, 1, 18, 21, 60,
    252–256
  of premodified nominal, 141, 142
  prototype, 191
Serbo-Croatian, xi, 90, 93–95

set terminal point, 34
singular reference, ix, 32
Slavic, ix, 46
Spanish, 87, 89, 167, 171, 172
stress patterns, 131
  discourse-conditioned vs. discourse-
    neutral, 134
  of argument-argument compounds,
    143
structure sharing, 309, 310
SUBCAT, 307–316
subject, 85, 308, 309
  postposing, 217
summativity, 39, 43
Swedish, 146
syntactic
  complexity, xiii, 184, 188, 207
  markedness, 188, 206

Telic predicate, viii–x, 30, 34, 35,
    61, 69, 74, 80
template, 313–317
temporal
  constitution, 29, 30
  order, 33
  trace, 33
thematic relations, viii–x, 1, 2, 11,
    19, 31, 34, 62, 71
theme, 14
θ-criterion, 274
θ-role, 270, 271, 274, 291
'though' clause, 213, 214, 231
time dependency, 101
time-span adverbial, 30, 51
topic, 212, 217
topic-focus structure, xiv, 209, 211,
    214, 217, 219, 223, 230,
    235
topicalization, 218, 286
tough construction, xvi, 269–283, 288–
    296
transformational rules, xv, xvii, 302,
    303, 305
transitivity, 76

Unaccusative, 11, 12, 57, 58, 73, 76
unbounded dependencies, xv, 241
unergative, 11, 12

unification, 313
uniqueness
    of events, 39, 46
    of objects, 39, 44
universal alignment hypothesis, 2
universal theta assignment hypothesis, 2

Variable, 241, 251–253, 256–258, 260, 265
verba efficiendi, 46
verb
    compound, 145
    frequentative, xiii
    nonstative, 3
    performance, 46
    periphrastic, xi, xii, 112, 122

    psych, 16
    quirky, 309
verbal modifiers, 218
VP-ellipsis, xvi, 241, 253, 259–262

Welsh, 170, 171
wh-construction, 270, 271, 277, 292, 293
wh-extraction case, xvi, 294
'while' clause, 225, 231
word
    affixed, 171
    atomicity, 172
    order, 209, 217

Zhuang, 171

CSLI Publications

Lecture Notes

The titles in this series are distributed by the University of Chicago Press and may be purchased in academic or university bookstores or ordered directly from the distributor: Order Department, 11030 S. Langely Avenue, Chicago, Illinois 60628.

A Manual of Intensional Logic. Johan van Benthem, second edition, revised and expanded. Lecture Notes No. 1. ISBN 0-937073-29-6 (paper), 0-937073-30-X (cloth)

Emotion and Focus. Helen Fay Nissenbaum. Lecture Notes No. 2. ISBN 0-937073-20-2 (paper)

Lectures on Contemporary Syntactic Theories. Peter Sells. Lecture Notes No. 3. ISBN 0-937073-14-8 (paper), 0-937073-13-X (cloth)

An Introduction to Unification-Based Approaches to Grammar. Stuart M. Shieber. Lecture Notes No. 4. ISBN 0-937073-00-8 (paper), 0-937073-01-6 (cloth)

The Semantics of Destructive Lisp. Ian A. Mason. Lecture Notes No. 5. ISBN 0-937073-06-7 (paper), 0-937073-05-9 (cloth)

An Essay on Facts. Ken Olson. Lecture Notes No. 6. ISBN 0-937073-08-3 (paper), 0-937073-05-9 (cloth)

Logics of Time and Computation. Robert Goldblatt, second edition, revised and expanded. Lecture Notes No. 7. ISBN 0-937073-94-6 (paper), 0-937073-93-8 (cloth)

Word Order and Constituent Structure in German. Hans Uszkoreit. Lecture Notes No. 8. ISBN 0-937073-10-5 (paper), 0-937073-09-1 (cloth)

Color and Color Perception: A Study in Anthropocentric Realism. David Russel Hilbert. Lecture Notes No. 9. ISBN 0-937073-16-4 (paper), 0-937073-15-6 (cloth)

Prolog and Natural-Language Analysis. Fernando C. N. Pereira and Stuart M. Shieber. Lecture Notes No. 10. ISBN 0-937073-18-0 (paper), 0-937073-17-2 (cloth)

Working Papers in Grammatical Theory and Discourse Structure: Interactions of Morphology, Syntax, and Discourse. M. Iida, S. Wechsler, and D. Zec (Eds.) with an Introduction by Joan Bresnan. Lecture Notes No. 11. ISBN 0-937073-04-0 (paper), 0-937073-25-3 (cloth)

Natural Language Processing in the 1980s: A Bibliography. Gerald Gazdar, Alex Franz, Karen Osborne, and Roger Evans. Lecture Notes No. 12. ISBN 0-937073-28-8 (paper), 0-937073-26-1 (cloth)

Information-Based Syntax and Semantics. Carl Pollard and Ivan Sag. Lecture Notes No. 13. ISBN 0-937073-24-5 (paper), 0-937073-23-7 (cloth)

Non-Well-Founded Sets. Peter Aczel. Lecture Notes No. 14. ISBN 0-937073-22-9 (paper), 0-937073-21-0 (cloth)

Partiality, Truth and Persistence. Tore Langholm. Lecture Notes No. 15. ISBN 0-937073-34-2 (paper), 0-937073-35-0 (cloth)

Attribute-Value Logic and the Theory of Grammar. Mark Johnson. Lecture Notes No. 16. ISBN 0-937073-36-9 (paper), 0-937073-37-7 (cloth)

The Situation in Logic. Jon Barwise. Lecture Notes No. 17. ISBN 0-937073-32-6 (paper), 0-937073-33-4 (cloth)

The Linguistics of Punctuation. Geoff Nunberg. Lecture Notes No. 18. ISBN 0-937073-46-6 (paper), 0-937073-47-4 (cloth)

Anaphora and Quantification in Situation Semantics. Jean Mark Gawron and Stanley Peters. Lecture Notes No. 19. ISBN 0-937073-48-4 (paper), 0-937073-49-0 (cloth)

Propositional Attitudes: The Role of Content in Logic, Language, and Mind. C. Anthony Anderson and Joseph Owens. Lecture Notes No. 20. ISBN 0-937073-50-4 (paper), 0-937073-51-2 (cloth)

Literature and Cognition. Jerry R. Hobbs. Lecture Notes No. 21. ISBN 0-937073-52-0 (paper), 0-937073-53-9 (cloth)

Situation Theory and Its Applications, Vol. 1. Robin Cooper, Kuniaki Mukai, and John Perry (Eds.). Lecture Notes No. 22. ISBN 0-937073-54-7 (paper), 0-937073-55-5 (cloth)

The Language of First-Order Logic (including the Macintosh program, Tarski's World). Jon Barwise and John Etchemendy, second edition, revised and expanded. Lecture Notes No. 23. ISBN 0-937073-74-1 (paper)

Lexical Matters. Ivan A. Sag and Anna Szabolcsi, editors. Lecture Notes No. 24. ISBN 0-937073-66-0 (paper), 0-937073-65-2 (cloth)

Tarski's World. Jon Barwise and John Etchemendy. Lecture Notes No. 25. ISBN 0-937073-67-9 (paper)

Situation Theory and Its Applications, Vol. 2. Jon Barwise, J. Mark Gawron, Gordon Plotkin, Syun Tutiya, editors. Lecture Notes No. 26. ISBN 0-937073-70-9 (paper), 0-937073-71-7 (cloth)

Literate Programming. Donald E. Knuth. Lecture Notes No. 27. ISBN 0-937073-80-6 (paper), 0-937073-81-4 (cloth)

Normalization, Cut-Elimination and the Theory of Proofs. A. M. Ungar. Lecture Notes No. 28. ISBN 0-937073-82-2 (paper), 0-937073-83-0 (cloth)

Lectures on Linear Logic. A. S. Troelstra. Lecture Notes No. 29. ISBN 0-937073-77-6 (paper), 0-937073-78-4 (cloth)

A Short Introduction to Modal Logic. Grigori Mints. Lecture Notes No. 30. ISBN 0-937073-75-X (paper), 0-937073-76-8 (cloth)

Other CSLI Titles Distributed by UCP

Agreement in Natural Language: Approaches, Theories, Descriptions. Michael Barlow and Charles A. Ferguson (Eds.). ISBN 0-937073-02-4 (cloth)

Papers from the Second International Workshop on Japanese Syntax. William J. Poser (Ed.). ISBN 0-937073-38-5 (paper), 0-937073-39-3 (cloth)

The Proceedings of the Seventh West Coast Conference on Formal Linguistics (WCCFL 7). ISBN 0-937073-40-7 (paper)

The Proceedings of the Eighth West Coast Conference on Formal Linguistics (WCCFL 8). ISBN 0-937073-45-8 (paper)

The Phonology-Syntax Connection. Sharon Inkelas and Draga Zec (Eds.) (co-published with The University of Chicago Press). ISBN 0-226-38100-5 (paper), 0-226-38101-3 (cloth)

The Proceedings of the Ninth West Coast Conference on Formal Linguistics (WCCFL 9). ISBN 0-937073-64-4 (paper)

Japanese/Korean Linguistics. Hajime Hoji (Ed.). ISBN 0-937073-57-1 (paper), 0-937073-56-3 (cloth)

Experiencer Subjects in South Asian Languages. Manindra K. Verma and K. P. Mohanan (Eds.). ISBN 0-937073-60-1 (paper), 0-937073-61-X (cloth)

Grammatical Relations: A Cross-Theoretical Perspective. Katarzyna Dziwirek, Patrick Farrell, Errapel Mejías Bikandi (Eds.). ISBN 0-937073-63-6 (paper), 0-937073-62-8 (cloth)

The Proceedings of the Tenth West Coast Conference on Formal Linguistics (WCCFL 10). ISBN 0-937073-79-2 (paper)

Books Distributed by CSLI

The Proceedings of the Third West Coast Conference on Formal Linguistics (WCCFL 3). ($10.95) ISBN 0-937073-45-8 (paper)

The Proceedings of the Fourth West Coast Conference on Formal Linguistics (WCCFL 4). ($11.95) ISBN 0-937073-45-8 (paper)

The Proceedings of the Fifth West Coast Conference on Formal Linguistics (WCCFL 5). ($10.95) ISBN 0-937073-45-8 (paper)

The Proceedings of the Sixth West Coast Conference on Formal Linguistics (WCCFL 6). ($13.95) ISBN 0-937073-45-8 (paper)

Hausar Yau Da Kullum: Intermediate and Advanced Lessons in Hausa Language and Culture. William R. Leben, Ahmadu Bello Zaria, Shekarau B. Maikafi, and Lawan Danladi Yalwa. ($19.95) ISBN 0-937073-68-7 (paper)

Hausar Yau Da Kullum Workbook. William R. Leben, Ahmadu Bello Zaria, Shekarau B. Maikafi, and Lawan Danladi Yalwa. ($7.50) ISBN 0-93703-69-5 (paper)

Ordering Titles Distributed by CSLI

Titles distributed by CSLI may be ordered directly from CSLI Publications, Ventura Hall, Stanford University, Stanford, California 94305-4115 or by phone (415)723-1712 or (415)723-1839. Orders can also be placed by e-mail (pubs@csli.stanford.edu) or FAX (415)723-0758.

All orders must be prepaid by check, VISA, or MasterCard (include card name, number, expiration date). For shipping and handling add $2.50 for first book and $0.75 for each additional book; $1.75 for the first report and $0.25 for each additional report. California residents add 7% sales tax.

For overseas shipping, add $4.50 for first book and $2.25 for each additional book; $2.25 for first report and $0.75 for each additional report. All payments must be made in US currency.

CSLI was founded early in 1983 by researchers from Stanford University, SRI International, and Xerox PARC to further research and development of integrated theories of language, information, and computation. CSLI headquarters and the publication offices are located at the Stanford site.

CSLI/SRI International   **CSLI/Stanford**   **CSLI/Xerox PARC**
333 Ravenswood Avenue   Ventura Hall   3333 Coyote Hill Road
Menlo Park, CA 94025   Stanford, CA 94305   Palo Alto, CA 94304

99 98 97 96 95 94 93 92   5 4 3 2 1

Library of Congress Cataloging-in-Publication Data

Lexical matters / Ivan A. Sag and Anna Szabolcsi, editors.
    p. cm. -- (CSLI lecture notes ; no. 24)
    Includes bibliographical references and indexes.
    ISBN 0-937073-65-2
    ISBN 0-937073-66-0 (pbk.)
    1. Lexicology. 2. Grammar. Comparative and general. I. Sag, Ivan A., 1949- .
II. Szabolcsi, Anna, 1953- .
P326.L384 1992
413'.028--dc20

90-28772
CIP

CSLI Lecture Notes report new developments in the study of language, information, and computation. In addition to lecture notes, the series includes monographs, working papers, and conference proceedings. Our aim is to make new results, ideas, and approaches available as quickly as possible.